LAW ENFORCEMENT PATROL OPERATIONS: Police Systems and Practices

Larry D. Nichols

South Plains College

McCutchan Publishing Corporation

P.O. Box 774
Berkeley, California 94701

ISBN 0–8211–1309–7
Library of Congress Catalog Card Number 90–62594

Printed in the United States of America

This text is dedicated to my students—past, present, and future—who accept the challenge to become professional peace officers and make their world a better place for peace-abiding citizens. In addition, this book is dedicated to my wife, Micheline, who provides support, encouragement, and love in my work and growth as a person.

Contents

Contents

Preface

Law enforcement patrol operation is the heart of a law enforcement agency. A peace officer on patrol must have a clear understanding of the special tactics and techniques designed to keep both him- or herself and the public safe, while ensuring that criminals are apprehended and brought to justice. Peace officers must make difficult decisions every day, and proper discretionary judgment results in deciding to make or not to make an arrest, to use or not to use force (including deadly force), and when and where to establish overt or covert patrol tactics, to mention but a few. These are often difficult split-second decisions, sometimes involving life and death, and they are made on the basis of officers' education, training, and experience. The courts may take years to determine if the officer made the correct decision—and then perhaps end up with a split verdict. Because of these considerations, your service as a professional law enforcement officer requires dedication, maturity, courage, training, education, and professional commitment.

Law Enforcement Patrol Operations: Police Systems and Practices was developed to provide an understanding of basic procedures and techniques that have proven successful in field-tested police operations. The contents of this text have been carefully organized and drawn from hundreds of sources, including material from professional texts cowritten by the author for use in colleges and police academies in the states of Texas, California, Illinois, and Florida. The author has also included materials from training bulletins and course outlines that he has used in teaching college law enforcement courses for over fifteen years. It is hoped that you will benefit from these experiences and the wisdom of others as you learn the philosophy, tactics, and techniques necessary to accomplish the difficult job of a law enforcement patrol officer in modern society.

The materials are presented as a compilation of guidelines rather than as a collection of arbitrary rules to follow. As you progress in your law enforcement career, you will learn that there is more than one way to accomplish any particular task. This text offers suggestions to help you during patrol operations; your task is to improve on these guidelines in practice as a modern peace officer. In addition to past challenges, the peace officer in the twenty-first century will face new challenges. For example, new computer technology will change the face of crime and the way that peace officers meet the demands of the police mission. Thus, in the future you will have an opportunity to expand and add to the body of patrol operations knowledge now available. You should establish a strong foundation in understanding your role as a law enforcement patrol officer and adhere to the Law Enforcement Code of Ethics to make wise decisions that advance the police mission. Then, by applying the time-tested field tactics suggested in this text to approach the difficult job of a patrol officer, you will establish a strong foundation to become a *professional* peace officer.

At the end of each chapter are a number of study questions and suggested activities to provoke conscientious examination to ensure application and understanding of the principles. Through diligent study of this material you will achieve a firm understanding of the requirements necessary to begin your career as a law enforcement officer committed to serving justice. Remember also that this is only the beginning of your study to achieve success; professional officers learn and add to their knowledge every day on police patrol. You must apply your education and training in the field and become experienced in handling the police mission.

The author gratefully acknowledges the efforts of literally thousands of professional peace officers who have contributed to the body of knowledge from which many of the ideas in this text have been drawn. The author would also like to thank Ray K. Robbins and Charles P. Runkle for use of selected sections of *The Texas Peace Officer*, *The California Peace Officer*, and *The Illinois Law Enforcement Officer* in this text. Their contributions, along with valuable experiences in co-authoring these texts, provided invaluable research for this book. The challenge in writing any text is not so much to develop new materials, but rather to organize and create a different viewpoint and approach to the subject in order to best explain and convey lessons from the past. This work is an effort toward achieving this goal, and it is sincerely hoped that it serves this end. However, because any writing is a "work in progress," the author would appreciate your feedback to enhance future editions of this text.

Law Enforcement Code of Ethics

As a law enforcement officer, my *fundamental duty* is to *serve* humanity; to *safeguard* lives and property; to *protect* the innocent against deception, the weak against oppression or intimidation, and the peaceful against violence or disorder; and to *respect* the constitutional rights of all people to liberty, equality, and justice.

I will keep my private life unsullied as an *example* to all; *maintain courageous calm* in the face of danger, scorn, or ridicule; *develop self-restraint*; and be constantly mindful of the welfare of others. Honest in thought and deed in both my personal and official life, *I will be exemplary in obeying the laws* of the land and the regulations of my department. Whatever I see or hear of a confidential nature or that is confided to me in my official capacity will be kept ever *secret* unless revelation is necessary in the performance of my duty.

I will *never act officiously* or permit personal feelings, prejudices, animosities, or friendships to influence my decisions. With no compromise for crime and with relentless prosecution of criminals, I will *enforce the law courteously and appropriately* without fear or favor, malice, or ill will, *never employing unnecessary force* or violence and *never accepting gratuities*.

I recognize the *badge* of my office as a *symbol of public faith*, and I accept it as a public trust to be held so long as I am true to the ethics of the police service. *I will constantly strive to achieve these objectives and ideals, dedicating myself to my chosen profession . . . law enforcement.*

1

Introduction to Patrol Operations

No single phase of police operations is as visible, vulnerable, or important as the patrol function. The primary responsibility of any law enforcement agency is to mobilize, equip, and maintain a knowledgeable, professional patrol section that provides security, protection, and service to the citizens of the community. It is at the patrol level that most citizen-police contacts take place and the ultimate delivery of police service is made to the community. Ill-trained or poorly equipped officers can quickly destroy years of good police-community relations efforts by improper or overzealous actions. Conversely, professional law enforcement officers give the community confidence in their ability to achieve the "police mission" and provide citizens a safe place to live and raise their families.

THE PROFESSIONAL LAW ENFORCEMENT OFFICER

Society does not easily bestow the term *professional* on any group or person. In general, "professionals" tend to have characteristics that give honor to their occupations, because group members have perfected their skills in a unique task, craft, or art. Members of society frequently put "blind faith" in a professional's ability to achieve a desired result. Doctors, lawyers, and educators seem to have achieved professional status; it is not uncommon to hear someone to refer to "my doctor," "my lawyer," or "my teacher." However, few people ever say, "That's my cop!"

Defining *professionalism* and applying the term to modern peace officers is not as easy as it may seem. The term implies more than just "being paid" to do a job. After all, many "jobs" are paid positions; however, not all workers are considered to be "professionals." What individual characteristics do doctors, lawyers, and educators share that separate these professionals from all other people? The answer to this question may help us understand what the "true professions" may have in common that separate them from other types of employment and, therefore, what other occupations must achieve in order to be accorded such status. Once we discover the "common core," we can then ask ourselves if the law enforcement profession shares any of these characteristics.

The most obvious characteristic common to the "true professionals" is a high level of education. The minimum entry requirement for some true professions is a bachelor's degree; however, master's and doctoral degrees are commonly required for job entry, advancement, tenure, and success. The requirements for such levels of education are frequently rewarded with higher salaries, which usually entail better living styles and conditions.

Generally, true professionals specialize in one specific type of endeavor. A proportionally large group of doctors tend to specialize in one area or another of medicine; even a "general practitioner" specializes in this type of medicine. Lawyers specialize in criminal law, or one of the numerous varieties of civil law practice. Teachers at public schools generally teach a wide variety of subjects; community colleges and universities employ "master teachers" who specialize in specific subjects such as English, history, government, and—yes—even criminal justice and law enforcement. Common sense suggests that there is a great deal of "pride" in being "professional" and ensuring that every task is given the utmost of attention to detail.

One characteristic that is equally required of professionals, but less well known, is the necessity for each member of the profession to adhere to a strict code of ethics. Doctors, lawyers, and educators are bound by professional ethics to achieve high moral standards of behavior, job performance, and professional conduct. Furthermore, each such group is represented by a professional association ensuring that professional conduct conforms to the standards of that association's code.

Last, but not least, professionals can transfer to another job or agency at an equal level of proficiency without "starting over" as a "rookie." This aspect of career mobility allows professionals to achieve their life goals by transferring to another job or for the purpose of obtaining a "promotion." (This aspect of professionalism exists only at the highest administrative positions in law enforcement.)

How does the law enforcement profession match up? If we apply the "true professional" criteria, there are both similarities and large discrepancies. The educational criterion for job entry for many departments is still a high school diploma or a GED (General Education Development) certificate. However, agencies across the nation have systematically moved toward encouraging and requiring higher educational standards from job applicants as a means of "professionalizing" their departments. Many agencies now require an associate's degree (or 60 hours of college) for career entry. Other agencies require some college hours (30 hours, 45 hours, and so on) of an applicant seeking employment as a peace officer. Many agencies also offer monthly monetary incentives for officers who achieve degree requirements and maintain competency. Some federal jobs, and many criminal justice positions (such as probation and parole officer) now require a bachelor's degree as a minimum educational credential.

In 1968, the President's Commission on Law Enforcement and the Administration of Justice completed a study that outlined deficiencies in law enforcement education. This study resulted in creation of the Law Enforcement Assistance Administration (LEAA), a federal agency organized to improve law enforcement and criminal justice for communities. One of the responsibilities of this agency was to oversee administration of the Law Enforcement Education Program (LEEP); this program continued throughout the 1970s and provided tuition, book, and other assistance for inservice and preservice law enforcement officers to return to or enter into college and acquire an education. Today, officers who were beneficiaries of this program serve in staff, supervisory, and command positions throughout the nation. Some officers have gone on to government programs, while others entered the field of law enforcement education. During the interim years, law enforcement education at colleges and universities has grown into major programs that serve the needs for law enforcement and criminal justice students across the nation.

Surveys of many state commissions that certify or license peace officers throughout the United States indicate a slight increase in the number of modern law enforcement officers who currently possess associate's, bachelor's, master's, doctoral, and law degrees. For example, in the state of Texas, the current status of law enforcement officers shows that they have acquired the following educational backgrounds:

Educational Level	Number	Percent
GED	6,977	10.9%
High School	46,779	73.3
Associate's	2,988	4.7
Bachelor's	6,253	9.8
Master's	538	0.85
Ph.D.s	161	0.25
Law	129	0.2
	63,825	100%

Note: These figures include regular peace officers, jailers, elected officials, and reserve peace officers.
Source: Texas Commission on Law Enforcement Officer Standards and Education (TCLEOSE), as of December 1, 1989, Austin, Texas.

It is an eye-opening fact that slightly over 84 percent of all personnel have a high school diploma or GED certificate, while only 16 percent have advanced degrees. Obviously, law enforcement agencies are still far away from achieving the numbers of degree-holding employees necessary for professional status across the board according to professional educational criteria. However, it is interesting to note additional statistics that specify the number of people in the law enforcement profession that have earned professional certification in the state of Texas. The figures are based on a combination of education, training, and years of service to the law enforcement profession.

Certification	Number	Percent
Basic certification	34,788	54.5%
Intermediate certification	9,766	15.3
Advanced certification	17,789	27.9
Pending (or not applicable) certification	1,482	2.3
	63,825	100%

Over 43 percent of currently employed officers hold intermediate or advanced certification. This level is significant, because the job of enforcing the law tends to appeal to young people. The high number of officers who have advanced to higher levels of certification indicates the strong commitment to excellence on the part of career officers in getting training and education and providing service to the communities.

It was noted that "true" professional people maintain a strict code of ethics as one criterion in achieving their status. This text begins by introducing the traditional law enforcement code of ethics, with specific text highlighted and emphasized. In studying the elements that promote professional law enforcement behavior, look at the action words in the first paragraph: an officer's fundamental duty is to "serve," "safeguard," "protect," and "respect." These positive action verbs suggest that there are "specialties" that law enforcement officers perform. No other occupation combines these four elements as a basis of its fundamental duty. Accepting this role involves a sworn duty that each officer dedicates his or her life to perform in the service and protection of all individuals. Officers not only have a sworn duty to safeguard lives and property, they must also ensure that the constitutional rights of all people are equally respected and protected. These requirements place law enforcement officers in the middle. Professional officers must serve society and protect all people from the illegal acts of a few; however, at the same time, peace officers also protect the civil rights and liberties of those few who may seek to violate the law. Such a course of action is called due process of law, or ensuring that all procedural requirements of the U.S. Constitution, law, and court rulings are complied with to the letter of the law. Certainly, we need true professionals to achieve this duty with integrity and dignity.

The second paragraph of the code says that the behavior of law enforcement officers should be "exemplary"—should set an example for others. This responsibility applies to both on- and off-duty conduct. Peace officers are constantly under public scrutiny; citizens expect law enforcement officers first to obey the law, then arrest others who violate the law. For example, if the law requires drivers to wear their safety belts when moving motor vehicles, citizens in the community will look to see if you are wearing your safety belt (in your patrol unit as well as your private automobile). Other drivers will check your driving speed when it appears that you are not handling emergency situations. Even after an officer has left the police service, the public expects exemplary conduct. In rare instances where officers or former officers have violated the law, newspaper headlines highlight the fact that a "law enforcement officer was arrested or accused of a crime"—even though many others may be arrested or accused of the same crime at the same time. Accepting the responsibility to be a professional law enforcement officer is a lifetime commitment—a commitment to excellence in both professional and private behavior.

According to the code, professional law enforcement officers must develop self-restraint and be constantly mindful of the welfare of others. Every officer is first a person; this means that each person brings to the job his or her strengths *and* weaknesses. Professional officers must absolutely know and understand themselves before they can successfully handle other people. By knowing and controlling your weaknesses (such as prejudice or short-tempered reaction to anxiety), you can become a good peace officer who treats every individual with respect. One axiom has been tested and found to be true time and time again: *You can't control others unless you can first control yourself!*

The code requires that professional officers not be gossips. Your job includes the responsibility to handle public and private matters in a confidential manner unless in the performance of your duty you must make reports, testify in court, or otherwise divulge information entrusted to you. Privacy is a sacred trust. Only people who have a "need to know" should be informed of the nature of your investigations, knowledge, and conclusions.

Professional officers do not act officiously. Citizens and other officers do not respect anyone—much less a law enforcement officer—who condescends to others. The fact that you wear a badge and a gun does not give you the right to feel, think, or act as if you were better than anyone else. Quite to the contrary, the privilege of wearing the uniform makes *you* a public servant and requires that you respect other people's feelings and enforce the law courteously and appropriately at all times. Even though the law gives you limited rights to use force to protect yourself and others, you are prohibited from using any force unless it is immediately necessary to prevent imminent hazard. Unnecessary force in the line of duty will subject you to both criminal and civil charges. Professional officers do not have to use excessive force to achieve their objectives. Professional officers obey the law and respect other people's right to life, liberty, and the pursuit of happiness.

The code notes that true professionals do not accept "gratuities." A gratuity is any reward, gifts, or favor received in return for services rendered. You are a public servant; as such, your community expects and deserves only your best duty performance. No officer has the right to "look the other way" when someone commits a violation or crime. Any officer who violates the public trust does not deserve to wear the uniform and the badge. Police frequently discuss the question as to whether accepting a "free cup of coffee" at a local restaurant amounts to a gratuity or not. The answer lies in "what is expected in return" for the coffee. If the waiter or waitress expects that an officer will not write a traffic ticket in exchange for the cup of coffee, that free coffee is a gratuity. However, if nothing is expected other than to encourage law enforcement officers to frequently visit the restaurant (and thus discourage would-be robbers), then no real gratuity is involved. In the latter case, professional officers usually leave a tip that covers the cost of the cup of coffee and eliminates embarrassment to both the officer and the establishment.

The last paragraph of the code notes that the police badge is a "symbol of public faith." By displaying the badge, you are telling everyone that you are a *professional officer* who will constantly strive to achieve the public's trust. However, saying you are "professional" is not enough; you must *earn* the title by closely adhering to the principles that deserve respect. Corruption is a cancer that can destroy both your life and the lives of your loved ones. Once an officer accepts a "bribe" or other favor and knowingly allows criminal activities to occur, that officer has sold his or her soul to the criminal world. No amount of remuneration can make up for sacrificing the public trust. Once an officer becomes a pawn of crime, that officer aborts self-esteem, integrity, and the trust of the community. Such actions also affect other officers and the integrity of the agency. Professional obligation demands that you must be above temptation. You have dedicated your life to helping others—make sure that you deserve that trust every day of your life.

Police professional associations primarily exist to provide a forum for exchange of ideas, information, and expertise. Organizations such as the National Association of Chiefs of Police (NACP) promote professionalism at all levels of law enforcement; however, this group primarily involves agency heads and not street officers. Although many associations have sought to represent peace officers as a whole, no one such organization represents all officers and is responsible for ensuring that every officer abides by a strict code of conduct. This fact, coupled with the idea that some "police associations" have become means of collective bargaining, rather than promoting police professionalism, is an obstacle to achieving complete "professionalism" in the police world. Unions in police ranks is a "hot topic" in many parts of the country. Some peace officers strongly feel they have no control over working conditions and professional growth unless they can use collective bargaining to prevent abuses from unresponsive management. Other officers look suspiciously at any organizations or affiliation that may have links to organized crime, or motives and objectives that foster grievances. These divisive collective feelings fail to unite law enforcement officers into one organization that unanimously speaks for police professionalism.

Being *professional* means many things to many people. To the professional law enforcement officer, it means more than just providing an honest day's work for an honest day's pay. It also means living up to expectations of public trust that each officer will strive to achieve high standards of conduct, education, behavior, skill, compassion, and empathy for public concerns. Earning the "professional" title demands that every officer achieve a high degree of personal commitment to goals and objectives of the department and strictly adhere to the code of ethics. Since the "professional" title must be earned, every officer bears an intrinsic responsibility to strive to reach this level of achievement. To be *professional*, you must *act* professionally. Every officer has the responsibility of living up to high public expectations of police trustworthiness. As a law enforcement officer, you will play a major role in creating the image of a professional in every contact, report, and investigation. Seek to perform your duty with dignity and integrity, and "constantly strive to achieve these objectives and ideals" by dedicating yourself "to your chosen profession . . . law enforcement."

THE POLICE MISSION AND OBJECTIVES OF LAW ENFORCEMENT PATROL

Patrol operations fulfill many objectives and purposes, although all patrol tasks tend to surround one primary goal—the protection of people and property. The way in which this goal is achieved determines the success or failure of the law enforcement agency in accomplishing its mission. Each officer plays a major role in achieving this goal. As a professional officer, you will be responsible for your beat and the maintenance of peace and order in that area of responsibility.

As a law enforcement officer, you must at all times be aware that your presence is a threat to those who would break the law and a blessing to those who seek police protection. On one hand, you must constantly think in terms of your safety; on the other hand, you must demonstrate courtesy and respect for the rights and dignity of all people with whom you come in contact. The ways you choose to handle this paradox will largely determine your standing as an up-to-date professional officer as well as determine the amount of respect the public bestows on the local law enforcement agency.

A paramount consideration for each officer is simply personal safety, because law enforcement work can be dangerous. So long as law enforcement officers are empowered to impose their authority over others, make arrests, control human conduct, and seek solutions to criminal and civil matters, the potential for violent confrontation remains a constant threat to the officer. The manner in which an officer meets these challenges can well be a matter of life and death.

Although patrol procedures vary from place to place and department to department, a common core of accepted procedures exists in all patrol functions. In all departments, the primary purpose of all patrols must be to effectively and efficiently carry out the six elements of the police mission:

1. *Preventing criminal conduct* by targeting patrol coverage to areas most likely to sustain criminal activity and so reducing the opportunity for criminal action or threats of crime

2. *Repressing crime* by instituting procedures for identifying offenders through effective investigative techniques
3. *Apprehending offenders* to deter crime by maintaining certainty of arrest and prosecution
4. *Recovering property* to help reduce the monetary losses due to crime, limit the profits of crime, and enhance the public image of law enforcement effectiveness
5. *Regulating noncriminal conduct* such as traffic control, performing traffic accident investigation, enforcing city ordinances, issuing oral and written warnings, educating through programs about crime prevention and traffic safety, and conducting juvenile programs designed to prevent misbehavior
6. *Performing miscellaneous services* such as operating detention facilities (which is a major function of the sheriff's office); offering emergency assistance to citizens; assisting or informing out-of-town visitors; answering animal calls; escorting parades; handling special events involving crowds; receiving complaints on city services; and protecting dignitaries

Ultimately, the basic duties of police patrol can be summed up in two words: *protection* and *service*. The police mission and patrol objectives must coincide to achieve successful, effective results. Therefore, most departments will list objectives similar to the following:

1. Protecting lives and property
2. Preserving the peace
3. Preventing unlawful acts
4. Apprehending offenders
5. Suppressing disturbances
6. Providing aid, relief, and information
7. Collecting and preserving evidence
8. Providing testimonial evidence in court
9. Resolving disputes and conflicts

These objectives collectively support the departmental goals of building positive, strong police-community relations, operating efficiently within budgetary constraints, increasing productivity, obtaining better salaries to attract and retain more professional officers, providing continuing education and inservice training, and ultimately reducing the crime rate and its effects on the community. Total realization of these goals and patrol objectives will result in a safe, secure, smooth-working community and satisfactory realization of the police mission, which is to maintain social order within carefully prescribed ethical and constitutional restrictions.

THE PATROL FUNCTION WITHIN THE POLICE ORGANIZATION

A police department's patrol function is the heart of all police operations. Patrols feed information to other sections of the department relative to crime rates, types of crimes, community attitudes, and other nonpolice information that enables management people to guide the department into "hot spots" or funnel resources to areas where they can best be used to reach departmental goals. The position of the patrolling officer—between the police and governmental management on one hand and the citizens of the community on the other—is difficult. It should neither be ignored nor be taken lightly. Patrol operations include more than merely apprehending offenders; officers on patrol must also provide for crime repression, crime prevention, recovery of stolen property, control of noncriminal conduct, and miscellaneous other services. Any overemphasis in one area could encourage increased problems in another area. The patrol section must balance its efforts in all areas of responsibility for maximum effectiveness.

The patrol operation of any law enforcement agency is its largest, most indispensable element, and it is the only function of the police machinery that is totally independent and can function on its own. As a rule, a minimum of 50 percent of all police personnel a department employs should be assigned to the patrol function regardless of departmental size or location. The patrol division is the nucleus of the department, around which the other services develop. For this reason, the patrol function is vitally important: "As the patrol goes, so goes the department." An efficient, productive patrol division reflects an efficient, productive department. By maintaining 50 percent or more of its strength in patrol operations, a department enhances its ability to deter, detect, and reduce criminal activity.

The Purpose of the Police Patrol

The basic purpose of police patrol is to eliminate both the actual opportunity for, and the confidence in succeeding at, misconduct by the criminal element of society. Although a thief's desire to steal is not

diminished by the physical presence of a patrol officer, the belief that
the criminal action will be successful is reduced in proportion to the
number of police patrols the thief observes in and around the target
area. A criminal's belief that he or she is likely to be caught in the act
is a good deterrent to any involvement in criminal activity. An
aggressive, highly visible, and mobile patrol division enhances the
criminal's insecurity, which in turn increases the overall security of
the community.

Unlike many occupations that target a special clientele in the
community, law enforcement officers serve the entire community. One of
your most important roles as an officer of the law will revolve around
your ability to successfully handle many "noncriminal" matters that
are inherent in police service. Patrol officers defuse arguments, medi-
ate issues in neighborhoods, answer calls in regard to lost children,
and provide information about community services. Officers mitigate
complaints regarding homeowners and apartment dwellers and provide information about agencies organized to alleviate hazardous and
unsanitary conditions. In many situations, you will be called on to
provide information about, or direct a complainant to, legal services,
rape crisis centers, child abuse agencies, and numerous other organizations such as the Salvation Army, Red Cross, and public welfare
agencies—to mention but a few.

On patrol you will observe many hazards—such as inoperative
traffic control signals and unsafe road conditions—that must be
promptly handled to prevent accidents. You will control crowds and
traffic in congested areas to reduce the possibility of injury to pedestrians and drivers. During emergency conditions (such as hurricane
warnings), special events (such as football, baseball, or other sport
games), or "routine" day-to-day activities, law enforcement officers
are viewed as the primary group of professionals who provide for
order and preserve a safe environment for every person in the community. Law enforcement patrol officers are mobile representatives of
city management. The patrol officer's activities decentralize municipal services by providing a mobile information dissemination and
collection medium for city management. Information goes out to the
public via patrol-citizen encounters, and feedback returns via patrol-
city management interaction. Because the police patrol is present and
mobile throughout the community around the clock, it serves other
functions of city management as well—such as reporting fires or fire
hazards; reporting hazardous conditions or broken water mains,

health hazards, traffic safety hazards; and checking occupational licenses. And this multiplicity of involvement is provided at little or no additional cost to the community! Truly, the purposes of police patrol are many and varied. Your role as a public servant—either in eliminating the opportunity for criminals to ravage the community or in performing numerous noncriminal roles—is one of the most important human activities. Your role as a *professional* law enforcement patrol officer is vital to the community. The ways in which you accept this responsibility and carry out its vital functions ultimately determine how effectively the police mission is performed.

Activities of the Patrol Division

Special job assignments for patrol officers are viewed in three ways. First is the technical skill that results from formal schooling and training. Second are the functional assignments an officer is given that include but are not limited to homicide and accident investigation—which are learned skills—crime prevention, traffic control, general patrol, dispatching, and fingerprinting. Third is workload distribution: keeping records and files and carrying out other duties such as determining what tasks need to be done, the duration and location of tasks, and the time of day or night they are best carried out. The officer on patrol alone in a patrol unit must make maximum use of all the special techniques learned or developed in the course of training. Patrol techniques vary according to the time of day, location of patrol, type of neighborhood, statistical crime rates, and so on. Also, tactics used by one-person patrol units vary greatly from those available for two-person units.

Preventive Enforcement

The first technical skills that patrol officers learn are the basic preventive patrol methods of law enforcement. Preventive enforcement is protection. In areas where police have made their presence continually known, the number of offenses declines. Preventive enforcement was first suggested by Sir Robert Peel in 1828 when he asked the British Parliament to form the Metropolitan Police. Since that time, preventive patrol has been the cornerstone of law enforcement patrol tactics and techniques.

Crime prevention patrol is the soundest of all criminological methods. By being seen frequently in the community, the patrol officer reduces criminal activity. Professional criminals, especially burglars, often admit that they avoid areas or communities where their "casing" has indicated heavy and thorough law enforcement patrol. Generally, preventive enforcement includes the following proactive tactics:

- Frequently checking business and residential premises
- Looking for and talking to suspicious people
- Varying the patrol pattern
- Keeping visibility in the area

Frequent checks of business and residential premises both protect property and help detect criminal activity. Searching spotlights may discover broken windows or other damages that need further investigation. Officers may check to see if doors are secure. Occasionally officers may detect, by feeling heat on glass windows, the presence of a fire that has not as yet been reported. Also, would-be criminals notice the peace officer's actions. When officers frequently check suspicious people, individuals who have criminal intentions begin to doubt their ability to successfully carry out the crime. By varying patrol patterns and being conspicuously visible in the patrol area, officers become unpredictably, yet noticeably, omnipresent. Both these facts weigh heavily on the criminal's mind before, during, and following a criminal episode.

Directed Enforcement

Patrol officers cannot completely cover all their assigned areas. Officers patrol many square miles of land; the task is complicated by heavy traffic, congestion, and geographical restrictions. Since one officer's ability to cover a patrol beat is limited, the logical solution is for the officer to go where the trouble is occurring or is most likely to occur. The officer's approach to crime prevention under the concept of directed enforcement is basically proactive and deals with specific violations or circumstances at the time and location of occurrence.

To be able to respond where trouble is most likely to occur, the patrol officer should be aware of the following factors. Knowledge of the beat or patrol district helps the patrol officer cover the area well. An officer working a normal shift cannot formulate an overall picture of criminal trends. Statistical charts and maps can show trends that occur 24 hours a day, seven days a week. Many departments now use computers and statistics to predict criminal activity. Directed enforcement allows an agency to better use its resources. These resources can be assigned to high-crime areas most of the time. Statistical research supplied to the patrol division can also be helpful on patrol.

Directed enforcement, combined with preventive enforcement and used in accident prevention, has proven highly successful. Personnel can be assigned duty depending on an analysis that indicates where an accident, incident, or crime is occurring or is likely to occur. For example, if studies show that a new prostitution group is setting up shop in an area, vice squad personnel may be assigned to cover the case. Another study may suggest that reports of rapes at a city park be assigned to a stakeout unit using decoy officers. Such assignments should be coordinated with the patrol division to avoid misunderstandings.

Some directed enforcement duties may be determined by geographical considerations. Rural crimes call for a different type of patrol assignment in some cases; such incidents may also require a special type of person or equipment to ensure success. Likewise, livestock thefts may require mounted patrol personnel used in a specialized manner. Different types of terrain require special equipment or vehicles. In some cases, helicopters or other aircraft may be the only forms of transportation ideal for patrol coverage.

Distribution of the Patrol Force

The demand for law enforcement services varies with the time of day and the need for service. Peace officers must be constantly available for response because the community relations aspect of poor response times is significant. Response times depend on the size of the area patrolled, the number of patrol units assigned to the area, the officer's knowledge of the area, and the type of calls received. Peak demand hours for services are the evening hours of 6 P.M. to 1 A.M., particularly on Fridays, Saturdays, and Mondays. Allocating adequate time to preventive patrol functions often results in significant savings in time needed to spend investigating crimes that occur during periods of low patrol coverage. Patrol time must be efficiently used and accurate reports must be filed to enable law enforcement administrators to maximize their effective use of patrol coverages. Accurate reporting of patrol coverages and responses gives administrators a true representation of law enforcement workload and helps them in preparing budget and personnel requests.

Knowledge of patrol area is crucial to the efficient and safe conduct of patrol function. Obviously, a hometown officer has a strong advantage in maintaining knowledge of the patrol area. A newcomer to the community is, however, probably more likely to be observant, at least initially, during orientation training in the city. In both situations, city growth and development constantly change patrol areas and add new hazards with which the patrol division must deal.

Other factors that affect the patrol division are the types of structures in the community and the types of people who live in the area. For example, communities with college campuses have an unusually large percentage of young people in their population, which brings youth-associated types of crime and disturbances. Border communities or coastal areas attract migrant workers, and law enforcement officers may encounter people who do not speak English. Military installations harbor large, rapidly changing populations. Such ingredients contribute to the need for planning and for developing the patrol division as well as for constantly changing tactics and procedures for effective preventive programs.

Types of Law Enforcement Patrol

Patrol officers are generally assigned duty with a specific shift. A shift is determined by several factors:

- Number of personnel available for duty
- Frequency of calls for police service
- Time factors based on frequency of crime occurrence

The shifts are constantly reevaluated in accordance with changing data and other variable factors. Occasionally officers are reassigned to new shifts to facilitate and enhance the agency's ability to meet and carry out the law enforcement mission.

Patrol assignment to a particular area is called a "patrol beat." The size of a beat is often determined by the following:

1. Type of patrol techniques used (foot, motorized units, boat, airplane, horse, and so forth)
2. Type of area covered, which may vary from high-density apartment complexes to rural farmland
3. The type of criminal activity in the area

4. Crime frequency
5. Personnel available for duty
6. Frequency of calls for service

Many types of patrol techniques are used in law enforcement today. Although patrol methods and tactics vary from area to area and community to community, they are dictated by the objectives the department establishes. The common methods in use include but are not limited to the following:

1. *Foot patrol.*
2. *Automobile patrol* by one- or two-person teams.
3. *Motorcycle patrol* and three-wheeled motorcycle patrol. This trend has somewhat diminished in many areas in favor of safer, smaller patrol vehicles.
4. *Canine patrols* are seeing more and more use nationally. They provide excellent, thorough coverage of buildings and open areas. Their abilities in bomb and narcotics searches are unsurpassed.
5. *Marine patrols* are used in coastal areas and areas adjacent to large bodies of water. They are effective in patrolling areas for enforcement of game and safety regulations.

Each of these patrol techniques has its own advantages and disadvantages.

Foot Patrol. Foot patrol offers the following *advantages*:

1. Provides the best opportunity for close observation of criminal activity within range of the officer (this may be the greatest advantage)
2. Increases good law enforcement-community interaction and potential for positive, long-lasting relationships (a secondary —but very important—advantage)
3. Allows more firsthand knowledge to be obtained, by expanding the eyes and ears of the department
4. Affords one of the most effective techniques for patrolling densely populated or congested areas
5. Provides the best coverage of "inspectional" tasks
6. Creates better information sources by repetitive contact between citizens and the officer

7. Allows the officer to become more familiar with the physical characteristics of the "beat"
8. Gives the officer—due to familiarity with a beat—more ability to anticipate and "read" conditions developing before any actual incidents occur
9. Deters criminal activity because of the high visibility of the patrol officer

The *disadvantages* of foot patrol are that

1. It is an extremely costly form of patrol, because of the limited area one officer can cover.
2. The mobility of the officer is restricted.
3. Officers are more susceptible to attack or ambush.
4. Activities are reduced or curtailed by bad weather.
5. The amount and type of equipment carried are extremely limited.
6. Supervision is difficult.
7. It can be negatively received and carried out when management uses foot patrol as punishment or disciplinary action against officers.
8. Overfamiliarity with people on the beat and/or acceptance of favors may compromise the officer's ability to administer proper police action equally.
9. In some instances, communications may be inadequate.

Basic techniques for conducting patrol tactics are much the same whether it is done on foot or in a vehicle. However, foot patrol provides officers the opportunity for much more detailed inspection than is possible from a car. For example, observations between buildings or in narrow passageways ordinarily cannot be made satisfactorily from a vehicle. For this reason, radio car officers should spend a sufficient amount of time patrolling on foot in areas where crimes are most prevalent and where detailed, close observations are suggested.

During the daytime, an officer on foot patrol should be conspicuous, provided that the type of patrol conducted allows such exposure. There are several ways to conduct a foot patrol, including the following methods:

1. Using fixed posts for traffic control, sporting events, parades, and so on

2. Using a line beat that concentrates heavily on the activity of pedestrians
3. Incorporating a random combination type of patrol with another type, to increase flexibility and effectiveness
4. Keeping toward the curb line during *daytime* patrol because you are more conspicuous, you have more flexibility of movement, and you can observe better
5. At *night*, keeping toward the building line, which permits you to inspect building interiors and take advantage of shadows that provide concealment
6. Avoiding any semblance of routine patrol coverage (stop and retrace your steps occasionally; cut through alleys; stop, listen, and observe; turn corners as often as possible for advantage of surprise; avoid coffee and food stops at the same location and/or times)
7. Maintaining contact with the public

Automobile Patrol. Automobile patrol has the *advantages* of being the most productive, safe, and efficient use of personnel. In addition, the high mobility of the automobile patrol provides

- Fast emergency response
- A wider range of services
- Greater coverage with fewer patrol personnel
- A greatly increased ability to pursue violators and criminals

The automobile patrol unit also offers increased protection from ambush or sudden attack, and such patrols can continue to function in bad weather, when foot patrols must be withdrawn yet requests for police services continue or accelerate. Other advantages of the mobile patrol are as follows:

1. Supervisory abilities are easier to carry out.
2. The patrol vehicle is capable of carrying many needed supplies and equipment beyond the ability of the foot patrol officer.
3. The mobile patrol does not suggest the negative image that officers often equate with being detailed to foot patrol.
4. This patrol is more comfortable and less fatiguing than foot patrol duty.
5. The mobile patrol creates an excellent environment for experienced officers giving on-the-job training to new officers.

The major *disadvantages* of vehicular patrols are that

1. Such patrols lack the close, intimate relationships that can develop between a "beat cop" and the local community. Along with this loss is an accompanying increase in mistrust of the police by the public because of the relative remoteness of the patrol unit.
2. Rapid movement through the patrol area requires fast, sharp observation skills.
3. Mobile patrol loses the "eyes-and-ears" sensitivity of the foot officer.
4. Sources of information lack depth and are more difficult to develop.
5. Vehicular patrol officers generally do not know their beat very well beyond the portion visible from the street.
6. The ability to "feel" the conditions of the community through interaction with the people on the beat is decreased.
7. The deterrent effect of patrol presence is limited to the period of its visibility in the area; larger patrol areas mean less frequent coverage of the area, which correspondingly decreases the possibility of detection of the criminal.
8. The criminal element is more likely to "read" the patterns of patrol by routine coverage becoming predictable coverage.
9. The priority shifts from the silence of the approach to the swiftness of approach. Rapid response by vehicular patrols often requires use of the lights and/or sirens to clear traffic, which announces police presence prematurely.

Specialized Methods of Patrol

Modern law enforcement agencies are adopting a flexible, coordinated combination of patrol techniques for optimum coverage at the lowest cost to the taxpayer. Efficient operation is the ultimate goal of most police managers. Inventiveness is important in developing strong patrol coverage. Methods of transportation and patrol methods are limited only by the progressiveness and open-mindedness of the departmental personnel. Although not exhaustive, the following methods of specialized patrol have been used successfully in many agencies.

Motorcycles. Motorcycles are used for traffic enforcement and control in congested urban traffic. Some agencies use parking control officers in three-wheel motorcycles. In cities where patrol officers provide funeral escort service, traffic control for sporting events, and other miscellaneous services, the mobility and quickness of the motorcycle offer many advantages over automobile units. As noted earlier, however, the motorcycle is not without its disadvantages and limitations.

Aircraft. Airborne patrol is becoming very popular as a way of providing coverage for large areas quickly with a minimum of personnel. Airborne patrol is, however, probably the most expensive patrol method currently being used. General uses of this specialized patrol are for traffic control, observation, and search and rescue operations. When used, helicopters can offer distinct advantages over fixed-wing aircraft in some situations; for example, the helicopter can become a backup unit when high-risk traffic stops, or other tactical operations, are engaged. Helicopters can provide versatile rescue and emergency transportation. Coupled with infrared devices, helicopters can conduct searches at nighttime that were impossible to do before with the same degree of success.

Bicycles and Small Vehicles. Because of their mobility, flexibility, and low cost, bicycles and other small vehicles are considered excellent modes of travel in confined or congested areas. They have been used successfully for law enforcement patrol on college campuses, housing areas, and other locations where the noise or size of vehicular or motorcycle patrol is not appropriate. In some warehouse districts, the quietness of bicycles is excellent for quick mobility in on-site surveillance for apprehension patrol; backed up by quickly responding motorized patrol units, the bicycle officer can direct placement and operation to apprehend criminals practicing their "trade." An added bonus for officers is the fitness that riding a bicycle can provide.

Mounted Patrols. In some areas, officers on horseback are used for park enforcement, mob control, and search and rescue operations, to mention but a few. Although specialized handling, training, and care are necessary in handling horses, they can contribute meaningfully to police-community relations and enhance the public's image of law enforcement if used correctly.

Television. Observation through use of television is not new to law enforcement. Many jails and prisons have complete television surveillance of prisoners. And many agencies also use the fixed observation capabilities of television in high-crime areas to alert officers to unusual activity. In some parts of the country, television has been used to monitor traffic moving on highways and to detect accidents. With the recent adaptation of video cameras, television is currently being used to photograph large group gatherings at fires and other disturbances, where follow-up investigation may identify a "firebug" or reveal which members of the group committed unlawful acts. The long-range application of television and VCR use for law enforcement is limited only by an officer's imagination.

Canine (K-9) Units. The use of specially trained dogs for law enforcement use became popular after World War II. The main advantage in using canines is *officer safety*. Dogs can be used in high-risk situations where an officer may be vulnerable to attack— such as in searching buildings for drugs, bombs, or people.

Dogs can also track humans more easily and more effectively than a human can and can also be used effectively for crowd control. The ideal conditions for using canine units for tracking purposes include situations where a wanted person is isolated from other people, in cold or cool weather, and in damp or high-humidity conditions. However, you should be aware canine units are used before other officers are permitted to enter some crime scenes. Because carbon monoxide covers up human scent, *turn off* the patrol car engine on arriving at the location where canine units are used. Recall that any evidence at a crime scene in which a canine unit is to be used should be touched only by the dog handler, to avoid confusing the dog. If you are assigned to accompany a dog handler at a crime scene, stay at least six to seven feet *behind* and slightly to the left or right of the dog in order to have a clear field of vision and fire.

Marine and Amphibian Patrols. Specialized marine and amphibian vehicles patrol beaches, waterways, shorelines, and harbors for crimes of smuggling and violations of game and fishing laws, and perform many other specialized functions. Because of these special conditions, patrol can be accomplished only with the aid of boats, amphibian vehicles, and helicopters. Officers assigned to these types of patrol are skilled in water safety tactics as well as life-saving skills.

Proactive Law Enforcement

*Pro*active law enforcement simply means taking positive preventive and enforcement action to anticipate when and where crimes or violations may occur and to distribute the patrol systems accordingly to confront the anticipated problem. In the past, many police systems tended to be *re*active—getting to the scene of the crime or collision after the fact. In proactive enforcement, law enforcement officers predict events by using collected data, computers, and even "common sense and instinct." They arrive at the scene to prevent harmful behavior or, failing this goal, enact timely enforcement action or assistance as the situation requires. To achieve this type of patrol system, professional officers must have foresight, use intuitive planning, and take initiative for responsibly patrolling their district or beat.

To properly cover a beat using automobile patrol, you should operate the patrol unit in a safe manner consistent with traffic conditions and departmental policy. When and where possible, drive at slow speeds that permit good observation; however, be careful not to impede traffic. Select an appropriate patrol pattern to use in covering the beat, and select the best lane that affords optimum patrol coverage. However, don't travel solely on main arterial roadways. When necessary for preventive or apprehension patrol, park the patrol car correctly according to department policy. By stopping periodically and parking the patrol vehicle among other cars on the street, you can observe activity that might otherwise escape your attention. If another patrol is dividing your area of surveillance, overlap each other to maximize the surprise element. When possible, get out of the car to deal with citizens.

Basic law enforcement patrol is usually referred to as "routine," although patrol should actually avoid *any* semblance of routine as much as possible. Basic patrol uses both preventive and directed enforcement techniques. If officers establish a predictable patrol pattern, their effectiveness in suppressing crime is virtually eliminated. Criminals are not stupid; people who plan to commit a crime will check the patrol pattern. Once they know the pattern or "routine," criminals believe they can avoid arrest. When the officer is unpredictable, criminals must weigh their chances of being caught if they choose to commit an act.

Consequently, the first goal of a patrol officer is to *consciously avoid* developing any type of systematic routine. Professional officers do not take the same streets or roads during preventive patrol activities. Furthermore, experienced officers do not take their "coffee breaks" or meals at the same time of the day, nor at the same restaurants, on a day-to-day basis. The professional officer is "predictably unpredictable" and creates doubt in the mind of the would-be criminals.

The flexibility of time and patrol location also increases the officer's visibility in the patrol area and allows the officer to be seen more often by more people. An added benefit is that law-abiding citizens appreciate good police coverage. Good law enforcement-citizen relations can open up lines of communications that provide officers with more information.

Patrolling at night creates both advantages and disadvantages for patrol officers. Use the darkness to maximize the advantages. For example, by stopping and listening for unusual sounds, you might detect breaking glass, barking dogs, and other noises that can alert you to unusual activity. Thinking officers minimize the disadvantages by understanding that sound from the police radio is more distinct at night. Furthermore, metal on the police uniform (badge, cap piece, hat band, and so forth) that reflects light will give away your position and presence unless you prevent that from happening.

Two-Person Versus One-Person Patrol. Officers in motorized patrol are assigned to either two- or one-person patrol units. With the possible exception of training situations (for example, where a field-training officer is supervising a rookie officer out of the academy), one-person patrol coverage is considered superior in many departments. However, special circumstances may warrant a two-person unit in unique circumstances. Generally, studies show that one-person coverage is better because

1. Reliance on a partner becomes a crutch that allows individual performance to suffer.
2. A high degree of admiration by one partner for another can cause the first officer to take unnecessary risks.
3. Resentment, jealousy, or fear of the partner can cause negative conduct by one or both partners.
4. Overzealous activity by one partner can result in the other's withdrawal and ineffectiveness.
5. One partner may cover up for another who is engaged in unethical, immoral, or possibly illegal activity.

6. It is difficult for supervisors to give credit or blame to the proper partner for good or bad performance.
7. The productivity of a two-person unit is half that of a one-person unit, while the cost of operation is almost doubled.
8. The additional cost of vehicles and their maintenance to provide one-person-unit coverage is offset by the increased productivity.
9. Nine of ten calls for police service can be effectively handled by a one-person unit.
10. The one in ten calls requiring more than one officer almost always allows enough time for the second unit to arrive.
11. One-person units encourage the officer to become more observant and subsequently less susceptible to accident or sudden attack.
12. One-person units make quicker, wiser decisions, and the officer assumes more personal responsibility for actions and decisions.
13. More and better care of vehicles and equipment is seen in one-person units.
14. One-person units tend to develop more accurate, detailed investigations and stronger court cases.

Combined Automobile and Foot Patrols. The most effective, productive method of patrol is a combination of the one-person unit coupled with periodic foot patrol in various areas. This method requires a well-trained officer and dispatcher team, coupled with adequate supervision. A one-person vehicular unit operating with occasional periods of foot patrol has rapidly become the accepted method of patrol in many areas of the country. Security checks provide a good example where such patrol tactics can be effectively applied.

Security Checks. Frequent checks of business premises and property are a preventive patrol or enforcement technique. Security checks of businesses and buildings are necessary patrol functions. During such checks, note the following:

- Broken windows
- Open doors
- Pry marks (learn to distinguish "new" marks from old marks)

- Suspicious vehicles and people
- Property damage
- Lights off that are normally on (or *vice versa*)
- Unusual groups
- Access to roof (such as ladders left in the alley)

Security checks of buildings within a beat area have three objectives:

1. Making the officer more knowledgeable about the layout of the businesses, and so forth, on the beat
2. Allowing officers to discover an open business or burglary
3. Employing effective crime prevention and public relations tools

When performing security checks, cover as much of the commercial area(s) as possible, constantly varying patrol patterns to avoid a routine. Checks should be thorough, with emphasis given to crime-prone areas. Motorized patrol should include foot patrol checks for versatility of coverage. To avoid detection and alerting criminals, use flashlights and spotlights properly. Overillumination not only alerts criminals that officers are present but also provides a target at which the criminal can fire a weapon.

Security checks should include alleys and streets, cars (or other suspicious vehicles), pedestrians, and any unusual conditions. If you discover a forced entry into a business, immediately take cover and notify the radio communications center. Because there is always a chance that a suspect may still be inside the building, *wait* for assistance, *maintain* surveillance, and *contain* the situation. *Under no circumstances should the officer enter the building alone!* When help arrives, search and secure the building. Ultimately all officers should return to service as soon as possible. The officer who discovers the forced entry makes the reports and notifications required by the department or agency.

If an open business is discovered where no forced entry is apparent, follow the same precautionary measures for forced entry situations. Once the building is checked, notify the owner if possible. Once the premises are secured, return to duty as soon as possible. However, note the time of discovery and date for future reference. If the premises cannot be secured, leave a note if the owner cannot be notified or does not wish to come to the scene. Maintain a frequent check throughout the shift, and alert the next shift to the situation.

JUSTICE AND DISCRETIONARY PREROGATIVES

As a law enforcement officer, you will make many decisions on choices that involve discretion. In this statement, the key words are *decisions*, *choices*, and *discretion*. For professional peace officers, the end product of this process must be that each person is fairly treated based on sound principles of common sense, equal treatment, and due process of law. This concept is called "justice." In fact, it is at the patrol level of police operations that the concept of justice can be best implemented. You will be entrusted with the power to make arrests, give warnings, make decisions about traffic law violations, handle disturbances of the peace, dispose of cases involving juvenile violators, and regulate vice and narcotics violations—to mention but a few activities that require decision making. Each activity involves making decisions about a number of choices. How you react and what decisions you make determine what kind of officer you will become. For example, while on routine patrol you may observe a driver slow, but not completely stop, at a stop sign when no other traffic is present; your decision to issue a citation or give a warning is a matter of choice. A citation will certainly teach the driver a lesson and remind him or her of responsible driving; however, you might also determine that a courteous "warning" might gain the driver's respect and achieve the objective of voluntary compliance of stop sign obedience in the future. Which course of action is best? It's a matter of discretion for the officer.

Discretionary decisions in police work are absolutely essential. Such decisions frequently change, depending on priorities and available officers. Although you might issue a citation for a red light violation during preventive patrol duty, you may have to ignore a similar violation occurring within the next five minutes when you are directed to proceed to an accident involving injuries. The accident has priority over the violation. Availability of time, demands for service, patrol strength, and ongoing investigations can influence decisions. For example, detective officers frequently choose which cases to work on, given solubility factors determined by the initial investigation. Because time and officer availability prohibit complete investigation of all cases, a detective must concentrate on those cases that can be most easily solved and resolved. Such discretion serves the best public interest and uses police availability most wisely.

Within the law enforcement profession, thousands of individuals bring their strengths, interests, and talents to the patrol job. Although field supervision does exist, each patrol officer basically works as an independent entity on patrol. Each officer's training, personal value system, interests, and idea of preventive enforcement or investigation ultimately determines the degree and type of police service rendered to the community. This element of surprise works to the patrol advantage because of differences among patrol officers. Would-be criminals try to guess what patrol officers will do and where they will go during the patrol shift. Because officers differ in techniques, tactics, and interests, would-be criminals cannot always be sure of what to expect from various patrol officers. This situation helps law enforcement officers perform their duties, provided they correctly apply the other patrol tactics discussed in this text.

As a law enforcement officer, you have the responsibility and authority to respond to many situations in a variety of ways to determine what may or may not constitute a crime. You must rely on your education, training, judgment, and knowledge of which situations actually involve criminal activity. Your actions, to some degree, are governed by the substantive and procedural laws of your jurisdiction and agency. Laws regarding the use of reasonable force, probable cause, and so on frequently involve value judgments. Until other reasonable people agree with your judgment, your use of sound discretion may determine whether or not justice will prevail in any given situation.

Discretion in Use of Force

One of the most serious discretionary decisions any officer makes deals with the use of force. The amount of force permitted in each situation is limited to the officer's ability to exercise good judgment and competence in accordance with the penal code and departmental policy. A law enforcement officer must have the basic knowledge and physical ability necessary to make wise decisions in applying the correct amount of force in any given situation. Whenever you are threatened with danger, your confidence, ability, instinctive reaction, mental alertness, and concentration—coupled with self-control over emotions and body reactions—will determine whether or not you survive the crisis. In addition, you must constantly be aware that superiors will closely scrutinize any use of force to determine if it was an appropriate response to the threat. The community will be quick to judge your actions and apply sanctions for inappropriate behavior. In some instances, both you and the department will be subject to liabilities should you fail to use "reasonable force" in performing police duties. Remember the legal aspects of using force in law enforcement work. When you use force, the action can result in death or injury—or in control of the situation. Force in law enforcement is used to *protect life* and to *enforce the law* within the "limits of the law." Whenever force is used, you must be certain at all times that your actions are necessary and justified. Courts will examine whether or not the act was *committed of necessity* in your performance of duty. Furthermore, courts will determine if you acted as a reasonable person and used the *minimum amount of force necessary* to take the suspect into custody. Failure to meet these minimum standards of justification exposes an officer and the police agency to possible lawsuits.

Discretion Versus Discrimination

As noted, justice best prevails in law enforcement when officers make good discretionary decisions based on logical reasoning. Professional officers, however, never base discretionary decisions on discrimination. Discrimination is the outward result of prejudice—a tendency to act based on a judgment or unfavorable, irrational opinion formed before the facts are known. Hatred or dislike for a particular group, sex, race, or religion can result in injury or damage to a person arising from a hasty and unfair judgment by others. *There is no room for discrimination or prejudice in law enforcement!*

Every person brings his or her personal value system to the job. Each person has both strengths and weaknesses. However, officers in law enforcement must understand themselves—their prejudices and weaknesses—and put aside any unfavorable personal feeling before putting on the police uniform, badge, and duty weapon. It is impossible to control the actions of others unless an officer first understands and controls his or her own shortcomings and actions.

In order to effectively apply discretion in any given situation, an officer must *know* that the treatment is based on solid principles of good police discretionary decision making and not discrimination. Ask yourself if you would treat every person equally in any given situation. In a traffic situation where a warning is indicated, would you treat every person in the same way? If you give a man a ticket while letting a woman go with a warning, you are not using discretion, but rather discrimination. If you would arrest a person of a different race for disorderly conduct, but let a person of your own race go with only a lecture, you are discriminating. Ethnic slurs, prejudicial "humor," and discriminating statements are the acts of ignorant people. Such actions have no place in professional law enforcement.

Law Enforcement Officers and Civil Liability

By its very nature, police work involves the necessary use of limited force to accomplish the law *enforce*ment role. Penal codes specifically outline that officers may use necessary force against someone when the officer reasonably believes it is immediately necessary to make an arrest or search, or to prevent escape after arrest. However, penal codes also limit the use of force. For example, if a peace officer injures or kills an innocent third person, the penal code justification for using force is *not* available to the officer even though he or she was attempting to make a lawful arrest. In effect, the officer can face both criminal *and* civil litigation for recklessly injuring or killing an innocent third person. In other words, because of their training, education, and experience, law enforcement officers are expected to know *when* and *how* to properly use force to complete the law enforcement mission. Any deviation from strict guidelines can be justification for criminal and civil sanctions.

But this is only *part* of the story. The fact that the use of force may be justified under the penal code does not keep anyone from seeking any civil remedy for acts committed by peace officers in the line of duty. In performing duties, officers use "necessary force." This force can be a matter of perception for both the officer and a person being arrested. On one side, the officer will be certain in his or her own mind that whatever force used was *justified*; however, to the person being arrested, any amount of force (including the use of handcuffs) may seem extreme and *unnecessary*. Such a person may well seek to bring the matter to civil suit and ask a magistrate or a jury to determine the merit of the case. Nothing in the law prohibits an officer from being sued in civil court. In fact, lawsuits are a regular part of police work in today's civil litigation-prone society. Some lawyers make a lucrative law practice in handling this type of case. Generally speaking, civil suits are directed at both the officer and his or her agency; the plaintiff (person bringing the suit) expects to get a great sum of money from the city, county, or state rather than from the individual officer. Such suits usually contend that the officer's action was an extension of "policy or custom" of the agency, or that the agency failed to properly train the officer. Generally, the courts have held that a single act of misconduct by a peace officer is not sufficient to establish "policy or custom" for municipal liability purposes (*Oklahoma City v. Tuttle*, 105 S. Ct. 2427, 1985). However, in other limited situations courts have held that a single decision by "the appropriate official" may establish "policy," even though not every decision will do so (*Pembauer v. City of Cincinnati*, 106 S. Ct. 1292, 1986). As a rule, most civil suits will be weighed in the officer's favor provided that he or she follows generally accepted procedures and guidelines of the agency. In contrast, however, officers who have gone beyond the limits of their authority have had to face the real fact of owing large sums of money to plaintiffs in civil actions.

Civil suits can happen in relation to almost any aspect of a peace officer's job assignment. In one instance, the Supreme Court held that even while working under the authority of an arrest warrant, a peace officer does not have "absolute immunity" from liability for damages. Consider the following case.

Malley v. Briggs, 106 S. Ct. 1092, 1986.

On the basis of information received from a wiretrap, law enforcement officers obtained arrest warrants for plaintiffs on felony drug charges. Plaintiffs were arrested, but the grand jury did not indict them, and charges were subsequently dropped.

Plaintiffs filed a federal civil rights suit pursuant to 42 U.S.C. 1983, claiming that the officer-defendant violated their Fourth and Fourteenth Amendment rights "by applying for arrest warrants."

The trial judge granted the officer's motion for summary judgment, holding that an officer who believes facts stated in a warrant affidavit and submits them to a neutral magistrate is entitled to immunity from damages. However, the Supreme Court held that peace officers acting pursuant to a warrant are not entitled to "absolute immunity." It said, "There was no absolute immunity for complaining witnesses at common law, and there is no reason to adopt it for police officers who obtain warrant."

The Court stated that qualified immunity provides ample protection. If officers of reasonable competence could disagree about whether a warrant should be issued, the officer should enjoy immunity. But if it is obvious that a reasonably competent officer would have concluded that a warrant should not have been

issued, the officer-defendant has no immunity. Objective reasonableness cannot be established by merely showing that the officer
believed the facts stated in the affidavit and presented it to a
magistrate for review. It depends instead on whether a reasonably
well-trained officer would have known the affidavit was insufficient.

In this case, the defendant-officer urged the court to adopt an
absolute immunity where a warrant has been obtained, much like
the immunity enjoyed by prosecutors for their acts. The Court's
rejection of this contention does not diminish the effectiveness of
the officer's having a warrant. As long as the officer acted with
"objective reasonableness" in obtaining a warrant, he or she will
be immune from damages. The availability of qualified immunity is
an important incentive to acting with a warrant.

In another case, the Supreme Court held that peace officers have
"qualified immunity" from liability for a prisoner's suicide.

Gagne v. City of Galveston, 805 F.2d 558, 5th Cir. 1986.

Galveston police officers arrested a man for public intoxication and took him to jail. The prisoner had scars on his wrists from
a prior suicide attempt. Despite a department rule requiring that
prisoner's belts be taken from them at the booking site, the
officers failed to do so and failed to investigate the prisoner's
suicidal tendency. On the night of the prisoner's arrest, he hanged
himself with his belt. His survivors sued pursuant to 42 U.S.C.
1983.

The Court held that police officers engaged in discretionary
functions enjoy a *qualified immunity* from suit. The violation by the
officers of the regulation related to taking belts from prisoners was
not enough by itself to deprive them of this qualified immunity. The
officers in this case were under no constitutional duty to protect
prisoners from suicide attempts. In the absence of such a constitutional duty, the violation of the departmental rule was insufficient
by itself to characterize their conduct as ministerial rather than
discretionary. The qualified immunity for discretionary acts by the
officers has in this case therefore not been lost.

The panel decision from the Fifth Circuit was a divided one.
The dissenting judge would have found that the officers' violation

> of the department regulation amounted to a "callous indifference" to the life of the prisoner. The decision could just as easily have gone the other way—and may do so on another day.

In some instances, people indirectly affected by a police-initiated action have filed civil suit against a law enforcement officer. One such case happened in the city of Dallas.

Dent v. City of Dallas, No. 5–85–478CV, Tex. App.—Dallas, Nov. 20, 1986.

A law enforcement officer stopped a vehicle being driven by a person suspected of attempting to pass a forged prescription. When the officer ordered the car to pull off to the shoulder, the suspect sped away. The officer and others pursued the fleeing suspect for less than a mile before he ran a stop sign and collided with a car, whose driver was killed because of the accident.

The family of the deceased sued the two officers who were chasing the suspect, and the city of Dallas. They claimed the officer initially involved was negligent for failing to arrest the suspect when he had first stopped him, for instituting a high-speed chase, and for pursuing without using his siren.

The court held that in every negligence suit the plaintiff must establish that the defendant has a legal duty that he breached, causing damage to another. A law enforcement officer has a duty to the public at large to enforce the criminal law, but ordinarily has no specific duty to arrest unless such a duty is established by law. The court noted that "to hold the defendant liable for failure to arrest the fleeing suspect would require imposing a duty on police officers to arrest all persons stopped for any purpose to prevent their possible flight and subsequent injury to others." The duty of the officers in this case was to the public at large, not to the traveling public or to the deceased specifically. Also, the cause of the death was the fleeing suspect's grossly negligent conduct in running the stop sign and violating traffic laws in his attempt to escape arrest. The officer was a nonjudicial government official performing a discretionary function in *good faith*, and he was therefore entitled to qualified immunity.

While this case restates what has generally been held to be the law in other states, it is a "case of first impression" in Texas. The court refused to recognize any special duty, found the suspect's negligence the sole cause of the death, held the officer was entitled to good faith immunity, and rejected the possibility of a federal civil rights claim because the conduct of the officer was not negligent. On another day, in another city, the judgment *could* be different.

These three brief examples demonstrate but a few of the many types of lawsuits brought against law enforcement officers every day. The fact remains that anyone can sue you for just about any reason. However, just because you are being sued does not mean that you are in the wrong and that a large settlement will be granted against you. You can ensure that you have positive protection and limited immunity against such civil litigation by doing the following:

1. Learn to correctly perform your duty as a law enforcement officer through education and training. This text is a starting point for professional police patrol tactics and procedures, understanding of the law enforcement officer's role, knowledge of hazards, and a rational basis for specific reactions to many situations. Beginning peace officers start their careers by building a strong foundation in correctly approaching any situation and solving the problem with maximum protection for all people. Veteran officers will tell you that they never stop learning new tactics and techniques to enhance their job performance.

2. Know and follow departmental policy and guidelines in performing your duty. Remember that the "good faith immunity doctrine" works in your favor. Provided that you are acting in *good faith* based on departmental policy, you have *limited immunity* from civil litigation. "Good faith" means that you acted reasonably based on your knowledge, training, and experience; it also means that you followed departmental guidelines to the letter and intent. "Limited immunity" means that the courts will protect you from unreasonable suits provided you can prove that you were doing your job as a professional law enforcement officer.

3. Document your actions through proper reporting procedures. You have a means to "tell your side" of a case first when you generate accurate and detailed reports regarding all activities. Don't be lazy

when writing the account of your activity. Professional officers are also reporters. The written account of your actions—detailing that your activities are in accordance with correct local and state procedural rules—is your best means to protect you against civil suits. The report and your related field notebook will contain facts that might otherwise be forgotten; these reports can be very valuable in preparing a defense against civil litigation.

4. Keep your supervisor informed up front. Your immediate supervisor is on your side—remember, he or she is a peace officer too. However, your supervisor cannot stand up for you if he or she does not have all the facts. If you acted correctly in accordance with departmental policy and guidelines, your supervisor will back you all the way. This kind of aid is necessary for both your morale and the department's support.

5. Align yourself with professional police associations that seek to improve the law enforcement profession. Look for those kinds of associations that will provide insurance and legal assistance or advice for officers facing litigation.

6. Know that you are in the right, and stand up for yourself. Professional officers are hard to come by, and the profession cannot afford to lose your experience.

Keep in mind that once on patrol, you are in charge of your own conduct and activity. You are responsible for the decisions that you make and the actions you initiate. Through the courts, society will constantly evaluate your job performance. The way you apply reasonable force will constantly be scrutinized. You must be your own worst critic—constantly evaluate and reevaluate your performance. Strive to improve your techniques, tactics, and knowledge. On the day you "hang up your badge and gun"—whether at retirement or any time before—be able to honestly say that your community is a better place for your service because you were a professional law enforcement officer in every way.

KEY TERMS

Automobile patrol
Civil liability
Code of Ethics
Crime prevention
Crime repression

Directed enforcement

Discretion

Foot patrol

Inspections

Limited immunity

Patrol beat

Patrol hazards

Patrol operations

Police mission

Preventive enforcement

Proactive law enforcement

Professionalism

Reasonable force

Regulation of noncriminal behavior

STUDY QUESTIONS

1. Write two examples for each statement noted in the law enforcement code of ethics, and explain how law enforcement officers should correctly act in each instance.

2. As a student of law enforcement, what can you do now to begin preparing yourself to set the example for others?

3. In your own words, restate the following: "Accepting the responsibility to be a professional law enforcement officer is a lifetime commitment—a commitment to excellence in both professional and private behavior."

4. Make a list of your own prejudices and indicate, if possible, why you have these feelings. Make a plan of action to consciously overcome these shortcomings and instead implant a positive course of action for the future. Remember, you can't control others unless you can first control yourself!

5. As a uniformed peace officer, you approach the checkout counter at a local restaurant to pay for your meal. Although several people are in front of you, the hostess tells you that the manager has taken care of your ticket and waves you through. What should you do?

6. You observe a speeding violator, and stop the vehicle. The driver of the speeding car says she is late for a plane and hands you a $20 bill along with her driver's license. What should you do?

7. Define the basic purpose of police patrol.

8. What is the police mission, and how do the objectives of police patrol seek to accomplish it?

9. Define the difference between preventive enforcement and directed enforcement. Give three examples of each type of patrol activity.

10. What is the citizen's role in assisting the law enforcement agency? What can you do to increase community participation in preventing and reporting crime?

11. Outline ten ways that law enforcement officers provide "services" for the community other than crime repression and apprehension of offenders.

12. Why is a peace officer considered to be "an ambassador" for his or her community? Outline five situations where an officer's duty could result in such a service.

13. Why do a majority of law enforcement officers work other jobs during off-shift hours and on weekends?

14. What are the advantages and disadvantages of foot patrol? Through group discussion, add to the list outlined in the text.

15. What are the advantages and disadvantages of motorized patrol? Through group discussion, add to the list outlined in the text.

16. Modern advances in technology continually add to new methods of police patrol. What contributions do you think computers will make to law enforcement of the future?

17. Define proactive law enforcement. How can officers best use proactive methods to control crime?

18. Why must officers consciously avoid developing any type of "routine patrol?"

19. What is the good faith immunity doctrine? When does an officer receive qualified immunity from civil litigation?

20. How can combined foot and automobile patrol be used effectively to achieve the police mission?

21. Define the concepts of justice and discretion. How can a professional law enforcement officer use these concepts to accomplish the police role?

22. How do discretion and discrimination differ?

23. If a peace officer uses excessive force to make an arrest, what are the

possible criminal and civil ramifications of such action?

24. Outline the methods discussed in the text to protect yourself against unreasonable civil litigation. Through discussion with instructors, law enforcement officers, magistrates, and other people, can you add to this positive list of ways to avoid civil liability?

ACTIVITIES

1. Organize two discussion groups. One group will advocate the two-person motorized patrol, and the other group the one-person motorized patrol. With an instructor or other person as a moderator, establish a dialog that will discuss the pros and cons of each method. After one person advocates a plus for his or her group, someone from the other group is given an opportunity to argue against the proposition. Then someone from the other group presents its argument for that position, and your group counters with an opposing view. Alternate the discussion groups as time permits. Use as many people as possible to enter into the discussion and present different views. After the open forum, each student writes his or her own evaluation of each position.

2. Research recent court decisions in your state or local area regarding civil litigation against peace officers. Prepare a short case brief detailing the events leading up to the suit and the court ruling or "holding" in each case. Critique the case, and evaluate the officers' actions in the situation. What lesson can other officers gain from the experience of the officers involved in the litigation?

3. Interview several peace officers and ask them to define "professionalism," and how the concept applies to their job performance. Outline your goals to become professional.

4. Conduct a survey of your local, county, or state law enforcement agencies to determine the level of educational background for officers assigned. Conduct a "professionalism survey" in the same community, and determine the community perception of law enforcement in the community. Correlate any reports corresponding to the educational background of the officers and community perception as to the professional behavior of the officers.

2

Police Systems and Basic Patrol Procedures

Teamwork and adherence to time-proven procedures form the bases of modern law enforcement tactics and techniques. Sound principles and logical approaches to police patrol systems and procedures develop out of many years of work to improve patrol tactics for law enforcement. Efforts of professional officers in the past form the foundations for specific procedures that modern officers follow to accomplish the police mission. This chapter overviews the interrelations of proven systems and suggests methods you can apply in accepting the patrol responsibility.

THE POLICE SYSTEMS APPROACH TO LAW ENFORCEMENT

Throughout the ages, policing has been a major function of organized societies in all countries. Law enforcement in the United States has generally developed from rudimentary organizations of great antiquity that originated in Europe. From the time people first began to live together in society, they have realized that laws are necessary to regulate the conduct of community members for the security and good of all. Otherwise the result would be chaos, and community life would be impossible. Furthermore, for the laws to be meaningful, communities have to provide ways and means of compelling observance and obedience. Accordingly, in every time and place where civilization has bloomed, certain people have been given immediate responsibility for enforcing community laws.

Development of Police Systems

In the seventeenth and eighteenth centuries, the system and structure of law enforcement that had become familiar in England was transplanted to the American colonies. Rural America, incorporating most of the colonial territory, became the province of the sheriff and the constable. The transfer was accomplished with the structure of those officers virtually intact as compared to their English counterparts; the constable had responsibility for law enforcement in towns, while the sheriff assumed charge of policing in the counties.

Local Law Enforcement. The first half of the nineteenth century saw phenomenal growth in U.S. towns, and with that growth and expansion, crime, violence, and lawlessness became commonplace. Because the situation rose beyond the constable's ability to deal with it, many U.S. cities responded to the threat of crime and disorder by developing organized metropolitan police forces of their own. Philadelphia was one of the first such communities. Wealthy philanthropist Stephen Girard died in 1831 and left a "substantial sum" of money to the city of Philadelphia for the purpose of establishing a competent police force. The city government, motivated by the windfall, passed an ordinance creating a force of 24 men to work during the day and 120 nightwatchmen. The force was placed under the command of a captain appointed by the mayor; promotions were based on merit rather than political favor. The entire system proved very successful, although short-lived. When the bequest was exhausted, the ordinance was repealed, and the police system in Philadelphia reverted to its previous status. Of course, it immediately became clear that the old system was unsatisfactory. However, not until 1854 did day and night forces merge under the command of an elected marshal.

In 1838, Boston established a day police force to augment its night watch. Cities were discovering that crime and violence were not just nighttime phenomena. These early two-shift police systems had inherent difficulties. Fierce competition between the day and night shifts was a major source of strife and created problems for the two separate administrators. Recognizing the harmful effects of having two separate and independent shifts, the New York legislature in 1844 enacted a law authorizing the merger of the day and night forces, an action that abolished the night watch system. Ten years later, Boston consolidated its day and night watches.

During the next decade, several cities, following the New York model, developed their own unified police forces, and by 1870 the nation's largest cities had full-time police forces. By the turn of the century, few cities of significant size lacked consolidated forces, which gradually came under the direction and control of a single chief or commissioner. These chief executive officers were often appointed by the mayor, sometimes subject to city council approval. Some gained the office by direct election.

Not surprisingly, these early organized police forces in U.S. cities faced many problems that police confront today. A constant need for additional personnel necessitated compromises in employment standards. Moreover, salaries for police were among the lowest in local government, which in itself blocked successful recruiting. The fact that police of the period were not respected should not be surprising. They were not strikingly successful and were not noted for their progressiveness and vitality. The major purpose of their existence was simply to keep the community peaceful and sufficiently trouble-free so as not to arouse public outrage.

Political control caused many problems that plagued these pioneer metropolitan police forces. Police eventually became identified with the graft and political corruption that marked local government during the era. In a serious effort to resolve these problems, responsible community and government leaders adopted police administrative boards or commissions to remove the control and direction of police operations from local politicians. These boards were given responsibility for appointing police administrators and managing police business. Unfortunately, these efforts at removing political meddling were unsuccessful, probably because the members of the administrative boards (judges, lawyers, businessmen) were incapable of dealing effectively with the range of problems that police faced.

Toward the close of the nineteenth century, another serious attempt at police reform was undertaken. State legislatures, noting that the problems of inferior policing existed primarily in the urban areas, and being dominated by rural legislators, required that police administrators be appointed by the state. Thus the state displaced local government in the control of law enforcement. This shift in authority was also unsuccessful, mainly because many further problems had not been anticipated.

Despite increased state control, large U.S. cities still had to pay for police service, and costs continued to grow. A major reason for rising costs was that police boards were not directly accountable to the local tax-paying entities they served. To make matters worse, in situations where state and city governments were on opposite sides of the political fence, friction usually increased. Certainly this was the case when a state-appointed administrator implemented policy in conflict with the views of the local population. Cities did not regain control of their police forces until well into the twentieth century.

In the last half of the nineteenth century, police forces and functions continued to grow and expand. After these sincere efforts at police reform, however, little notice was made of the changes that had necessitated expansion. Nor was there analysis of the effects of such broad social changes on the role of the police. The Pendleton Act of 1883 established civil service for government service, including law enforcement; it was a breakthrough that spread to local police agencies and alleviated some of the more serious problems of political interference.

County Sheriff. The word *sheriff* was derived from under the Anglo-Saxon form of government in ancient England. In each shire, or county, which frequently represented an old petty kingdom, an alderman represented the ancient royal family and acted as titular head of the area. The word *shire* was derived from the Saxon *scyre*, or "squire"; *county* came from the Old French *comte*, or "count."

Because the alderman was inclined to uphold local interest against any attempt at centralization, the king eventually placed alongside him a new official called the king's reeve, who answered to the king and not to the alderman. The word *reeve* meant "keeper" in Saxon. This official became the principal officer in the shire under the name of "shire reeve" or, as we know it today, *sheriff*. Eventually taking the alderman's place completely, the sheriff, within the limits of his county, exercised powers akin to those of a viceroy. (A viceroy is the governor of a province or county who rules as a representative of the king—*roy* means "king.")

The sheriff's duty in receiving and interpreting the king's mandates were military, judicial, fiscal, and executive. For example, he was responsible for the military forces of the county and for keeping the public peace. For help in this effort, he was authorized to muster the *posse comitatus* (under the English common law, the sheriff could summon all men over 15 years of age to help enforce the laws). The concept of the U.S. West "sheriff's posse" was based on this principle.[1] As the king's bailiff and steward, the shire reeve had responsibility for collecting county revenues, executing writs, operating the jails, and protecting the king's forest.[2] Because he was the judicial president of the shire, administrator of the royal domain, and the executive arm of the law in the county, the whole plan of local government centered in the shire reeve's office.

Under Norman rule, the sheriff continued his control over police administration of the county as a royal officer of great dignity and power. After the conquest, the conquerors tended to strengthen the sheriff's authority on a systematic basis. But in time the Norman kings began to reduce the sheriff's power. Even before the thirteenth century, he had begun to lose some of his authority, and the Magna Carta removed his judicial authority in 1215. Gradually, the sheriffs, instead of being the colleagues and equals of the king's justices, became assistants to the judges. Between the thirteenth and nineteenth centuries, the English sheriffs were slowly but surely stripped of virtually all the great powers they had once exercised. About all that remains today in England of their once extensive power is the authority to call out the *posse comitatus*. Although responsible for prisoners condemned to death, they have nothing to do with jails. The principal duty still retained today is that of executing the writs addressed to the sheriff by the courts.

In the colonial United States, the rural areas of the South designated the sheriff as the chief law enforcement officer of the county. However, because of the position that the sheriffs had held in old

---

[1] The Posse Comitatus Act of 1878 prohibits the use of U.S. Army (or other military) personnel for the purpose of helping civil authorities enforce civil law.

[2] The story of Robin Hood concerns this era when the king's forest was reserved for royal people. Ordinary townspeople were not permitted to hunt game in the forest, and it was the shire reeve's job to prevent such poaching. Robin Hood's chief rival was the Sheriff of Nottingham (one of the larger shires in ancient England).

England, the general populace was suspicious of giving too much power to one person. Thus, the county sheriff in most areas of the United States is an elected official—through their vote, citizens of the county can either keep or remove any sheriff who does not abide with the will of the county voters. Today, the sheriff in most jurisdictions is responsible for enforcing law in the unincorporated areas of the county. The sheriff also manages the county jail, provides security in the county courts, and serves the civil process of the county.

State Police. State police agencies developed later than local or municipal police forces. The Texas Rangers were established in 1835. In those days, the Rangers were more a military unit than a law enforcement agency. Massachusetts was the first state to appoint "state constables" to enforce state laws in 1865. In 1903 Connecticut established a state law enforcement agency, but the first actual state police agency was organized in Pennsylvania in 1905.

The states had organized militia, and the National Guard was available to be used as an emergency enforcement arm. However, these tools were inadequate and inappropriate for the extensive tasks connected with effective police work. At the turn of the century, large U.S. cities were growing larger, and the developing metropolitan areas created tremendous crime problems with which sheriffs and constables could not cope. Moreover, as the local jurisdictions developed their own police forces, state officials—particularly governors—began to realize that they had no control over law enforcement in their states. Furthermore, the failures of local authorities to control vice and labor violence, enforce laws in the rural area, and patrol the increasing miles of roads and highways all became painfully evident to state authorities. As a result, state efforts eventually developed efficient state agencies to handle these and other problems. Today, many state law enforcement agencies exist with specialized divisions to accomplish law enforcement mission efforts at the state level.

Federal Law Enforcement. The U.S. Constitution reserved the general police powers for the states. The federal government was restricted by the Constitution to enforcing certain federal laws having to do with taxes, commerce, post offices, and counterfeiting of U.S. currency. Federal law enforcement was very slow in developing because the states feared a strong federal law enforcement program. The first federal law enforcement agency was the U.S. Marshal's

Service in 1791, which provided protection and service to the federal courts. During the western expansion in the United States, the Customs Service was organized in the late 1700s to protect the nation against smuggling. Other major federal agencies were formed later in response to dealing with specific problems. Some of these include the Internal Revenue Service to enforce internal tax laws; the Bureau of Alcohol, Tobacco, and Firearms to enforce alcohol, tobacco, and gun laws; the Secret Service to investigate counterfeiting of U.S. currency; the Border Patrol to combat illegal alien traffic; and the Federal Bureau of Investigation, in 1925, to investigate various other federal offenses.

Current U.S. Police Systems and Practices

Law enforcement activities in the United States have always been fragmented; that is, no one body of government oversees the totality of organizing and controlling law enforcement efforts throughout the United States, or in any one of the individual states. Enforcement activities are vested in numerous agencies with overlapping jurisdictions. For example, dealing with a bank robbery in one city will most likely involve cooperative efforts of federal, state, county, and local law enforcement officials to identify, locate, apprehend, and prosecute the guilty offenders. Law enforcement efforts thus are a result of "teamwork," starting with the higher echelons of administration and management and working down to the patrol level at the street. It is therefore not surprising that the term "team policing" has developed in this field.

Team policing has been experimented with in many forms. The early method of using a ward system was an attempt at team policing. For example, the Statute of Winchester, issued by King Edward I in 1285, was a genuine effort to establish a systematic police patrol system in divided areas—called "wards"—both in and out of London. Based on the old "hue and cry" system,[3] this system required every town to supplement its forces by deploying men at each gate to watch continually all night "from sun setting unto sun rising." Large areas were divided into wards, and residents performed night watch (or

---

[3] The "hue and cry" action required every able-bodied man to join in the common chase for offenders; this process was the origin of our current process of *citizen's arrest*.

patrol) within the section. For the purpose of safety, some watchmen grouped themselves together and formed a *marching watch*; this may have been the beginning of "police patrol" activity as we know it today. In the early American colonies, ward systems were used, reinstating night watch programs. However, early systems failed because the nightwatchmen were bored with the duty and failed to execute their responsibility. The duty tended to be given to the elderly, sick, or lame. Ultimately, the constable on patrol (perhaps the origin of the acronym *COP*) became the predominant type of law officer in the northern counties, while the sheriff performed essentially the same service in the rural South.

In many large U.S. cities, administrators have again adopted a ward-type system to decentralize police into precincts or districts. The traditional district command under team policing is simply an extension of the district team concept; that is, in each division several district teams have general responsibility for almost all police service. In this system, the commander is responsible for most police services within the district, and thus conventional functions such as patrol on the one hand and investigation on the other are no longer carried out by separate divisions.

The traditional district, sector, or team area is a geographic area in which a single team operates. Generally the team is commanded by a lieutenant, with five or six sergeants, a number of detectives, and nine to as many as forty patrol officers. A division, or area, would consist of several teams, usually under a captain or major. The beat, response zone, or zone is the area within a district that is the responsibility of a single officer but may also include overlapping jurisdictions of several officers working at the same time in the district. Usually, these terms apply to the area for which an officer is responsible for the conduct of follow-up investigations within the district. Police personnel are apportioned throughout the day in time units and are assigned to a watch or shift; the tour of duty may be consecutive eight- or ten-hour shifts and may overlap other shifts to meet unusual or peak-load periods of time. Some jurisdictions have used a platoon system where personnel are assigned to one shift or watch. The platoon, ordinarily commanded by a lieutenant, may serve the entire city or a district thereof. It may be composed of several squads assigned to sectors for the city or the district. Divisions that have personnel on duty for more than one shift divide them into platoons on the basis of the hours of the day they are on duty, without regard to the number on duty or the rank of the supervising officer. This procedure facilitates making assignments.[4]

Team policing in modern times has taken on new meanings. In small law enforcement agencies, team policing is the basic tactic used on a day-to-day basis. However, in larger departments, traditional district command concepts do not apply in the case of team police. Law enforcement has moved into an era of specialization in many of these agencies. For example, a special weapons and tactics (SWAT) team is one type of specialized team policing. Officers assigned to SWAT teams come from regular police operations and react to potentially dangerous situations as required. Personnel receive special training in tactics and weapons to be used against people who have taken a hostage or in other violent circumstances where a high potential for violence exists. The purpose of such a unit is to resolve the crisis situation in a manner that employs the least amount of force, harm, injury, or death to all people involved in the incident. Other examples of specialized team efforts are as follows.

1. *Tactical units.* Unmarked police patrol units used primarily for surveillance and apprehension of criminals. These units use *covert patrol* and are usually directed against special crime problems such as burglary, robbery, and sexual assault cases.

2. *Canine (K-9) units.* Officers working with specially trained dogs to supplement and support other tactical or patrol units. The dogs can be effectively used for search tactics and backup units in the field.

3. *Domestic violence specialists.* Law enforcement teams are now being trained to specialize in handling domestic violence crimes and help in settling civil as well as criminal disputes.

4. *Rape crisis (also called "sexual assault") teams.* These officers specialize in investigation of various types of assaults, including rape. Special interviewing techniques, the need to obtain sensitive evidence, and compassion toward the victim are all foci of unique efforts to concentrate team training to handle these crime problems.

5. *Other specialized investigation units.* Within the detective division of many departments, teams specialize in crimes against persons, crimes against property, criminal intelligence, organized crime, and many other specialized units as need exists in the area. Such problems

---

[4] Summarized from O. W. Wilson and Roy Clinton McLaren, *Police Administration*, 4th ed., (New York: McGraw-Hill Book Company, 1977), p. 72.

may include gambling, prostitution, book making, and loan sharking, to mention a few.

6. *Neighborhood team policing.* In this model, a squad or team of officers is responsible for providing almost all police services within a specific area on a 24-hour-a-day, seven-day-a-week basis. This concept expects officers to become part of the community in which they patrol and to use police-community relations and crime prevention to the maximum in their concentrated area of patrol. The premise is that people are territorial and will protect their home turf from hostility. When police personnel are assigned to an area and are kept there for a good period of time, those officers will learn to care for and protect "their" territory. Instilling the same fervor in the minds of the residents in that area, thus gaining public approval and support of police action, helps police to complete their mission.

Pros and Cons of Specialization in Police Work

Team policing appears to be effective in many areas of the country. As noted, most smaller agencies are organized as teams. However, efforts to specialize teams for specific concentration in larger agencies can have both negative and positive effects on the agency or department. Many problem areas tend to involve communication and coordination between specialized units and traditional patrol units. In order for neighborhood team police to be effective, operations must be planned to coordinate team efforts, emphasizing communication between the specialized team and other components of the patrol force. Furthermore, to eliminate overlap of supervision, the team's territorial integrity must be regulated so that responsibility for almost all police operations is fixed within the agency. Officers assigned to conduct follow-up investigations must work closely with patrol officers and be accountable to the same team commander; this action promotes positive management concepts of unity of command; that is, only one person commands each situation or officer. When one person is in command, each officer knows to whom he or she is directly responsible within the chain of command, thus eliminating confusion and instituting harmonious working relationships between personnel. Coordination of efforts is crucial when various command components are involved in working together toward a similar police operation. In such cases, the plan should consist of designating one officer in charge or command of the entire operation to avoid confusion and conflicts.

Active community relations programs with emphasis on meetings and other contacts with neighborhoods must expand to ensure citizen participation. A means for educating and informing the public in setting team objectives is essential to seeking community support.

Pros in Favor of Specialization

Specialization is a natural progression in an advanced, highly technological society. Industry as well as government agencies have found that specialization provides many positive advantages. Some of the arguments in favor of this approach are

1. Training can be focused for members of the "team" that will directly handle specialized incidents. For example, members of the SWAT team may receive specialized training in various assault rifles, rappelling from buildings or other high places, drug raids, hostage negotiations, and approaches to dangerous situations, to mention a few.

2. Specialization instills "esprit de corps" in members of the unit. This pride improves morale in the unit and evokes the best from each officer.

3. Training is expensive; intense training designed for specialists reduces the relative cost of training the entire department.

4. The professional results of working specialists reinforces the community's belief that the law enforcement agency can effectively deal with problems and bring about positive conclusions to crime and/or area dilemmas. Publicizing the existence and success rate of the special team is useful to deter crime and solicit support from the community (although it is wise in most cases to keep the identity of assigned officers anonymous). For example, publicizing the fact that undercover officers are posing as prostitutes to combat excessive offenses on the street will likely reduce the number of such crimes because the offenders will know they run a high risk of being caught.

5. Responsibility and authority for handling law enforcement actions can be delegated to a subordinate official who answers to the agency head. In this manner the chief or sheriff fixes the responsibility and knows whom to specifically contact in order to give direction or obtain answers about certain investigations or police actions. In addition, the agency head can act as a coordinator between various specialized groups when combined unit action is contemplated.

6. When a team works together in training exercises, each member knows his or her role and understands what the other team

members are doing. This coordinated effort results in safety for the members and positive results for the team.

7. Officers in the agency will have something to strive toward in their career development. The opportunity to work with a specialized unit is the reason why many people seek to join the law enforcement profession in the first place. Many rookies want to have a positive effect in society by working to eliminate drugs or to help juvenile offenders.

8. Specialization can use the special skills that each officer brings to the career field. Skills such as computer expertise, piloting helicopters or airplanes, and driving high-powered automobiles (to list a few) can be used in a positive way to accomplish the police mission.

The Cons or Negative Results of Specialization

Generally, the positives outweigh the negative aspects of specialization. However, specific action is required to prevent the following negative reactions:

1. Any act to specialize generally requires labor power from another part of the law enforcement force—most frequently from patrol. Therefore, too many specialized forces pull people from routine patrol and can result in understaffing preventive patrol efforts and increasing response time to incidents, accidents, or other patrol responsibilities, including backup efforts. Remember that at least 50 percent of the uniformed officers of any department or agency should be assigned to patrol duties.

2. The creation of an "elitist" attitude among members of the special teams can be a problem, especially when the special unit is given credit for accomplishing a mission at the expense of the work of the regular patrol units. It is imperative that the chief administrative officer, as well as team leaders, prevent "empire building" within the specialized group. Such empire building not only can create problems within the department but can also have negative effects on citizen support.

3. Promotions within the team may remove a valuable member of the squad who has had extensive training in a specialty. On being promoted to sergeant, or a higher staff position, the member may be required under labor power rules to assume new duties. This void must be filled from the patrol division and necessitates training a new person in the specialty.

4. When communication and coordination fail between specialized units or within the agency involving patrol units, this dangerous situation can create animosity among departmental functions. This animosity can have devastating long-range effects on future operations.

PREPARATION FOR PATROL DUTY

Law enforcement patrol operations fulfill many objectives and purposes, though all the patrol tasks tend to surround one primary goal—protection of people and property. The way this goal is achieved determines the success or failure of the police department in accomplishing its mission, and each officer plays a major role in achieving this goal. Each officer is responsible for his or her district and the maintenance of peace and order in that area of responsibility.

Initial Strategy for Patrol

Peace officers use specific criteria in determining a strategy for covering the beat (patrol) area. You must be aware of the characteristics of the beat and accordingly prepare to meet the demands of the job ahead. Knowledge of special problems inherent on the beat, understanding of the population distribution, understanding of hazards, and the ability to tap community resources allow the patrol officer to develop awareness and accountability. Seasoned officers develop specific beat information that enables them to be proficient on the job. Information can be gathered regarding the population, geography, location of emergency facilities, crime hazards, and community habits. For example, the following information is generally relevant to the officer:

1. *Population.* How many people live in the area? What are the racial characteristics? What is the general age displacement (juvenile, elderly, and so forth)?
2. *Geographic data.* Where are the thoroughfares, freeways, railroads, lakes, reservoirs, and dams? Does the terrain contain swamps, ravines, dangerous animals, and so on?
3. *Emergency facilities.* Where are the hospitals, fire stations, community mental health offices, and other community resource

agencies? The professional officer will have readily available a list of the addresses and phone numbers of such agencies.

4. *Crime hazards.* Are the business and residential areas burglary-prone? Which establishments are robbery-prone? What areas are attractive to auto theft suspects? Are some areas prone to acts of petty theft or malicious mischief? What kind of drug-related activity is present?

5. *Community habits.* What are the traffic patterns in the beat area? Is the area a community dealing with seasonally oriented visitors, such as a beach or resort location? Does the area sponsor sporting events such as football or baseball games? Is the area a retirement community?

By answering these questions, officers begin preparing for the patrol responsibility.

Two areas need to be considered in preparing for patrol duty: (1) physical preparation and (2) mental preparation. Both require careful forethought and planning. Neglecting either can lead to disastrous consequences for the officer.

Physical Preparation. Before each shift, check yourself for the following:

1. *Cleanliness*
2. *Personal grooming*—fresh shave; neat, clean hair; and so on
3. *Uniform:*
   a. Tailored to fit as well as possible
   b. Clean, pressed, and in good repair
4. *Equipment:*
   a. Leather gear
   b. Duty weapon, shotgun
   c. Mace
   d. Baton, helmet (if appropriate)
   e. Flashlight with fresh batteries and spare bulb
   f. Badge and name plate
   g. Clipboard
   h. Notebook and both pen and pencil (*note:* pencil may be necessary during inclement weather when ballpoint pen does not work)
   i. First-aid gear
   j. Vehicle

k. Required materials for duty, such as arrest, incident, and accident forms; citation and traffic warning books; impound and recovery forms; juvenile contact and arrest forms; and other relevant items

5. *Personal actions:*
   a. Maintain good posture; always walk and stand erect; do not slouch.
   b. Keep hands out of pockets.
   c. Avoid stuffed pockets; keep carried items to a minimum.
   d. Do not smoke or chew tobacco while confronting the public.
   e. Wear headgear properly, not cocked to one side or on the back of the head.
   f. Remember that a direct relationship exists between appearance and attitude, both yours and the public's.
   g. *Esprit de corps* is higher among officers who belong to a sharp, snappy outfit!

Mental Preparation. The single most important factor in officer safety is mental conditioning. The transition from civilian work to employment as a peace officer necessitates some mental and emotional conditioning to adapt to the psychological pressures of law enforcement work. Because these elements are internal to the individual concerned and cannot be seen or monitored, this item is most frequently overlooked or misunderstood by supervisors and/or other officers. Many of the following factors are involved in psychological preparedness for law enforcement work:

- Attitude development and preparation
- Sociological and psychological maturity
- Both formal and informal education
- Personal value system

Avoid developing attitudes that are counterproductive to job performance. Such *poor* attitudes include

- Isolationism and ostracizing others
- Becoming paranoid and regarding all people suspiciously as would-be criminals
- Withdrawing from or failing to be a normal part of the community

Before beginning a shift, orient yourself to that particular shift. Shift orientation involves such areas of preparation as

1. Keeping abreast of any changes in departmental policy or procedures
2. Maintaining current knowledge of court rulings pertinent to job performance
3. Checking lists of wanted people and noting any additions or deletions
4. Noting items reported as lost or stolen and keeping a current list of serial numbers, if applicable
5. Maintaining information pertinent to stolen automobiles
6. Keeping up-to-date information on incident reports from previous shifts, such as
   a. Disturbance or disputes in your patrol area
   b. Crimes committed in your patrol area and methods of attack used
   c. Auto accidents or special traffic problem areas
7. Maintaining a current list of home checks or business checks of vacationers, and so on
8. Knowing about vacant or newly constructed homes and businesses in your patrol area
9. Conducting follow-up investigations of reports from previous shifts as necessary and filing supplemental reports
10. Preparing for changes in assignments or stakeout details
11. Maintaining current knowledge of arrest warrants to be served
12. Obtaining an indepth briefing from the previous officer on the patrol about current problem areas

Officers generally gather information through reports and briefings: Reports may include

- Daily incident log
- Daily crime log
- Computer printouts
- Officers' journals
- Crime desk
- Investigations unit

Briefings may involve

- Squad conferences
- Detective briefings
- Inservice training
- Intersquad-intrasquad information exchanges
- Internal memoranda

PATROL TECHNIQUES AND PROBLEM AREA PATROL

In choosing the type of patrol technique to be employed at any time during the tour of duty, consider the special problem areas on the beat. Common patrol techniques used by patrol officers are "preventive" (or conspicuous) patrol and "apprehension" (or nonconspicuous directed) patrol coverage; these concepts were introduced in Chapter 1. The specific techniques used depend on a number of factors, including the types of problem to be dealt with. The basic difference between these two approaches depends on whether officers wish to be visible to the public and/or the criminal element or not. In preventive patrol, the objective is "high visibility," to discourage potential problems. In apprehension patrol, the aim is to arrest the violator or criminal in the act.

Preventive patrol can be very effective in combatting certain kinds of problems. Once an officer has identified specific problems (accidents, violations, and so on), he or she may plan to be seen as much as possible. Preventive patrol has two distinct advantages: (1) it increases citizen confidence in the police, and (2) it reduces the opportunity for crime, thus reducing citizen anxiety and dissatisfaction and the cost of prosecution. Apprehension patrol may be used for the more difficult or serious problems such as burglary, robbery, and drug or sex offenses. Officers use stakeouts and other covert operations to observe without being seen by the would-be criminal. Gathering information and intelligence on narcotics and gambling operations may be a part of the specific technique. Establishing tactical units to deal with a warehouse burglary or convenience store robberies is another example of this tactic. You may follow up on an informant's lead to observe an alleged meeting between a narcotics dealer and young high school customers in a parking lot. If a "sale" is made, you can then take action to make an arrest or call the situation to the attention of narcotics specialists.

The decision to use preventive or apprehension patrol is frequently left up to the patrol officer. However, communication between the officer and other officers (including the supervisor) is needed to coordinate efforts. The decision you make will depend on the seriousness of the crime involved. If the crime is serious, you will want to apprehend the criminal. If the crime, or offense, is less serious, your presence may be enough to discourage or prevent the activity from occurring.

In addition to the sight and sound of the patrol unit, other factors will help determine how aware other people are of police presence. These factors involve the way you handle your patrol vehicle. One of these factors is the use of lights. Department policy outlines whether or not officers may patrol without headlights at night; certainly, there are certain liability concerns to take into consideration should the patrol vehicle be involved in an accident while operating covertly. If you plan to patrol without headlights, you must avoid activating brake lights, interior lights, spotlights, and the flashlight. Any unexpected flash of light will betray your presence.

Techniques of Patrol

In addition to the basic types of patrol and the factors of citizen awareness that determine effectiveness of patrol activities, specific patrol techniques can increase the effectiveness of crime detection. For example, patrol speed can have a direct effect on the problem. For normal street patrol, most authorities agree that approximately 20 mph is the most effective because it provides maximum opportunity to observe while maintaining effective control of the vehicle. This speed also contributes to citizen awareness of the officer's presence and maintains a good police image.

In general, select a parking location to accommodate your plan of patrol activity. If you want the patrol unit to be visible, the parked vehicle should be conspicuous. If you plan to apprehend a potential offender, choose the parking location after considering the legal, as well as the visibility, factors.

Patrol Patterns

There is more to covering a police beat than simply driving through in the patrol vehicle and responding to radio calls. In order to achieve the goals of citizen awareness, crime prevention, and apprehension, you need to have many different plans. One of these plans is the pattern of movement you use in driving through the assigned area. The plan should be certain to cover all streets assigned while ensuring that the patrol method is *not* predictable. The lack-of-predictability objective is obviously aimed at keeping potential criminals off balance—uncertain whether the officer passing a certain location will be back in five minutes or at some later time.

When patrolling the beat, make appropriate decisions about which lane to drive in. The Number 1 lane (nearest the center of the roadway) lends itself to effective observation. From here, you have a clearer view between buildings on both sides of the street. In addition, you can observe oncoming traffic more effectively. However, sometimes you will want to drive in the lane nearest the curb, especially if you are traveling slowly. At these times, stops at the curb can be made more readily, and the curb lane affords a better view of street-front windows, sides of buildings, and potential hiding places. The curb lane also lets you focus attention on one particular area longer than if you had to worry about traffic coming toward the patrol unit, or from some other direction.

Once in the field, gradually develop a patrol plan that provides complete coverage without predictability. Generally, professional officers use a combination of three basic patrol patterns—circular, double-back, and random.

Circular. In this pattern, the car is driven either from the approximate center of the beat in ever-increasing "circles" or from the outside of the beat in ever-decreasing circles. (Obviously, the pattern is not truly circular, but approximately so. See Figure 2-1.)

Double-Back. This plan is methodical and is also helpful in learning the beat. As with the circular plan, unpredictability can be provided by varying the starting-point and occasionally either looping a block or making a double-back run on the same street just covered, as shown in Figure 2-2. Double-back runs are particularly helpful in problem areas or in cases where you have spotted something on the regular run that needs another look. You may even want to stake out the suspect area for a while on the opposite side of the street.

Random. There are as many ways of achieving a random pattern

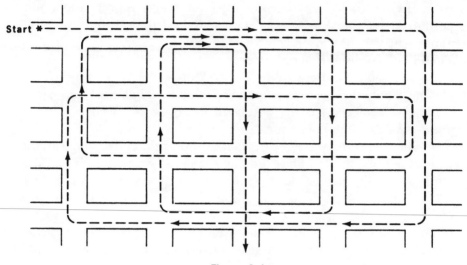

Start *

Figure 2-1
Example of circular patrol pattern

as there are beats to be covered and officers to patrol them. The random pattern is actually a *combination* of the other two, and is the one you will probably use once you get to know your beat. (See Figure 2-3.) For example, you may choose to build your random approach around the type of problem you are trying to resolve. However, whichever pattern you select, it must provide for complete coverage.

Patrol Hazards

Police hazards are any condition that could lead to an incident calling for police intervention or action. The four basic kinds of police hazards are (1) people, (2) places, (3) property, and (4) situations. Each of these can in turn be aggravated by conditions such as weather, seasonal changes, population density, or other factors. Remember that both animate and inanimate hazards often appear together.

Elemental factors that create hazards can include the presence, absence, or condition of certain things, the human element, or an element of time including the hour of the day, the day of the week, and the season of the year. Hazards can result from any conditions, such as

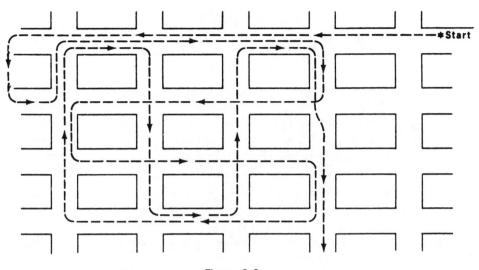

Figure 2-2
Example of double-back patrol pattern

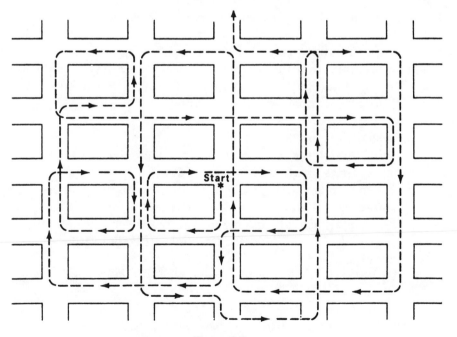

Figure 2-3
Example of random patrol pattern

- Poor visibility resulting from inadequate or excessive lighting or view perception
- Inadequate physical security of premises or property
- Uncontrolled people, animals, and so on

Other factors can also affect hazards, such as the frequency of occurrence, the value of materials involved, the opportunity or desire for the hazard involved, and the temporary or permanent nature of the hazard or its duration. Hazardous factors can be eliminated or corrected by physical changes, additions to or changes in regulations, public education about the hazard, or merely by the physical presence of the law enforcement officer. Hazard factors are a major determining condition in assigning law enforcement patrol personnel. Personnel are assigned by priority according to the significance and frequency of the hazards in the area.

Avoid the hazard of silhouetting. This hazard is created when you place yourself (or others) in a position that provides the suspect(s) with a definite, identifiable target. Such targeting outlines your exact location and tells the suspect(s) how many officers are present, their fire power, and direction of approach. Furthermore, silhouetting allows suspect(s) time to plan alternate courses of action and transfers valuable lag time from the officers to the suspect(s). You might use one or more of the following techniques to avoid becoming a "silhouette" for the criminal to use as a target:

1. Select locations for high-risk vehicle stops away from street lights and off the main traffic route, where lights from oncoming vehicles create a backdrop of light.
2. Backup units should turn out lights (headlights, and red and amber lights) on approaching the primary unit.
3. Position a flashlight in such a way that it will not illuminate your body (do not hold the flashlight directly in front of your body).
4. Do not stand in doorways and hallways or peer openly through windows.

Tell-tale noises are distinctive sounds that alert suspects to the officers' presence and location. Such sounds might come from the patrol vehicle (engine, safety belts, doors, etc.); the police radio; keys and whistles; the baton or shotgun; or unnecessary conversation.

These tell-tale noises not only alert suspects, but also provide them with advantages similar to those discussed for silhouetting. To avoid making tell-tale noises, you can do the following (to mention a few positive actions):

1. Secure pocket keys.
2. Do not park the patrol unit too close to the scene.
3. Carefully secure safety belts.
4. Do not let the vehicle door slam shut.
5. Turn the volume on the radio down to a level that can be heard only by the officers.
6. Communicate with other officers only when necessary, and use nonverbal communications if possible.

The suspect's hands are always potentially hazardous to the peace officer. The guilty suspect may try to hide contraband (evidence) in pockets, or possibly in the armpit area. Even more dangerous to the officer, the suspect may be attempting to conceal a weapon. Some suspects try to conceal their hands to hide identifiable marks, scars, or tattoos. Always keep the suspect's hands in sight to protect against this type of hazard.

Stopped vehicles also present dangerous situations for law enforcement officers. Use proper vehicle-stopping techniques, and take special precautions in approaching vehicle occupants. This topic is covered in more detail in Chapter 8, "Vehicle Pullovers."

In some instances, a law enforcement officer can become a hazard to other officers. For example, a uniformed officer may observe a plainclothes officer talking to a group of other people on the street. By speaking too quickly, the uniformed officer could "burn" (give away the officer's true identity) the undercover officer who is attempting to make a drug buy. The uniformed officer should treat the undercover officer the same way other citizens are treated, unless the plainclothes officer acknowledges the beat officer. If the plainclothes officer does not acknowledge the other officer *first*, the uniformed officer should complete his or her activity in a normal manner and depart from the area.

Reporting Hazards

While engaged in routine preventive patrol, the officer uses powers of observation and perception to accomplish many tasks. One such task is to locate, identify, and report any hazardous conditions. A patrol officer is in an advantageous position to observe hazards in the roadway as well as faulty traffic control devices. Roadway hazards can include any obstruction, ranging from vehicles in the roadway to debris or dead animals. Remember, however, that many officers are injured, and some are killed, while lighting flares on highways, dealing with stalled automobiles in the roadway, dragging broken furniture that has fallen from trucks and other vehicles off the road, to mention but a few such situations. In each of these situations, along with numerous hazards where officers are working in the roadway, *you will be subject to danger!* In fact, such instances are a *major cause* of officer injuries. If you can remove the obstruction immediately, that is the best course of action. Stalled vehicles will need the protection of the patrol vehicle displaying its emergency visual equipment; in some cases, a stalled vehicle may be either pushed off the roadway by the driver or picked up by a tow truck. *Do not use the patrol vehicle to push another motor vehicle unless it is an emergency!* Each agency issues policy guidelines regarding actions that you *must* follow. It is your responsibility to know and comply with departmental policy regarding use of the patrol vehicle. By using the patrol vehicle in an unauthorized manner, you subject yourself and the department to civil liability resulting from damage to private property. Ensure that this does *not* occur by *following all department regulations!*

To have dead animals removed from the streets or highways, the officer (or the law enforcement agency) should notify the animal shelter or similar agency equipped to handle such situations. Since dead animals cause a health hazard to the public, this matter requires immediate attention. Do not try to remove the animal carcass alone without special tools and equipment.

Faulty traffic control devices also require immediate attention. The devices were installed to establish and maintain a safe traffic flow; so whenever such devices are inoperative, damaged, or have been removed, the potential for accidents increases. During periods of peak traffic flow or when the risks are immediate, you may need to set up a temporary traffic control point until a technician can repair the problem.

An officer on patrol may also have occasion to observe and report home and building crime hazards. While making routine building checks, an officer frequently sees open windows and doors that the owner may have carelessly failed to secure. You might notice a ladder or other object lying on the ground or leaning adjacent to the structure that the owner forgot to put away. These conditions make the burglar's job too easy! Once assured that the structure has not been the target of criminal activity, take action to secure the area and notify the owner. In some cases, you may leave a courtesy note notifying the owner of the hazard and relating your actions to secure the building. If a situation requires immediate attention, the owner should be notified by telephone and asked to come to the location of the hazard. In either case, the owner will realize that you are attentive and concerned about the safety of the owner's property. This public service work reinforces good community relations, and that makes your job much easier.

Pedestrian Approach Procedures

Law enforcement officers frequently initiate pedestrian contacts on the patrol beat. An individual may act suspiciously or may be a known criminal. Be mindful of hazards associated with such stops before confronting the pedestrian(s). Determine the safest method to conduct the contact that includes

- When to stop the person
- Where to stop the person
- The best method to use in stopping the person

Without knowing and understanding the principles behind these determinations, you will be unable to conduct lawful pedestrian contacts. On the contrary, improper contacts will result in improper arrests (or detentions), which will lead to unsuccessful court prosecutions. Evaluate the following tactical considerations before approaching a pedestrian:

1. *The person's appearance.* Does the person's appearance generally fit the description of a person wanted for a known offense? Does he or she appear to be suffering from a recent injury or to be under the influence of alcohol, drugs, or other intoxicants?

2. *The person's actions.* Does the person act suspiciously (such as running away from an actual or possible crime scene), or is the person otherwise behaving in a manner indicating possible criminal conduct? If so, in what way? You should be able to describe specific behavior that drew your attention to the suspect. These observations will

become part of your "probable cause" statement if an arrest is warranted.

3. *Prior knowledge of the person.* Does the individual have an arrest or conviction record, or is the suspect otherwise known to have committed a serious offense? If so, is the prior offense similar to the one that has just occurred, or that is suspected to occur imminently?

4. *Area of the stop.* Is the person near the area of a known offense soon after it occurred? Is the area known for criminal activity (a high-crime area)? If so, is it the kind of activity the person is thought to have committed, be committing, or is about to commit?

5. *Time of day.* Is it the time of day during which criminal activity of the kind suspected usually occurs? Is it usual for people to be in the area at such an hour (perhaps at a very late hour in a warehouse district)?

Carefully evaluate these factors *before* deciding to approach the suspect. In many cases, a backup unit should be alerted and properly positioned before you approach the suspect.

Where to Stop the Pedestrian. Take care in selecting the proper location to stop a suspect. The interview should take place in a location that has the least number of

- Escape routes (avoid intersections, use well-lighted areas, etc.)
- People that could be injured
- People that could be used as hostages
- Locations that produce additional risks to an officer, such as known trouble spots (bars, night clubs, discos, etc.)

On Foot. General procedural policy dictates that officers *never* initiate a suspect pedestrian contact while seated in a patrol car. Officer safety demands that you exit from the patrol vehicle and make the pedestrian contact on foot. To do otherwise would place you at a serious tactical disadvantage.

The initial officer position depends on various tactical situations. You may elect, for example, to conduct a stop from either the suspect's front or rear. Always be mindful of the suspect's hands, furtive movements, bulges in clothing, and his or her behavior. Use the patrol vehicle to maximize safety for yourself and the public; proper positioning of the patrol car can maximize your tactical advantage while you keep the pedestrian in view at all times.

While there is no one conventional approach that is always appropriate, do avoid the "Hey, you, come here!" approach. Your communication must reflect both command and courtesy. Words incite more confrontations than do actions; carefully chosen words, however, can also solicit cooperation.

The standard field interview position—also referred to as the "interrogation" position—maximizes an officer's advantage while contacting pedestrians (suspects). The position is achieved by approaching a suspect at a 45-degree angle with your weapon away from the suspect. At a position just outside the suspect's reach (about one arm's length), place your weak foot forward; place the other foot perpendicular to the front foot and distribute your weight equally between a shoulder-width stance. By bending your knees slightly, you can maintain balance if the suspect attempts to push or pull you. Your strong hand (gun hand) should remain free, and you must be mindful of the surroundings at all times. *You must watch the suspect's hands!*

If you must approach two or more people, address yourself to the dominant person and take the field interview position. Do *not* permit the suspects to close in, or surround, your position. Again, keep your strong hand free and watch the suspects' hands.

As noted, it is generally desirable to acquire backup assistance before approaching suspects, if possible. When two or more officers are present, the chance of encountering confrontations is greatly decreased. The primary officer contacts the suspect(s), as previously stated. The second, or backup, officer assumes a position that allows maximum visibility of the suspects. The second officer should also adopt the standard field interview position at a place that permits maximum observation. However, this officer does not get involved in lengthy conversations with the subject(s), which would detract from the cover responsibility. If a threat or hazard to the primary officer is initiated, the cover officer communicates the potential threat and reacts accordingly. However, prevent any situation where you risk crossfire.

OFFICER SAFETY AND SURVIVAL CONSIDERATIONS

Today, perhaps more than ever before, law enforcement officers must be cognizant of the dangers they face daily in police work. Peace officers often approach people engaged in many activities (including drug-related activities and crimes in progress, to mention a few) that call for investigation and they often make stops for violations. These contacts involve officers in inherently dangerous situations. The rate of felonious assaults on officers has risen in recent years. The trend is complicated by the fact that many officers have the feeling that "It can't happen to me" or "It won't happen to me!" Such officers may become complacent and develop a false sense of security. A passive attitude is too often reenforced when officers handle false calls for police service, such as faulty alarm calls or a phony robbery report. Such officers begin to relax, treat calls as "routine," and take chances. This mistake can be deadly, because officers who are not vigilant at all times run a strong risk of being injured or permitting a fellow officer to be seriously injured or killed. To prevent such consequences, *officer safety* must be the *number one priority* at all times.

Officer safety results from a conscious effort by professional peace officers. The ability to survive intact depends on your physical conditioning, alertness, caution, skill, and planning through proper preparation. For example, your physical conditioning is a matter of both personal pride and safety. The law enforcement job can create many stressful situations, and each stressful situation in turn causes physiological changes in your heart rate, blood pressure, and adrenal gland action—to mention only a few. Officers in good physical condition can cope with such drastic changes in body chemistry more readily. Unfortunately, officers in poor physical condition have had heart attacks or strokes while engaged in highly stressful confrontations.

The patrol officer must be alert at all times in order to observe, analyze, and detect actions and behaviors that threaten the safety and property of people in the community. The officer must guard against fatigue, which can cause a deterioration in alertness. Too frequently officers take on a second job. Moonlighting does supplement the family income, and the "police personality" is such that an officer may feel the need to be actively engaged in some form of activity, even off duty. Officers are often employed (with the permission of their agency) in security-related roles such as being a department store security officer, or in private enterprise such as construction work. The officer might also become involved in college classes and higher education as a means of improving both the knowledge and ability needed to handle the multifaceted roles of an officer of the law. Each such outside activity can be tiring and could cause the officer to be sleepy or inattentive. You must achieve a balanced schedule in order to ensure sufficient rest before assuming the responsibilities of a peace officer.

Although officers must take positive action in any situation that is or might be an emergency, it is equally important to distinguish between immediate action and impulsiveness. Mature *caution* prompts professional officers (among other precautions) to

1. Consider waiting for assistance while attempting to keep a suspect in view.
2. Secure the patrol vehicle keys before leaving the unit unattended, to prevent access to the vehicle and the shotgun.
3. Check for hidden suspects in stopped vehicles.
4. Use preparation and planning before taking action.
5. Avoid allowing an incident or contact to become "routine."
6. Stay alert at all times, using good observation and perception techniques.

Concentrate and make a continuing effort to remain aware of the possibilities inherent in each contact with citizens. Never treat any contact as routine! As the shift reaches the half-way point, some emotional and physical drain on an officer is inevitable.

Once you are physically and psychologically ready to approach the law enforcement role, your skill—gained through preparation and planning—will ultimately affect your safety. Your skill in reducing hostility between yourself and the subject will increase your safety because it reduces the intensity of the subject's desire to commit an assault. Developing this skill should be a primary effort of every law enforcement officer. In addition, a brief moment of preparation and planning may make the difference between a safe contact and a dangerous incident. When you consciously evaluate a situation, you can begin to plan for safety.

Safety Tactics

Be prepared both mentally and emotionally for a possible shooting situation. Professional officers develop a state of mental readiness that gives them an edge in a shooting situation. The "how" in developing a state of mental readiness begins with planning. Try to "see" a shooting situation in your mind, and anticipate how you would react in the situation. For example, you might ask, "If this happened to me, what would I do?" Then think your way through the situation.

In the physical realm, control the field contact situation by not letting subject(s) move around. Stay constantly aware of the suspect's hands, to keep them in view. Communicate well with your partner, and understand the role each will assume in a contact situation: the contact officer will search while the cover (or backup) officer guards the suspect(s); the contact officer will approach the driver's side of the vehicle and the cover officer will guard at a safe location; and so on. Understand the need to maintain both verbal and visual contact with your partner, and approach each call with caution.

Develop "tactics for survival," and maintain a "will to live" at all times. The following recommendations are only beginning steps to safety; the veteran officer will have developed many tactics by the time retirement is near.

1. *Minimize the possibility of entering into an ambush setup.* Treat all calls as if they could be setups, but don't become paranoid. Even though a call may seem to be about a minor problem, it is always possible that the call was faked to draw an officer to the scene. By varying the patrol pattern and avoiding easily observable habits, you can avoid compromising situations. A safety-conscious officer not only plans the approach to the scene, but is also aware of distracting movements that may place him- or herself in a position of disadvantage.

2. *If you come under sniper fire when on foot,*
   a. *Take cover and/or concealment.* A tree, a post, or a fire hydrant, for example, may provide good cover—anything that will protect you from the assailant's firepower. Even if such items are not close, you might hide behind a bush or other object for a temporary time (concealment) until cover is obtainable. *Don't stand in plain view looking for the subject!*
   b. *Look for the assailant's location from behind cover or concealment.* Smoke from the suspect's gun, noise, and reflected light are some ways to determine the point of attack.
   c. *Assess the situation.* Check the surrounding area to determine the extent of the problem. Look for innocent bystanders, escape routes, protected and unprotected areas, the need for assistance, and so on.
   d. *Warn bystanders.* Direct bystanders either to seek protective cover or to leave the area—depending on the situation.
   e. *Call for assistance.* Report the nature of the emergency, the

suspect's location, your location, and any other relevant facts the backup officers will need to know. The officer under siege may suggest the safest entry points for responding officers, as well as possible escape routes that the sniper might take.

f. *Isolate and clear the area.* Once backup officers arrive at the scene, the general locality of the hostile actions should be safely cleared and isolated. Once the area is cordoned off and secured, law enforcement negotiators will work to end the emergency.

3. *If you come under sniper fire when in a vehicle,*

a. *Accelerate through the "kill zone."* This action should be instantaneous. The idea is to get out of the line of fire as quickly as possible.

b. Another option is to turn the vehicle left or right into the nearest available cover. Move without hesitation to the safest possible area. While in the vehicle, use the best advantages the patrol vehicle can provide for cover. For example, place the engine block between you and the assailant. In addition, temporarily lie down in the seat for concealment while escaping the assailant's fire.

c. Once the vehicle is parked, abandon it for better cover, but avoid becoming a good target for the sniper. By moving low, in a "zigzag" manner, at unpredictable times, you will be able to assess the situation better and protect yourself.

d. An alternate surprise movement in the "kill zone" is to put the vehicle in reverse gear and quickly accelerate out of the area. Along with a straight reverse movement, you might make a U-turn or a J-turn. A J-turn is usually superior because of speed and the area needed to execute the movement. With practice, you can quickly reverse directions of travel safely, to the dismay of the would-be assailant.

4. *If your vehicle is hit by a firebomb,*

a. Quickly accelerate from the area.

b. Roll up windows if they are not already up.

c. Abandon the vehicle after the initial flame blast if the vehicle is inoperable.

Safety Guidelines

Certain standards of personal safety are axioms in police patrol operations. First, never approach a potentially dangerous situation without first notifying communications, and without a backup, if needed. The law enforcement profession is *not* made up of individual heroes; rather, the professionals are team players who are trained to provide safety for their fellow officers.

Second, never go without a backup officer into a building or structure where criminal activity is suspected. The backup officer not only provides security, but also both officers are thus protected from allegations of illegal activity that might arise if an officer were alone.

Third, maintain constant awareness of your duty weapon. Always keep your duty weapons in good operating condition and securely fixed in their holsters unless you need them in the line of duty. Safety must be given the highest priority both on and off duty. Off duty, take measures to secure your duty weapon and educate your families in safety precautions.

Finally, practice good officer safety techniques day in and day out. Never let a drug case, a crime in progress, or even a traffic stop become routine. Respond to each call with the same regard for safety, using all the proper techniques of suspect encounters, building or vehicle approaches, cover, and concealment. These techniques are designed to keep officers alive!

Communication Factors

Keep the communications dispatcher informed at all times of your status and location. In a one-person unit, the communicator is the patrol officer's partner. The communications expert has the responsibility for knowing the whereabouts of each patrol officer during the tour of duty. Communications must also know immediately which units are available for backup service or for responding to calls for assistance.

The law enforcement role is a team effort. Each officer must depend on fellow officers to be available whenever a call for help is put out. Even when one officer is making a "routine traffic stop" in which a backup unit is not normally needed or requested, other units in the vicinity of the stop normally drive toward the stopping area to provide support, if they are not assigned another call.

Avoiding Job Fatigue

All too frequently an officer enters the law enforcement role expecting excitement from the moment of coming on shift until finishing the last report for that tour of duty. The "TV cop syndrome" projects an image that a law enforcement officer is actively engaged in crime fighting every minute. Veteran officers know that the real world is quite different. There are many periods when you will be engaged in preventive patrol activities, and such times can seem dull if you are looking for continuous excitement. You may get lulled into a condition of job fatigue and can become complacent and inattentive. Then you will be in serious trouble. A complacent officer takes risks, is careless when approaching suspects, responds leisurely to alarm calls, and does not notice unusual conditions on the beat. Each of these attitudes is contrary to all the officer's training.

Recognizing the dangers of fatigue is one of the first steps toward becoming an alert and cautious officer. In some instances, inactivity lulls an officer into a false sense of security and keeps him or her from making mature decisions. To avoid job fatigue, you must become involved with expanded areas of responsibility. Times of inactivity provide opportunities to get out of the patrol car and get to know the people on your beat. This police-community relations aspect of your role will pay dividends in your ability to obtain information during investigations and open lines of communication that would not otherwise be available. The professional officer is also curious and gets to know not only the people, but also the vehicles and buildings in the patrol area. Through active preventive patrol, you can make note of the strange and different and become curious when a situation is not as it should be—an open window that is normally closed or a light turned off when it should be illuminated. Such aggressive and creative patrol eliminates job fatigue. If you become sleepy during a tour of duty, contact the sergeant or supervisor.

There are additional ways in which you can compensate for fatigue. For example, you might change drivers (in a two-person unit), stop for coffee, or use a combination foot-and-motorized patrol mode to change the routine. Needless to say, good diet, proper rest, and maintaining a high level of physical fitness are imperative to achieve the goal. However, in some cases, sheer discipline can overcome "giving in" to poor tactics. In fact, more than one officer's life has been saved by his or her determination to use good tactics even when he or she did not feel like doing so.

Officer Survival Considerations

One of the saddest experiences for every officer is to learn that a fellow officer—no matter where—has died in the line of duty. Officers from all around the country will attend the funeral of a slain officer, even though the officers have never met. Officer deaths and injuries frequently happen while conducting traffic stops or responding to disturbance calls, and while the officer was not expecting trouble. In fact, more than 70 percent of the time fatal confrontations erupt during so-called routine patrol. Studies have shown that many officers die needlessly because of lack of training, carelessness, lack of planning, and overconfidence. All these deaths could be prevented!

True survival readiness involves a number of interrelated factors that each officer can consciously develop to *prevent* tragedies and survive dangerous confrontations. These factors and skills include

- Mental and physical conditioning
- Tactical preparedness
- Shooting skills
- Defensive tactics skills
- First-responder skills
- Proper training and retraining

Under stress, human beings instinctively revert to the way they have been trained. Unfortunately, poor training and sloppy efforts on the part of trainees can result in bad habits that lead to officer error, injury, and death. Conversely, conscientious and diligent efforts and concentration given to good training lessons will teach techniques designed to promote safety.

To *survive* the hazards of law enforcement work, learn from fatal errors that have killed other peace officers. At least in this way, their death can have some purposeful meaning. Such fatal errors include the following.

1. *An apathetic attitude.* Peace officers are caring people; this is why they get into law enforcement in the first place. One of the saddest sights is to observe a law enforcement officer who has lost his or her "zeal" for the job. Apathy, or no longer caring, is a warning sign that an officer can be a danger to him- or herself, and to others.

2. *Tombstone courage.* Some officers, especially young and inexperienced officers, believe that the badge and gun will "protect the just"

no matter what. Being "gung ho" may seem fine in stories and on television, but in real life such courage can—and sometimes does—lead to an early grave. Airline pilots have an old saying that can be borrowed: "There are old pilots, and there are bold pilots; but there is no such thing as an 'old, bold' pilot." A similar statement can be aptly applied to law enforcement officers and their careers.

3. *Not getting enough rest.* The very nature and psychological makeup of law enforcement officers suggest a personality that consciously seeks added work experiences, formal education to advance, and additional activities to avoid inactivity. Although many of these activities achieve enrichment and reward, each can have a telling effect on your ability to be sufficiently rested for the law enforcement role. Allocate enough time to achieve personal goals without sacrificing needed rest time to be alert.

4. *Taking a bad position.* Your training will stress over and over again the need to constantly seek cover and concealment in hazardous situations. Unprotected officers provide too good a target for an assailant who has nothing to lose. In some instances, bad positioning can result in injuries and death attacks in a "blind spot" that the officer did not consider. For example, an officer may be talking to the violator about an infraction and forget to observe a passenger in the car. If you turn your back and ignore others on the scene, you may never see the fatal blow coming.

5. *Missing danger signs.* Inattention, laziness, carelessness, and apathy can all have their down sides. And when the "down side" prevents you from seeing—or "sensing"—an obvious danger sign, the consequences can be fatal! Your law enforcement education and training will be dedicated to alerting you to as many "danger signs" as possible in the time and space available. You have the responsibility to yourself and your loved ones to learn these danger signs and to be constantly alert when such hazards confront you.

6. *Failure to watch the suspect's hands.* If a suspect is going to hurt you, he or she will probably do so with his or her hands or feet. The hands are by far the more dangerous. When a suspect is allowed to put his or her hands into a coat pocket, glove box, or other hidden area, the chances of the suspect obtaining a weapon to use against you are too great. Officers who ignore such obvious hazards can be seriously injured or killed and never know what happened.

7. *Relaxing too soon.* Many criminals will wait to commence an attack until they think an officer's guard is down. Such people con you

into thinking the situation is well in hand so that you will let down your guard. Once suspects have an opportunity, they will take full advantage of it to escape—and they won't blame themselves because you relaxed too soon and gave them the chance!

8. *Improper use of or not using handcuffs.* Agency policy generally requires officers to handcuff all people who are arrested, to control the individual and protect the officer. However, many officers make discretionary decisions *not* to handcuff, or in some cases do not apply handcuffs in accordance with recognized acceptable procedure (behind the suspect's back, palms turned outward). This is another instance where the suspect waits for his or her opportunity to take advantage of the lack of control and to attempt escape. In some tragic situations, a suspect has taken away an officer's duty weapon while seated in a patrol unit and used it against the officer.

9. *No search or improper search.* The mechanics of arrest mandate a thorough search once the suspect is handcuffed. Searching officers *must* locate and secure all weapons. Too frequently, a searching officer may find one weapon and *assume* that the suspect has no others. That can be a fatal mistake! An even more deadly error is never searching at all. Veteran officers can tell many horror stories about guns, knives, and other weapons and contraband discovered at the detention facility, or in the patrol unit, following booking (an initial administrative recordkeeping procedure) of a person who was "searched" in the field.

10. *Dirty or inoperative weapon and equipment.* Your tools of the trade cannot be taken for granted. You may never need to use your sidearm in the line of duty, but are you willing to risk your life on that bet? Some officers who died in the line of duty did draw their duty weapon—only to find that it did not work properly when they most needed it. Neglecting equipment maintenance, or failing to take time to do it right, reflects on just how much risk you are willing to take with your life!

11. *Failure to maintain proficiency with equipment.* As noted earlier, people are creatures of habit. What you learn, and how you practice what you learn, will become the instinctive habits you will revert to under stress. When you need to use equipment in an emergency, you will not be "instinctively" proficient with your duty weapon, and other equipment, unless you have taken the time to practice correct procedures. Your training center will conduct proficiency and inservice training. You will be required to demonstrate efficiency with

equipment at periodic intervals. However, does any one honestly think that these sessions once, or twice, a year can produce professional proficiency? The answer is obvious. To be proficient, you must conscientiously practice on your own time.

12. *Mental preoccupation.* "Preoccupation" is not the job you had before becoming a peace officer; it is thinking about that job, or anything else, when all your senses should be concentrating on surrounding hazards. Most of us daydream at one time or another. However, for some officers who daydream—including officers who were "just driving"—the dream never ended, because they never woke up!

13. *Poor physical fitness.* The law enforcement job can be stressful. Your lifestyle can become sedentary. Your routine will be such that you quickly eat meals so that you can get back on patrol. The hours that you work will be varied and sometimes changing. Each of these, along with other physical disablers, will take their toll on your health. An officer who is not physically fit to handle the increased physical stress of chasing after an armed robber may easily drop dead! Not from anything that the criminal did, but rather because his or her body could not stand the added stress and the officer suffered a stroke or heart attack. Physical fitness is a personal, as well as professional, consideration that is your individual responsibility to ensure for your own health.

Each of the above fatal errors can be prevented by professional people seeking conscientiously to strive for excellence. To prepare for emergency situations and survive, discuss hypothetical situations with a partner. Veteran officers love to tell "war stories" that can serve as valuable lessons on how—and sometimes how *not*—to handle actual situations properly. Remember, you can learn from others' mistakes as well; officers who have been involved in everything from shooting situations to traffic stops can and will allow you to profit from their experiences to help you survive as well.

Officers who survive have a plan of action. These officers have already made up their minds to seek cover and concealment in hazardous situations. They watch for danger signs and the suspect's hands; alert officers never relax too soon and use proper handcuff and searching techniques. By maintaining their weapons and equipment in proper order and maintaining proficiency with them, they are mentally prepared as well as physically ready to take on the role of being a peace officer. Above all, the professional's attitude remains constantly alert; the "love for the job" and caring about other people are rewards that few other professions can offer.

Survival Tactics

Alertness is the key to survival, along with avoiding the "fatal errors." Fatigue is an inevitable hazard that constantly stalks you. To combat fatigue in a two-person patrol unit, you might change drivers. For some officers, stopping for coffee or a soft drink is enough to refresh them and overcome drowsiness. At other times, a brief meeting with your immediate supervisor (usually a sergeant) can prove beneficial and he or she can suggest ways that can help you pass the "sleepy" time. Without a doubt, people who eat well-balanced meals and get proper rest have superior ability to overcome "fatal fatigue." Maintain a high level of physical fitness, and encourage your fellow officers to do the same.

As noted earlier, to minimize the possibility of entering into an ambush setup, treat all calls as if they could be a setup. Don't relax too soon because the call appears to be a minor problem. Don't fall into easily observable habits that allow criminals to predict what your next move will be; do not patrol the same way every day. Plan approaches to crime, accident, and/or incident scenes. Above all, when dealing with suspects, constantly *watch the suspect's hands* and body movements.

If you are approaching a dangerous situation, anticipate danger. Let the circumstances dictate the tactics and be prepared to instinctively carry out the plan. Use tactics that are unexpected. Be alert for clues or danger signs by effectively using your eyes and ears. Maximize your distance from the potential danger area, and "think survival"! If other officers are on the same scene, be aware of their location and avoid crossfire with fellow officers.

When approaching a building, have a clear objective in mind to apprehend the suspect. Take an unexpected approach, and assess the situation. While using cover and concealment, be conscious of your surroundings. For example, use corners of a building to your advantage. At all times be alert; stop, look, and listen to maximize your perception and observation. Communicate with your partner and other officers on the scene.

Doorways are particularly dangerous. Use extreme caution at all times. Never stand in front of a door; by standing to the side of a door and delaying entry, you can gain an advantage in hazardous situations. If a complainant answers the door, try to determine whether or not he or she is armed.

The duty weapon is both a constant companion and hazard. Maintain peak alertness at all times. If any life is in danger, or in the event of a high-risk situation, always have your duty weapon ready. Under no circumstances should you walk into a high-risk situation with just a handgun; use the shotgun! Be familiar and proficient with all firearms authorized and employed at your agency. Critique all shooting incidents to find out what went right and what went wrong. As *you* become a veteran, you will pass on vital information that may save another officer's life!

Shooting situations do have their special lessons. Those who have been there will tell you, "*Do not rush!*" If you have fired your duty weapon, reload if necessary, but do not put the weapon away. If a suspect appears to be submitting, do not assume that he or she really is giving up. Watch the suspect's hands, especially hands that are not visible. Expect the unexpected!

If you encounter and attempt to disarm an armed suspect, do it from a position of cover and safety. Command the person to remove his or her finger from the trigger, lay the gun down slowly, and step away from the weapon. As always, watch the suspect's hands. Do not move out from behind cover until the suspect is disarmed. Under no circumstances should you leave cover to accept a weapon directly from a suspect.

By using good common sense, relying on your instinctive training, and having a "will to live," you can enhance your ability to survive. Often an officer can survive being shot or seriously injured merely by mentally refusing to give up or to accept death. Instead of giving in, fight back to live. Officers who do survive follow some basic survival tips, including the following:

1. Practice reloading with your "off" hand.
2. Do not hold a flashlight in front of you; rather, hold it to your side.
3. Carry an extra concealed handcuff key.
4. Call out, "Police—don't move!" to challenge suspects.
5. For searches, one officer should cover while the other officer completes the search.
6. Remember to look up as well as around.

7. Open doors fully before entering.
8. Practice counting shots; never totally empty your duty weapon; if possible, practice reloading quickly.
9. Avoid tunnel vision—the tendency under stress to focus totally on one place or person.
10. Always handcuff the suspect *first*, and *then* search.
11. "Expect the unexpected."

KEY TERMS

Apprehension patrol (nonconspicuous directed)
Circular patrol pattern
Communications
County sheriff
Covert patrol
Double-back patrol
Esprit de corps
Fragmented police systems
Hue and cry
Neighborhood team policing
Officer safety/survival readiness
Patrol patterns
Platoon system
Police systems
Posse comitatus
Preventive patrol (conspicuous)
Random patrol pattern
Response zone
Safety/survival tactics
Specialized unit
S.W.A.T. team
Tactical units
Team area
Tombstone courage

STUDY QUESTIONS

1. In colonial America, what were the two main forms of law enforcement positions employed to control society? Why was one form more prominent in the North while the other was more prominent in the South?

2. What was the significance of the Pendleton Act of 1883?

3. What are some problems that can occur when struggles for political control of law enforcement agencies arise?

4. What is the origin of the word *sheriff*?

5. Why is the sheriff still an elected position in most areas of the United States?

6. What is the *posse comitatus*, and when was it first used as a law enforcement tool? According to the Posse Comitatus Act of 1878, what group of people cannot be subject to joining a *posse*, and what is the rationale for this law?

7. Why did governors in various states develop their own police forces?

8. Why was federal law enforcement slow to develop, compared to state and local police systems?

9. Why are law enforcement activities in the United States considered "fragmented"?

10. What is the *ward system*, and what was the significance of the Statute of Winchester issued by King Edward I in 1285?

11. What is "team policing"?

12. Why is team policing more difficult to organize in large agencies than in small departments?

13. What is one possible origin of the acronym *COP*? Can you suggest any other possible ways in which *COP* might be interpreted?

14. What responsibility did Anglo-Saxon people have when they heard the "hue and cry"? Of what significance is this concept in today's society?

15. What is a district, sector, or team area? How has it been traditionally organized?

16. What is a beat, response zone, or zone? Who is responsible for this area of police duty?

17. What is a platoon system, and how does it function?

18. List and define the responsibility of five types of police teams organized to handle special operations.

19. Describe the neighbor team policing model. How is it organized, and how is it supposed to function to achieve the police objective? Do you think this is a valid approach to accomplish the goals and objectives of the law enforcement mission?

20. List and describe six positive aspects of specialization in law enforcement work.

21. List and describe four negative aspects of specialization in police work. What action(s) must be taken to overcome these shortcomings?

22. What are major considerations that you should take into account in preparing for a strategy for patrol?

23. What are the two major areas of preparations that each officer should constantly be conscious of when preparing for a tour of duty? Describe the necessary components of each element.

24. What distinct advantages specifically relate to preventive patrol?

25. What is the purpose of apprehension patrol?

26. What is the most effective speed for preventive patrol in a residential area, and why?

27. Describe three different types of patrol patterns, and when and why each would be used during routine patrol.

28. What are four basic kinds of police hazards? Give an example of each.

29. What hazard exists for officers who do not avoid the problem of silhouetting? What considerations should be taken into account to avoid this hazard?

30. What physical objects in the patrol unit or on an officer's person create noises that could alert suspects about the officer's presence? What actions can you take to avoid these noises?

31. Suspect confrontation in the field can have hazardous consequences for law enforcement officers. In handling a suspect, what part of the suspect's body must you closely watch? Why is this precaution important?

32. What should you do if you see a plainclothes officer talking to a group

of other people on the street? Why is your action crucial to the other officer's safety?

33. What are your responsibilities as a patrol officer in dealing with roadway hazards? What dangers may you encounter in handling such hazards?

34. What should you do if you find a dead animal on the roadway?

35. If you observe a potential building security problem or hazardous condition while making routine building checks, what actions should you take? What is the purpose of leaving a courtesy note for the owner once the situation is secured?

36. What hazard elements of the stop should you consider before approaching a pedestrian to make a field contact investigation?

37. In evaluating tactical considerations before approaching a pedestrian, what should you specifically note about the suspect before making the stop? What can you learn from this evaluation?

38. Why should you approach pedestrian suspect(s) on foot rather than interviewing them while seated in the patrol car?

39. Describe the interrogation position. What is the role of a backup (or cover) officer in a pedestrian suspect approach?

40. In your own words, list the main keys to officer safety and survival.

41. What type of police attitudes contribute to officer injury and death in the field? What should each officer do to prevent such incidents?

42. What problems does moonlighting create for law enforcement officers? How can this be handled to ensure officer safety?

43. What types of precautions should mature officers take in handling dangerous situations?

44. How can you mentally prepare for a hazardous situation in the field?

45. How can you minimize the possibility of being ambushed?

46. If you come under sniper fire while on foot patrol, what actions should you immediately take, and why? What additional considerations and actions should you make relative to the situation?

47. What actions should you take if you come under attack while driving the patrol unit or if your vehicle is hit by a firebomb?

48. What are the axioms of personal safety standards in police patrol operations?

49. Why is the communications officer an important part of the patrol officer team?

50. If you become sleepy or tired while on patrol, what positive actions can you immediately take to compensate for the fatigue? What actions can you take before coming to work, to avoid this condition?

ACTIVITIES

1. Write a research paper on the development of various patrol systems used in cities during early U.S. history. What was the origin of the police uniform, and how did it develop into a symbol of professional law enforcement?

2. Either individually or in groups, make a random survey of your city or town and make a list of various types of hazards that law enforcement officers could, or should, note and take positive action to alleviate. Compare notes in a class session, and suggest ways and means of patrolling that could increase the number of hazards that officers observe.

3. In a role-playing situation, conduct a field inquiry stop of a pedestrian suspect with a backup officer. Be sure to properly use an interrogation position and ensure officer safety by watching the suspect's hands.

4. Develop four hypothetical situations that might involve hazards for patrol officers, and suggest what actions you might take to handle each situation. Compare notes with other students in class, and conduct a group discussion regarding your conclusions.

5. Obtain current event articles from the newspaper or magazines regarding incidents where law enforcement officers were hurt or killed during the line of duty. Discuss what actions the officer might have taken to avoid the injury and how you might have reacted differently in the same or similar situation.

3

Observation and Perception Techniques

Law enforcement officers must become trained observers. The average person sees less than 20 percent of the action that goes on around him or her. Peace officers are "expected" to see and make note of people, places, and things that the rest of society would not ordinarily notice. Most "rookie" officers are taken quite by surprise during their initial patrol duty with a training officer; the veteran officer will quickly make a turn in pursuit of an offender or a wanted suspect, or check an irregularity, and leave the rookie officer wondering, "What's going on?" When the training officer explains the problem or situation, the rookie officer is astonished that the training officer saw the problem when the rookie was not even aware one existed. Thus the new officer's training begins with lessons in observation and perception.

INTRODUCTION—ALERTNESS AND OFFICER SAFETY

Alertness is one attribute of the professional patrol officer that contributes to officer safety. Officers are constantly acquiring information through the five senses: sight, hearing, feel, taste, or smell. Such awareness is perception, the process of organizing and attaching meaning to sensations so that the sensations can be interpreted as part of observation. The analysis process results in an evaluation. Obviously, people differ in their perception of objects and events because they organize and attach different significance to many factors that can affect and distort perception. These factors include but are not limited to

1. Past experience and education of observer
2. Maturity
3. Mental condition (such as stress and personal problems)
4. Emotional involvement
5. Environmental conditions
6. Training
7. Cultural and ethnic background
8. Prejudice and bias of observer
9. Physical condition of observer (such as poor eyesight, color blindness, depth perception problems, and fatigue)

For example, a witness who is unfamiliar with firearms will not recognize the difference between the sound of a shotgun and that of a pistol. Furthermore, a witness who is extremely prejudiced against a man because he is blond, a teenager, or a member of a different race, religion, or ethnic group, will tend to perceive that man's action unfavorably. In addition, an emotionally overwrought victim of a vicious crime might be temporarily incapable of giving any useful information whatsoever. In each of these examples, one or more of the key factors affecting perception influenced the information that was ultimately available. Another person under the same or similar circumstance would have perceived the situation very differently because a key factor was changed for that person.

An officer constantly faces the need to evaluate the reliability of witnesses. It is understandable that two witnesses observing an accident or incident can develop different impressions. Someone who observes an accident from 150 yards down the street will not, in all likelihood, give the same report as a witness standing on the sidewalk just a few feet away. Similarly, a witness who saw the situation developing and who realized that an accident was going to happen will give a different story from that of a witness whose attention was first attracted by the crash. In some cases, a witness who is a close friend of one of the parties to the accident very likely will provide an account that is significantly different from that of a neutral witness. Yet all these witnesses may feel that they are describing the situation in a complete and truthful manner.

Observation is the accurate noting of what is presented to the five senses through keeping in view, taking notice of, or giving attention to people, things, or circumstances. The two parts of a complete observation are (1) receiving a stimulus, and (2) being aware of the stimulus. Ultimately, a person must respond to the stimulus in a way that is appropriate to the situation.

INTERPRETING OBSERVATION AND PERCEPTION

We gain most of our information through the senses of sight and hearing. What we do with the information and how it is interpreted depends not only on the stimuli but also on how it fits with our past experience, attitudes, and needs. In order for the sensations received through the sense organs to be useful, they must first make an impression on you; in other words, you must be conscious of the existence of the action, sound, or other stimuli. The degree of attention given to the stimulus may vary from nothing, or a very vague awareness of its existence, to the most intense concentration possible.

Law enforcement officers must have good understanding of human nature. You should acquire knowledge of psychology, sociology, culture, the principles of human behavior, and how people react to things, events, and other people in a changing world. You must be able to accurately evaluate people's behavior in order to correctly interpret their actions. Furthermore, you should develop a thorough knowledge of the principles of human behavior, to anticipate how people may react in a variety of situations. To survive the hazards inherent in police work, you should be able to recognize behavior as unusual, unstable, or suspicious. Professional officers base their perceptions on standards of justice and fairness, rather than on prejudice and personal likes or dislikes. One of the first lessons any officer learns is to understand his or her own weaknesses and then to put the "professional self" in place of the "personal self" as a law enforcement officer.

It is also important to understand that there are practical limits on most aspects of human performance. Be suspicious of any claims that exceed these limits. For instance, if a witness gives an exceedingly detailed description of a criminal where opportunity for observation was limited, an aware officer should suspect that the witness is exaggerating, either consciously or unconsciously.

The Problem of Illusions

Human performance is also affected by the fact that things may not always be what they seem to be. Illusions, a common experience, are false or distorted perceptions. Figure 3-1 shows various illusions that illustrate how the apparent size of an object is related to other objects among which it appears. These pictures show that the orientation or pattern of the object observed affects the perception of relationships. This phenomenon can be significant in witness interviews.

Because perception can vary so widely among witnesses, experimental evidence shows that the average of the composite judgments of several witnesses is generally more trustworthy than the individual judgments. For example, if six witnesses were to guess how long a 40-feet space appeared, they might estimate distances of 20, 40, 25, 50, 60, and 75 feet. The average of these estimates would be 38 feet and 4 inches, which is nearer the truth than all but one of the individual estimates. In one simple experiment, a group of trained investigators estimated the height and weight of two men. Man A was shown to the group, and they gave their estimates of his height, which ranged from 69 to 74 inches. The average of their estimates was 70.26 inches, which was close to A's actual height of 70.5 inches. The group was then asked to make the same estimates for B, who was known to all the men but who was not present for them to look at. The estimates of B's height ranged from 70 to 76 inches, with an average of 73.76 inches; his weight was estimated at from 150 to 200 pounds, with an average of 183.4 pounds. B's actual height and weight were 73.25 inches and 185 pounds. Such results indicate that composite descriptions are likely to be more accurate than those given by individuals. Perhaps such experimental evidence simply proves that two heads are better than one—especially where estimates are in question.

Contrasting colors of objects also produce false perceptions. An object of bright color often appears larger than the same-size object of dull color. Figure 3-2 illustrates this phenomenon.

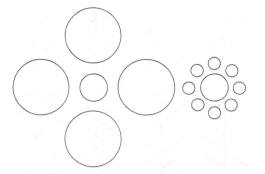

(a) The central circles are the same size, although they look different because of the size of the surrounding circles in each case.

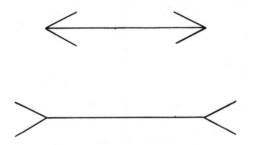

(b) Here, the two central lines are equal in length. The pattern in which an object is viewed affects judgment of its size.

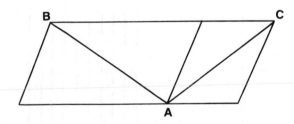

(c) In this parallelogram, lines AB and AC are equal in length.

Figure 3-1
Illusions

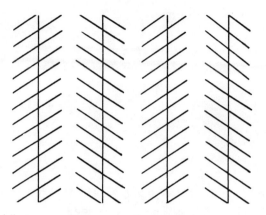

(d) The vertical lines are drawn exactly parallel.

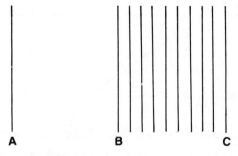

(e) These horizontal and vertical lines are of equal length. Vertical distances seem longer than horizontal distances, and witnesses may therefore tend to overestimate height and to underestimate breadth.

A   B   C

(f) The distance from A to B is identical to the distance from B to C; the latter distance looks larger because it is interrupted. A witness is likely to underestimate such a distance in an open field.

Figure 3-1, *continued*

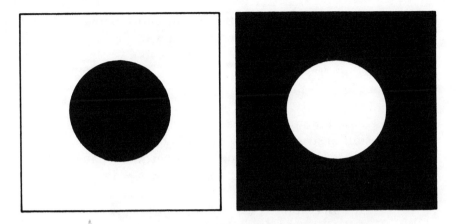

Figure 3-2
Contrast. In this figure, the white circle looks bigger than the black one although they are of exactly the same size.

Using Personal Senses

Sight is the most crucial of the senses in law enforcement. Law enforcement agencies place a high degree of importance to a person's ability to see well (with or without various aids to vision) when establishing criteria to hire new officers and screen potential candidates for the job. However, no matter how good a person's ability to see may be, various factors, including the following, affect all officers' vision.

1. Visual acuity depends largely on distance or proximity, size (of objects), and light conditions.
2. Dimly lit objects tend to become indistinct, particularly if their colors blend with the background.
3. Slowly moving objects are more difficult to see at night.
4. Movement may be noticed from the corner of the eye almost as well as from straight on; stationary objects are not noticed as well from the corner of the eye.
5. Nearsightedness is more of a disadvantage for observation than farsightedness.
6. In full moonlight, you must be within 10 or 11 yards of another person for visual recognition of facial features.
7. Depth perception requires proper coordination of both eyes.

8. Colors are not seen equally over the entire retina of the eye.
9. Lighting can distort color perception (for example, sodium vapor or fluorescent lamps distort colors).
10. Tinted glasses affect color perception, particularly at night.
11. Blue objects will appear larger when red and blue objects are compared.
12. The observer's position may affect how he or she sees things.
13. Physical obstructions may partially or fully block sight.
14. Adaptation to darkness does not occur immediately.
15. Weather conditions (rain, high winds, fog, etc.) can distort vision.
16. Visual observation is affected by "mental set" (or how the officer is conditioned).

Of vital interest to law enforcement officers is the fact that perception of colors is greatly affected by the background in which the colors are observed and, in some cases, by color blindness. For example, dark red may appear black in dim light, such as dusk. In the retina of the eye, cells called *cones* contain a light-sensitive substance that responds to colors of red, green, and blue, or a combination of these colors. The absence of light affects the ability of the cones to correctly perceive color. The most common form of color blindness is an inability to distinguish between reds and greens in dim light. The second most common form is to have the same inability to distinguish these colors even in adequate light. Defects of color vision affect men far more often than women. The defects are almost always hereditary and present from birth.

Darkness is a continuing hazard for law enforcement officers on patrol. Therefore, alert officers use adaptation techniques to compensate for the lack of light, such as

- Stopping momentarily after entering darkness and allowing eyes to adjust to the available light
- Keeping one eye closed (if it is safe to do so) when going from darkness to a lighted area and then back to darkness
- Looking slightly above, below, or to one side of an object to prevent fadeout of its image at night

Hearing and Other Senses. Errors in interpreting sensations are by no means limited to the visual field. People can also make errors in perceiving sounds, odors, feeling, or taste, the passage of time, and even social relationships. For example, time may seem to fly quickly when a person is engaged in some interesting pursuit; however, time may appear to drag when a person is forced to wait his or her turn in line for movie tickets or at the grocery store. In the social area, most people would see nothing unusual about a man in a crowd, carrying an overcoat over his arm and holding a newspaper in his hand, bumping into another man. However, a law enforcement officer, because of experience, would perceive that this may be a pickpocket operating his "trade."

The following factors may affect an officer's hearing:

- The origin of a sound may be determined if one ear is slightly closer to the origin or if the head is turned when the sound is equidistant from both ears.
- Distance from a sound is judged by absolute intensity.
- An officer must know the nature of sounds and associate them with experience (such as noises, voices, motors, or engines).
- Sounds carry over a greater distance at night.
- An object that makes noises appears larger.

Many substances can be identified by their odors (gasoline or petroleum products, natural gas, gun powder). However, officers understand the following affect an officer's sense of smell:

- Substances such as gasoline and ether temporarily deaden the sense of smell.
- Nasal congestion will reduce sense of smell.

The following factors affect an officer's sense of touch:

- The sense of touch can be affected by adaptation; for example, lukewarm water will feel cool if the hand is immersed in hot water first.
- Sense of touch can be affected by abnormal events (this can happen, for example, during a fight).

Factors affecting an officer's sense of taste include the following:

- Taste is closely associated with smell.

- Sense of taste can determine only sweet, sour, salt, and bitter).
- Taste must be used with discretion, to avoid potentially hazardous situations—perhaps even cyanide and drug poisoning.

Making an Observation

In order for people to observe or perceive an object or a situation, it must command their attention. Generally, this is a matter of selection. People tend to pay attention to things that interest them; since interests differ among people, the observed situation will appear different to them even though they are looking at the same scene. Therefore, careful questioning of several witnesses normally brings out different things they might have noticed. Females, for example, may provide superior information about clothing, while a male witness may have more accurate information on automobiles, weapons, and so on.

A person's span of attention is limited. It is impossible to pay attention to everything present in any given location. A person cannot note and remember everything that occurs. Moreover, a person's attention is constantly shifting from one thing to another, and many things go unnoticed because other objects or events crowd them out. You cannot get a meaningful report from a witness of something that has not claimed his or her attention. The more fleeting a perception is, the less reliable is the observer's report.

So people's perceptions are only as good as the completeness and accuracy of their observations. Appreciate and allow for the fact that errors in perception may arise in several ways:

- Due to peculiar or unusual patterns of stimuli in the outside world
- From the preoccupation and resultant inattention on the part of the observer
- From defects in the witness's sense organs
- Because the witness has developed certain mental outlooks or habits and customarily perceives according to those expectations
- Due to prejudice, expecting things to happen in certain ways and interpreting what is observed in such a manner that supports bias
- Because of lack of experience with the thing observed

- Because of failure to observe details through lack of interest

Common circumstances can affect perception and observation. For example, an officer or witness may focus attention on the

- Louder or larger element in a given situation
- Unusual or out-of-place element
- Object, individual, or element that appears more than once
- Movement as opposed to stationary objects or elements
- Persons, objects, or elements that are familiar or can be identified

Very few people are trained observers. Witness estimates of distance, height, weight, and so forth can be poor; however, good questioning can improve the reliability of information obtained from witnesses. Ask specific questions to obtain more accurate witness observations, and consider conditions under which the observations were made. Avoid leading or suggestive questions. For example, the leading question "Was the suspect carrying a gun?" might be better phrased as "Was the suspect carrying anything?" Also, try to evaluate the witness's statements in light of his or her abilities and/or special interests.

Peace officers are trained observers. Technically, "observation" means more than just seeing something. It involves using all the senses to become aware of surrounding elements. Develop and improve your observation and perception skills daily. Novice officers can develop their skills by looking at a picture of a street scene, people, crime scenes, license plates, or a video for a few seconds, or even parts of a second, which simulates real observation time. Then write down what you saw, and compare the notes with the actual scene. Continuous practice will improve your ability to remember more details.

Much of the data you gain through observation will not be immediately and directly useful; however, you cannot always know in advance which of the things observed at the time will be useful and which will not. Effective observation can significantly contribute to good law enforcement. Observation is important as a means of preventing crimes as well as catching criminals in the act. Good, effective enforcement includes protecting the public from a variety of hazards that arise from natural causes, negligence, and other factors—here, again, observation plays an important role. Since police work frequently involves a great deal of personal danger, officers who are skilled, alert observers are likely to live longer and stay healthier than those who are not.

Two basic problems arise in making accurate, useful observations. First, much of what is important to the peace officer is often obscured by irrelevant objects or events. Second (as noted) it is often difficult to tell, at the time of an occurrence, what will be important later. To become a competent, skilled observer, you can develop several different techniques:

1. Improve your basic observation skills (the ability to see everything there is to see and to take it in quickly and accurately) by rigorous self-training and practice.
2. Learn "where to look." Avoid tunnel vision, and look beyond the obvious. Then put your observation skills to work against a background of irrelevant stimuli.
3. Learn your own beat area; coming to know what is usual for the area will let you recognize the unusual when it occurs.
4. Specific techniques for developing observation skills can include looking at store windows, pedestrian descriptions, arrest reviews, discussions with other officers, interviews with people in custody, study of crime scene photos and mug shots, and vehicle descriptions (including license tag information).

Making Complete Observations

Complete observation consists of two parts: *receiving* some stimulus and being *aware* of it. Complete observation consists of sensing and awareness occurring at the same time. For example, a driver may see (receive a stimulus from) the windshield of a car every time she drives; however, she may not actually be aware of the windshield. As such, this occurrence does not qualify as an "observation," since it lacks the "awareness" element. On the other hand, if the driver becomes aware that the windshield is dirty, she has made an observation, because now she is consciously aware of what she has sensed.

Complete observation develops into a "conscious" memory. However, most people also have a "sensory," or unconscious, memory. This phenomenon allows the mind to store an image of a stimulus that might be called up later and studied in the same way the conscious memory was studied. The use of hypnosis works on this principle.

Peace officers need all the observation skills available in order to do their job correctly and safely. Making accurate and complete observations permits you to become aware of surrounding incidents and events. Then you can make decisions on correct responses; you may decide to discard the observation, commit it to the conscious memory, or make a written record of the observation. The practical use of the sensory memory is to establish the "big picture" of a person, event, or scene in the mind. To take advantage of this technique, first look at the scene to get a complete once-over, without stopping to study anything in detail. This kind of observation takes a lot of training, because it is not a natural way to look at something. However, with this method you can get a full picture of the event and thus avoid the trap of staring too hard at one item or detail and failing to observe other important items or details.

The sensory memory applies to the senses of hearing, touch, taste, and smell as well as sight. The auditory (hearing) sensory memory works the same as the visual (sight) sensory memory, and it can be trained in the same way—appropriately modified for hearing instead of sight. The other senses can likewise be trained. For example, the sense of touch can detect vibrations as an indicator of someone's presence, or heat as an indicator of fire; a familiar example is touching the hood, tires, or muffler of a parked automobile to determine how recently it was driven. The senses of smell and taste are limited in the range of useful information they can provide. Although an officer may smell burning marijuana, other senses are needed to support an investigation of the odor, because the sense of smell weakens very quickly. Although the use of taste is also limited (tasting is *not* the best and safest way to test for a chemical or narcotic), there are some useful purposes to which it can be put to use. For instance, the sense of taste can determine whether sugar or salt was spilled on the table at a crime scene; however, since tasting any unknown substance may be dangerous, other testing methods may be safer. The observant officer makes use of all the senses in both the conscious and sensory memory.

WITNESS OBSERVATION AND PERCEPTION

As a patrol officer, one of your major sources of descriptive information will be complainants and witnesses at a crime or accident scene. Your ability to gain meaningful facts and data from these people will frequently determine how successful an investigation will be and whether or not justice is accomplished. To be certain, your job is complicated by the fact that witness perception is limited by both external and internal complications; some of these (as noted earlier in the chapter) are experience and education, maturity, mental and emotional conditions, bias, and so on. In addition, however, keep in mind that the average citizen does not consciously "observe" specific and significant facts, especially under highly stressful conditions. Too frequently, for example, the fear of looking down the barrel of a firearm totally consumes the victim's attention, and he or she will not be able to adequately describe the person holding the gun. Also be conscious that a person who gives you "too good" a description is either filling in the memory gaps to please you, or is totally fabricating the story to cover up his or her own illegal actions—such as a false robbery report to cover up an employee theft.

Three facts must be considered when evaluating information supplied by a complainant or witness: presence, consciousness, and attentiveness. First of all, the witness must be present at the scene. Presence can be acquired through use of any of the five senses. For example, an apartment dweller using binoculars from his or her room can "see" a crime committed in another building; thus, the witness has "presence" as defined under the law. Similar examples have been noted in case law for the other senses as well.

Second, the witness must be conscious of what he or she believes to have perceived. Awareness is crucial to an observation, as noted in the example of noticing a dirty car window. Seeing alone is not sufficient unless a specific consciousness of awareness is also present. In some cases, skilled hypnotists can help someone to "look" into his or her subconscious to remember something that the conscious mind does not recall. For example, witnesses have recalled license numbers and other facts under hypnosis that the conscious mind could not recall. However, even under hypnosis, the fact remains that the person must first have *seen* the license number in order to recall it. In one case, a witness did recall the license number; nevertheless, the witness could not describe the person sitting inside the car behind tinted glass, because the witness saw only a form and did not actually "see" the person.

Thus the third criteria, attentiveness, also plays a big role in witness perception. Most people look at situations, people, places, or things that interest them or attract their attention. A person who is genuinely interested in sports cars may never "see" the driver or passengers because his or her perception was focused on the car and not the people. A male witness may recall only the description of the woman when asked to give a description of a man and woman who were walking in the park.

Stress is a real factor in dealing with a witness's memory of an event. High stress frequently focuses attention on the stressful event, to the exclusion of other facts. A witness who gives vivid details about one aspect of an investigation may not be able to relate information about relatively observable data surrounding circumstances. For example, the victim may give a general description of the firearm pointed at him or her but not be able to describe the person holding the gun. The stress in this situation comes from the dangers that the weapon could inflict; the victim's focus is directed to the gun rather than the person holding it. Interestingly enough, however, the person may be able to give you very good information about the gun, which may be indelibly etched on his or her conscious mind.

Descriptions of People

While on patrol, you may receive a call regarding a "robbery in progress." You quickly proceed to the area following standard practices for this type of response (see Chapter 9, "Crimes in Progress"). You safely arrive at the scene and learn that the suspect fled the scene on foot. After determining that the victim is unharmed, you quickly begin the interview by asking the witness to generally describe the suspect and relate any fact(s) that stands out in the witness's mind about the suspect; for example, the victim may instantly recall a tattoo, scar, voice accent, or other irregularities to help identify the subject. These distinctive observations, along with a general description, then may be quickly broadcasted to local units searching near the immediate area of a crime for a fleeing suspect.

After the cursory description, you conduct a complete investigation to acquire a complete description of the wanted person. Standard descriptions of people (see Figure 3-3) usually start at the top of the individual and work down. Not only will you develop a technique to avoid missing any part of the descriptions, but most people will see others this way. Do not be surprised if a witness begins to become vague as the description moves toward the lower extremities and clothing. Most agencies provide a description questionnaire for of-

Standard Description of Person

Start   Finish

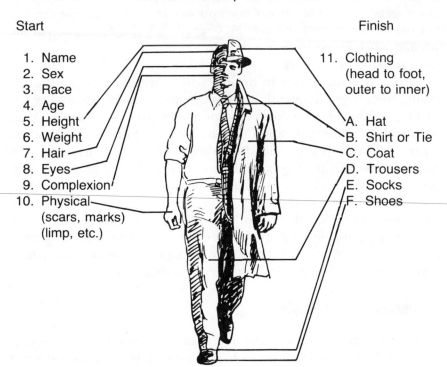

1. Name
2. Sex
3. Race
4. Age
5. Height
6. Weight
7. Hair
8. Eyes
9. Complexion
10. Physical
    (scars, marks)
    (limp, etc.)

11. Clothing
    (head to foot,
    outer to inner)

A. Hat
B. Shirt or Tie
C. Coat
D. Trousers
E. Socks
F. Shoes

MEMORIZE THE SEQUENCE!
  Use it on the air,
  on the telephone,
  and in taking
  descriptions.

GET IT ON THE AIR!
  Seconds count.

DON'T TALK TOO FAST!
  The other person
  has to copy it.

BREAK FREQUENTLY!
  (On long descriptions.)

Figure 3-3
**Example of standard description of cars and people in radio communication.
For vehicles, you give the CYMMBALS (symbols): *c*olor, *y*ear, *m*ake, *m*odel
*b*ody, *a*nd *l*icense number, followed by the *s*erial number (if known).
Descriptions of people start with the name, sex, race, age, height, weight,
color of hair, color of eyes, complexion, physical characteristics (marks,
tattoos, or limps), and finish with a clothing description (starting at the top
and working downward).**

Standard Description of Cars

Start at top and move down.

C. COLOR	RED OVER WHITE
Y. YEAR	78
M. MAKE	CHRYSLER
M. MODEL	CORDOBA
B. BODY	2 DR HARD TOP
A. and	
L. LICENSE	AB 1234
S. SERIAL	166736S123456
	(VIN)

Figure 3-3, *continued*

ficers' use in making witness inquiries. Standard information used in describing people outline brief but accurate data that are necessary to the investigation. The general form follows accepted application of description principles used in law enforcement agencies throughout the United States:

1. *Name*, if known, including nickname or alias (frequently listed as "a.k.a." or "also known as"). If available include first, middle, and last name, along with any distinguishing addition such as "Sr.," "Jr.," "II," and so on.

2. *Sex*. Keep in mind that a disguise (such as a female impersonation) might be used, and that the witness's perception could be in error.

3. *Race*. Ethnic distinction is a useful investigative tool to eliminate people of other ethnic backgrounds from the search and focus on

a particular suspect. Ethnic characteristics may also be noticeable through accent or dress. Standard abbreviations help reduce time in note taking; however, such abbreviations may change from one locale to another, and you should specifically learn the format used in your department or agency. Generally, use "W" for *White* or *Caucasian*— this designation may also be used for people who do not fit another designation; "B" for *Black American* (this has become more popular than "N" for *Negro*, which may still be used in parts of the country); "M" or "H" (depending on the area) for people of *Mexican* or Latin heritage, or *Hispanic*; "O" for people of *Oriental* (Asian) heritage.

4. *Age*. If known, an exact age is helpful; however, most witnesses will be able to only "estimate" age, and this can be difficult in some cases. The investigator might use a technique of "comparative" guessing; that is, ask the witness to compare the suspect's age to other people present and make comparisons—older, younger, etc.

5. *Height*. Victims and witnesses usually tend to overestimate a suspect's height. Many convenience stores have installed height measures near store exits to help clerks make accurate height descriptions. Again, the technique of comparative guessing can help the witness to assess the subject's height—"Was he (she) taller or shorter than me?" If there are a number of witnesses around, an average of all the "guesses" may be more accurate than one person's guess. In general, a man is considered to be short if he is less than 5 feet 6 inches, medium if 5 feet 6 inches to 6 feet, and tall if he is over 6 feet. In contrast, a woman is considered to be short if she is less than 5 feet 2 inches, medium if 5 feet 2 inches to 5 feet 6 inches, and tall if she is over 5 feet 6 inches. A final police description for a wanted suspect frequently indicates both a minimum and maximum range: "Suspect is between 5 feet 6 inches and 5 feet 11 inches tall."

6. *Weight*. Another category open to conjecture is weight. Witnesses may tend to use "light," "medium," or "heavy" designations rather than specifically guess at a person's weight. The term *light* for men usually indicates someone under 150 pounds; for women, the term may be used for someone under 100 pounds. A *medium* description for men may indicate someone between 150 and 185 pounds; women between 100 and 130 may be classified in this category. Men are *heavy* if they are over 185 pounds and women over 130 pounds might likewise be classified. It may be more difficult to generalize about a woman's classification because the height-to-weight ratio largely determines the body build. Additional terms that might be

applied to subject description are "slim," "stocky," "obese."

7. *Hair.* The most "individual characteristic" of personal appearance is hair—style, color, cut, length of hair, and so on. A person may be totally bald or have a distinctive hairline, such as a receding hairline at the front of the scalp or a "bald spot" at the back of the head. A witness may note the length or absence of a suspect's sideburns. The texture of the hair might be described as fine or coarse, kinky, curly, or straight. If possible, determine where the hair is parted (left side, right side, middle, or not at all). Keep in mind that a suspect may "mask" hair characteristics by wearing a wig or hat; given enough time he or she may change the style or color to avoid detection.

8. *Eyes.* A person's eyes are distinctive. Although color is the most obvious characteristic to ask about, remember that people can change the color appearance by wearing contact lenses. However, the description of the eyes should note more than just color. Consider the shape and form of eyes, as well as their size. Did the suspect have "bags" under his or her eyes, watery eyes, or bloodshot eyes that might result from an illness or intoxicating beverage? Do not overlook the fact that the suspect may have cross eyes, a false eye (marked by a shiny appearance), slanted eyes, or squinting eyes. If the suspect was wearing glasses, you should obviously get a full description: color, size, bifocal or trifocal lenses, or other noticeable characteristics.

9. *Complexion.* This item applies to the color and shade of the skin (fair, dark, ruddy, chalky, pale), as well as distinctive characteristics such as birthmarks, freckles, scars, pockmarks, acne (including blackheads and pimples), blotches, sunburn, skin grafts, and so on. Seek to list and determine their location and number and degree.

10. *Physical marks or characteristics.* Examples of typical physical marks or characteristics you should ask about include scars, limps, deformities, type and location of facial hair (beards and moustache), and missing or unusual teeth (some people have gold ornaments or other distinctive markings or stained teeth). In addition, visible tattoos on hands, arms, or other body limbs or locations serve to readily identify a suspect. Determine, if possible, whether the suspect was right- or lefthanded—in which hand did he or she hold the gun or weapon? Include any unusual characteristics about speech, actions (crying, nervous, angry, or other emotion), or any other visible part of the body.

11. *Clothing, jewelry, or other accessories.* Starting from the top and

working down, have the witness describe applicable items of headgear, shirt, tie, coat, dress or pants, shoes, and socks. Each item should include color, material (if known), style, design, and condition (cleanliness, tears, holes, distinctive marks, and so on). The suspect may have worn a mask or hosiery over his or her face and head as a disguise. Various hats (baseball cap, hat, beret) and neckties are very distinctive and may have inscriptions or designs printed on the article. Jewelry might include rings, bracelets, watches, necklace, and earrings (if only one worn, which side?). The location, description, color, or other relevant notation of this jewelry can help to identify the suspect even if he or she attempts to disguise the face. Other accessories might include scarves, noticeable checkbook or billfold protruding from pockets (note location), combs, purses, bags or bundles, and so on. Each fact should be identified and documented.

12. *Personal characteristics.* A suspect may have a distinguishing accent (either foreign, in which case you associate it with country of origin, or domestic regional—southern, midwestern, northeastern, New York or Boston, etc.). Other individual traits that might point to a specific subject are enunciation of words ("educated" or "uneducated"), speech impediments, distinctive tone or pitch of voice, talking speed (slow or fast), or specific language usage (cursing, colloquialisms, "jargon," and so on), to mention but a few. The witness may note distinctive movements such as the subject's walk—athletic, limping, shuffling, bowlegged, flatfooted, or pigeon-toed. Many people have "nervous habits" such as chewing fingernails, cracking knuckles, twitching, scratching the face, or wrenching of hands, etc. Each such unconscious or conscious movement can be like a "fingerprint" when combined with all other information to identify and locate the suspect.

To assist in criminal identification, law enforcement agencies employ a number of tactics such as "photo identification kits" and "police artists" to use witness descriptions to create a likeness of a suspect. Logically, you should remember that these sketches or combination photographs try to reasonably depict a suspect and may, or may not, recreate a precise likeness. Use these aids only to acquire a general idea of what the person may look like.

Eyewitness Identification

Law enforcement officers use a variety of techniques to identify crime suspects. Obtaining a verbal description, or *portrait parlé* (French for "word picture"), is still considered a reliable identification aid. The officer's skill and technique in interviewing witnesses and acquiring the "word picture" will help in locating a suspect. Even though the initial information may be somewhat vague, it will serve as a starting point to eliminate others in the area that do not match the initial description. More complete descriptions may suggest a known criminal or permit identification of a suspect at a later time.

Field Identification. If a suspect is located within a reasonable period of time near the scene of the crime, you are permitted to bring the person back to the location for witness identification. However, remember that the field identification process should not unnecessarily suggest that the person in custody is, in fact, the suspect. Allow the victim, complainant, or witness to determine whether or not he or she can identify the suspect without suggestion, duress, or coercion. In rare instances, you may detain an innocent person only to learn that he or she was not the subject of the investigation. Even though this can be embarrassing, you have at least eliminated that person as a suspect. Apologize and explain the detention in such case, and express your appreciation for the citizen's cooperation in the investigation.

In attempting to obtain a field identification, recreate similar conditions (lighting, location, etc.) to those that existed at the time of witness-subject interaction. Avoid suggesting that the person in custody is a suspect, and make it clear that the person's guilt or suspected participation in the crime should not be implied as the basis of the field identification process. Attempt to locate the witness and suspect in approximately the same positions as the initial contact took place. The suspect should be present without restraints, if practicable; however, this may not be practical if the person is combative or uncooperative. Record the witness's comments regarding any identification. In addition, assure yourself that the witness could logically make the identification under the environmental conditions then present.

Photographic Identification. Showing victims or witnesses a series of photographs is permissible provided there is a similarity between the photographs or there are enough pictures (as in a "mug book") to eliminate the possibility of suggesting a particular suspect. Based on investigative leads, you might discover several suspects in your *modus operandi* (MO) file of known offenders that might fit the suspect's description. The courts have upheld this identification procedure if a series of ten or more similar pictures are shown to the witness, or if the witness picks the suspect out of a random sampling of a large number of pictures. In some instances, investigators have deliberately shown witnesses a group of pictures that do not contain the suspect, to prevent any suggestibility of improper influence; the fact that this routine was used can be presented in court to substantiate witness reliability.

Witnesses should view the photographs separate from other witnesses; do not let the various people discuss the photographs among themselves. Explain to each witness that they should not be influenced by the fact that you are showing photographs, nor should they believe that the suspect will necessarily be among the pictures reviewed. Each witness should be informed that there is no obligation to identify anyone and that he or she should be reasonably certain of any identification. If a witness makes an identification, retain the group of photographs for later use to demonstrate the fairness and impartiality of the procedure. If several witnesses make similar identification, consider stopping the photographic identification process and using an in-person lineup for other potential witnesses.

Lineup Identification. The purpose of a "lineup," or "show-up" as it has sometimes been called, is to eliminate the power of suggestion as a factor in suspect identification. This identification step differs drastically from a field identification or photographic identification procedures. It is considered to be a "critical stage of the criminal proceedings," and thus a criminal defendant has the right to have an attorney present during the lineup process, to ensure the fairness and impartiality of the procedure. However, in accordance with the 1967 Supreme Court cases of *Wade, Gilbert*, and *Stovall*, the suspect does *not* have the right to refuse to participate in the lineup, give voice samples, or wear specific clothing or items of cosmetic alteration to simulate a crime situation.

In *United States v. Wade* (388 U.S. 218, 18 L.Ed 2d 1149, 87 S.Ct. 1926, 1967), the majority of the Court held that police lineups constitute a "critical stage of the prosecutorial process," and the Sixth Amendment right to counsel attaches at that time, applicable to the states through the due process clause of the Fourteenth Amendmend. Thus, an accused person has the right to have a lawyer present during the lineup. A second 1967 case, *Gilbert v. California* (388 U.S. 263, 18

L.Ed 2d 1178, 87 S.Ct. 1951) stated that an accused person's Fifth Amendment privilege was not violated by placing the person in a lineup and having him or her repeat phrases used by the person who committed the crime at the time he or she committed it. In a third case in the same year, *Stovall v. Denno* (388 U.S. 293, 18 L.Ed 2d 1199, 97 S.Ct. 1967), the Court ensured a fundamental fairness approach in relation to law enforcement procedures. *Stovall* made it clear that right to counsel at a lineup identification applies to preindictment stages. These three cases expanded the 1966 *Schmerber* doctrine (*Schmerber v. California*, 384 U.S. 757), so that the net effect of the cases is that one can be compelled against one's will to appear in a lineup (notwithstanding the right to have an attorney present), to furnish a handwriting exemplar, to put on clothing or, as in *Wade*, to put strips of tape on one's face and, at least inferentially, to speak for voice identification. This latter act, along with possibly other performance such as walking or taking a particular stance, would seem to have some limitations.

As noted, the right to have an attorney present at a lineup has been well established. However, it should be noted that the attorney cannot advise his or her client not to participate in the lineup; rather, the attorney's presence is to ensure the fairness of the lineup procedure and point out any unfair conditions. This not only provides due process of law for the suspect, but it also assists the law enforcement agency to ensure that a lineup identification will not be challenged in court. It is the law enforcement officer's job to ensure that the accused person has the opportunity to aid of counsel. Prior to the lineup, tell the suspect that he or she has the right to have an attorney present; if the subject indicates that he or she cannot afford an attorney, inform the person that the court will appoint a lawyer without cost. If the suspect asks for an attorney, delay the lineup until counsel for the accused can be retained. If the suspect waives his or her right to an attorney, have the suspect sign and date an acknowledgment of rights and waiver statement (every agency has forms available for this purpose); the waiver should be witnessed by the officer in charge of the lineup and second witness. If the suspect cannot write or sign his or her name, ask the person to make his or her personal mark[1] and

---

[1] Do not tell the suspect to make an "X" when signing any document. This may or may not be the way that the suspect makes his (her) normal sign and could be challenged in court.

then witness the action yourself, along with two disinterested people who are not peace officers.

Guidelines designed to ensure due process of law for lineups include the following:

1. All witnesses should be kept separate from each other and not allowed to compare notes or discuss subject identification.
2. At least six people of similar sex, age, racial characteristics, height, weight, and so on, should be assembled for the lineup. The suspect should have the right to choose his or her spot in the line.
3. Ensure that all people in the lineup have been advised of their right to have counsel present.
4. All people in the line should be similarly dressed; that is, one person should not be wearing shorts when all the others are wearing long pants.
5. All people in the lineup should be unknown to the witness(es) to avoid any suggestibility, unless the suspect was already known by the witness.
6. At the lineup, attempt to duplicate similar conditions (visibility, lighting, relative distances between the suspect and witnesses) to replicate the witness's perception situation.
7. Each person in a lineup should be required to perform same actions, repeat same phrases, put on same item of clothing, and so on, to prevent any suggestion that might focus on one subject.
8. Make a photographic or video record of the lineup for use in court at a later time, if needed.
9. Each witness should be interviewed after the lineup to determine his or her response to witness identification. If the witness makes a positive suspect identification, determine what characteristic(s) the witness specifically noticed or recalled in making his or her choice. A tape recorder is useful during this interview to ensure that specific details of the identification are not lost.
10. If a witness cannot make a specific identification at the lineup, express appreciation for his or her assistance and assure the person that you will continue your investigative efforts. Do not suggest that another witness did make an eyewitness identification.

11. If a witness picks out a person in the lineup who could not possibly have committed the offense (individual was in jail at time of offense, etc.), determine what features in this person reminded him or her of the suspect. You may gain new investigative leads that the witness failed to communicate in the initial investigation.

Description of Property

Accurately describing items that have been stolen enhances your chances of locating the property and subsequently returning it to the rightful owner. Learning to describe property takes time, because most people take various characteristics for granted. Law enforcement officers must learn how to describe an item of property to the exclusion of all other similar items. As a minimum, the description of any stolen item should cover the following:

1. *Quantity of the articles.* Item should be given a listing number and itemized by the quantity of missing items. For example,

Item Number	Quantity	Article
1	(2)	rings
2	(3)	handguns
3	(8)	twenty-dollar bills

2. *Kind of article.* Indicate if the item is a "man's watch," "a woman's ring," etc. Denote the purpose or who most frequently uses the item, if applicable.
3. *Physical description.* Include model, style, design, shape, size, and trade name. Report identifying serial numbers, initials, engraved driver's license number(s), symbols, or other significant marks that apply to this specific item to the exclusion of all others.
4. *Describe the material used in the item.* Gold, silver, diamonds, jewels, wool, silk, and so on. If the item has various quantities of precious metals or jewelry, describe each thoroughly. Determine if the owner has photographs or other video materials that depict the item(s).
5. *Color(s) of items,* such as "blue steel revolver," "yellow 14-K gold," or "brown and beige television."

6. *Condition of the item*, including age; determine when item was purchased and its current state of repair. Any "age marks," scratches, bumps, or missing parts should be noted to describe the specific item for identification.
7. *Value*. Indicate whether this is owner's cost or replacement cost, or how otherwise the value was determined. If money was involved, attempt to ascertain how the amount was determined (for example, "based on a register count two hours prior to the robbery").

Some of the more frequently stolen items are stereos, VCRs, televisions, firearms, and jewelry. These items, and other valuables, can generally be quickly traded, or exchanged for cash. When possible, obtain significant identification data from sales documents, warranty papers, or operating manuals that may have accompanied the items when purchased. In some cases, the owner may be able to obtain useful information from the seller or dealer where the item was purchased.

For firearms, the make, caliber, and serial number, the type of finish (nickel-plated, blue, etc.), and the length of barrel are specific pieces of information needed to complete the description. If possible, determine when and where the weapon was purchased; this information can help verify the model and serial number and other relevant information.

For stereos, televisions, VCRs, and so forth, find out specific information regarding dials, program bands (AM, FM, short-wave, and so on), modes (VHS, Beta), and other significant data in addition to brand names, model, and serial numbers. Determine if the items are portable, table model, and so forth. Specific types of control knobs and dials can be useful information to an alert investigator. For cameras, include the lens description (the most valuable part of the camera), size of film used, covering materials or cases, in addition to type and model, serial number, and color.

Jewelry should be specifically identified as pins, clips, earrings, lockets, rings, necklaces, and so forth. Each item should be detailed to indicate whether it was probably made for a man or woman (if applicable), the number and type of precious stones, type of metals used, and value. If possible, ascertain the type of stone cut—baguette, briolette, marquise, pendeloque, square, fancy star, to mention some of the more conventional styles of gem cutting. The owner of the jewelry may be a good source of this information; however, a picture of the item, or a dealer, may be more valuable in many cases.

VEHICLE INSPECTION FOR WEAPONS AND CONTRABAND

Your ability to apply good observation and perception techniques is especially important when conducting vehicle inspections for weapons and contraband. To safely and effectively apply vehicle search principles, follow time-tested procedures for officer safety and complete searches:

- First, properly remove and control vehicle occupants.
- Second, systematically search both the suspects and their vehicle(s).

Small areas of an automobile yield well to a general systematic search approach. The basic technique is to start at one predetermined point and proceed to another, in as direct a line as possible. For example, in searching a vehicle start at the top and work down. Another approach starts from the front and works to the rear; or begin from the inside and work to the outside. Whichever plan is used, the search must be planned. The primary consideration in planning the search will be the nature of the area to be searched and the nature of the object being sought (contraband, weapons, evidence, etc.).

Inside Vehicle Search

Vehicle interiors provide many hiding places. To begin the interior search, thoroughly search the cowling for anything that might be attached to it. Empty the glove compartment, and check each item before replacing it or seizing evidentiary items. Check under the dashboard, paying particular attention to the maze of wiring under the dashboard to see if anything is attached to it. Check the back of the ignition switch to see if the vehicle is being operated properly or has been "jumper wired" ("hot-wired").

Check the back of the rubber cover of the brake pedal, clutch pedal, and accelerator pedal for anything that might be attached. A popular hiding place is behind the firewall and the side kick panels; the kick panels are usually covered by cardboard of fiberboard, fastened down by small clips or screws. In addition, the air ducts or the ventilation system are excellent places for concealing illegal items. Furthermore, check the steering column for anything that may be taped to it.

Empty the contents of the ashtray onto a sheet of paper, since many items can be hidden in the ashes. The ashes may also constitute evidence of marijuana or other controlled substances. Scrutinize the cigarette lighter and the housing into which it fits. Knobs on the dashboard might operate hidden compartments located in the vehicle. Check all courtesy lights on the dashboard or roof of the vehicle, especially if they do not light when activated.

Whenever possible, search under the floor carpet and floor mats. The sun visor can hide numerous items; check both sides, and look between a mirror and the sun visor, and between registration holder and the sun visor, for checks, money, narcotics, and so on. The floor area under the front seat is a popular storage place for weapons and contraband. However, also check for anything attached to the underside of the front and rear seats, as well as between the seat and kick panel located on the right and left sides of the front seat.

Another popular hiding place is the crevice area down between the seat cushion and the seat back. Examine the upholstery of both seats for any tears or seams that have been opened and resewn. If the vehicle has seat covers, make sure that nothing is concealed between the seat and the seat cover.

Finally, check the door paneling for signs of removal; many items can be hidden in the lower portion of the doors. By checking the surface of the doors and window handles, you may discover items attached to them; narcotics may also be hidden inside a handle or armrest in the vehicle.

Exterior Portions of the Vehicle

Outside the vehicle, carefully search under surfaces of front and rear fenders for anything that might be hidden or attached there. Inspect the area behind the rear bumper and the rear license plate and the area where the neck of the gas tank is located.

Under the hood, check the engine compartment and motor accessories, paying particular attention to the area between the radiator, grill, and lower portion of the hood. Outside accessories and "ornaments" may be false and provide hiding places for contraband.

Check the vehicle trunk thoroughly. Look inside the spare tire coverings, and check boxes, bags, tool box, and containers that are found in the trunk. If you find clothing in the trunk, check the pockets and other areas for illegal items.

Check all taillight assemblies for items that may be hidden there. In addition, hub caps are popular areas to conceal contraband and other objects. Check the center post to determine if it is stationary or not. Some burglars remove the center post and weld it in position to the front or the rear doors on the right side of the vehicle. When the rear door is opened, the front door and center post open with it, providing ample room for loading stolen goods such as television sets or safes.

Finally, check any trash containers found in the car, attached to the doors, dashboard, and so on. Examine all miscellaneous items found inside the vehicle. If items are found in a container, examine each item as it is removed. Do not overlook the obvious when searching a vehicle: books, blankets, and clothing may contain evidence of criminal activity for which you are directly or indirectly looking. Ultimately, your thoroughness, observation, and perception will determine whether the search is successful or not.

KEY TERMS

Alertness
CYMMBALS
Eyewitness identification
Field identification
Illusions
Lineup identification
Modus operandi (M.O.) file
Observation
Perception
Personal senses
Photographic identification
Physical marks or characteristics
Portrait parlé
Sensory memory
Stress
Vehicle search/inspection tactics

STUDY QUESTIONS

1. What is the difference between "observation" and "perception"?

2. Which of the five senses is the most useful? Why?

3. Which of the five senses is the least useful? How can this sense nevertheless be used in police work?

4. List six factors that can distort perception. Explain how each factor might apply to you.

5. Why might two witnesses who saw the same accident give different accounts of what happened? Does this necessarily mean that one witness is lying?

6. What are the two parts of a "complete observation"? How does an officer on patrol use both parts?

7. Why must law enforcement officers have a good understanding of human nature and behavior?

8. In your own words, explain the statement "One of the first lessons any officer learns is to understand his or her own weaknesses and then put the 'professional self' in place of the personal self as a law enforcement officer."

9. How could each illusion depicted in Figure 3-1 apply to law enforcement field operations?

10. Why do people have more difficulty distinguishing colors in dim or dark light?

11. How does the presence of other colors affect perception of another color? Why?

12. How can various types of lighting affect colors? Why is this important to law enforcement patrol operations?

13. As a patrol officer, how can you prepare yourself to increase your visual acuity on entering a dim room from a lighted area?

14. How can you improve on your sense of hearing to become a better law enforcement officer?

15. What dangers should you be aware of in using the sense of "taste" in law enforcement work?

16. How can you improve your observation skills?

17. Good observation skills can protect the public from various hazards

before they adversely affect others. List various hazards that you might observe on routine patrol, and note what action you should take regarding each hazard.

18. What is "tunnel vision"? How do you avoid this condition?

19. Devise a systematic approach to searching a vehicle. Make a check-list that you could use during a vehicle search.

20. When evaluating a witness's statement, what three facts should you consider in determining whether or not the person can provide meaningful information?

21. What role does the subconscious play in observation?

22. What role does stress play in observation and perception?

23. What are the standard elements used to make a description of a person? Describe yourself, using this formula.

24. In describing clothing, why should you start at the top of the person and work downward?

25. What should you expect if a witness gives you *too* good a description?

26. Make a list of various "personal characteristics" that a patrol officer might ask a witness about a crime suspect.

27. What is a *portrait parlé*?

28. When and how would a patrol officer use a "field identification" technique to identify a possible suspect? What should you do if you have the wrong suspect?

29. What requirements are necessary in order to lawfully use a photo-graphic identification technique in witness interviews?

30. Can a suspect refuse to participate in a lineup? Justify your answer.

31. If a suspect wants a lawyer prior to a lineup, what should you do? What happens if the suspect cannot afford an attorney?

32. What are your legal requirements if a suspect waives his or her right to an attorney prior to a lineup?

33. How can you verify that a suspect waived his or her constitutional rights if the suspect does not know how to write?

34. What role does the suspect's attorney serve at the lineup?

35. List the correct procedural steps in holding a lineup.

36. If a witness picks a person out of a lineup who cannot possibly be the

criminal sought, what information can you gain from this incorrect identification?

37. Using an item of personal jewelry (a ring, watch, necklace, etc.), completely identify it to the exclusion of all other similar items.

ACTIVITIES

1. Create small groups of five to six members. Have a person unknown to the class appear before the class for a few minutes. Have each group "guess" at the stranger's height and weight; have each group "average" their responses. Compare each group's "average" to the person's actual height and weight.

2. Distribute a potato to each student in class, and ask each to describe the potato in detail to the exclusion of all other potatoes. Collect the potatoes and individual writings. Read several of the descriptions, and have various students try to pick out the individual potato described. Have the class evaluate the descriptions. Ask students to determine why some descriptions are better than others. How can each person improve on describing property? How does this apply to law enforcement investigations? Repeat experiment using items of jewelry.

3. Show one or more pictures to the group for a minute. Have each student write down what he or she observed. Compare the written observations to the actual picture. Have the students evaluate their papers in reference to what they did *and* did not observe, and ask them to evaluate reasons for their lack of description or deletion of objects.

4. Have students observe parked cars in a parking lot (shopping center, campus parking lot, etc.) for fifteen minutes. Make a list of the number of observable out-of-state license plates, expired license plates, obscured license plates, and expired vehicle inspection stickers (if applicable in your state). Compare results in class. How does this project relate to law enforcement patrol operations?

5. Have students describe a well-known person in public life. Read the descriptions, and ask the class to "guess" at the person's identify.

4

Law Enforcement Communications Systems

Funk & Wagnall's Standard Dictionary defines the word *communicate* as a verb meaning "to cause another or others to partake of or share in; impart" or "to transmit or exchange thought or knowledge." The noun *communication* is "the act of imparting or transmitting; the transmission of ideas, information, etc., as by speech or writing; a message; a means of passage or of transmitting messages between places or persons; the science of communicating."[1] Day-to-day patrol operations, police investigations, interrogations, complainant and witness interviews, intradepartmental intelligence and coordination, interdepartmental exchange of information, interpersonal communications, and police-community relations are all parts of law enforcement communication "operational links" to ensure officer safety and survival. Communication is the lifeline for all officers. Each officer must seek to know, understand, and properly use communication sciences to achieve the police mission and personal safety.

---

[1] *Funk & Wagnalls Standard Desk Dictionary, Vol. 1: A–M* (New York: Funk & Wagnalls Publishing, 1979), p. 128.

Expert communications results in causing others to partake or share in information that is vital to police operations. Exchange of ideas and information is not always easy. Every time we share information with others, we risk putting ourselves on the line and being accountable for our actions, words, feelings, and concepts. One excellent proverb says,

Be careful of the words you speak,
Be sure to keep them sweet—
You never know from day to day
Which ones you'll have to eat!

Without communication, however, no action would ever be taken; officer safety would cease to exist. The inability to learn and impart thought and knowledge would signal the end not only of efficient police operations, but also of society as we know it. Efficient communication is the "lubrication" that makes the machinery of society— and certainly the law enforcement agency—work. Each element of the law enforcement agency is linked together to form a combination of specialties collectively working to achieve common objectives. In addition, every law enforcement agency is linked to other police services through intricate computer network systems and personal communications involving interchange of knowledge, information, and ideas. The degree and quality of mission success can be directly focused on the extent of information exchange and communications efficiency between each "linked" entity.

Recent advances in law enforcement technology, particularly in areas of communication—radio, teletype, computers, telephone, and so on—give rise to excitement in the law enforcement profession as we begin to move into the twenty-first century. Technological innovations in the past forty years far exceed those of any prior period of history. Peace officers now can maintain constant communications with operational headquarters and other officers—an ability many officers take for granted. Patrol officers access radios and computers, both at the station house and in their patrol units, to instantly communicate and acquire information necessary for officer safety and to accomplish their duties. Quick access to the central data processing centers for information on wanted people, vehicles, and other property gives officers up-to-the-minute feedback.

However, the real excitement in technology is still on the horizon. Technology is still in its infancy. Although it is difficult to imagine all the devices yet to come, it is relatively easy to predict that law enforcement officers of the future have much to look forward to in the way of new technology. For example, the wrist television and communications device that the comic strip character Dick Tracy uses will certainly become a reality; however, the device will probably be expanded to include computer capabilities and accurately record all law enforcement activity. It will be an exciting era in which to be a law enforcement specialist.

This chapter examines communications from an operational perspective. Beginning with criteria for developing two-way interaction and essentials for police communication, important concepts of human relations and community interaction are reviewed in the context of departmental and interpersonal relationships. Use of the field radio and computer operations are introduced, along with federal and state communication information systems. Guidelines for speedy and reliable communications are presented as a way to begin preparing for careers as modern peace officers. Finally, we look at how to deal with the public media and conflicts concerning the right to privacy.

TWO-WAY COMMUNICATIONS—ESSENTIALS FOR POLICE OPERATIONS

As noted at the beginning of this chapter, the science of communication is the act of imparting or transmitting ideas and information between places or persons by various methods including verbal, nonverbal, and written means. A frequently overlooked fact is that communication is most effective when "two-way communications" exist; that is, information flows in both directions to clarify misunderstanding and provide opportunity for both parties to ask questions and receive appropriate responses. Conversely, one-way information inhibits communication and lacks the essentials for effective exchange of information and ideas.

Figure 4-1a is a flowchart of a one-way communications model. Box A represents a mind that formulates a thought to be transmitted. The mind selects the best means to encode the idea and sends the

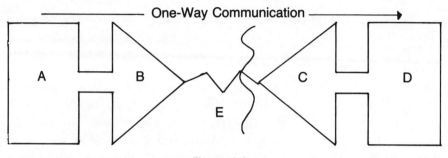

Figure 4-1a
One-way communication flowchart model. A is the "encoder" that initiates the idea to be communicated; the thought is encoded and transmitted at B (voice, written document, nonverbal communication, etc.). The message flows until it reaches C, a receiver (ear, eye, etc.) that in turn transmits the message to D, the decoder. The middle area, E, represents the transmitted medium that is frequently hampered with "noise," such as distractions, interference, and so on.

message via a transmitter (B); typical transmitters involve the senses of sound, sight, ability to write, and so on. Some transmitters unconsciously operate to send messages that the conscious mind is not even aware of. Body language, for example, is an example of nonverbal communication that can be detected if a receiver (C) is functioning and alert. The receiver typically is the eye or ear; however, one of the other senses may also be involved. The receiving device does not operate to "understand," which is the job of the decoder, D.

Various problems inhibit communications in this form. Noise (E) can take many forms—distractions, not paying attention, and so on. If any "noise" inhibits transmitting the message, it probably will not be decoded. This typically occurs, for example, when an instructor is lecturing to a class; if a person enters the classroom (or some other disturbance results) during the lecture, students' attention turns toward the distraction and anything being taught at that moment is lost unless repeated without distraction. In addition, problems occur in translating information between the receiver (C) and the decoder (D). For example, the receiver (an ear) may clearly hear words spoken in another language; however, if the decoder (the brain) does not recognize that language, no communication has occurred. Without the ability to seek "feedback" or clarification, the quality of any "real" communication is poor at best and completely lost at worst.

Have you ever heard a person say, "What I said was not what I

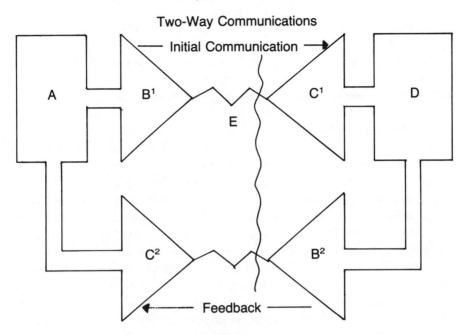

Figure 4-1b
Two-way communication flowchart model. In this model, communication flows both ways. Once the initial idea or message is received by D, the opportunity for feedback is added to complete communications. B^2 represents transmitting a question or clarification about the initial message to C^2, which in turn receives and decodes the communication.

meant"? Is the spoken or written word itself "the thought," or is the word merely a symbol of a thought? If the spoken or written word is a *symbol*, it is possible that the mind selectively can choose the incorrect symbol in some cases, creating errors or confusion in the communication. This confusion suggests a problem between the encoder (A) and the transmitter (B). We frequently ask for clarification for another person to ensure understanding. This clarification or confirmation process is called *feedback*, which serves to ensure complete communication. Figure 4-1b adds the ability of feedback to the one-way communications model. The same initial problems of confusion and misunderstanding occur in the two-way model as they do in the one-way model—inability to effectively encode and decode. Now, however, the receiving person can encode a question for clarification, "Did you mean to say . . .?" Repeated interaction leads to clearer understanding and good communications. However, understand that "noise" continues to disrupt and prevent communication at all times. Efforts must be taken to eliminate as much noise as possible. For example, an officer interrogates a suspect in a closed room that does not contain a telephone; other people in the area are instructed not to disturb the interrogation until the interviewing officer is through. Taking steps to eliminate as many interruptions and distractions as possible greatly enhances the ability to reduce noise and effectively communicate. In some cases people let others seek feedback, and rely on their questions for clarification. This process can be effective in limited situations such as a court of law, where a jury listens to questions and answers between lawyers and witnesses; however, such a process is limited by the quality of the questions. In a criminal investigation, as an investigator "you" must ask the "right questions" in order to get the "correct answers" that provide evidence in a case.

How does all this affect the street patrol officer? You work with people every day—they are your business. Your ability to effectively communicate on all levels will determine your status as a respected law enforcement officer. Within your agency, you will use the police radio, operate computers, communicate with other officers to exchange information, and write reports concerning your investigations of incidents, accidents, and arrests. On the street you may talk to complainants, victims, witnesses, or perhaps a neighbor mowing his or her lawn. You will testify in court before magistrates, lawyers, and jurors. Each of these situation involves opportunities for communication. For example, by using two-way communications in a criminal trial, you may be able to clarify a defense lawyer's question before offering an answer that may result in a criminal conviction. In another instance, your supervisor and other officers can offer feedback regarding your written reports to ensure completeness, accuracy, and avoid misunderstanding or suggestion of improper police procedure. Professional officers continually seek new and inventive ways to improve communication techniques. You will have many opportunities to successfully achieve your goals in law enforcement if you learn to use communications to your advantage.

Essentials for Law Enforcement Communications

Law enforcement communications systems have developed from "state of the art" technological advances in radio and computer telecommunications. However, the sophistication and efficiency of the mechanical and technical means used in the transmission of information is of little value if the information is not clearly expressed in the first place. Clarity will not be improved in the transmission. Furthermore, a clear message transmitted through equipment improperly used will probably be distorted. Therefore, officers must be careful not only to structure their message properly but also to know how to use their equipment. Hence, various "essentials" can be noted as crucial to operations of law enforcement communications systems.

Proper *training* in the use of various types of communications equipment is essential. Every agency has standard operating procedures to ensure proper use of equipment. You will receive on-the-job practical application of devices in the field. Learn to correctly use the equipment, and follow departmental regulations regarding its handling. In the meantime, however, begin to prepare for patrol operations by learning to use two-way communication techniques for complete understanding and commit the ten-signal code and phonetic alphabet (see Figure 4-8 on field radio operation) to memory.

Needless repetition of messages causes wasted air time. Much of this loss can be eliminated by not transmitting with a pencil, chewing gum, or some other object in your mouth; speaking too rapidly; slurring words; or transmitting during excessive interference from passing planes, trains, trucks, sirens, and so forth. Learn good radio technique and discipline. For example, do not attempt to key the microphone and transmit a message when another person is using the radio. Even in emergency (10–33) situations, trying to use the radio over another transmission is useless; you only succeed in blocking out both transmissions.

Learn to observe and increase communications from body language—also called "interpersonal communications." Your ability to develop good human relations and interact well with your community will pay great dividends. You gain a tactical advantage by understanding vertical and horizontal methods of communication within your agency and following the "chain of command." These essentials of law enforcement communications form a foundation for growth and advancement. The next sections expand more on these topics.

The Johari Window

One way to explain how two-way communications can effectively work in law enforcement is by adapting the Johari window communi-

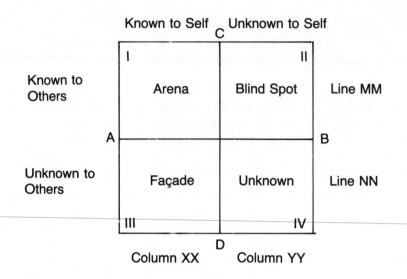

Figure 4-2a
The Johari Window applied to law enforcement patrol operations. Line AB represents exposure, or one-way communications. Line CD represents feedback used in two-way communications. The Arena amounts to information that is shared between oneself and another; the Blind Spot indicates information known to others but unknown to oneself. The Façade involves data known to oneself but unknown to others, while the Unknown can be a danger to both parties.

cation design to police communications. This information-processing model is applicable to many different types of feedback and exposure. Figure 4-2a outlines the basic standard plan of the window, which establishes the pattern for understanding relationships. The four quadrants are divided by Lines AB and CD, which cross in the middle. Line AB represents "exposure" or one-way communication; for example, a peace officer seeking information by opening lines of communication to ask about an incident, crime, or other significant investigation. Line CD represents "feedback," or two-way communications in response to inquiry.

Notice that Column XX encompasses the total length of the left-hand side of the diagram; this space indicates information that is "Known to Self," data that you are aware of. Column YY, on the right-hand side of the diagram, represents information that is "Unknown to Self," or knowledge that you do not have. Line MM across the top portion of the diagram represents information that is "Known to Others," while Line NN on the bottom of the plan is labeled "Unknown to Others."

Thus, the four quadrants or regions are created. Quadrant I is called the Arena; this block represents information that is known to you *and* to others (a cross and combination of Column XX and Line MM). This is the most desirable block to operate within and seek to expand. Sharing appropriate information eliminates misunderstandings, misinformation, rumor, and other impediments to communication. Quadrant II is called the Blind Spot. This information is known to others but unknown to yourself. To gain this knowledge, you must seek and gain a greater amount of feedback from the other person.

Quadrant III is called the Façade. This block represents information that you know, but which is unknown to others. A great deal of information you acquire in police work is confidential, and you cannot share the knowledge "unless revelation is necessary in the performance of your duty." However, there are other means of expressing "exposure" in this context; compassion, empathy, sympathy, understanding, a desire to listen and help—these are but a few of the ways you can expand this part of the Arena without compromising your duty. Block IV is the Unknown; this area indicates data that are a mystery both to you and to others. In many instances, the Unknown can be a dangerous place to be; "what you don't know *can* hurt you."

Expanding Your Arena. Law enforcement work is a people-related profession. To effectively work with people, you must be able to *expand your Arena*, by giving and receiving as much information and understanding as possible to accomplish your goal and objectives in the police mission. If your Arena is too small, you are not doing your job. Therefore, let's look at ways to expand the Arena. There are two obvious ways to accomplish this task—extending your exposure and acquiring feedback from others.

Figure 4-2b represents the basic "window" where you have exerted effort to communicate with others by extending your "exposure." Look at what happens when positive efforts are made to open lines of communication by widening your "exposure." First of all, your Arena considerably grew by knocking down some of the Façade that hinders openness to others. Your caring, compassionate demeanor in handling victims, witnesses, complainants, and other citizens will facilitate and express your desire to efficiently and effectively handle their

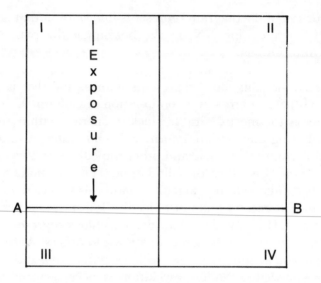

Figure 4-2b
In this variation, the exposure area has increased to expand the Arena in one direction. This exposure can amount to limited appropriate information, a caring, compassionate attitude, empathy, and willingness to be a good listener. Notice that the Blind Spot can increase as well without feedback; however, the Unknown and Façade did diminish.

problems. When you handle, interrogate, or deal with crime suspects, an honest and forthright approach indicates your eagerness to conduct a professional investigation in a fair manner. However, keep in mind that negative exposure can have exactly the opposite effect that you desire to achieve; a condescending attitude only serves to increase the Façade and limit opportunities for communication.

The other obvious effects of magnifying your exposure is a proportionate increase in your Blind Spot (which can become a disadvantage depending on information you exposed) along with the decrease of the Unknown (a desirable task). Of these two quadrants, the Blind Spot is your most immediate concern. Once you know what the other person knows, you will be able to increase your Arena again. This is accomplished by acquiring information through "feedback."

Figure 4-2c represents the region where you acquire only feedback without effort to extend any of your exposure. In this diagram, the area is definitely in your advantage; however, the increased Façade may also lead you into falsely assuming facts that are not true or

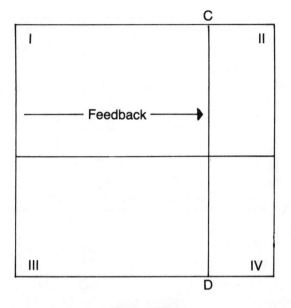

Figure 4-2c
In this example, feedback expanded without any exposure. The Arena and Façade increase in size, with an accompanying decrease in the Blind Spot and Unknown. However, this situation can leave the other person dissastified and unwilling to cooperate at a later time.

leaving the other person unsatisfied with the communication. You may get a witness's story but fail to gain his or her respect; future opportunity to acquire information from that source may already be damaged. You may acquire necessary information to fill out a burglary report, but the complainant feels dissatisfied with the manner in which the investigation was conducted. A criminal who gave you information during "an interrogation" will probably allege coercion at a later time. In addition, the feedback you obtain will probably be incomplete and inaccurate, and lead you in the wrong direction. These are but some of the problems associated with this form of one-way communication.

Figure 4-2d represents the best effort of two-way communication. Note that in this example, both exposure and feedback work together to expand the Arena. An associated decrease in the Blind Spot and Façade proportionately expand that part of the plan that imparts understanding, compassion, and caring to achieve positive feedback that works to everyone's advantage. Also note what happens to the

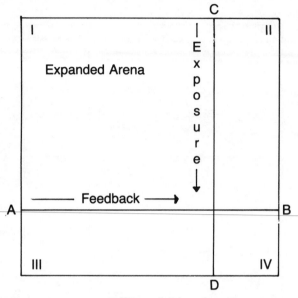

Figure 4-2d
In this example, both exposure and feedback are used to expand the Arena to achieve best results in two-way communications. Note that the Unknown is greatly diminished, while the Blind Spot and Façade also decrease in size.

Unknown—it virtually diminishes, to become almost insignificant. This is highly desirable for law enforcement officers seeking to become professionals, and it can have safety applications as well.

Consider some other applications of the expanded Arena in criminal justice work. Appropriately enough, this is the method used by our adversary court system to let jurors decide cases. Jurors usually begin by working in the Unknown. Each side presents evidence and seeks feedback regarding the validity of the testimony and physical facts. By the time each side has presented its case, the jurors are well within the Arena and able to decide the issue before them.

Other obvious examples involve communications between a radio dispatcher and a patrol officer. Without proper exposure and feedback between these "partners," this operational Arena can be very small—and dangerous. Officers participating in a drug raid must know and understand what other officers are doing to ensure safety and operating effectiveness. Coordination with the patrol division is also important to prevent misunderstanding and ensure mission effectiveness.

In another example, consider your position while seeking to learn about law enforcement police operations. The size of your Arena will vary directly with your past exposure to law enforcement officers and the amount of feedback you have already obtained. You continue to gain knowledge through exposure and feedback by using this texbook and participating in discussion and exercises. You never stop learning; it is a lifelong process designed to expand your Arena and enable you to become a complete and knowledgeable professional.

HUMAN RELATIONS AND COMMUNITY INTERACTION

Police officers must work with other people in order to maintain peace and order within the community. Although the officer must have a thorough knowledge of laws, rules, procedures, and techniques in order to perform police functions efficiently, the officer must also understand that at the point marking delivery of service he or she is dealing directly with people. Any professional interaction between human beings involves communication and human relations. Thus to be a competent police officer, you must be able to relate well to other people, both inside and outside the police department.

Police work is inherently stressful; stress is generated through contact with people outside and within the police agency. But stress can be either positive or negative. Positive stress motivates employees to strive for goals. Negative stress stands in the way of accomplishing objectives and the police mission. The professional peace officer learns to deal effectively with stress and to use the positive motivating factors advantageously while overcoming harmful or negative stress.

The police agency is a family. Strong ties connect officers in a sense of kinship and mutual respect. As we noted earlier, many peace officers will attend the funeral of a fellow officer slain in line of duty, even though the officers did not personally know the deceased officer. These relationships extend through a lifetime. Police officers are people who care about all people.

This police-to-police relationship is generally positive and can have a strong positive effect on the community. Peace officers must, however, guard against a closed-door syndrome that can develop as a side effect of strong police-to-police relationships. Frequently officers can become paranoid because of the criminal element they must deal with on a day-to-day basis. An officer may grow to feel secure only when he or she is with other officers. Thus the officer begins to close the door and exclude anyone who is not a member of this close personal or professional family. When the closed-door syndrome takes over the officer's personality, the potential for poor police-community relations intensifies.

The key to avoiding poor police-police relations, poor police-community relations, and the closed-door syndrome is *professionalism*. This word means many things to many people. To the peace officer, professionalism means more than just getting paid to do a job. The police professional holds the position in high esteem but does not expect special treatment because of this position in society. The peace officer seeks justice through service to the community and efficient enforcement of society's laws. Peace officers develop and apply a professional attitude toward each day's work by building a career that adheres to the edicts set forth in the Law Enforcement Code of Ethics.

Police-Police Relations and Police-Community Relations

A simple theory of relationships serves well to demonstrate how police-police relations equal police-community relations: PPR = PCR. In this equation, the way in which officers relate to one another has a direct bearing on the way in which the police relate to the public. This "pass-it-on" concept states that whenever "officers are frustrated and resentful over mistreatment by other police personnel [they] will vent that resentment and frustration in the community where it is safer to express themselves without the consequence of being insubordinate to higher ranking officers."[2]

PPR = PCR creates a circular pattern of interaction. Whenever poor morale problems within the department are passed on to the citizens within the community, the citizens in turn respond negatively through their feedback to the department. While not all citizen complaints are valid, an increased number of complaints regarding one or more officers is an indication of poor police-police relations. If the morale problem is not solved within the department, citizen complaints will create more negative communication within the police

---

[2] Paul F. Cromwell, Jr, and George Keefer, *Police Community Relations*, 2nd ed. (Saint Paul, Minn.: West Publishing, 1978), p. 157.

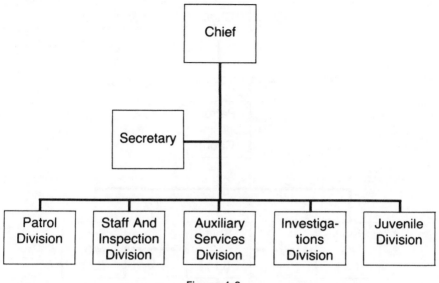

Figure 4-3
Organizational chart of a small police agency showing lines of communication, which is also the chain of command.

department, resulting in continued expressions of resentment and frustration when the officer deals with the public at large.

If the equation of PPR = PCR is a valid expression of interaction, it is equally valid to say that positive police-police relations will result in positive police-community relations. Positive relationships are built on open lines of communication, trust, and professionalism. A department's organizational chart defines the structure of the agency. The following organizational chart might be implemented for a small agency. (See Figure 4-3.)

In Figure 4-3, each division is connected to the chief of police by a chain of command indicating lines of supervision within the agency. These lines of command are also the lines of communication within the agency. Subordinate units within the divisions would communicate with the chief of police through their divisional commanders. When the lines of communication are open, the officer has the opportunity to share ideas, express problems, and gain meaningful advice and guidance of superiors. If the lines of communication are closed, frustration and anxiety grow into hostility and aggression.

Horizontal communications, indicated in Figure 4-4 by a broken line (---), aid coordination and information sharing that in turn

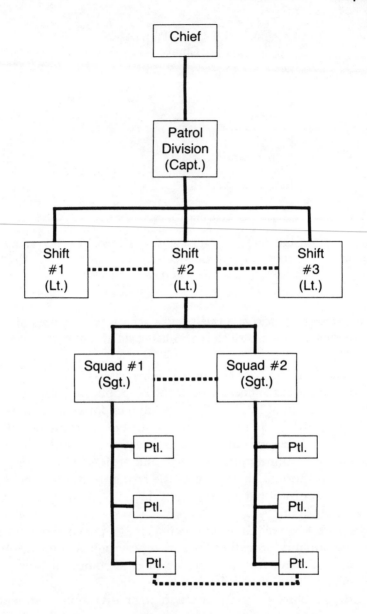

Figure 4-4
**Example of chain of command for Shift 2, showing vertical lines of authority
and lines of communication from patrolperson (Ptl.) to the chief of police.
The solid line indicates the route of formal communications; the broken line
shows avenues of coordination.**

promote the objectives of the police mission. An open policy of helping through communication results in good police-police relations.

Using the code of ethics as a foundation, officers can achieve professionalism by exercising positive attitudes while performing a multitude of roles. The officer must be able to make the transition between roles smoothly and effectively. For example, the officer might be called on to arrest a felony suspect in one part of town, then be called on to help an elderly person who is lost in another area. Such quick transitions in roles create their own kind of stress for the officer. The ability to cope with constantly changing roles effectively is the essence of a positive professional attitude.

The quality of professionalism is enhanced by pride in oneself and one's profession. The job of being a peace officer requires that the officer enjoy the work and have an attitude that anything less than the best effort is not good enough. As a result, the officer's attitude is reflected in job performance, concern for other people rather than just self-interest, and an honest desire to be a public servant and to ensure that justice, above all else, is the objective of the police role.

POLICE-COMMUNITY RELATIONS

Every contact that a law enforcement officer makes with a member of the community is an opportunity for developing good police-community relations. When the police officer is receptive to the needs of people in the community, the officer reinforces positive police-community relations. When the officer is courteous and fair in dealing with citizens, the officer makes friends for the department—not adversaries. Each encounter is a chance for the peace officer to cultivate friendships. Such encounters open doors to effective communication and frequently help develop sources of information.

Elements of Police-Community Relations

Good police-community relations are built on the interrelationships between public service, public relations, and community participation. Each of these elements is vital to establishing and maintaining open lines of communication and feedback between the community and the police agency. With police professionalism serving as a strong foundation, a sturdy structure of police-community relations is built

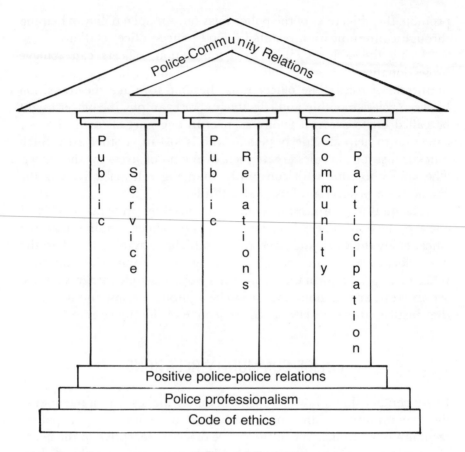

Figure 4-5
**With police professionalism serving as the foundation, strong pillars of
public service, public relations, and community participation support a sound
structure of police-community relations.**

on the pillars of public service, public relations, and participation.
(See Figure 4-5.)

Public Service. Public service is designed around the concept of
the police mission. A police department is expected to (1) prevent
crime, (2) repress crime, (3) apprehend offenders, (4) recover stolen
property, (5) control and assist in areas of noncriminal conduct, and
(6) perform miscellaneous services. Police manner and methods determine the degree of public service to citizens, who pay for the police
services.

The ability of the police agency to prevent crime can be measured by comparing types and frequency of crimes. By using selective conspicuous and nonconspicuous patrol, the police department can prevent specific offenses. An active program of operation identification—where police help citizens mark valuables for positive identification in the event of theft—not only is a positive prevention tactic, but also reinforces good police-citizen contact.

Crime repression involves investigating a criminal offense, identifying the perpetrator of the crime, and locating that person. Many benefits spring from good crime repression. First, the criminal is brought to justice quickly. Quick, efficient police action creates a positive image in the community, which in turn places more confidence in its police department. Second, when the police agency has a reputation for quick, efficient repression of crime, criminals expect less success. Good crime repression becomes powerful crime *prevention*. The final benefit is in apprehending the offender, which is the next element of the police mission.

Apprehending offenders takes up a small but important part of the police mission. Peace officers usually spend less than 5 percent of their time in making actual apprehensions. Whenever an apprehension is accomplished, though, it is imperative that the officer follow precise rules of procedure in establishing probable cause, obtaining warrants, making arrests, conducting searches, and making seizures. Nothing is more demoralizing for a peace officer than to spend hours, days, weeks, and maybe months investigating a criminal offense only to lose the case by failing to follow proper procedural guidelines established by the Constitution and Code of Criminal Procedure. To ensure that justice prevails, the arrest of offenders must be legal and above reproach.

Citizens of the community expect the police to locate and return property taken unlawfully. Members of the community report theft, robbery, and burglary to the police agency, expecting that the officer investigating the offense will be able to locate and return the property. Although the citizen needs police reports for insurance purposes, the property owner would prefer that the lost property be returned. To help in this endeavor, the officer should encourage everyone to mark valuables for identification using a driver's license number, which is easily traced. Such efforts by property owners and police officers can increase police efficiency and ability to meet this demanding task and service.

The police responsibility for control of noncriminal conduct can take from 85 to 90 percent of the patrol officer's time. In this capacity the officer helps citizens, establishes safe traffic corridors, maintains crowd control, and generally protects the community. In this capacity the police officer achieves the purposes for which he or she became an officer: to help others and make the community a safe and happy place for families to live and raise their children. What better purpose is there? In controlling noncriminal conduct, the officer has many specific opportunities to create good police-community relations and develop a positive feeling between the citizens and the police agency.

The police agency might also have to handle a number of miscellaneous services. Although the agency head must minimize such requests for additional duties in order to maintain proper police patrol objectives, the department will probably be asked to provide special services when another governmental agency is unable to complete the task. These services could involve escorts, animal control, security of public areas (such as the parks and cemeteries), and other incidental tasks. The officer performs such duties with the same professionalism required of any other daily tasks.

Public Relations. Public relations relate directly to the ability of the police to effectively communicate with the community. In order to create and maintain an effective flow of information, the police department must open two-way communication. Two-way communication involves not only talking to the public about police problems, but also listening to each segment of the community as it expresses its needs for police services and suggestions for improvement in police-community relations. Many departments assign a supervisory officer to a police-community relations unit. The purpose of such a unit is opening and maintaining positive communications with the community. In addition, such a unit can be effective for police recruiting, handling complaints and grievances, and securing effective informants. Such a unit always seeks community support for police goals and objectives through effective communication.

Community Participation. You have a responsibility of citizenship within the community. You not only serve the community but are also a part of the community. The community is not separate from the police, nor is the police agency separate from the community. It is imperative that police officers take an active part in community affairs, social events, and civic pride.

Too frequently the peace officer can grow to believe that the only worthwhile social contacts are other peace officers. This is not so; the professional peace officer should not permit social contacts to be limited to other peace officers. To be effective, you must get to know the members of the local community. You can do this by participating actively in church activities, civic groups (such as the Lions Club, Rotary Club, or other civic organizations), or working closely with youth athletic programs. Since each officer's personality is different, the civic activity that you enjoy will vary. The important point is that you become involved.

Involvement leads to a number of advantages for both the officer and the department. The primary advantage for you is feeling a part of the community and knowing that the people you serve are living, caring individuals. Whenever you become limited only to contact with other peace officers and the criminal element, there is a real danger that you can become paranoid and untrusting of anyone other than another law enforcement officer. When such an attitude develops, you close doors to effective communications and become suspicious of the motives and mannerisms of everyone. Such a state of mind is not police professionalism. When you get to know fellow citizens, you are promoting good police-community relations and helping achieve the goal of the police agency.

TELECOMMUNICATION DEVICES AND INTERPERSONAL COMMUNICATIONS

For many citizens, an interview with a law enforcement officer is a frightening experience. The person may view the law officer as having authority and power. Circumstances that push someone to contact a peace officer can in themselves be overwhelming, and the individual may be extremely excited or emotionally upset. All these elements can add up to become an important event for the citizen seeking police assistance. Your attitude at such times is vital. To begin with, you must be an attentive listener and observer. At such times your effort to learn the information from the complainant or victim must supersede any other goal. You must ask for feedback to clarify the facts of the contact and must be truly interested in the citizen's problem.

Professional officers are expert in the science of communication, including use of telephone devices and understanding interpersonal communications. However, you must also be concerned with difficult aspects of communication, including (but not being limited to) the hearing and visually impaired. This section outlines ways to approach these types of law enforcement communications.

Telephone Contact

Frequently, the only contact that the community has with the police department comes via telephone conversations. Since such a contact is important to the caller, the person answering the telephone call must be attentive, interested, and professional. Incoming calls must be answered promptly. No aspect of an emergency is more demoralizing than to call for help and listen to a phone ring and ring and ring. Once the phone is answered promptly, the officer must use proper communication techniques. Identify yourself and agency so the caller knows he or she got the right number. Record the request, and pinpoint exactly what the caller wants in the way of service. If it is necessary to leave the line to handle another important matter, inform the caller and request that the caller remain on the telephone line. Any such interruption should be made only as a matter of greater priority and should be for only a short period of time. Once back to the original line of communication, thank the caller for waiting and get any additional information necessary to the investigation or complaint. Your choice of words must be polite, courteous, and interested. When the call is ending, leave the caller with the impression that action will be initiated right away, being certain to express thanks for the complainant's cooperation.

If you must make an outgoing telephone call, it is extremely important that you use proper telephone procedures here as well. Be courteous, identifying both self and agency. During the initial part of the call, explain the purpose of the call and request specific information. Here, again, your choice of words is extremely important. The person at the other end of the telephone line will respond positively to a courteous tone. In ending the call, express appreciation for the help and cooperation received and ask permission to recontact the citizen if needed for further information.

Follow these simple, but important, telephone rules that lead to favorable telephone conversations:

1. Answer the telephone promptly, and identify yourself and your agency. Let the caller know that he or she has reached a person who can help. If you are answering an emergency line, ask, "What is your emergency?" If the phone is for other routine calls, ask, "How can I help you?"
2. Let the caller talk and give the facts. You need complete information in order to make a correct judgment.
3. Speak at a moderate rate; vary your tone of voice. The listener does not have the benefit of watching you, of seeing your gestures and changing expressions. Speak slowly and distinctly to ensure understanding the first time.
4. Speak into the mouthpiece. It is not necessary to shout or even talk loudly if properly using the phone.
5. Ask the caller to repeat names and number, for the sake of accuracy while making notes.
6. Sound alert and interested. Give the caller individual attention. The voice that reflects a personal interest affects the listener as being pleasant, friendly, cordial, interested, and helpful.
7. Assure the caller that his or her request for assistance, report of criminal activity, and so on will be expeditiously handled.
8. Thank the caller for the telephone call, and give any appropriate follow-up instructions as needed. For example, tell the complainant to stay inside his or her house rather than leaving and looking for a prowler suspect, because the responding officer might mistake the complainant for the suspect—or vice versa.

During the course of a conversation, you may have to leave the telephone to perform a variety of functions that require your immediate attention. When such situations arise, avoid using abrupt phrases like "Hold on" or "Wait a minute" when leaving the telephone. When you recognize that a search of files may take longer than a minute or two, ask the caller's permission to return the call. You might also ask the caller to call back at a prearranged definite time. Generally, a waiting period should be limited to about a minute. A longer period not only removes the phone from service as it cannot receive additional incoming calls, but may be very irritating to the caller.

When you ask a caller to wait, put the phone gently down on the desk. This not only eliminates an unpleasant crashing sound but also protects the instrument from unnecessary wear or damages. If at all possible, put the telephone in a downward position on a blotter or papers. In addition to cushioning the sound of laying the phone aside, this position also helps to block out some of the background noises.

Be careful what you say or what may be said by others when the phone is left off the hook, as it may cause embarrassment. Simply placing a hand over the mouthpiece or resting the telephone face down on a desk are not effective methods of preventing speech from being picked up. The basic safeguard against embarrassment is not to say anything that may offend or cause concern while the phone is off its stand. However, sometimes you cannot control other people's conversation, so use the hold button if the phone is equipped with one.

When answering the telephone for someone else, give appropriate information in answer to the inevitable question "Is he (or she) there?" Volunteer the information about the person's whereabouts and probable time of return, rather than force the caller to ask additional questions. If you do not know where a person may be, you may satisfy the caller and avoid embarrassing the person. Experience has shown that such replies are tactful and effective. Since they are helpful in tone, they encourage the caller to leave a message or to ask for help from the person who has answered. In either case, the caller leaves the conversation feeling satisfied that the matter will receive proper attention.

If you take a message for another person, ensure that it is delivered. Failing to pass on a telephone message properly often creates an uncomfortable situation and personal irritation. A misunderstanding arises either from the failure to write down a message or from the person receiving the message writing it down on a totally inadequate scrap of paper that is later accidentally discarded.

Write messages on forms specifically designed for that purpose. Such forms usually elicit certain essential facts that can be readily checked. If a department has no telephone message forms, write down any instructions, information, or requests received for another officer on a full sheet of paper at the time the message is received. Do not try to commit it to memory. Make certain a message is complete and correct by verifying all numbers and names. Do not hesitate to ask a person to repeat his or her name, to verify the spelling. The caller would rather spend a few seconds more and make sure that you have the correct information than not receive a return call at all.

Interpersonal Communications

During one-on-one personal contacts, you should understand that demeanor, tone of voice, and professionalism are all immediately obvious to the average person. In each contact, approach the conversation in a courteous way and help make the person feel comfortable. During the conversation, be attentive, a good listener, friendly, and positive. If you can't help the complainant, refer the individual to the proper authority who can help in handling the problem.

During such contacts, do not make any promises that are impossible to keep. If you promise service or follow-up action, you have a responsibility to recontact the citizen, to tell him or her the outcome of such an inquiry. In all cases, be concerned with the problems of the other person and realize that, to that person, it is the most important event that you are involved with at that time. The way you handle the contact will be retold by the complainant over and over to many others. This is how departmental image develops and becomes established in the minds of local citizens.

Body language frequently speaks as loud as, or louder than, actual words. Your mannerisms, stance, and use of facial and bodily expressions will communicate a great deal to the citizen with whom you are dealing. For example, if you are standing with your arms folded while talking to a complainant, you may be expressing a desire not to be open to communication. Closed hands tend to express a closed mind or disinterest, while open hands demonstrate compassion and empathy for the person's problems. You can demonstrate your willingness to listen to others by unbuttoning or removing your coat, uncrossing your legs and leaning forward, or by stretching out your arms and leaning back. Each of these action indicate your willingness to relax and listen. You must be aware of this kind of expression while interviewing a crime victim, complainant, or suspect. Each changing look communicates your interest, concern, and honesty in dealing with the situation at hand.

When you are interviewing a suspect, watch his or her eyes. If the suspect will not look you in the eye while talking to you, that may be an indication that he or she is lying to you. By the same token, take positive action to make eye contact with other people to communicate the sincerity of your intentions, behavior, or communications. You can use these techniques of positive nonverbal communication in every aspect of law enforcement work, whether it is for a job or promotion interview, speaking before a group of citizens, interviewing witnesses, interrogating suspects, or testifying in court. Your exhibition of openness through your nonverbal actions will communicate your confidence, experience, command of the situation, and professionalism.

Be aware of other nonverbal signs in a suspect's behavior that will tell you that he or she is not telling you the truth, or only part of the truth. The person is avoiding your questions if he or she looks up to the right or left (to avoid your eyes) and scans the perimeter of the ceiling. A suspect who rubs or "wrings" his or her hands is showing indications of extreme nervousness. Eye twitching, inability to sit in one place without constantly moving, a constant tapping of fingers on a chair or desk, and other nervous actions may well tell you more than the suspect is willing to verbally communicate.

Experienced law enforcement officers learn to "read" body language and people. By carefully observing people while they experience various moods, emotional response to stimuli, or reactions to stressful experiences, you can learn which approach best suits the moment. People react differently to different approaches. For example, you may perceive the need to handle one person gently with understanding and compassion to gain that individual's trust and cooperation. However, this approach may be completely inappropriate with a gang of angry youths carrying chains and tire irons; firm and direct language aimed at gaining control of the incident will be required. Keep in mind that your words and actions must not incite more anger, but rather solicit obedience based on respect and your command of the situation. Curse words, racial slurs, and other inappropriate actions or gestures will only excite others to a breach of the peace, and they have no place in professional law enforcement. In addition, avoid using the words "Shut up" when dealing with angry people; this phrase only makes combatants more angry. Words such as "Please be quiet a moment" or "Everyone can help by being quiet" may ease the tensions of the moment and let you gain control of the conversation. Choose your words and actions wisely to gain cooperation and solicit support.

Law Enforcement and the Hearing Impaired

Deafness is a complex and often technical disability. A deaf person's reaction to law enforcement officers, and to society in general, is based on such factors as audiological capacity, educational background, and communication philosophy.

The personalities of deaf people are as diverse as the mainstream of society. The common bond among deaf people is their hearing disability. The real handicap of deafness is being cut off from the normal means of transmitting and receiving language. This isolation affects the sophistication of a deaf person's world and raises personal, social, educational, and occupational obstacles. Most deaf people have been able to cope with this "communication loss" by using such auxiliary means of communication as sign language, lip and speech reading, reading, and writing. Two factors affect the use of these communication techniques: (1) the age at which the person became hearing impaired and (2) the severity of the impairment.

The term *prelingual* or *early-onset deafness* refers to being born deaf or having become deaf in early childhood. People in this category use sign language as their principal means of communication. People with postlingual deafness have become hearing impaired later in life, after they have mastered spoken language. The hearing impairment may have occurred for a variety of reasons, including age. People in this category have been known as the "hard of hearing." It is impossible to generalize about the type of communication used by these people. Many do not know sign language, and many have comprehensible speech. You may understand these people's voices; however, these people may not understand *your* voice. Furthermore, lip reading can be used only with a limited degree of success. Every hearing-impaired person copes with the communication loss in a different way.

Deaf people are unusual as a disability group in that, among themselves, they are not disabled. This naturally encourages formation of a separate deaf community and culture. The deaf community, like any other minority group, is held together by common experiences. Deaf people attend residential schools, enroll in special deaf programs, and share a culture of language, jokes, drama, and traditions passed from one generation to the next.

American Sign Language (ASL, or Ameslan) is the "native" language of the prelingual and early-onset deaf (See Figure 4-6). It has its own grammar and vocabulary and is a completely visual

Hurt
"Are you in pain?"

Help

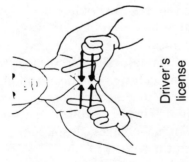

Driver's license

Police

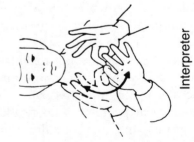

Name
"What is your name?"

Interpreter

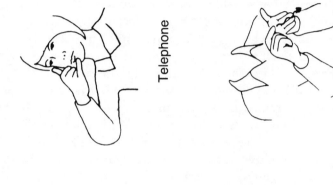

Telephone

Stop

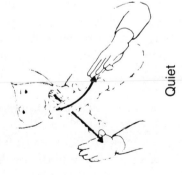

Quiet

Write

Ticket

Thank you

Figure 4-6
American Sign Language (Ameslan)

language. Because it has its own syntax, the written English of deaf people often appears awkward; it is not a code for English.

Fingerspelling, signed English, and oralism are also modes of communication for the deaf. Finger spelling (see Figure 4-7) and signed English are often used in conjunction with American Sign Language, while oralism involves a very different approach to communication. An officer who encounters an "oral" individual should not be fooled into believing that person can understand everything the officer says. Even people who are trained in the oral method can actually comprehend only about 30 percent of what is said.

In any situation involving the victim of a crime, one of the first priorities is to get a description of the suspect. With a deaf victim, you must decide on the method of communication immediately. Lip reading is the least reliable communication method; only about 30 percent of what is said can be lip-read. Writing is an effective means of communication, although the grammar of the deaf is often difficult to understand. Writing notes requires a great deal of patience on the officer's part.

Sign language is the preferred method of communication, and officers should seek the services of an interpreter, whenever possible. A friend or family member may be nearby; if not, the law enforcement agency's dispatcher should have a roster of interpreters available in the area. After any violent crime, it is difficult to obtain information from a witness who is obviously upset. The services of an interpreter will usually facilitate the communication process compounded by the individual's deafness.

A deaf witness to a crime or an incident may actually be more helpful than a hearing person. Deaf people may observe more than a hearing person viewing the same event. They are more dependent on visual cues to understand their environment. Law requires that an interpreter be provided for courtroom proceedings involving deaf persons.

Officers may be called to an accident scene in which a deaf person is involved. That individual's behavior may provide clues that the person is hearing impaired. For example, he or she may appear alert but fail to respond to the sounds. The deaf person may point to the ears, or the ear and mouth, perhaps while also shaking the head. The individual may speak in a flat or harsh, unintelligible monotone.

Communication with the deaf requires more time and patience; however, it is essential for the fair determination of what happened.

Deaf people have observed that officers tend, or seem, to exclude them from the conversation at an accident scene. Investigating officers should listen to both sides of the story and face the deaf person when speaking to him or her. This practice, if followed in addressing both parties, should help overcome misconceptions. A deaf person may also be able to understand some of the conversation if he or she can lip-read.

Keep careful, detailed notes, making certain that the deaf person is aware of important parts of the conversation. Instruct the deaf person concerning required follow-up procedures.

Law enforcement officers must, of course, maintain personal safety whenever stopping and apprehending traffic violators. Situations have occurred in which deaf people stopped by police have been shot and killed because they made a quick move for a pen and pad in their coat pocket or glove compartment. Such unfortunate incidents are preventable by mutual awareness that overcomes the loss of communication. Deaf community groups and law enforcement agencies are attempting to teach the deaf proper conduct when stopped by officers, such as keeping their hands on the steering wheel until officers understand that the person involved is deaf. Not every deaf person is aware of the officer's position—but the officer must be aware of the deaf person's.

Since deafness may affect a person's sense of balance, officers should, in cases of suspected driving under the influence of alcohol and so forth, use alternative field sobriety tests instead of the curb or straight-line tests.

When dealing with a deaf suspect, officers must be extremely cautious to avoid unintentionally violating civil rights. Cases involving deaf suspects have been improperly handled in the past, resulting in inadmissible evidence. A hearing-impaired suspect who prefers sign language has a legal right to a professional interpreter, and that individual should be summoned immediately. Family members or friends are not acceptable as interpreters in such cases, and written *Miranda* warnings may be insufficient. *Miranda* warnings are written at an eighth-grade level, a level many deaf people do not achieve. In fact, an average deaf person reads at fifth- or sixth-grade level.

Never attempt to question a deaf suspect without an interpreter, who should be used at initial and subsequent questioning. All questions should be directed to the deaf person, not the interpreter. Many interpreters, although certified, cannot effectively communicate with

F

K

P

E

J

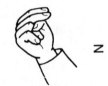

O

D

I

N

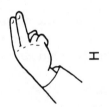

C

H

M

B

G

L

A

 U

 Z

 T

 Y

S

X

R

W

Q

V

Figure 4-7
Fingerspelling: the American Manual Alphabet

all deaf persons. Always make certain the deaf person understands what is taking place.

Suspects have the right to make a phone call using a telecommunication device for the deaf (TDD). Many law enforcement agencies in most states have these devices, including sheriff's departments and state police stations.

Law Enforcement and the Visually Impaired

Blind people are perhaps the most patronized members of society. This is due largely to historical misconceptions of the blind as being inferior and helpless, an attitude that has blocked understanding of blindness and of what a blind person can accomplish. Law enforcement officers have responsibilities to treat all citizens with equal consideration under the law. This is the single most important consideration when encountering a visually impaired person.

There is no such thing as a "typical" blind person, and, of course, not all are totally blind. In fact, 80 percent have some remaining vision, and the extent to which this vision may affect mobility depends on the individual. For example, visually impaired people with tunnel vision may be able to identify an officer approaching, but may still need help spotting oncoming cars when crossing the street. They are not all musical, and they may not have a mysterious "sixth sense." No compensating factor takes over when a person loses sight. Naturally, the use of other senses becomes intensified, but this is a result of a blind person's need to adapt to the environment, not because of some biological "superhearing" or "supersmell."

Unlike the case with most other disabilities, age is a significant contributing factor to the incidence of blindness. Ten percent of all blind people are under 18 years of age; 30 percent are between 18 and 64, inclusive; and 60 percent are 65 or over. Many law enforcement encounters with the visually impaired involve senior citizens. When dealing with an older blind person, be aware that sometimes a person who has lost vision later in life may not be trained to deal with this handicap.

Of the many misconceptions about blindness, one is that blindness is a handicap of vision. Actually, the situation is not so simple. Rather, the real handicaps of the blind are problems of mobility and negative public attitudes toward the blind. Mobility is a daily issue in the lives of the blind. It affects self-concept, self-confidence, personal and social relationships, and education and employment opportunities.

There are two primary ways for a blind person to achieve mobility: the guide dog and the long, or "white" cane. A visually impaired person using a guide dog is always totally blind. A guide dog is trained to respond to the master's commands and to exercise "intelligent disobedience"; that is, to refuse a command that could bring harm to the master. For example, a guide dog may refuse to cross the street if there is oncoming traffic. Approximately 7 percent of the visually impaired population use guide dogs.

The long cane is the more commonly used mobility tool. Orientation and mobility training are necessary to acquaint the visually impaired person with the long cane. The "white cane law," first adopted in 1930, gives the right of way at an intersection to a blind person carrying a white cane.

In addition to their mobility problems, blind people are frequently confronted with a condescending attitude by the general public. Unfortunately, the old joke about someone raising his or her voice when talking to a blind person is all too true and frequent. Blind people can hear and understand what is said as well as a sighted person. Similarly, visually impaired people do not need "interpreters" to participate in a conversation.

In an interviewing situation, talk directly to the blind person, not to a third party. There are no "taboo" figures of speech; "look," "see," and "read" are part of a blind person's vocabulary. The degree of success with which you are able to communicate with the visually impaired depends on your particular attitude.

Generally speaking, one out of every 200 people has a severe visual impairment. Consequently, your chances of encountering blind people while on the job are significant. Law enforcement officers are most likely to encounter blind people when such persons appear to be lost or when they need help. If, while on patrol, you meet a blind person, he or she may welcome assistance. Identify yourself, saying, "I am a police officer. May I help you?" This approach at once puts the blind individual on an equal basis with the officer, thus avoiding embarrassment and establishing an appropriate relationship.

Officer identification is important; contrary to popular belief, blind people do not always recognize another person's voice. When assisting a visually impaired pedestrian, ask the person to take your arm. Then the blind person can follow the movements of your body.

And, when approaching a curb or a set of steps, the blind person can feel you rise or descend, moving easily beside him or her. Of course, it is an extra help to say something like "Here's the curb," and so forth. In such situations, never push the blind individual ahead of yourself. When a blind person takes your arm, walking may become less difficult for him or her. You may even ask sighted people on the beat to help by clearing a path for the blind person. This added courtesy allows the visually impaired person to walk without fear of tripping over objects. An officer performing traffic duty in the center of an intersection may be inclined to wave a blind person through with a hand signal before realizing that the person cannot see the officer. Instead, identify yourself and give verbal direction.

An officer investigating a case involving a blind victim should recognize that the victim is as capable of describing the suspect as any other victim would be. Of course, not seeing does create special fears. Officers should be aware of this when assisting the victim, and when obtaining a description of the suspect. Obviously, blind people are at a disadvantage during personal attacks because they cannot see their attackers or anticipate where they are going to be struck and defend or protect themselves accordingly. Similarly, they cannot see if they still need defense or protection after the original attack. If you notice such fears, offer calm assurance that your presence will guarantee the person's safety. Consider making follow-up phone calls for a week or two after such an incident. If extreme fear persists, counseling should be recommended. Furthermore, a blind person may experience disorientation in his or her own neighborhood or environment after a crime. Knowledge of the surroundings will put a blind person at ease.

If it is necessary for the blind individual to testify in court, the officer may need to educate the attorneys and judges about the credibility of blind witnesses. Also, be conscious that blind people cannot read or fill out law enforcement agency forms and other printed documents. They will need assistance in reading these materials.

Many blind people read through a system of raised dots known as Braille. The Braille system is as effective for the blind as printed words are for the sighted. Notify court personnel that notices to appear in court and related documents should be printed in Braille, if possible, or communicated by phone. Although most blind people arrange to have mail read to them, documents in Braille or a phone call are an additional courtesy.

FIELD RADIO AND COMPUTER OPERATIONS

Problems of communicating with officers on the beat was an early concern in law enforcement patrol operations. Early forms of communication between foot patrol officers involved forms of the old "hue and cry" and a carryover of the old England "rattle watch" system, where patrolling officers used noise-making devices to call for assistance. However, late nineteenth-century implements for the "cry" would be a nightstick (baton) struck on the sidewalk or fence at nighttime, when the sound would carry a long distance to another officer privy to understanding the meaning of a prearranged signal. In addition, officers used whistles, hand signals, and voice alerts as signaling devices. These officers knew nothing of the advantages that future portable "walkie-talkie"-type communication devices could provide. They depended on each other and on a signal light located atop a tall structure to receive alerts for various calls for assistance. Through a system of coded light flashes, a police dispatcher at headquarters communicated with street officers. On seeing the coded signal lights, officers depended on land-line telephone devices to determine the location of crimes, criminal descriptions, and other relevant crime information. Various departments were linked to other agencies through the telegraph, which was an early form of the teletype still frequently used to exchange information. Understandably under these conditions law enforcement officers in the nineteenth century were limited in ability to quickly respond and effectively stop criminals in the act. Patrol officers of that era depended on their own observation and perceptions to apprehend criminals in the act—perhaps more than modern officers do so.

In the twentieth century, two vastly important technical achievements enabled law enforcement to come out of the doldrums of antiquated patrol tactics and enter into the new age of technological police patrol. These innovations were the (1) development of the automobile for police patrol and (2) the adaptation of police communications systems for mobile use. Police patrol tactics and techniques changed more thoroughly than during any preceding period of time.

As early as 1904, the Indianapolis Police Department started to replace horse-drawn "paddy wagons" with automobiles. However, not until 1917 did the Detroit Police Department begin using automobiles with two men to a car. They did not go out on patrol as we now know it—they were stationed in "police booths" along the street, and left the booth on receiving a telephone request for assistance. Not until the advent of the workable mobile radio receiver did police vehicles became patrol units as we now think of them.

Detroit Police Commissioner William P. Rutledge was instrumental in establishing the first workable police radio system. On April 7, 1928, after seven years of research and development, the Detroit Police Department went on the air as Station W8FS using a receiver installed in Police Cruiser Number 5; the transmitter was installed on Belle Isle, an island in the Detroit River.[3] Although this was only a one-way receiver (much like a radio without capability of speaking back), the initial results were exciting for that time in history. Officers in police cruisers were catching holdup men, car thieves, and burglars within minutes after the crime was reported. Soon police departments in Cleveland and Indianapolis, and the State Police in Michigan were on the air. In 1931, the first police motorcycle was equipped with a police radio receiver. Units could finally patrol the streets without standing by a telephone booth waiting for a call to action. However, there certainly were problems. A radio dispatcher was never sure that the patrol units received a message until a telephone call confirmed a successful communication. Therefore, the dispatcher repeated the message until he or she was assured that the unit heard the message. In addition, static, "dead zones," receiver instability, and lack of sensitivity hampered good radio reception.

As exciting as the new technology was, it was nothing compared to expanded expertise that resulted in two-way communications capabilities. By 1933 the Bayonne New Jersey Police Department went on the air with the first two-way mobile police radio system. However, this system was imperfect due to static and other interference.

Daniel E. Noble of Connecticut State College developed the first frequency modulation (FM) system in 1939. In 1940—merely twelve years after the first radio receiver was placed in a patrol unit— Motorola President Paul Galvin authorized the perfection of a two-way FM system for Motorola Police Radio Sales. This development used the remarkable "differential squelch circuit" that demonstrated

---

[3] This and other historical communications facts are summarized from George T. Payton, *Patrol Procedure*, 4th ed. (Los Angeles: Legal Book Corporation, 1971); pp. 123–126.

a vast improvement in radio range and clarity. By the year 1945, the Federal Communications Commission allocated frequencies for FM, and FM became the established system for police radio communications. With these major steps in police radio usage dawned a new age in experimentation that eventually evolved into advancements in portable radio capabilities, computer technology, and many other advancements now used by modern peace officers.

Radio Communications and Law Enforcement Response

As police radio communication begins to enter into the twenty-first century, we can marvel at the technological advances that have taken place since that first receiver was installed on Detroit Cruiser Number 5 in 1928. Today officers have multichannel radio capabilities. The majority of agencies have three-way radios where the patrol car in the field may not only carry on a two-way conversation with the base radio, but may also carry on the same type of conversation with other patrol units in the field. Officers carry portable radio units (sometimes called "walkie-talkies") on their belts, an innovation that rivals carrying a duty weapon as the most important defensive weapon in the police arsenal. Officers can now patrol on foot or leave their patrol units and maintain constant communication links with headquarters and other officers in the area. These small transistorized portable units enable you to call for immediate assistance—whether immediate medical assistance for an injured person or assistance in apprehending a burglar inside a building. This immediate transmission of information aids proper and efficient accomplishment of the police mission.

In 1968, the President's Commission on Law Enforcement and the Administration of Justice reported that the police departments' ability to catch a criminal in the act is directly related to officer "response time." Obviously, the quicker an officer arrives, the greater the possibility of locating and apprehending the offender. When a call for services reaches the complaint center at police headquarters, it can be recorded and quickly relayed to field officers. Their response is then delayed only by travel time from the point of receipt of the message to the scene. According to one study,[4] law enforcement

---

[4] Lubbock (Texas) Police Department Radio Communications, *Lubbock Avalanche-Journal*, February 5, 1989.

officers in the field are informed of an emergency call on an average of 1.3 minutes after the information is received from the victim of a major crime. Generally, it takes about 3.5 minutes for a patrol unit to arrive at the scene, depending on traffic and road conditions. Thus about 4.8 minutes elapse from the time the victim of a major crime contacts the police dispatcher until an officer arrives. One continuing challenge of future law enforcement operations is to constantly seek improved communications and reduced response time.

A priority system frequently differentiates calls for emergency service that must receive immediate attention, and other calls that must receive quick attention. Emergency response—Priority 1—traditionally involves emergency medical calls, offenses involving violence, and crimes in progress. Priority 2 calls include such nonemergency situations as domestic and civil disputes in which no violence has yet been reported, but the situation could become violent. The average dispatching time for this type of call is between 2 and 2.5 minutes; officer response time averages about 4 minutes for a total elapsed time of about 6.3 minutes.

Priority 3 calls are assigned to nonemergency calls where rapid response is not judged to be appropriate. Such calls include accidents without injuries and nonviolent crimes such as "cold burglary" calls (reported hours after the actual event) in which the immediate apprehension of a suspect is not possible. Depending on the time of day, or day of the week, Priority 3 calls are usually dispatched within 15 minutes after the call is received; if the delay could last longer than 15 minutes, the police dispatcher should call the reporting party and explain the situation. If all police units in a certain area of town are busy handling other calls, any additional Priority 3 calls in that area of the city will be held until an officer is free to respond. It can take an officer up to 7 minutes to arrive after receiving a Priority 3 call, resulting in an average response times of about 30 minutes for nonemergency calls. While these times seem commendable on the surface, it is understandable that a complainant who waits 30 or more minutes—in some cases up to an hour—for a law enforcement officer to report may not be ecstatic about police reaction to service requests. Most departments note that delayed response time to Priority 3 calls is a sign of not having enough officers available in the field to handle requests for service, rather than of inadequate communications ability.

Consolidated Emergency Communication Operations

Many communities are beginning to consider consolidated communications centers for police, fire, and other emergency response teams. Many U.S. communities have implemented the Emergency 911 network systems. General arguments in favor of consolidated communications facilities are as follows.

1. Efficiency is improved by having a larger group of dispatchers who are cross-trained to work on either the fire department or police department radios. Such cross-training minimizes the effects of personnel turnover by allowing trained dispatchers to maintain the vital communications process while training newly hired dispatchers, who must undergo at least six months of training before being allowed to work unsupervised.

2. Maintenance costs are reduced by having all communication equipment in a single location where it is readily accessible and protected.

3. Dispatchers and the radio equipment are protected in secured facilities—in some cities (such as Lubbock, Texas) in below-ground locations. Secured facilities reduce vulnerability to attack by "crazed persons" or by organized crime groups that might seek to disable emergency communications, to facilitate the commission of a crime. In addition, secured facilities are less vulnerable to weather-related disasters that might otherwise hamper communications.

4. From a management standpoint, a consolidated facility reduces overall operating costs and increases ability to handle calls for service. And other innovations will certainly help reduce call-response time in the future.

A consolidated communications facility is not, however, without problems. Some perceivable problems are as follows.

1. The FBI and state law enforcement agencies require that teletype equipment and the personnel who use it be under control of a law enforcement agency. Putting such equipment and personnel under the control of a nonpolice communications department creates difficulty in meeting official law enforcement communications security requirements. This problem can be ultimately handled through regulation agreements.

2. Secured communication facilities are generally located away from the agency headquarters. Therefore, communications personnel cannot readily access files and records that may be needed by field

officers. Various advances in computer technology may be implemented to overcome this perceived weakness.

3. Communication specialists that are required to work extended shifts could create a hazardous situation for street officers. Studies show that if a dispatcher has been at the console for more than eight hours, he or she starts to lose the concentration that is needed to keep track of all the street activity.

4. Communications that are not under the direct control of a police agency could result in compromise of mission tasks. For example, in one case undercover officers from the police street crimes unit were preparing to conduct a drug raid at a city residence. As was the policy at the time, the undercover officer notified the radio room and the leader of the patrol shift on duty that a search was about to occur at a certain address. The radio room employee who took the call recognized the location as her brother's address; the woman apparently was able to notify her brother by phone before the officers reached the address, and the house was empty when the officers arrived. Understandably, the communications person lost her job when the police learned of the tipoff. Even though this "worst-case scenario" was an isolated incident that may never happen again, it outlines potential problems that could develop when different city organizations are involved in dispatching police calls. Policy and tactics to prevent such occurrences should receive priority attention.

Police Radio Procedures

A police radio system is only as efficient as the people who use it. When its limitations are recognized, and it is prudently used, it will generally provide many years of satisfactory service. The basic components of police radio equipment are the microphone, the transmitter, and the receiver. When a radio message is to be sent, remove the microphone from its bracket, hold it about an inch away from and about 45 degrees to the side of your mouth, depress the microphone switch, pause briefly, and start the message. The switch activates the transmitter and should be fully engaged in the "on" position so that the transmitter motor reaches full speed before the message commences.

When requesting information from the dispatcher, frame your question so that it can be answered with yes or no whenever possible; if possible, you should use the telephone rather than the police radio when lengthy communications are anticipated. To properly use the radio, speak slowly, clearly, and deliberately when you communicate, using established codes whenever they apply; for example, see Figure 4-8. Spell out difficult or unusual names. Repeat lengthy numbers— such as telephone, house, Social Security, operator's license, motor, serial, and other numbers. If long radio transmissions are necessary, break frequently to give other units an opportunity to transmit emergency messages, or to ensure that the receiving person can keep up with the needed information.

Whenever practicable, follow the sequence of information used in the report forms for particular crimes to describe the suspect, to simplify the dispatcher's task in recording the data. When seeking information about several suspects or vehicles, ask the dispatcher for a clear frequency. Describe only one vehicle or person at a time. Identify juveniles as such if their records are kept separate from adult records. When you need to pass information on to another officer, give the dispatcher a general reason for the request. When you need service from street maintenance crews, the coroner's officer, or public utilities agencies, or when an ambulance or fire equipment is necessary, specify the reason for the request so that appropriate equipment can be sent. When backup units, supervisors, or investigators are needed at the scene of an incident, give the reason in sufficiently specific terms so that they may assess the urgency of the call. When the need no longer exists, cancel requests for service.

Do not make police calls for help unless help is urgently needed. Calls for help ("10–33" or "May Day" calls) should be reserved for those situations involving an officer in immediate danger or actual emergency circumstances. Responding or assisting patrol units frequently proceed to an "officer help" call with all urgency—sometimes inappropriately disregarding all safety concerns as they travel to the scene. Therefore, calls of this nature should not be made lightly. A "call for assistance" does not imply the same degree of urgency as a "call for help."

Personnel can clutter a completely adequate system with poorly planned, nonessential, or conflicting broadcasts. This clutter considerably weakens the operational efficiency of patrol operations. When two or more units on the same frequency try to use it at the same time, the dispatcher or communications cannot understand either one, and must waste air time requesting repeat messages. Save radio air time by listening for a few seconds to ensure the frequency is

Ten Signals

10-0 —Caution
10-1 —Unable copy—change location
10-2 —Signal good
10-3 —Stop transmitting
10-4 —Acknowledgment (OK)
10-5 —Relay
10-6 —Busy—unless urgent
10-7 —Out of service
10-8 —In service
10-9 —Repeat
10-10—Fight in progress
10-11—Dog case
10-12—Stand by (stop)
10-13—Weather—road report
10-14—Prowler report
10-15—Civil disturbance
10-16—Domestic problem
10-17—Meet complainant
10-18—Quickly
10-19—Return to . . .
10-20—Location
10-21—Call . . . by telephone
10-22—Disregard
10-23—Arrived at scene
10-24—Assignment completed
10-25—Report in person (meet) . . .
10-26—Detaining subject, expedite
10-27—Driver's license information
10-28—Vehicle registration information (VIN)
10-29—Check for wanted
10-30—Unnecessary use of radio
10-31—Crime in progress
10-32—Person with gun
10-33—EMERGENCY
10-34—Riot
10-35—Major crime alert
10-36—Correct time
10-37—(Investigate) suspicious vehicle
10-38—Stopping suspicious vehicle
10-39—Urgent—use light, siren

10-40—Silent run—no light, siren
10-41—Beginning tour of duty
10-42—Ending tour of duty
10-43—Information
10-44—Permission to leave . . . for . . .
10-45—Animal carcass at . . .
10-46—Assist motorist
10-47—Emergency road repair at . . .
10-48—Traffic standard repair at . . .
10-49—Traffic light out at . . .
10-50—Accident (F, PI, PD)
10-51—Wrecker needed
10-52—Ambulance needed
10-53—Road blocked at . . .
10-54—Livestock on highway
10-55—Suspected DUI
10-56—Intoxicated pedestrian
10-57—Hit and run (F, PI, PD)
10-58—Direct traffic
10-59—Convoy or escort
10-60—Squad in vicinity
10-61—Isolate self for message
10-62—Reply to message
10-63—Prepare to make written copy
10-64—Message for local delivery
10-65—Net message assignment
10-66—Message cancellation
10-67—Clear for net message
10-68—Dispatch information
10-69—Message received
10-70—Fire
10-71—Advise nature of fire
10-72—Report progress on fire
10-73—Smoke report
10-74—Negative
10-75—In contact with . . .
10-76—En route . . .
10-77—ETA (estimated time of arrival)
10-78—Need assistance
10-79—Notify coroner

10-80—Chase in progress
10-81—Breathalyzer
10-82—Reserve lodging
10-83—Work school crossing at . . .
10-84—If meeting . . . advise ETA
10-85—Delayed due to . . .
10-86—Officer/operator on duty
10-87—Pick up/distribute checks
10-88—Present telephone number of . . .
10-89—Bomb threat
10-90—Bank alarm at . . .
10-91—Pick up prisoner/subject
10-92—Improperly parked vehicle
10-93—Blockade
10-94—Drag racing
10-95—Prisoner/subject in custody
10-96—Mental subject
10-97—Check (test) signal
10-98—Prison/jail break
10-99—Wanted/stolen indicated

Key:
F   = Fatality
PI = Personal injury
PD = Property damage
DWI = Driving while intoxicated
ETA = Estimated time of arrival

Figure 4-8
The ten-signal system and the phonetic alphabet used by many law enforcement agencies

Phonetic Alphabet

Since it is difficult to understand unusual words, proper names, and addresses, they must be spelled phonetically.
EXAMPLE: Barry, B-Boy a-Adam r-Robert r-Robert y-Young.
Do not say, B *as in* Boy, A *as in* Adam, etc.

A Adam	J John	S Sam
B Boy	K King	T Tom
C Charles	L Lincoln	U Union
D David	M Mary	V Victor
E Edward	N Nora	W William
F Frank	O Ocean	X X-ray
G George	P Paul	Y Young
H Henry	Q Queen	Z Zebra
I Ida	R Robert	

Figure 4-8, *continued*

clear and by planning your broadcast. Outline in your notebook the essence of your message *before* attempting to broadcast. If the situation is not urgent but still requires much conversation, use a telephone. You maximize your use of the equipment by using sound, logical communication practices.

In the standard two-way system, only one officer at a time can communicate with the dispatcher on a single frequency. Thus, any unnecessary transmissions may deprive other officers of air time that they might urgently need. The adverse effects brought about by the misuse of the radio by one unit may not, in themselves, be crucial; however, if all units on that frequency do not exercise restraint, the entire system might become ineffective.

The problem becomes much more crucial with three-way systems in which radio units can communicate with each other without supervision by the dispatcher unless he or she intervenes. This is important when the officer has an emergency message, and the patrol officers are conversing about less important matters. All units on such frequencies can monitor all other units' transmissions. One inexcusable, unprofessional, and poor radio procedure is repeatedly keying the microphone in response to what some poorly trained officers believe is humorous or laughable. Such officers are only expressing their own ignorance by doing so. Closer supervision over the use of this car-to-car equipment is needed than with the two-way system, in which the dispatcher can exercise some control over field units. Unnecessary communications between units misuse air time that might be needed by other units, and may interfere with other broadcasts from central dispatch. So officers *must* refrain from using police radios for any nonessential purpose.

When the frequency is quiet for an unusually long period, officers are sometimes tempted to make a check over the air. The transmitter may be in good working order, but if the receiver is malfunctioning you usually cannot receive broadcasts. Repeated calls to the dispatcher only interfere with other units on the same frequency. The problem is sometimes due to a burned-out fuse on the receiver, a defective vibrator, or foreign objects such as metal paper clips. These often adhere to the speaker magnet when they are jammed into the speaker grill, and cause a malfunction.

Radio reception is sometimes distorted by noise. This may result from improper adjustment of the audio controls as in a standard radio or television. For example, radios equipped with a squelch control, in harmony with the volume control, can usually be easily corrected by turning the volume fairly high, then—when the station is off the air—slowly turning the squelch control clockwise to a position where noise is heard, and finally reversing the squelch control counterclockwise to a point where the noise ceases.

Transmitter failures may be caused by a blown fuse or relay or an improperly connected battery, causing reverse polarity. The transmitter motor will not turn in the proper direction, and broadcasting will be impossible. These minor problems can be easily adjusted or corrected by a mechanic or radio technician.

Interference—and, in some cases, embarrassment to the officer—may occur if he or she carelessly puts the microphone in the hanger or jams it into the glove compartment in such a manner that the broadcast switch remains open. This can also occur if the microphone is left on the vehicle seat and the officer happens to sit on or near it, causing the microphone to be "keyed." With some equipment, the receiver is off when the microphone switch is on, thus making it impossible for one officer to receive a call for help in a life-threatening situation. When the switch is engaged, the dispatcher cannot inform the involved officer of his or her open microphone. Other units on three-way systems and the dispatcher on two-way systems can hear conversations and noises from within the patrol car but have no practical means of informing the officer involved.

Officers preparing for a "stakeout" should follow departmental policy regarding notifying the dispatcher of the location. In some instances, such a notification could help avoid "burning" the operation if street patrol units inadvertently drive by. In areas with consolidated communications facilities, notifications of undercover operations may be prohibited. However, once the stakeout or operation is over, the unit should immediately notify central dispatch to relay the message to other units.

Technical or design problems sometimes contribute to interference that results from improper use of the equipment. Engineering problems have been reduced considerably over the years; however, some persist. For example, radio car broadcasts in one part of the country sometimes interfere with those in another, due to a phenomenon called a "skip" effect. Interference with other systems may extend far beyond the immediate area in which the transmission is clear enough to be useful, but these are problems for the engineer to resolve; the officer can do little to eliminate them. You can, however, reduce the interference for which you yourself are responsible.

The radio patrol officer sometimes cannot transmit or receive a clear message, due to a "dead spot," where waves are blocked by large buildings, power lines or devices, hills, and so forth. Modern equipment has largely eliminated this problem, and you can often easily correct it merely by moving your vehicle.

To achieve maximum advantage of radio communications, follow these basic rules:

1. Ensure the *accuracy* of radio transmissions by planning your transmission and thinking before you act.
2. Be *brief*; keep radio transmission as short as possible, using correct ten-signal codes when possible.
3. Be *courteous*—do not cover another officer's transmission.
4. Be *clear* and avoid misunderstanding; avoid poor pronunciation and distinguish between words and letters with similar sounds such as "QU," "MN," "BEPTVZ," and so on, by properly using the phonetic alphabet.
5. *Follow rules* of professionalism and radio discipline; use correct unit identification and avoid humor and horseplay.
6. Be completely *familiar with agency radio procedures and properly use all equipment*; treat it as though your life depended on it—it *does*!

Hand-Held Equipment

Police use of hand-held broadcasting equipment has increased considerably during recent years. In the past, the limited range and the problem of "dead spots" have restricted the value of "walkie-talkie" radios small enough to be conveniently carried. However, these problems have been virtually eliminated in more sophisticated and efficient equipment such as the inexpensive mobile relay repeater.

With this equipment, a patrol car transmitter can readily be converted from a standard radio unit into a repeater that relays broadcasts from a portable radio through the car transmitter to the dispatcher. Such a system allows the officer to leave a mobile unit to patrol on foot or perform other police work some distance from the unit, and still communicate as though he or she were in the car. The flexibility of the equipment is limited only by the number of cross-connection facilities installed at the central control.

Officers can use this equipment to communicate with each other, as in the standard three-way system, either directly or through the dispatcher. This small portable equipment is extremely valuable in stakeouts, where officers must maintain constant contact with each other; in civil disturbances, where officers can transmit intelligence from within the crowd itself; and in major disasters, where communications are imperative between rescue services. It is equally useful in searches conducted in open, wooded, or bushy areas to maintain contact with each other, and for many other tactical situations where portable radio communications are needed. It is a must for officers deployed at sites where suspects have barricaded themselves and in many other potentially dangerous situations.

Other Technological Devices Adapted for Law Enforcement

Law enforcement agencies across the nation have adapted many technologies in the fight against crime. Through the Law Enforcement Teletypewriter Services (LETS) network, transmission equipment quickly transfers up-to-the-minute information on wanted people, stolen vehicles, and other property. This basic link daily brings together more than 4,500 law enforcement agencies. Data on criminals, stolen weapons, wanted vehicles, and literally hundreds of pieces of information crucial to police operations are continually disseminated among agencies. Because this information is generally highly confidential, system integrity is protected by regulation. For example, terminals are available only to criminal justice agencies, and security provisions must be taken at the terminal site. A limited number of people have access to these terminals; this is a major problem that must be resolved in consolidated communications facilities. All people who have access must be thoroughly screened and trained in proper operation of the data base, to ensure file accuracy.

Recent advances in television technology have many tactical law enforcement applications. It has been appropriately adapted for jail and prison security, as well as prisoner observation. Law enforcement agencies use it for lineups, especially when it is difficult for witnesses to travel long distances to view suspects. Television monitors have been used on highly traveled sections of freeways to quickly spot accidents for a number of years in some locations. Video cameras have been used in booking operations, at civil disturbances, near fires where a person suspected of arson might be spotted in the crowd, and in many other activities involving large numbers of people where on-the-spot identification would otherwise be difficult or impossible. Television cameras can be used in tactical operations, even from helicopters, to survey large areas at the same time for criminal activity. Adaptation of television video capabilities enhances law enforcement training in both academy and college or university settings. Many companies now offer satellite transmission for up-to-date training techniques for law enforcement agencies.

Law enforcement communication facilities now have the capability for sending photo facsimiles (fax) from agency to agency. Pictures and artists' conceptions of wanted people and other data can be quickly transmitted across the country—indeed, throughout the world—if necessary. Such devices can be used to transmit and identify handwriting samples, forgeries, fingerprints, sketches, maps, diagrams, photo identification composites, and so on; the list is limited only by our own imaginations.

Law Enforcement Computer Adaptation

Indeed, we live at a tremendous time on the "cutting edge" of history as we experience the developing adaptation of computer technology. Space-age computer technology has catapulted modern society into a microchip world of data capture and information use. Obviously, this technology has not escaped the attention of law enforcement application. Moreover, we are just now learning the advantages of using word processors, criminal history file research, computer-aging (age enhancement) of lost children, rapid search of fingerprint files, and numerous other law enforcement computer applications. Law enforcement agencies routinely access state and national data banks on a daily basis.

Patrol officers already have patrol vehicle computers capable of searching data banks for relevant information on wanted people and stolen cars. Teleprinters in the unit receive and store written messages for officers whether they are in or out of the unit. This innovation of the LETS network ensures complete communications and eliminates errors that might otherwise occur while an officer is attempting to drive the patrol unit and write down pertinent information regarding a wanted criminal or vehicle. Speed is the most important advantage of computerization. As noted earlier, police response time directly supports law enforcement capability to catch criminals in the act. Computers speed the transmission of information; in fact, messages can be transmitted and received ten times faster than they would if sent verbally. In addition, security from outside monitoring of verbal communications improves officer safety and tactical expediency. Computer messages can be forwarded on the LETS network without the delays resulting from radio usage during busy times. Delays and misunderstanding resulting from semantics and phonetics of words and sounds can be eliminated. Names and identification numbers are accurately printed for officers who may be responding quickly to a crime in progress. The future of law enforcement computer technology belongs to people who have the foresight and imagination to apply new and innovative computer uses to accomplish the police mission.

FEDERAL AND STATE COMMUNICATION INFORMATION SYSTEMS

The Individual State Crime Information Center and the National Crime Information Center (NCIC) are automated data collection computers that can be accessed by every agency. Each state operates its own data collection center on wanted people, stolen vehicles and vessels identification data, criminal history records, and stolen property (guns, cameras, and so on). In addition, the computer banks also include a Missing Children Information Center (MCIC). Each agency uses the systems both to enter information into and to query the computers regarding investigative data. Information entered into state network systems or MCIC is automatically entered into NCIC. Therefore, every law enforcement agency in the United States has instant access to information about stolen property or wanted people; likewise, area law enforcement officers can access information about such matters even though the property or person is wanted in another state.

NCIC is managed by the Federal Bureau of Investigation (FBI) and is based in Washington, D.C. Each state in the United States, most U.S. territories, and Canada all access the NCIC data system. Stolen and embezzled vehicles nationwide are entered into the system, which provides a national data system on many people as well as property.

Using the State System

Information used in various state systems is derived from many sources, including

1. Criminal history data from arrests, fingerprint reports, and corrections reports
2. Wanted and missing people data entered directly by user agencies through their terminals
3. Stolen property data entered by users
4. Driver license, vehicle or vessel identification data available through links with departments of motor vehicles and other pertinent registration agencies

There are limitations on the uses of the information systems terminal. For example, operators should be trained before using the system. Any data obtained through the various information centers may be used only for criminal justice purposes; in fact, all communications capabilities are restricted to matters of criminal justice importance. Each agency entering data is responsible for maintaining and removing data that are obsolete or no longer needed.

Ensure efficient and effective use of the information centers by learning the systems' capabilities. You will receive training in using these systems if your duties involve such communication techniques. If you are entering data into the system regarding people, provide all available identification information, such as name, race, sex, date of birth, physical description, Social Security number, and driver's license number. For vehicles, include the make, model, year, color, tag number (include year issued, if known), vehicle identification number, and so on. Officers in the field requesting data information should have the terminal operator repeat the requested information, to ensure correctness. By having all available identification data at hand when making an entry into the system, the operator can quickly get needed information.

Wants and Warrants

Every officer should understand wants and warrants. A *want* is generally placed on a suspect before a warrant is issued and is based on probable cause. A *warrant* is a document issued by a magistrate of appropriate jurisdiction for a specific charge. More specifically, a *warrant of arrest* is a magistrate's signed order commanding the arrest of a specifically named person (or persons) who is (or are) accused of an offense. Another type of writ or process commanding an officer to take a person into custody is called a *capias*, which can be issued by the court clerk (based on a grand jury indictment or other legal grounds) or a magistrate. A magistrate is empowered to issue warrants and *capias* if he or she reasonably believes that the wanted individual has committed an offense within the magistrate's jurisdiction. To obtain an arrest warrant, officers must

1. Have probable cause—specific facts and circumstances that lead a reasonable and prudent person to believe that a crime has been or is about to be committed
2. Know the time and place of the offense
3. Describe the nature of the offense
4. Provide the name or description of the accused person
5. Sign the complaint or provide the signature of the complainant

If you are serving a warrant, confirm the following *before* executing it:

1. Name of the court from which it was issued
2. Name or specific description of person to be arrested
3. Specific description of the charge (felony or misdemeanor)
4. Date on which the warrant was issued
5. Signature and title of authorizing magistrate

To properly execute a warrant, proceed to the location with appropriate backup; notify the dispatcher before arriving at the location. On contacting the person to be arrested, identify yourself as a law enforcement officer and state the reason for the arrest, indicating that a felony (or misdemeaor) warrant has been issued. Arrest the person and inform him or her about the pertinent constitutional rights (*Miranda* warnings). Then handcuff, search, and transport the individual to the magistrate or appropriate detention facility. Complete the return section of the warrant, sign it, and return it to the judicial officer with an explanation of what was done in carrying out the order.

In some instances, an officer may be aware of the existence of a warrant by prior knowledge or through verification with the communications dispatcher. You should understand that you do *not* need to have the warrant in your possession at the time of the arrest, but on request from the arrested person you are required to show it as soon as practical.

The wants and warrants files can be used to determine if the license number of a vehicle is wanted in connection with a crime, or to determine if a warrant is out for a car in connection with a stolen vehicle. Officers on patrol frequently check vehicle license numbers of suspicious vehicles to see if there are any "wants" or "warrants" outstanding on people and/or property associated with the check. To speed up the process, many agencies have put their crime files into computer memory banks or have available information of crimes in manual files. In addition, most agencies can access major agency computer files, such as the files in departments of highway safety and motor vehicles. In agencies that have computers, each communicator or radio telephone operator is linked to the computer system through a CRT, or cathode ray terminal (a computer input-output device) at the station or communications center. In such cases, a license number can be checked directly from the inhouse computer system. Manual filing systems, while good, require more time to complete the check.

Three different types of information can be stored in files: wants and warrants, auto theft information, and the motor vehicles and/or vessels files. Each file covers a different range of information that can provide invaluable aid to the officer.

Wanted Vehicles. As noted, the wants and warrants (local manual or automated system) files can alert officers to vehicles used in connection with a crime. Always run a "want" check on suspicious vehicles. Auto theft information systems list cars that are stolen, recovered, impounded, or repossessed; in addition, the files contain vehicle identification numbers (VINs) of vehicles and/or plates that are wanted for other reasons. Generally, request checks on both wants and warrants as well as auto theft information systems, if you think the vehicle was stolen.

A variety of information on stolen, recovered, repossessed, lost, and found vehicles and license plates are included in the data systems. Furthermore, stolen transmissions and engines are entered into the system, as are embezzled vehicles. When vehicles (or parts) are found and recovered, the system must be updated without delay.

State Agency Handling Motor Vehicle Records. State vehicle agency files can provide you information regarding the year, make, model, and vehicle identification number of vehicles registered in that state. Furthermore, the computer system can give the name and address of the registered and legal owner(s) (if any) of the vehicle(s) in question. Although an officer may not always check the files at the same time a check is conducted for wants and warrants, including auto theft information, the information is useful in other situations. The files can tell you to whom a vehicle is registered or alert you whether or not a license plate is displayed on the correctly assigned vehicle. A request for a "10–28" will provide you with information about the year, make, and model of the vehicle to which the plate is registered; and, in addition, provide you the VIN and the names of the registered and legal owner(s) (if any), as well as any other relevant data.

Basic radio procedures vary from department to department. However, the procedure for making all the checks just outlined is the same. Start by giving the communication center your *unit designation*, and by telling the center what information you need. The request should state, "10–29 requests want on license number . . ." or "Request 10–28 on license number . . ." After pausing a second, read the license number, using the specific numbers and letters of the suspect vehicle. When quoting letters over the radio, use the phonetic alphabet pronunciation (see Figure 4-8) to avoid errors and misunderstanding. Once you have initiated the request, wait by the radio without transmitting. Generally speaking, the information reply will return within a few seconds unless communications tells you that there will be some delay.

Wanted Persons. Be aware of the following tactical considerations when requesting wants and warrants, or other information on people. When it is warranted, request a backup unit. Once the assisting unit is in place and the suspects have been secured, pat them down to find any weapons. Do the want or warrant check out of the suspect's hearing. If you are handling multiple suspects, a telephone is considered best to conduct checks. However, if a radio is the only means of communication, request a clear frequency and alert the dispatcher that more than one person needs to be checked, and give the number of people involved. Once communications gives you the go ahead, state the suspect's name, address, driver's license number, date of birth (DOB), and physical description (this list may vary from agency to agency). Remember to start the radio transmission with the unit designation, since the dispatcher may need to know your unit number as part of the query. If the driver's license is from another state, indicate the state first, then the number; if the license is from your home state, simply give the number. If there is a match, or a "hit," on a warrant, the computerized warrant teletyped abstract may be identified even if the warrant is listed under an alias used by the suspect.

Once the first suspect has been checked, the radio dispatcher may tell you to begin transmitting information on the second suspect. However, it is important for you to wait for an answer on Suspect 1 *before* asking for a query on Suspect 2, unless communications directs otherwise. Since a computer can handle only one piece of information at a time, each suspect will need to be identified individually.

In some cases, suspects may have more than one address and/or aliases (names assumed and used by subjects other than their proper name). When requesting information on warrants, determine if a subject has moved from the address indicated on the driver's license. If the subject's address has changed, give the most recent address on the license first, then relate additional addresses (if any). Likewise, give any known aliases that the suspect may use. It is not uncommon that a "hit" on a wanted person may be listed under an alias unknown to the officer at the time of the warrant check.

As noted, you may arrest suspects based on radio information that a warrant is outstanding, even though the warrant is not in your hands. On returning to headquarters, or the communications center, identify your teletyped abstract by looking for your unit designation on the document.

THE MEDIA AND RIGHT-TO-PRIVACY CONFLICTS

Handling news media personnel effectively takes tact and diplomacy. The First Amendment of the U.S. Constitution guarantees freedom of the press. However, officers have a duty to protect a crime or incident scene until it can be processed thoroughly and correctly. Furthermore, citizens generally enjoy a "right to privacy" and expect these rights protected in accordance with law. In some instances, these rights and duties may conflict. Follow your department's guidelines in handling the public media.

Media Relations

An adverse crowd control situation, riot, or crime scene is news. The news media feel a responsibility to report such newsworthy events to the public, both as a service and as an obligation. In fact, the news media frequently monitor law enforcement communications and arrive at crime scenes at the same time as the investigating officer. The manner in which the media perceive the law enforcement officers' performance of duty can drastically affect how the public views and relates to the law enforcement agency. An adverse image is difficult to overcome; conversely, a positive media relations effort can gain public support for law enforcement goals and objectives.

Officers are expected to perform duties in a professional manner. By using professional tact, you can frequently gain cooperation and assistance of news media personnel at various scenes. For example, most media personnel understand the danger of driving up to the front door of a residence where a man is holding his wife and children as hostages, following a domestic violence dispute where neighbors have reported shots fired. Most media personnel will cooperate with law enforcement requests to remain safely out of danger until the situation is under control. However, in other, unusual situations, officers have perceived media personnel as uncaring and disrespectful; for example, when they attempted to film video coverage of an accident scene where the female driver was partially unclothed after the collision. Such situations require cool tempers, understanding, compassion, and tact tempered with diplomacy.

In many departments, a specific officer may be designated as the spokesperson for the agency. This person may be trained in handling media interviews and understands what information may, or may not, be released immediately for media use. Generally, officers should refer media questions to the designated media relations officer or to a supervisor. Do not make independent statements or speculations without authorization. If they lack training in media relations, officers may inappropriately reveal the name of people who are under investigation, injured, or under age. Such lapses could subject the department to lawsuits and embarrassment.

Right to Privacy

According to the fundamental philosophy of the U.S. constitutional form of government, public policy dictates that all people are entitled to full and complete information regarding the affairs of government and the official acts and policy of those who represent them as public officials and public employees. Such access is necessary to enable the people to fulfill their duties of discussing public issues fully and freely, making informed political judgments, and monitoring government to ensure that it is being conducted in the public interest.

Public "right to access" policy, however, is not intended to be used to violate individual privacy, nor to further a commercial enterprise, or to disrupt the work of any public body independent of fulfilling any rights of the people to access to information. For example, every state prohibits disclosure of a juvenile suspect's identity. A child's conduct is generally considered to be a "civil violation" (unless certified as "criminal" by a court of competent jurisdiction); therefore, a child has the right to privacy from public identification. In these jurisdictions, the child generally has the right to have all records "sealed" and prohibit access to past records for employment checks or record searches. Law enforcement officers should be cognizant of the exemptions from inspection and copying restrictions applicable to information, files, and data in their possession:

1. Information that, if disclosed, would constitute a clearly unwarranted invasion of personal privacy, unless such disclosure is consented to in writing by the individual subject of such information
2. Personnel files and personal information maintained with respect to employees, appointees, or elected officials of any public body or applicants for such positions
3. Information revealing the identity of people who file com-

plaints with or provide information to administrative, investigative, law enforcement, or penal agencies

4. Investigation records compiled for state or local administrative law enforcement purposes or for internal matters of a public body, but only to the extent that disclosure would
   a. Interfere with pending or actually and reasonably contemplated enforcement proceedings
   b. Deprive a person of a fair trial or an impartial hearing
   c. Unavoidably disclose the identity of a confidential source, or disclose confidential information furnished only by a confidential source
   d. Disclose unique or specialized investigative techniques other than those generally used and known
   e. Constitute an invasion of personal privacy
   f. Endanger the life or physical safety of law enforcement personnel or any other person

5. Criminal history record information maintained by state or local criminal justice agencies, except the following:
   a. Chronologically maintained arrest information, such as traditional arrest logs or blotters
   b. The names of an adult person in the custody of a law enforcement agency and the charges for which that person is being held
   c. Court records that are public records
   d. Records that are otherwise available under state or local law
   e. Records in which the requesting party is the individual identified, *except if such records endanger the life or physical safety of law enforcement personnel or any other person* (*Note*: "Criminal history record information" means information collected by criminal justice agencies on people consisting of identifiable descriptions and notations of arrests, detentions, indictments, or other formal criminal charges, any disposition arising therefrom, sentencing, correctional supervision, and release. The term does not apply to statistical records and reports in which individuals are not identified and from which their identities are not ascertainable.)

6. Records of state and local law enforcement agencies and correctional agencies that are related to the detection and

investigation of crime or the security and operations of correctional institutions

The conflict between the media's right to access information in the public interest and an individual's right to privacy are major concerns for peace officers. As a rule, the initial report filed by a peace officer is a chronological record of events, incidents, arrests, and so on. These documents, therefore, are open to media review and a file is generally maintained for this purpose. However, follow-up investigative reports are subject to confidentiality, especially while an ongoing investigation is in progress. As a rule, the names of involved people (suspects, complainants, victims, witnesses, and so on) are *not* used in the narrative body of the initial police report; instead, labeling terms such as "Subject 1," "Witness 2," or "Complainant 1" are used to represent involved people. In this manner, a person's identity is protected under his or her "right to privacy," while the media (and hence, the public) still has access to appropriate information regarding incidents. However, officers use the person's real name in supplemental reports for clarity, rather than the labeling term used in the initial report.

For emphasis, it should be noted that only designated officers are authorized to provide information to the media regarding an ongoing investigation. Remember the code of ethics rule that says, "Whatever I see or hear of a confidential nature or that is confided to me in my official capacity will be kept ever secret unless revelation is necessary in the performance of my duty."

KEY TERMS

American Sign Language (ASL, or Ameslan)
Capias
Chain of command
Communicate
Communications
Community participation
Community relations
Consolidated emergency communication operations

Decode
Encode
Exposure (Johari Window)
Feedback
Fingerspelling (signed English)
Horizontal communications (coordination)
Human relations
Interpersonal communication (body language)
Johari Window
Law Enforcement Teletypewriter Service (LETS)
Media relations
Missing Children Information Center (MCIC)
National Crime Information Center (NCIC)
"Noise" in communications
Operational "links"
Police-police relations
Phonetic alphabet
Public relations
Public service
Response time
Telecommunications
Ten-code
Three-way radio communications
Two-way communications
Walkie-talkie radios
Wants and warrants

STUDY QUESTIONS

1. Why is communications considered the "operational link" between peace officers and police agencies?

2. Explain what the following verse means: "Be careful of the words you speak, /Be sure to keep them sweet; /You never know from day to day, /which ones you'll have to eat!"

3. Describe the components of a two-way communications system, and how the system works.

4. What is the basic difference between two-way and one-way communication systems?

5. What communications problem has occurred when a person corrects him- or herself and says, "What I said was not what I meant"?

6. What problem does "noise" create in a communications system? Give three examples of different types of distractions that can constitute noise.

7. List six different types of situations where effective two-way communications can benefit you as a law enforcement officer.

8. What is body language, and what application does it have to law enforcement communications?

9. Explain the statement, "Police work is a people-oriented profession."

10. List two types of internal and external stress that law enforcement officers face on a daily basis.

11. Explain what "PPR = PCR" means and how it applies to daily police work.

12. Explain what horizontal and vertical communications are in relation to the police organization.

13. What is a chain of command? How is it shown in an organizational chart?

14. What three concepts form the basis or foundation of a strong police-community relations structure?

15. Define the elements of public service as it relates to PCR.

16. What is public relations, and how does it apply to PCR?

17. Outline the reasons why peace officers should become involved in community participation as a part of PCR.

18. Describe the proper procedures for answering a telephone call as a peace officer.

19. What should you do if you have to leave the phone conversation to handle another important matter?

20. Why is it important to be a good listener as a peace officer?

21. In a one-on-one interview, what can you suspect about a person who folds his or her arms and will not look you in the eye?

22. What types of body language indicate that a person is being truthful

and honest? What interpersonal communications indicate deceit and dishonesty?

23. Why should you not say, "Shut up" in dealing with angry people? What words could you use instead, to gain cooperation and solicit support?

24. What is the best way to obtain a suspect's description from a deaf victim? Why?

25. How should a law enforcement officer deal with a deaf person when investigating a motor vehicle collision between the deaf person and another motorist?

26. How should you handle an investigation involving a deaf person who is suspected of committing a crime?

27. Explain the statement "Blind people are perhaps the most patronized members of society."

28. What additional concerns should you consider before conducting an interview with a visually impaired witness?

29. Describe the methods used for law enforcement communications in the nineteenth century.

30. What was the significance of frequency modulation (FM) to police radio communications?

31. Describe the difference between two-way and three-way radio communications capabilities.

32. Why is response time so important to law enforcement operations? What are the major impediments to response time in modern police work?

33. List the advantages and disadvantages of consolidated emergency communication operations.

34. Distinguish the difference between Priority 1, 2, and 3 situations in radio dispatch of various types of calls. Why is a priority system needed?

35. Describe the proper way to use a police radio to make a transmission. What factors should you consider before making the transmission?

36. What advantage does telephone communication have over radio communications? Under what circumstances should you use the telephone for tactical advantage?

37. What is the purpose of the ten-signal system and phonetic alphabet used by many law enforcement agencies?

38. How would you phrase a radio message to obtain a vehicle registration check and check for wanted on license plate ABC 123?

39. What is the difference between a call for assistance and a 10–33 call for help?

40. What are some frequent causes of transmitter failure, and how should you handle these problems?

41. Why is it important to correctly replace the microphone in its hanger after each radio transmission? What type of embarrassing situations might occur if the microphone is accidentally keyed inside a patrol unit?

42. What is a skip effect problem in radio transmissions?

43. List the basic rules for correct radio transmissions.

44. What advantages does the hand-held radio provide for law enforcement patrol officers?

45. What is LETS, and what is its significance for law enforcement communications?

46. How can television and video help modern peace officers become more effective and efficient?

47. What role do computers play in modern law enforcement? How may future computer technology be applied to accomplish the police mission?

49. What is NCIC, and what role does it play in assisting law enforcement agencies? What is the name of the related information center in your state?

50. What types of data can be retrieved from state and NCIC data banks?

51. As an investigative officer at the scene of a downed civilian aircraft, how would you handle media people seeking information for local news?

52. List the types of materials and information that are exempt from media information systems.

53. How would you identify involved parties in the initial and supplemental reports regarding a local robbery you investigated?

54. What does the law enforcement code of conduct require regarding confidentiality of law enforcement information?

ACTIVITIES

1. Determine what the "chain of command" is in your city's local law enforcement agency. To whom is the chief of police or sheriff responsible for agency effectiveness?

2. With permission of a local law enforcement agency, visit the communications center and communications specialists. Find out what complaints these people have about officers attempting communications in the field.

3. After practicing the American Sign Language techniques, create a role-playing situation where a student "peace officer" stops a "deaf person" for the purpose of issuing a traffic citation.

4. Interview a local newspaper journalist or other media personality, and get his or her views on First Amendment rights to freedom of the press. Determine how this person handles the conflict between the public's right to know and an individual's right to privacy when public events occur.

5. If available, contact an organization representing deaf and/or blind people and find out what the agency is doing to improve the quality of life for affected people. What advice can they provide on how law enforcement officers can best assist and deal with deaf or blind people during an investigation or interview?

6. Divide the class into discussion groups. Ask each group to brainstorm and compile a list of how officers can expand their Johari Window Arena in law enforcement patrol operations. Have the groups compare their lists in open discussion.

5

Reporting and Records

Successful police work requires a businesslike professional approach to every work assignment. Such an approach demands teamwork and cooperation from everyone concerned. Your notebook and police reports are among the most important tools of the profession. This is true whether you are a patrol officer, criminal detective, or accident investigator.

Any investigative effort will be of value only if you maintain accurate and complete records throughout the process. Officers conducting investigations should realize how important this part of their work is, and the importance of reporting detailed aspects of police reports cannot be overemphasized. Days, weeks, and months of good law enforcement investigations ultimately are recorded in a cumulative permanent record of the events, actions, and results of a criminal action. These records become the basis for formal accusations of guilt and build the foundations for the state's case. In addition, as the author of the police report, you can use the report in court as an aid for testifying; your personal notebook likewise can be used to refresh your memory in the courtroom. Officers who know the requirements necessary for good reports and exercise sound tactics in recording the facts ultimately help achieve the objectives of the system—justice.

POLICE REPORTS—WRITE FOR THE READER

One of the first rules in police report writing is "Write for the reader." Keep in mind that others—your supervisors, attorneys, and the courts, to mention but a few—are going to read what you have written. You want to relate all the necessary facts required to tell who, what, where, when, why, and how. You must tell the story in a manner that will cause another person to understand exactly what happened and to feel as though he or she (the reader) were seeing the action in his or her mind. For example, consider the following letter:

Dear Sir:

I am writing in response to your request for additional information. In Block Number 3 of the accident report form, I put "Trying to do the job alone was the cause of my accident." You said in your letter that I should fully explain how the accident occurred, and I trust that the following details will be sufficient.

I am a bricklayer by trade. On the day of the accident, I was working alone on the roof of a new six-story building. When I completed my work, I discovered that I had about 500 pounds of brick left over. Rather than carry the bricks down by hand, I decided to lower them in a barrel by using a pulley that fortunately was attached to the side of the building at the sixth floor.

Securing the rope at ground level, I went up to the roof, swung the barrel out, and loaded the brick into it. I then went back to the ground and untied the rope, tightly holding it to ensure a slow descent of the 500 pounds of bricks.

You will note in Block 11 of the accident report form that I weigh 135 pounds. Due to my surprise at suddenly being jerked off the ground, I lost *presence of mind* and forgot to let go of the rope. Needless to say, I proceeded up the side of the building at a rather rapid rate. In the vicinity of the third floor, I met the barrel coming down. This explains the fractured skull and broken collarbone.

Slowed only slightly, I continued my rapid ascent up the building and I did not stop until the fingers of my right hand were

---

> two-knuckles deep into the pulley. Fortunately, by that time I regained my presence of mind and I was able to tightly hold onto the rope in spite of my pain.
>
> At approximately the same time, however, the barrel of bricks hit the ground and the bottom fell out of the barrel. Devoid of the weight of the bricks, the barrel now weighed approximately 50 pounds. I again refer you to my weight in Block Number 11.
>
> As you might imagine, I began a rapid descent down the side of the building. In the vicinity of the third floor, I met the barrel coming up. This accounts for the two fractured ankles and the lacerations of my legs and lower body. The encounter with the barrel slowed me enough to lessen my injuries when I fell onto the pile of bricks, and fortunately only three vertebrae were cracked.
>
> I am sorry to report, however, that as I lay there on the bricks—in pain, unable to stand, and watching the empty barrel six stories above me—I again lost presence of mind, and I let go of the rope!

To write a successful report, "tell a story." Although the above account is a whimsical version of how an imaginary accident occurred, the writer brings the reader into the story. You can almost "feel" what the bricklayer was going through during each stage of the encounter—and feel empathy for him as he lies there, in pain, watching the barrel six floors above him. The story is retold in chronological order; the writer tells what happened first, second, third, and so on in proper sequence or order.

In police report writing, relate the events that occur, beginning with your initial involvement in the incident. You might use the following common opening (adjusted for the appropriate situation) to begin your report:

> While on patrol at 0816 hours, 14 August 19____, investigating officers (IOs) received a radio call in reference to a reported robbery at 123 Main Street, Anywhere City, Texas. On arrival, IOs contacted the complainant who stated that . . .

This opening, modified to meet your location or situation, tells the reader what you were doing, how you received the call, when you were notified, where and what the complaint was about, and what you did. In some cases, especially if there is a long delay, you may wish to annotate your arrival time. Following arrival, tell the story in chronological order. What did the complainant say? What actions did you take? Conclude the report with your last actions involved in the incident, and make sure you have noted all proper dispositions of people, property, and evidence.

The body of the report is a logical summary of the important facts that you gathered at the crime, accident, or incident scene. You will no doubt include many bits of information in your field notebook that will serve as investigative leads, facts, and nonessential data for future reference. The police report that you write will be a product summarized from the important details of your field notebook. Therefore, before you can begin to write the police report you must note all details and take good notes. This is an art in itself and a skill that can be learned and improved with practice.

FIELD NOTE TAKING—GET ALL DETAILS

A good memory is a valuable asset to the peace officer, but even the best memory is not enough to keep track of all the details, incidents, and activities the officer becomes involved in. The best and most practical memory aid is the officer's notebook.

The habit of taking notes on the spot or soon after will help the officer develop powers of discriminating observation. Then the officer will be able to give orderly attention to facts and information that are essential to successful prosecution. Careful note taking eliminates confusion and loss of time as well.

The officer who develops the habit of taking proper notes reflects this good work in filing high-quality reports. Notes taken at the scene of an incident establish the clarity, completeness, conciseness, and accuracy of the report the officer later files with supervisors. Complete and accurate notes have been credited with successful criminal prosecution. In contrast, inaccurate or inadequate original notes have led to unnecessary acquittals. This in turn brings criticism and discredit to the agency and embarrassment to the individual officer.

The purpose of all criminal investigation is to produce proof that stands up in court. You are not expected to memorize the many details of a case; this would be impossible. You are, however, expected to write down all details in their notebooks—clearly, completely, concisely, and accurately.

Who, What, When, Where, Why, and How

To be clear, notes should be written neatly and be legible and understandable. To be complete, notes should include the who, what, when, where, why, and how of the situation at hand. Information concerning "who" includes the victim, suspect, driver, and so forth, "What" questions relate to property, weapons, evidence, vehicles, and such. Questions dealing with "when" involve dates and times connected with the offense, the suspect, the evidence, and any people associated with the investigation. "Where" questions determine the location of the crime or accident as well as the location of any arrest or other involved people. "Why" questions address the motive or reason for the offense or incident. Finally, "how" questions treat the manner or method in which an offense or incident occurred.

Your notes should be concise, brief without being skimpy. Include all facts but omit unimportant or unrelated information. You will have to make decisions as you take down notes. Use only standardized abbreviations, and then only with great care. If you use your own personal "shorthand," be certain someone else can decipher it if necessary.

Accuracy is a most important quality in taking notes. Be both correct and exact when recording names, addresses, and other identification on all people contacted or involved. Give careful attention as well to the names and badge numbers of officers present. Recording descriptions of suspects, vehicles, and witnesses as well as times and dates is essential. Also important are accurate descriptions and details of crime or accident scenes, including measurements, serial numbers, locations, and identification marks on any evidence.

A Sketch of the Scene

The officer usually makes a crime scene sketch in all investigations of major crimes and accidents. Sketches, easily made in the officer's notebook, are one of the best ways to depict a great deal of information concisely. A good accurate sketch can "say" many things. You need not be an artist to do a simple sketch, and no special equipment is necessary. Since the rough sketch is not a work of art, but only a reproduction of the crime scene, the only prerequisite is that you have the knowledge and experience to include any articles that bear on the case. Examples include the location of doors and windows, the position of furniture, and the placement of any physical evidence.

Police sketches usually cover the immediate crime scene, the adjacent area, and the general locality. The sketch or sketches provide accurate information about distances and are essential to a proper investigation. The sketches should include only what the investigating officer deems necessary and should omit unrelated or unimportant details. Precise measurements are essential.

Rough sketches made at once in your notebook provide a lasting picture of the crime scene. They will help you review the circumstances of the case long after the original scene has been changed or destroyed. Sketches also help witnesses accurately recall their original observations about the positions and locations of other witnesses or participants in a crime.

Notebook Styles

Police agencies sometimes regulate the type of notebook officers can use. Some require a bound notebook; others prefer the loose-leaf type. Most departments, however, allow individual officers their choice of notebook type. Where an option is given, consider several factors before choosing your notebook.

Bound notebooks offer the added security of having firmly fixed pages. The continuity of notes is also maintained easily since the pages cannot be moved around. One drawback, though, is that the bound notebook could be a source of embarrassment or needless questioning in court because the entire notebook is subject to examination if you refer to it while testifying or if the defense attorney requests it.

In contrast, a loose-leaf notebook allows you to select specific notes required for a particular case. Removing pages in this way could, however, cause the defense attorney to allege that portions of notes favorable to the defense have been removed deliberately. Such allegations can be avoided by consecutively numbering notebook pages before using them. (See Figure 5-1.)

Selecting a notebook is largely a matter of choice, and each type is a proven method of maintaining notes for future use. The main point is to use some type of notebook for note taking during investigations.

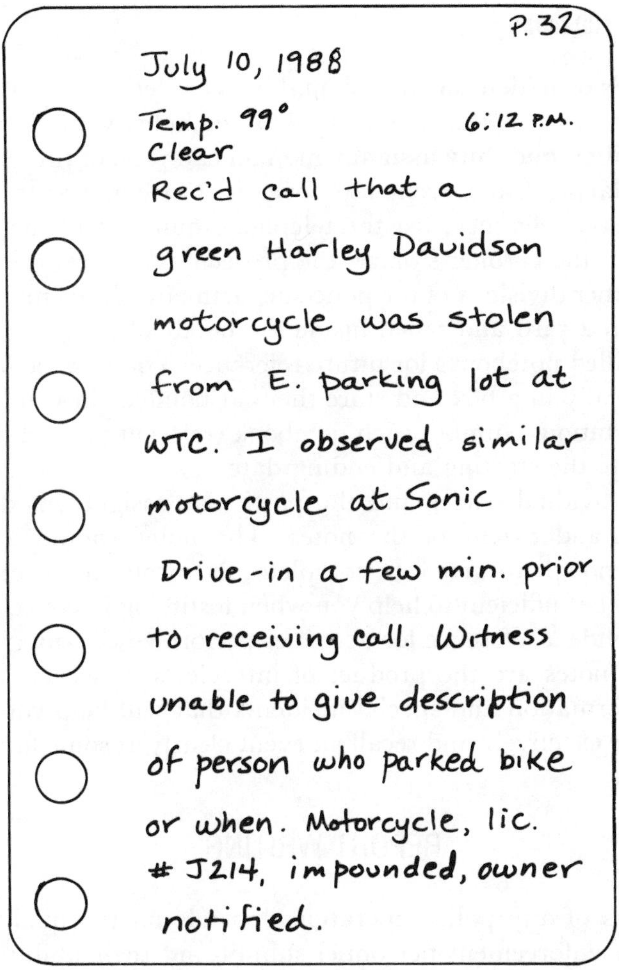

```
                                                    P. 32
          July 10, 1988

   O      Temp. 99°                 6:12 P.M.
          Clear
          Rec'd call that a

   O      green Harley Davidson

          motorcycle was stolen

   O      from E. parking lot at

          WTC. I observed similar

   O      motorcycle at Sonic

          Drive-in a few min. prior

   O      to receiving call. Witness

          unable to give description

   O      of person who parked bike

          or when. Motorcycle, lic.

   O      # J214, impounded, owner
          notified.
```

Figure 5-1
Sample page from loose-leaf style police officer's notebook

Never make notes on slips of paper or on any random material available such as match covers, index cards, or folded sheets of paper. Such poor note-taking practices negatively affect the quantity and quality of the notes. And disorganized methods of keeping notes—in pockets or in envelopes—soon make the notes meaningless. Always establish and maintain a workable system of note taking. Such a system is appropriate for long-term retention of important information, and as a professional the officer remains faithful to good note-keeping practices.

Using a Notebook

The officer's own identification should be recorded on the inside cover or the first page of the notebook. This includes your name, rank, badge number, and duty assignment. You can protect this entry from wear by placing transparent tape over it. Further, inside the notebook, for easy reference, list the telephone numbers of the local fire department, the coroner's office, the prosecutor's office, towing vehicles, and other divisions of the police department. These numbers can be typed on a card and taped inside the notebook.

Keep filled notebooks for future reference. You can file notebooks chronologically in a box and store them at home or in your locker at the police station. Number each notebook consecutively on the cover, and indicate the starting and ending dates.

The individual officer and the particular assignment determine the nature and extent of the notes. The notes should always be adequate enough to generate complete and accurate reports. They should also be sufficient to help you when testifying in court, and they should provide a reference for activities performed on any given duty day. Most notes are the product of interviews; however, also note general information and special incidents that will help you perform duties more effectively and recall an event clearly at some future time.

REPORT WRITING

The success of any police operation depends on the quality of the reports law enforcement personnel submit and their ability to write effectively. Reports are the principal means of transmitting official information to supervisors, command officers, co-workers, the courts, and other criminal justice organizations.

Because reports are so important, police officers must be able to communicate in writing. This cannot be overemphasized. Some officers consider this fundamental activity a drudgery and evade the task whenever they can. Their apparent lack of understanding about how significant reports are is often reflected in poorly written and incomplete documents.

Other law enforcement officers possess an unusual command of the language and understand the power of words. To these people, writing provides a chance to demonstrate their talents but in such a way that their reports are too elaborate and hard to understand. Such people, though gifted, also fail to understand the real purpose of police reports.

Finally, some individuals recognize the value and importance of effective writing, and they know the significance a sound reporting system has to the entire police operation. These officers try neither to shun their responsibilities nor to overwhelm their readers. Rather, their aim is to communicate in writing to the best of their ability. Often, however, this important goal needs some practical assistance.

What Reports Do

Reports provide a permanent record detailing the business of a law enforcement agency. In so doing, reports form the basis of the agency's entire record-keeping system. From an administrative standpoint, reports provide the valuable factual data necessary to prepare for and justify budget and staffing needs. Reports also offer information concerning crime problem areas. This enables researchers to develop crime trends from these data. An effective reporting and records system provides the names and pertinent histories of criminal offenders as well as detailed facts useful in verifying or invalidating citizen complaints. Administrators and supervisors are better able to coordinate field activities and use personnel effectively, given information originating from field investigation reports.

Superiors often base their overall judgment of the individual officer's job performance on the strength of his or her ability to write good reports. Because the report is one of the few tangibles in an officer's normal workday, many administrators consider it a useful yardstick in assessing the individual officer's competence and productivity.

To the officer, reports are a valuable tool of investigation. They can also become a vital piece of evidence when introduced at a trial. Naturally, a report containing obvious mistakes, improper construction, and misspelled words is likely to be worthless as evidence. If introduced at all, it is vulnerable to attack by opposing counsel and not only could discredit and embarrass the officer, but also could result in the defendant's undeserved acquittal.

Most of its readers accept an officer's report at face value as representing a truthful and accurate account of an investigation. An individual officer's training, dedication, and professionalism are all reflected in the quality of the submitted report. You should be committed to excellence in every aspect of performing regular duties. This rule holds true for writing reports in particular.

Types of Reports

The initial report is a product of the information the officer gathers during the preliminary investigation. The sources of information—crime scene, witnesses and victims, record search, personal observation, and so forth—will naturally vary depending on the particular assignment. Regardless of the source, note relevant details during any investigation. These include, for example, names, addresses, dates, times, and descriptions. Also include such additional information as a description of a suspect or vehicle in the notes of the investigation. The patrol officer first assigned to investigate a reported offense or incident occurring within an area of patrol responsibility usually prepares the initial report. This report then forms the basis for any further investigation.

Supplementary reports provide additional and follow-up information. Officers who gain information relevant to the investigation after the initial report is forwarded submit supplementary reports. Submit all such information, regardless of its seeming insignificance.

The case file includes all materials associated with the ongoing investigation. Officers should supply sketches of the crime scene and diagrams of buildings and other structures as attachments to supplemental reports. This requirement also applies to photographs of victims, damaged property, points of entry, as well as any other materials pertinent to the case.

The Writing Process

After officers have gathered all possible information in their preliminary investigation, they should arrange their notes and organize them in a logical order. Set aside irrelevant material at this point. This sorting process takes practice to perfect, because the officer cannot always easily determine immediately what is relevant and what is not. Generally, an abundance of noted information has no bearing whatsoever on the investigation, and such information should be separated out from the pertinent details.

Many successful report writers prefer to start organizing their information by using an outline. The advantage of an outline is that it makes the writing job much easier. An outline forces the writer to organize her or his thoughts and to decide what information is important enough to include and what is the best order of presentation. Then in the subsequent writing process, the officer expands each point of the outline into a paragraph. This process of determining paragraphs serves to develop one idea at a time.

In agencies that require officers to submit handwritten initial reports, legible writing is essential. Such departments usually require officers to complete a report form that a typist then transposes onto a standardized departmental report form. When this form is completed and the supervisor approves it, the investigating officer signs the report.

One of the worst weaknesses in police reports is the abundance of misspelled words. One legitimate reason for this is the complexity of the English language. Although some fundamental rules or guidelines aid proper spelling in English, the many exceptions to these spelling rules can make them less than perfectly helpful.

Spelling. Misspelled words, especially common words used in day-to-day communications, reflect negatively on the individual officer and the officer's department. Misspelled words can also confuse the reader and make the report difficult to understand. Sometimes such a report can bring the officer's credibility into question, especially in areas where the officer may need to testify as an expert witness. Remember that police reports are permanent official documents. Unless the officer takes proper care to ensure correct spelling, misspelled words can become part of documents preserved for years in a records system. This can embarrass everyone affected by the report.

Officers who spell poorly usually operate on one or more of three mistaken assumptions: (1) spelling is unimportant; (2) nothing much can be done to improve spelling skills; (3) the only way to learn how to spell is to spend hours memorizing long word lists. None of these assumptions is valid. Spelling is, in fact, important, and most people can train themselves to be reasonably good spellers in one or two months.

Many spelling errors result from simple carelessness. Most are caused by laziness, while some are the product of ignorance. The careless individual will omit a letter from a word or use a word other than the one intended. The lazy speller does not know the correct spelling of a word, and in lieu of making the effort to look up the word, simply guesses or asks another officer, who could be an even worse speller. Finally, the writer who operates in ignorance actually believes he or she knows the correct spelling but in fact does not. Thus, this individual consistently misspells the same words, meanwhile taking pride in doing a thorough job.

Recognizing the value of properly written reports, all proffesional officers should pursue every means of improving their competencies. It is essential that the officer be able to spell words commonly used in the everyday performance of police work. A small, inexpensive paper-back dictionary should be a part of every officer's regular duty equipment. The old high-school argument that it is hard to look up words when one doesn't know the first few letters is not valid. You can always start by looking up the first letter and go from there.

A dictionary, like the officer's weapon, is a working tool. The officer writing a report should faithfully consult it any time a question arises about how to spell a word properly. This is the only insurance against looking stupid in print.

Word Usage and Grammar. Two other major concerns in writing police reports are proper word usage and correct grammar. Because reports form the principal means of police communication, they must be clear and understandable. To achieve this, use short sentences with common everyday words. Peace officers are unfortunately notorious for using ambiguous words and phrases. This only intensifies the risk of being misunderstood. For example, why use the phrases "maintain surveillance" or "visually monitor" when the word *watch* is clearer and more forceful. The word *fight* works much better than "altercation" or "physical altercation."

The first goal of any official written communication is to convey a message so clearly that it cannot be misunderstood. The writer's selection of words will, to a degree, determine the effectiveness of any report. For this reason, you should use specific, definite, and concrete words, and adapt your writing to the language level of the reader. The unnecessary use of unusual or complex words hinders quick under-standing. The officer who writes, "After a comprehensive appraisal of all circumstances pertaining to the case," simply means, "After a careful review of the facts." "We shall endeavor to ascertain the data" would be better as "We shall try to learn the facts." Because the nature of police work brings officers into contact with lawyers, judges, and other criminal justice personnel, officers tend to start incorporating legal terminology into their reports. Sometimes this is necessary, but more often it is unnecessarily confusing, as legal jargon is not straightforward and clear. It is better to replace legalisms with more common words and phrases. In addition, officers must avoid using the 10-Code or other ambiguous police terminology in reports.

Police officers writing reports should choose the best word order to present their ideas and to give the reader an accurate picture right from the start. Construct paragraphs so that each completely develops one idea. Then arrange paragraphs in logical order, placing important ideas in important positions. The opening and closing sentences in paragraphs are positions of power. Sentence structure should be simple and to the point. Long, complicated sentences are probably the greatest cause of misunderstood reports. Avoid them.

Most report writing could be improved if the officer worked a little harder to choose appropriate words. Good writing depends on knowing the options of the language. Using the proper words enhances the quality of reports.

One of the best ways to increase your command of the language is by reading. For sharp, clear writing, the officer needs to know the difference between such terms as *capias* and *subpoena*, *verify* and *confirm*, and *victim* and *complainant*. As you develop good reading habits, you will find many words that are familiar but not part of your working vocabulary. Regular practice in their correct use will allow you to introduce them into conversation and writing so that eventually they become readily available to you.

Using a dictionary to check the meanings of words will also increase your word power. The dictionary habit is a valuable aid to the serious officer who sincerely wants to become an effective report writer.

Accurate Information. Information is the stock in trade of police work, but inaccurate or incomplete information is usually worse than no information at all. A good report ensures that information is available when needed, and to be a good report it must be complete and accurate.

Loss of time, effort, and, in many cases, even vital information follows from either incomplete or inaccurate information in the report. This could in turn lead to the inability to close a case. Criminal investigation specialists waste many hours following up these inaccuracies. An excellent guideline is that the officer should write the report as if she or he were going to do the follow-up work.

The officer's report must present a well-organized and readable word picture of the investigation. Departmental policy usually sets forth procedures for presenting such information. Most reports, however, include the following sections: the face sheet or initial page, the narrative section, and the conclusion.

The initial page or heading contains the administrative data necessary to identify, control, and accurately file the report. It usually begins with a case number. This case number facilitates filing, makes reference easier, and fulfills other administrative purposes. The date on which the report is actually submitted is always included. The status section (see Figure 5-2) refers to the condition of the case. When a case is still under active investigation, it is considered *open* or unsolved. A case that is completed or ordered closed by a superior officer is considered *closed*. When a suspect has been arrested and charged, the case status is *cleared by arrest*; however, a case cleared by any other means than arrest is regarded as *exceptionally cleared*. This status classification is used in cases where, for example, the suspect charged is already in custody, deceased, or insane.

The name, rank, and badge number of the investigating officer are recorded in the administrative section of the report. When a team of officers works together, the reporting officer's name is listed first. Under the heading *offense*, the reporting officer names the specific offense—burglary, theft, sexual assault, and so forth. Some departments also require the number of the penal code violation in this section.

Next list the names, addresses, phone numbers, and aliases of all people involved in the investigation on the appropriate section of the report form. This includes victims, witnesses, and any persons arrested.

Example: MILLHOUSE, Arthur J., alias "Frog," 5432 Argosy Trail, 555-9876.

The synopsis of the report gives the reader a brief case summary. It will contain all the essential elements of the incident in a brief,

OFFENSE REPORT
POLICE DEPARTMENT

CASE NUMBER ——————
CLASS NUMBER ——————
DATE OF REPORT ——————

OFFENSE	ADDRESS OF OCCURRENCE			
PLACE OF OCCURRENCE	TIME	DATE	HOW REPORTED	
COMPLAINANT	ADDRESS		PHONE	
REPORTED BY	ADDRESS			
REPORT RECEIVED BY	TIME	DATE	OFFICERS ASSIGNED	

PERSONS ATTACKED

PROPERTY ATTACKED

HOW ATTACKED

MEANS OF ATTACK

OBJECT OF ATTACK

VEHICLE USED

TRADEMARK

PERSONS ARRESTED

DETAILS OF OFFENSE (Use plain sheet of paper if needed)

CASE IS:——————OPEN——————UNFOUNDED——————CLEARED BY ARREST——————
EXCEPTIONALLY CLEARED ——————————— INACTIVE (not cleared)——————

COMMANDING OFFICER —————— DATE —————— INVESTIGATING OFFICER —————— DATE ——————

STOLEN PROPERTY

QUANTITY	DESCRIPTION	EST. VALUE	RECOVERED DATE	VALUE

BY WHOM RECOVERED	OWNER NOTIFIED BY	TIME AND DATE	TOTAL VALUE STOLEN	TOTAL VALUE RECOVERED

I HEREBY ACKNOWLEDGE RECEIPT OF THE ABOVE RECOVERED ARTICLES DELIVERED TO ME BY	SIGNED

Figure 5-2
Sample offense report

DESCRIPTION OF SUSPECTS OR PERSONS WANTED

	NO. 1	NO. 2
NAME		
ALIAS		
ADDRESS		
RACE, SEX, AGE		
HEIGHT AND WEIGHT		
COLOR OF HAIR		
COLOR OF EYES		
COMPLEXION		
NATIONALITY		
OCCUPATION		
DRESS AND OTHER MARKS		
WHY SUSPECTED OR WANTED		

FINAL DISPOSITION:

Figure 5-2, *continued*

concise statement using the who, what, where, when, why, and how
guidelines. Examples:

1. "The victim reported that at approximately 9:30 P.M., two
   armed gunmen entered his store and forced him to open his
   safe, stealing $5,000 in currency."
2. "The victim stated that an unknown suspect forced the rear
   door of his store last night and ransacked the place. It is not
   known at this time if anything was stolen."

Each succeeding paragraph in the *narrative section* relates in detail
the events as they occurred according to the victim. The reporting
officer maintains continuity in the report, even if the victim's account
is fragmented or out of sequence. A separate paragraph should cover
each step in the investigation so reviewers can understand exactly
what happened.

Use separate paragraphs for each witness or suspect interviewed
or interrogated. This enables proper identification of each individual
and easy location of information in the report.

The narrative section of an investigation report should contain descriptions of people, including age, sex, race or color, height, weight, build, posture, head shape, face, neck, shoulders, waist, hands, fingers, arms, and feet.

List property primarily according to classification of article; for example, watches, furs, automobiles, and so forth. You can class certain categories of property readily according to serial number. For example, watches, cameras, typewriters, and automobiles usually have serial numbers. In describing property, include the following basic information:

- Kind of article
- Physical appearance
- Material or substance from which it is made
- Brand name
- Number of articles
- Identifying marks

A large part of the narrative section is devoted to details of the offense and the investigator's and other participants' actions. For example, a burglary report would develop the following information:

- Who discovered the crime
- The location of any evidence
- The owner of the stolen property
- A description of the premises
- The method and point of entry
- Any damage to the premises
- The type and value of property damaged or stolen
- Other relevant details of the investigation

The final report usually contains the following data as well:

- A list of the evidence
- Its chain of custody
- Circumstances of the arrest
- Written statements from witnesses
- Personal information about witnesses
- Any pertinent information and remarks concerning undeveloped leads
- Reasons any sources have not been investigated

Finally, after describing all the details of the investigation, the investigator may list reasons the case should be closed or unfounded. This is the *conclusion* of the report. The officer may also recommend some remedial action through referral to another agency such as in cases involving juvenile violators or another police jurisdiction. Conclusions and recommendations should always be based on facts presented in the report. Conclusions should also be realistic and conform to relevant statutes and departmental policy.

Supplemental reports are submitted as officers conduct further investigations and develop more information. The format and content of any subsequent report should follow the same pattern as the initial report to maintain continuity and enhance readability.

Grammar Notes and Spelling Tips

Correct use of the English language can work to your advantage. Because your reports will be seen by your supervisors, the courts, lawyers, insurance companies, and even the media—to mention but a few—correct use of punctuation marks and spelling words will create a strong first impression on others. Common writing errors can be eliminated with basic editing skills and understanding of elementary grammar rules. The following type of errors frequently occur in police reports.

Commas. Improper use of the comma frequently is a writing problem for many people, including police report writers. The following simple rules will help to check your comman usage.

1. The first rule of comma usage is "When an independent clause is separated from another independent clause by a conjunction (and, but, or) *use a comma* to separate them."

Example: *"George was lonely at first,* but *after a while he came to like having the whole house to himself."*

Both of the italicized sections are *independent clauses*; either statement can stand alone and be understood without additional information. These independent clauses are joined by the conjunction *but*; thus, a *comma* is needed in this example.

2. The second rule of comma usage is "When an independent clause is separated from a dependent clause by a conjunction, *no comma* should be used."

Example: *"We could enter the house* or stay where it was hot."

In this example, the italicized portion of the statement is the independent clause. However, the words following the conjunction *or* constitute a "dependent clause"; the words "stay where it was hot" cannot stand alone with meaning unless the first part of the sentence (the independent clause) is coupled with the conjunction *or*. Thus, in this statement a comma is *not used*, resulting in a statement that is considered a whole thought.

3. The third rule of commas is "Use commas with nonrestrictive (parenthetical or nonessential) modifiers, but do not use commas with restrictive (defining or essential) modifiers." Nonrestrictive and restrictive modifiers are frequently used in police report writing for clarity and understanding.

Example: "The reporting officer, Jones, contacted a white male *later identified as Witness 1*, who stated that he observed an unknown subject break a lock."

The name "Jones" is a nonrestrictive, or nonessential, modifier because there is only one reporting officer; thus, commas were used around the name "Jones." However, the italicized portion of the sentence is a defining, or essential, modifier because many people could be "a white male." The modifier tells the reader who this white male person is. In addition, the reader understands that only later did the investigating officer identify this person.

Consider another type of essential modifier used in the following statement:

> Example: "Jill and her teacher Mrs. Martha Jones worked on the class project until noon."

Commas are not used around "Mrs. Martha Jones" in the sentence because her name is a restrictive (essential) modifier that specifies which of Jill's teachers was working on the project. Therefore, commas are not used to set off this defining modifier in the sentence.

An example of nonrestrictive (nonessential) modifier demonstrates when commas are used:

> Example: Jill and her teacher, Mrs. Martha Jones, worked on the class project until noon.

In this example, *Mrs. Martha Jones* is a nonessential modifier because Jill has only one teacher, and therefore commas are used.

4. The fourth rule of commas is "When two independent clauses are connected, but not by a conjunction, *do not use a comma*; use a semicolon (as in this sentence)."

Use of Quotation Marks. Reporting officers use quotations when the exact words used by a person at a crime or incident scene are relevant to the case. For example, a spontaneous oral exclamation made by a suspect can be an exception to the hearsay rule and admissible in court. Therefore, the suspect's *exact words* should be quoted in the report. However, you should know and properly use correct punctuation rules for quotations.

1. Periods, commas, and other ending punctuation marks are always placed *inside* of quotation marks when they are part of the quote.

> Example: Responding officers arrived at the scene and observed a person, Subject 1, run out of the home yelling, "Hurry, get an ambulance; I just shot my wife!"

In this example, the excited statement is quoted exactly as Suspect 1 stated the words. Since this is an excited statement, an exclamation mark was used instead of a period at the end of the sentence. Note that the quotation mark is outside the ending punctuation mark. Also note the comma preceding the quote following the word *yelling*—this comma tells the reader where the exact quote begins.

> Example: Officer Jackson informed the suspect of his constitutional rights in the presence of Officer Myers. The suspect stated that he understood his rights and did not want a lawyer. In addition, the suspect said, "I want to get this off my chest; I shot Jim because he owed me money and wouldn't pay up."

This is a confession. You need the suspect's exact words in case he or she later decides not to put the statement into writing. Again, notice the comma after the word *said* and proper use of the quotation marks. However, note also the use of paraphrasing where the suspect's exact words were not used as they relate to the waiver of rights, including access to an attorney. In this statement, the specific waiver acknowledgment can be backed up with the suspect's own confession that contains exact language of the waiver.

2. Semicolons are placed outside of quotation marks.

> Example: The witness stated she heard the victim say, "Don't shoot"; however, Suspect 1 pulled the trigger and shot the victim.

3. Question marks go to the inside of the quotation marks if it is part of the quotation.

> Example: The suspect asked, "Did the lady die?"

This quote is a question, thus the question mark is "part of the quote" and is placed inside the ending quote mark.

> Example: Was the gun found near "the strip"?

This quoted term is not a question, but rather a jargon term to describe a place. Therefore, the question mark is placed outside the quote mark.

Semicolon and Colon. Two separate (complete) but closely related ideas can be joined together with a semicolon (;). This punctuation mark can be used when a period would otherwise be applicable. It infers a strong bond between the two clauses but maybe not enough to make them one sentence. This punctuation mark can be extremely useful to police report writing; however, do not "overuse" the semicolon. Because many investigations involve "cause-result" situations, the use of semicolons can help your report "come alive for the reader." In other words, the reader will see and feel the close connection between the two ideas. Two separate, but closely related statements, can be joined as "one thought" while giving the reader a "breath in the middle" by using the semicolon rather than a period. However, be careful not to combine more than *two* thoughts or sentences with one semicolon.

A second use of the semicolon is to connect complicated clauses when confusion could result because of use of essential modifiers to describe or identify people, property, and so on.

> Example: The complainant stated that the following items were missing: a gold set of earrings, valued at $1,000; a Zenith 19-inch color television, serial number XYZ 1234567; and a man's Rolex watch, serial number ABC 98765.

It is obvious that three items were taken in the incident. Using a semicolon makes it clear that the essential modifiers (descriptions or serial numbers) pertain to a specific item.

Note also, in the last example, use of the colon (:). In this example, the colon alerts the reader to "a listing" of stolen property.

You would start the phrase following the colon with a capital letter only if it makes a complete sentence; otherwise, use a lower-case letter.

Other Grammatical Notes

Adverbs and Adjectives. Adverbs and adjectives are words that modify (describe) verbs and nouns. Generally speaking, place the adverb or adjective before the verb or noun.

Example: The complainant lives in a *white* house.
The noise was *closely* associated with gun shots.

The words *white* and *closely* modify the noun and verb that follow. They communicate a clearer meaning that expresses understanding and feeling to the reader.

Numbers. When using numbers, spell out the numbers one (1) through ten (10), but use the numerical value for 11, 12, and so on. Numbers 1–10 should be written as numbers when used with units of measure or in a mathematical context.

Percent and Percentage. Use the word *percent* only with a number. When you use it with a word, use the term *percentage.*

"It's" versus "Its". Frequently misused, the contraction *it's* means "it is"; you can avoid confusion by writing out the two words rather than use the contractions (except in a direct quote). The word *its* is possessive (no apostrophe); for example, "The vehicle had damage to its front end."

Parentheses. Use parentheses to explain or add to something. The explanation can even be a whole sentence. A period goes *outside* the last parenthesis mark unless the whole sentence is in parentheses, in which case put the period *inside* the closing parenthesis mark. Do not place a comma before or after the parenthetical remark.

North, East, South, and West. Do not capitalize the first letter of *north, east, south,* or *west* when using these as words *directions.* However, when used to describe a location they are capitalized: North Carolina, Southwest Drive, East Arden Street, and so on.

"Due to" versus "Because of." Use the phrase "due to" when the verb *was* or *is* comes before the phrase; otherwise, use "because of."

Example 1: "The injury was due to multiple hits with a club."
Example 2: "Because of the injuries, the victim was taken to the hospital."

"Who" versus "Whom." The word *who* is the subject of an action, while the word *whom* is the object of an action. To test correct usage, try substituting *him* or *her* for *whom*, to see if the sentence still sounds right.

"That" versus "Which." Use the word *that* if the addition that follows is needed. However, use the word *which* if what follows is not needed, and in this case use *commas* on each side of the clause.

Example: The suspect stated that she was not at home during the evening.
The gun, which was on the table, was in plain view.

Common Spelling Errors. Spelling errors plague many writers. Your high school teacher probably told you long ago, "If you don't know how to spell it, use a dictionary." This advice is still valid for correct, professional writers. Some common words are frequently misspelled, and you should know the difference without going to a dictionary. For example, consider *there, their,* and *they're.* Often people write *there* when they should have written *their* and do not know the difference! The word *there* indicates place: "put the book over *there.*" The word *their* indicates possession: "it is *their* book." The contraction *they're* stands for "they are," which should be written out fully in formal writing unless it is part of a quote.

Another common spelling error is confusion between *to*, *too*, and *two*. Most people do recognize that "two" is the number 2. However, confusion frequently exists between *to* and *too*. The correct usage of *too* can easily be distinguished by two tests. First, ask yourself if the word *also* can be substituted for *too*: "I want to go too (also)." A second use of *too* is to compare or contrast: too big, too small, too tired, too heavy, too high, too low, and so on. If the word does not fall into one of these categories, it will be used with an action word, as an infinitive: "I want to go to the store." By closely reading your report, you should be able to quickly spot these common errors.

Another common error concerns the word *regardless*. The colloquial "irregardless" is not considered good usage.

Only a few examples of common spelling errors have been outlined here for quick reference. However, remember that many people will read your police report—judges, juries, attorneys, and your supervisors, just to mention a few. Your report reflects both yourself and your professionalism. The few moments that it takes to ensure that words, punctuation marks, and grammar rules are correctly used will affect whether others regard you as a "professional" peace officer. The time is worth the effort.

Report-Writing Tips

The following guidelines will assist you in writing police reports.

1. Write in past tense. Your investigation, and the report you write, happen after the actual events occurred. Therefore, your report should be written in a style (tense) that tells the reader what happened.
2. Type or print your reports; many people's script writing is difficult, if not impossible, to read.
3. Use *black* ink or typewriter ribbon to complete reports.
4. In original (first) reports, use a label to refer to people rather than identify them by name; for example, C-1 for a complainant; S-1, S-2, etc. for suspects or subjects of the report; RP-1 for reporting person; W-1, W-2, etc. for various witnesses; IO for investigating officer, or RO for reporting officer; and so on. Use your agency's own codes and follow accepted practices.
5. In a supplemental report, do *not* use labels. Instead, use the person's name. (*Note*: Supplemental reports are not subject to

public or media scrutiny, and proper names are more clear than labels when telling the story.)

6. If a list of property, or other identifying data, exists in another place on the report, direct the reader to refer to the attachment for details (serial numbers, descriptions, license, or vehicle identification numbers, etc.).

7. After writing your report, ask another officer to proofread and edit your draft. By sharing editing responsibility, you can eliminate writing (grammatical and spelling) errors that may be embarrassing.

8. For a quick reference, keep a notebook of words that you often misspell. If you are not sure how to spell a word, look it up in the dictionary.

9. Use simple, common, everyday language, and keep your sentences short. A paragraph should not be long and cumbersome.

10. Use paragraphs to change ideas. Do not write your report as one long paragraph. Such paragraphs not only make it difficult to concentrate on the story, but are also detrimental to good report-writing style. Paragraphs should be kept short and related to changes in topic.

KEY TERMS

Accident reports
Arrest reports
Chronological order
Field notes
Incident report
Police reports
Sketch (crime/accident)
Supplemental reports
Writing for the reader

STUDY QUESTIONS

1. What is the purpose of field notes?

2. What are the 5-W's and H of report writing? Give three examples of each.

3. Where is the "rough sketch" generally completed during a criminal investigation? What items should the rough sketch indicate?

4. What are the advantages of the bound notebook used by law enforcement officers? What are the disadvantages?

5. What are the advantages and disadvantages of the loose-leaf notebook?

6. What different types of people will look at your police report?

7. Why is it as important to make a good and accurate report as it is to do a good and complete investigation?

8. Summarize the various types of reports that officers make during the tour of duty.

9. Why is spelling important to ensure accurate reports?

10. The field notes are used as a basis for completing the police report. What is the rationale for using some information in the field notes, but not necessarily all recorded information?

11. What are the three mistaken assumptions that poor spellers often use to explain why they misspell words? Are these assumptions valid? Explain why or why not.

12. Explain the four rules for properly using commas.

13. When is the semicolon used, and how can it be used as an effective tool in writing police reports?

14. What are "essential" and "nonessential" modifiers? When are commas used in relation to these parts of a sentence?

15. Describe the proper way to use quotation marks when a suspect makes a statement that you want to repeat exactly. Where do the comma and quotation marks go in relationship to the quote?

16. Explain when a question mark is used inside and outside a quotation mark. Do periods and other ending sentence punctuation marks go inside or outside the ending quotation mark?

17. Explain what "writing for the reader" means.

18. What is "chronological order" in writing? Why is this style generally used in police report writing?

19. When should you capitalize *north*, *east*, *south*, and *west* in a sentence?

20. Explain the proper use of the words *that* and *which* in a sentence.

21. How do you know when to use the words *who* or *whom* in a sentence?

22. Give three properly written examples each of the following words in a complete sentence: *there*, *their*, *too*, and *to*.

ACTIVITIES

1. Given the following information, write an opening paragraph in a vandalism police report. Supply additional information as needed to show how the vandalism was reported and what actions were taken.

Who?	Subject(s) unknown. Victim: Mark M. Jones, 6707 10th Avenue, Anywhere, _____ (your state).
What?	Damage of private property. Unidentified persons cut the vinyl top of Jones's 1989 Cadillac Coupe de Ville (license number _____) and scratched the painted finish. (*Note:* Be sure to describe the cuts—length, depth, etc.)
When?	Between 11:30 P.M. September 20, 19____ and 7:30 A.M. September 21, 19____.
Where?	The parking lot adjacent to the Cinema parking lot in Town and County Shopping Center, 1400 College Avenue, Anywhere, _____ (your state).
How?	With an unidentified sharp object.
Why?	Unknown.

2. Use the given information as the basis for a complete report. You should supply any details needed to write the report.

You are alone in a radio car working in a small city (pick one). Your unit is the only one on the road. At 4:30 P.M., Saturday, October 1, 19____, you are dispatched to Dagwood's Department Store to investigate a reported shoplifting.

You arrive at the store and are met at the curb by the store security guard, Earl E. Turize. Turize tells you that he saw a suspect pick up a packaged sweater. The suspect then slipped the sweater under her jacket and walked past the cashier without paying for the item before the guard could catch her. Turize stated that he ran outside after the suspect but lost her in the crowd. Turize then returned to the store to call the police.

You get a description of the suspect and the stolen sweater. You check the area for several minutes but you are unable to locate anyone fitting the suspect's description.

3. Use the given information as the basis for a complete report. Supply any details you need to complete the assignment.

You are in a two-officer patrol unit. At 2:30 P.M., January 5, 19____, you are dispatched to 1575 Banana Street to investigate a reported burglary.

On your arrival, you are met by the reporting party, Jane Wade, 419 Elm Street, Anywhere, _____ (your state). Wade tells you that her parents' (complainants) home was broken into and directs you to a bedroom window on the west side of the house. You see pry marks (be sure to describe) on the outer window casing, apparently made when the suspect(s) pried the screen from the window. The metal-framed screen, also with pry marks visible on the edges, is lying on the ground beneath the window. You find no other physical evidence outside the house. Inside the house, you find a bedroom closet door open; the closet is empty. There are pry marks on the door casing, and the door's edge is splintered in the area of the lock. You photograph and measure the pry marks.

You interview the neighbor at the house adjoining the west edge of the victims' property at 1565 Banana Street. The neighbor tells you that he did not hear or see anything that might aid in the investigation.

> You ask the reporting person (Wade) to call her parents (complainants) to determine what may be missing, if anything. You also tell Wade that she will be contacted by the detectives later and that she is not to disturb anything in the house.

4. Use the given information (supply any needed details) as the basis for a complete report.

> You are working alone in a residential area. At 9:00 A.M., Sunday, December 14, 19____, you receive a radio call to investigate a theft at 1999 Apple Street, Anywhere, _____ (your state).
>
> You are met by the complainant, Buck N. Bronk, who tells you that three bicycles were stolen from his front porch during the weekend. You check the unenclosed porch, but you do not find any evidence as to who may have taken the bicycles.
>
> Complainant stated that he and his family went away for the weekend; they left home at approximately 6 P.M., Friday, December 12, and returned home at 8:30 A.M., Sunday, December 14, when they discovered that the bicycles were missing. All three bicycles are 26-inch Schwinn girl's 10-speed bicycles. Two are blue in color, and the other is green. The complainant stated that although he does not know the tag numbers nor the stamped identification numbers, each bicycle is registered with the police department.
>
> You talk to various neighbors who were home over the weekend. One neighbor (supply details) reported that he saw a yellow pickup truck with a green top over the bed parked in front of the complainant's house around 10 P.M., Saturday. However, the neighbor did not see anyone in the truck and assumed it belonged to a guest or visitor in the neighborhood.
>
> You return to police headquarters and obtain the tag numbers and stamped identification numbers (supply needed information) for the bicycles.

6

Interviewing Techniques

Law enforcement officers share one common characteristic—they are inquisitive. However, smart officers also know the preliminary safety requirements essential for correct approaches to field and/or vehicle stops before gathering information as noted in other sections of this text. Officers constantly seek data and gather information from people—victims, witnesses, suspects, informants, even other officers. The ability to acquire information requires that an officer be able to *listen* to both nonverbal and verbal communications. Such skills are mandatory for field interviews as well as interrogations. Inquisitive officers understand the legal limitations necessary to ensure proper foundations for gathering information. This chapter outlines fundamental concepts of interviewing techniques once officer safety considerations have been ascertained.

INTRODUCTION TO LAW ENFORCEMENT INTERVIEWS

Police investigations involve gathering and evaluating information from both things and people. Of these, the more difficult is to acquire information from people. Properly collected and preserved, physical things such as weapons, fingerprints, and burglary tools speak for themselves without risk of perjury or impeachment. In contrast, people are strongly affected by many physical and emotional factors that can call into question the validity of the information they give to the police. Emotions can move a person to give incorrect information, to falsify, or simply forget what happened. Physical limitations, distances, or lighting can affect the accuracy of peoples' interpretations of events.

Officers trying to discover the truth must evaluate the information obtained from people very carefully. You must be able to recognize individual differences and limitations and be attuned to personal motives that prompt individuals to give information. When seeking information about a case, you must also use the necessary skills to persuade the uncooperative or obstinate witnesses to cooperate.

The interview is one way of obtaining information from people. Questioning is an important feature of interviewing, but the interview is much more than just asking questions. In essence, an interview is a conversation between a police officer and anyone other than a suspect who could provide information concerning a case under investigation. The interview is a conversation with a purpose, however. The police interview is designed and intended to discover information about people believed to have been involved in the crime or to obtain background information on a particular individual.

FIELD INQUIRY CONTACT

The police officer is in the people business, and people provide information. Thus a major function of the police officer's job is to obtain information from people. The field inquiry-contact report is one source of police information. This effective tool can be used with both adults and children.

Frequently an officer has occasion to investigate suspicious persons under suspicious circumstances. Such contacts often do not lead you to a probable cause determination that justifies an arrest, a search, or a seizure. In such instances, you are, however, justified in completing a field contact report, which documents the who, what, where, when, and why of the situation. The contact report is not a complaint; rather, it creates a record of the incident and provides information about the people, their vehicles, and the time and location of the contact. Such reports often help update known offender locator records and provide records for future use in investigations. A traffic ticket, especially late at night, provides much the same information and can be useful in identifying known offenders and placing them at, or near, the scene of an offense on that date.

Sources of Information

To obtain information, an officer must open lines of communication with informants, people living or working within the local patrol area, and other police officers. Your ability to make contact, establish rapport, and deal fairly with other people will relate directly to your ability to obtain information. In dealing with informants, you should understand the nature and purpose of the informant's information. The informant may expect cash or other rewards for information; in such cases, you must follow departmental guidelines and directives in handling such matters.

Many informants are merely good citizens who want to aid the police department in locating and identifying criminals. In such cases the informant may be credible, but you might use the information only to begin an investigation. Also make follow-up visits with such informants. These visits will assure the informant that you are acting on the information provided and will give the informant another opportunity to share additional information with you.

One of the officer's best sources of information is other police officers. Officers who are just going off duty can tell the officer coming on about any problems to be wary of, suspected criminal activity, and any other unusual situations the duty officer should know about. Members of the detective division, juvenile division, or other tactical units in the police department can be a major source of information for the on-duty police officer. Officers in each of the units of a police agency must work together closely and share information in order to achieve the overall agency goals.

THE POLICE INTERVIEW

An interview differs from an interrogation in several ways. The purpose of an interrogation is to determine the extent of a person's involvement in a particular offense. Thus the interrogation takes place between the officer and the suspect. The purpose of the interview is to collect all available facts about an incident, to substantiate information already obtained from other sources, or to provide additional information. The person the officer interviews could be the victim, the complainant, a witness, or any other person who might be able to help the police officer gain a better understanding of a case.

The capable interviewer is conscious of others' feelings and can read individual reactions to quickly determine an appropriate method for dealing with them. Your resourcefulness is quickly tested when an individual is uncooperative. Then you probe to find the reason for the reluctance in order to reverse the situation and gain cooperation. To do so, you may appeal to the person's pride, civic or patriotic duty, family interests, nationality, and even emotions and motives.

The skillful interviewer knows how not only to keep the subject talking but also to keep the talk focused on the problem at hand. Always maintain control of the interview, and do not allow it to be led away from the pertinent information. If you are interviewing someone about an incident, learn to answer a question with a question or to repeat or restate the comments of a talkative subject to confirm your understanding. You can also guide the reluctant subject by asking questions in the area you want to discuss.

Standardizing interviewing techniques into a set of rules is impossible. People's individuality does not permit a formal package of "dos" and "don'ts." You can, though, take heed of certain basic guidelines when preparing for an interview.

Interview Conditions

Generally speaking, the best and most appropriate time to conduct an interview is as soon after the event as possible. Circumstances often work against this, though, and then you must recognize the necessity to delay interviews. An example would be in the case of an emotionally upset person. If the person cannot settle down, postpone the interview. A direct relationship links emotions and memory—when emotions increase, memory decreases. For this reason you will get a better interview when the other person is relatively calm.

Physical discomfort also bears heavily on an interview. For example, a cold, hungry, sleepy, or otherwise uncomfortable person will not make a good interview subject. A person who is uncomfortable will be much more interested in the issue of comfort than in being questioned by a peace officer. Make every effort possible to prevent or eliminate any condition that distracts from your search for the truth. Let the interviewee rest and eat first, if such needs are evident. Furthermore, never awaken a person from a sound sleep to immediately begin an interview. A few hours' delay will enhance the value of any information you gain and is worth the wait in most cases.

Interview Setting

One major factor in conducting an interview is the location and proper setting of it. Of course, you can't always exercise choice in selecting an ideal place for an interview. In fact, the urgency of a situation often requires you to conduct an interview under almost all conditions, most less than ideal. For example, when investigating a traffic accident you must obtain as much information as quickly as possible right at the scene. In other serious situations, large crowds can gather, tempers can ignite, and emotions run free. Sometimes onlookers can hamper the investigation by eavesdropping and even contradicting witnesses' statements. Under such circumstances, obtaining an accurate and complete account of the incident is very difficult. The same holds true for the officer at the crime scene, who is somewhat at a disadvantage in having to interview witnesses while events are still fresh and clear in their minds.

In situations loaded with confusion and distractions, stick to those immediate concerns necessary to identify suspects, alert ·another officer, and find the initial details of the crime. In accident cases, immediately obtain the driver's identity, the extent of injuries, and so forth as well as some general information about the accident. In either situation, you can add more information through follow-up interviews conducted later under more favorable conditions.

When obtaining information at the accident or crime scene, where adverse conditions are present, adjust to a negative situation and do the best job possible. Some officers, though, have the chance to conduct an interview in better surroundings and fail to take full advantage of it. Often officers try to interview a person over a counter at police headquarters or in a hallway or in a meeting room. Any of these locations can be as distracting as a busy street. Phones ring, people pass, and the noises and general activity of a police station surround and distract from the interview.

In fact any location subject to outside interference detracts from an effective interview. When distraction and confusion work at the subject, it is extremely difficult to keep focused on the questions. Without privacy, the witness's fear of being overheard will outweigh any desire to speak freely. Third-party interruptions, ringing telephones, or other interferences can also derail the witness's train of thought.

An improper setting can disrupt thought processes and cloud the memory or destroy it entirely. Sometimes even a cooperative witness will temporarily forget the topic of conversation when interrupted by some outside interference or become nervous due to a lack of privacy.

Distractions also add to the overall emotional strain, which further handicaps the success of the interview. Tension can start when the interviewing officer notices that the person being questioned is more interested in the surrounding activities than in the interview. This may be natural for anyone in a new setting. Then the situation becomes aggravated when the subject fails to recall facts that are common knowledge, and this can add to the officer's irritation with the subject. The officer may think the witness is deliberately being uncooperative when in fact the real problem stems from the officer's poor judgment in selecting such a setting for the interview in the first place.

The need for privacy cannot be overemphasized. A conversation between more than two people is difficult, and when eavesdroppers are present, open conversation is virtually impossible. Both firmness and diplomacy are needed. Never hesitate to ask another officer for privacy in order to conduct an interview.

Interviewing Juveniles

Juvenile cases present special problems. The officer must inform the parents of the youth about the need to question their child, and they need to understand that their presence can create problems for the officer trying to reach the truth. When departmental policy mandates, a parent must be present during an interview of a juvenile. You can reduce the distracting effect of their presence by having the parent sit across the room from or behind the child. You can also achieve an atmosphere of privacy by having the parent sit just outside the room with the door open and the youth inside, back to the door. In this way the parent can witness the interview, yet the child is not overly distracted by the parent's presence.

Follow-Up Interviews

It is best to conduct routine follow-up interviews at the home or business of the person to be questioned. Ordinarily, the familiar surroundings will not distract the person or cause the cooperative person concern. In familiar settings, the interviewee can give full attention to the officer's questions and her or his responses.

Always make an appointment ahead of time to ensure that the person will be available. If securing a private place in the person's home or work place is impossible, postpone the interview until conditions are favorable.

In serious cases, it may be better to conduct the interview at the police station. This is especially true when you have an uncooperative witness or when the person you plan to question is known to be a friend of the suspect. The unfamiliar surroundings of the police station can cause anxiety and weaken the subject's resistance. At home or in other well-known surroundings, the reluctant witness is supported by the psychological reinforcement of familiar surroundings and could be strengthened in his or her reluctance. A strange location might weaken the witness's defenses.

Of course an ideal location for an interview is a private office equipped for just that purpose. Such quarters offer privacy and are free from distracting noises and phones. Such an interview office should have a desk and at least two comfortable chairs. It should also be well lighted, clean, and heated or cooled as needed. In such a setting, the officer can initiate the interview on a positive note.

Interview Objectives

The interviewing officer's immediate objective is to establish a good relationship that will aid communication. One simple way of achieving this goal is to eliminate barriers that divide. This means physical barriers such as a large desk, as well as the distance between the interviewer and the subject, even if they face one another in chairs. Any dividers also increase the social distance and so hinder communication.

In view of the fact that physical barriers and distance psychologically separate people, consider the furniture arrangement seriously in preparing for an interview. Seat the person you are interviewing along the same side of the desk as you. In the follow-up interview conducted at a witness's home or business address, do not seat yourself too far from the witness. As in the office interview, minimize physical distances.

Preparing for an Interview

The uniformed officer who thinks preparation for an interview is unnecessary often assumes that a special personal technique supercedes proper preparation. Such an attitude only makes the officer's lack of understanding highly apparent. Planning is crucial to the success of any venture, and the interview is certainly no exception.

Before starting an interview, first go over all the available information. An interview that wanders and lacks direction is seldom productive, and it reflects a lack of both information and preparedness. Under such circumstances, the reluctant witness who quickly recognizes your unpreparedness knows you are at a disadvantage. Likely the witness will voluntarily give only information you already have. An unprepared interviewer cannot control and direct the interview, and certainly an officer in this position will not be able to assess the value of information obtained.

The amount of background information necessary is directly related to the seriousness of the offense. The type of information sought and the attitude of the person interviewed also influence how much background data are necessary before the interview. Background information is less significant when dealing with a cooperative individual. The reverse is true with the reluctant witness, however.

In preparing for an interview, generally review all relevant case reports and evidence. Study each case in its entirety, and become thoroughly familiar with the evidence, the scene, and any earlier statements. In serious situations when there is sufficient time to prepare, develop personal information about the subject and secure as many facts as possible concerning the case. This thoroughness will impress the subject and will aid in evaluating the subject's personality. Furthermore such preparedness and knowledge put you in a better position to control the interview.

An interviewer's success is largely determined by attitudes and impressions formed during the first contact. If this contact is strained and awkward, the party being interviewed can feel distrustful and stifle the interview. Sarcasm, a curt dismissal of offered information, or outright rudeness will all expose the officer's attitude. Antagonism from the officer, whether real or implied, soon causes the subject to withdraw and become uncooperative. Make a determined effort to create a friendly, relaxed atmosphere that will put the subject at ease and lead to a good rapport.

Starting the Interview

Because the first contact creates such a strong impression, getting acquainted is a crucial part of the interview. The officer's initial approach can be either formal or informal, depending in part on the circumstances and person being interviewed. The introduction can begin with a pleasant greeting and a showing of credentials if you are not in uniform. Give the subject time to become accustomed to the surroundings and familiar with you. Trite remarks, especially concerning health and weather, will rarely generate any real interest. People enjoy talking about themselves and the things they care about. Such initial conversations should be relaxed, natural, and mutual. Never carry them on merely for form.

In developing rapport or establishing a harmonious contact, the officer sets the mood and pattern of the officer-subject relationship. You can enhance this relationship by showing sincere interest in the person to be interviewed. Anyone can recognize either shallowness or some type of "tough guy" approach from an officer, and these could create an unbridgeable gap. Be respectful, control personal feelings, show no reaction to anything the subject says, and demonstrate some understanding of the person being interviewed.

The ordinary citizen may find the police interview awkward and uncomfortable and may be unsure of what is expected. The newness of the surroundings can generate apprehension and even fear. Sometimes the mere presence of uniformed officers causes a witness to become overly cautious and to withhold information. The additional prospect of deeper involvement in a criminal case and the possibility of becoming a court witness can also influence witness cooperation.

The officer's personality and resourcefulness are sometimes severely tested during the preliminary phase of the interview. The uncooperative witness must be convinced that his or her testimony is necessary.

Conducting the Interview

Once the officer is satisfied that the witness is in a communicative mood, the focus should turn to the information being sought. You can now steer the interview toward the desired topic.

As the interviewing officer, always bear in mind that your primary purpose at this point is to keep the subject talking. From time to time you can pose specific questions to focus on the topic and keep the person talking. It is best to start, though, by allowing the subject to give you a complete account without interruption. You should be alert to catch inconsistencies and omissions during this recital.

Often an interviewer will find that what a person says is less important than the way in which it is said. What is *not* said can be significant, too. Recognize that appearances are often a key to what is going on inside a person, but apparent mistakes could be simply unintentional. Often a subsequent review clarifies these.

Sudden silence could indicate that the subject is deliberating whether or not to reveal certain information. Recognize and correctly interpret signals that suggest the conversation is becoming sensitive. Sudden confusion or uncertainty can signal touchy issues. When the interview reaches such a point, you could choose to review the entire sequence of topics that preceded the silence or apparent memory lapse.

Sometimes a witness may shift unexpectedly from the topic at hand to a completely unrelated subject. This behavior often indicates that the person is avoiding information too painful or embarrassing to get into. During interviews, attempts to withhold information due to guilt feelings often become manifest in sudden emotional outbursts of anger or indignation. Tactful, understanding, and sincere inquiry will often uncover the reason why a witness wants to evade a particular area of conversation.

You can often detect a subject's emotional stress through bodily responses. Nervous laughter, hand wringing, or twisting a handkerchief can express anxiety, tension, and apprehension. A change in skin color such as sudden blushing or paleness can indicate anger, fear, or embarrassment. Surprise shows as widened eyes, a dropping lower jaw, or a sudden glance at the interviewer. Noting such involuntary responses can be valuable since a person may be able to control his or her statements but can rarely manage to control all bodily responses at the same time.

Once the subject has begun to talk, do not interrupt. The slightest distraction can break the flow of conversation and hamper any intention to offer further information. Some witnesses feel reluctant to talk when they know their conversation is being recorded. This does not mean that you cannot make brief notes. Jotting down a name, a phrase, an address, or a phone number can be very useful, serving as reminders when additional and more detailed information is needed later.

Questions that are specific tend to divert and limit the interview rather than allow the subject to open up and tell the complete story. Direct questions can also indicate what you consider to be important. Nods or shows of approval after specific responses while ignoring others also tell the subject what you are interested in. Based on such cues, a witness may purposely omit important information, believing that you consider it unimportant. Once the witness has completed the initial narration, the skilled interviewer can then use direct questions to clarify or examine earlier statements.

Asking Questions

Most questions cannot be answered with a simple yes or no, and explanations are usually essential to learn all the facts. They can also open paths to more information. However, the yes-or-no type of question can help a reluctant witness get started since it leads to an answer of some sort but limits the answer as well. Keep in mind that some people will agree with the interviewer just to be agreeable or because they do not understand the question, and sometimes subjects agree because they are afraid to disagree. Simply because a subject agrees to a question does not necessarily mean the person is telling the truth.

Leading questions clue the desired answer with their phrasing. They can have the same effects as yes-no questions since they prompt a witness to say what she or he thinks the officer wants said.

To the inexperienced interviewer, rapid-fire questions appear to be appropriate, but the veteran investigator knows this type of questioning creates emotional tension. Beginning one question before the witness has finished the preceding one is not smart, only confusing. It can also provide an uncooperative subject a perfect opportunity to hide information simply by cutting off a full reply.

Allow the subject to talk without interruption. When the conversation slows or stops because the subject needs time to recall or even withhold the facts, the interviewer can use open-ended questions, the nondirective approach, or even long silent pauses to stimulate the subject's continued narration.

If you ask many questions early in the interview, you give the impression that you will ask about anything you want to know and, worse, that anything you do not ask about you probably are not interested in. By asking only a few questions leading into the conversation, you can give the subject the feeling that everything he or she says is important. Allow the response to flow freely, and hold off any questioning of the subject's narrative until it is finished.

Open-Ended Questions and Silences

Typical open-ended questions include such things as "Tell me what you saw" or "then what happened?" The general nature of this type of question promotes lengthy responses.

Use the silence that descends immediately as soon as conversation lags to keep the subject talking, or it may lead to you losing control of the situation. Many people find conversational gaps unsettling. During such a silent period, the inexperienced officer may become unnerved and put words in the subject's mouth. Or impatience may lead the officer to dominate the conversation or get upset. Long blank spaces in the conversation may embarrass the officer who feels responsible for keeping the conversation going. Given this attitude, the officer may jump in with some comment just to fill the gap. Some subjects know that if they are merely silent, this type of officer will step in and do more and more of the talking.

Fortunately, long pauses are usually equally embarrassing to the witness. Cultivate patience and wait. Soon the subject will resume the conversation and often actually volunteer additional information just to break the awkward silence.

Nondirective Interviewing

The nondirective approach is an interviewing technique that turns the subject's statements into questions that call for more information. To use this method, merely repeat the subject's last phrase, adding a rising inflection on the last word to change it into a question.

In conducting this type of interview, be careful to control your emotions and do not register either surprise or anxiety. Merely restate the subject's statements. This technique has the effect of drawing further information without providing the subject direction or restricting the subject's thinking, as direct questioning does.

Close of Interview

When it is apparent that the interview is ending, close the conversation in a friendly and courteous way. Never end the interview abruptly or with a curt dismissal. You might want to summarize what has been discussed and ask if the subject has anything else to add or emphasize. Express your appreciation for what the subject has done and for her or his valuable assistance. Such sincere expressions of courtesy during and after the interview not only create a favorable impression, but they also enhance the subject's willingness to cooperate. Courteous treatment of the subject or witness helps to ensure future cooperation if you need more interviews or the individual has to testify in court later on.

The general purpose of all interviews is to elicit information from the person being interviewed. In police work, the usual specific purpose is to obtain information about the maintenance of law and order. In short, the officer is concerned with information that will shed light on the commission of a crime and the identity of the person responsible for that crime.

INTERROGATION

Interrogation is one of the more useful tools of the police investigator because a valid confession can often mean the difference between conviction and acquittal. In recent years, though, the U.S. Supreme Court has dramatically redefined the legal guidelines for conducting the police interrogation. Granted that these court rulings call for police reappraisal and development of new procedures, they do not mean that police should restrain their investigative efforts. On the contrary, the responsibility remains the same though the task has become more challenging. The confession has not lost its evidentiary appeal, and at times it is the only solution to a crime. When admissible, a confession is the best proof of guilt. The purpose of interrogation is to determine the identity and responsibility for the offense and to obtain if possible a lawful confession or admission.

In contrast to a proper interrogation, a confession obtained in violation of constitutional and statutory restraints destroys the prosecution's position because it violates the law and cannot legally be used in evidence. A confession should never be used as a shortcut to close an investigation. The professional officer continues to seek additional evidence that will further connect a suspect to the offense. Such added effort pays big dividends and may provide the only incriminating facts if a confession is not allowed in evidence.

The *Miranda* Warnings

The Supreme Court's decisions challenging the legality of various police practices during interrogation have changed over the years. At one time a confession's voluntariness was the only test of its admissibility. Since then the Court has extended the arrested individual's right to counsel to the police station and has reinterpreted the constitutional guarantee that a person must be brought before a magistrate without unnecessary delay. The arrested person must also be warned of her or his constitutional right to remain silent.

In the case of *Miranda v. Arizona*, the Court ruled that the accused's right to counsel exists before the interrogation starts. It also held that the failure of the accused to request an attorney is not a waiver of rights, whereas the failure of the police to inform the suspect of his or her rights invalidates any confession they have obtained.

The *Miranda* decision established the rule that officers must give a felony suspect four pieces of information before interrogation: the suspect's right to remain silent, the information that anything the suspect says may be used against her or him, the suspect's right to counsel during the interrogation, and the suspect's right to appointed counsel. These are called the *Miranda* warnings.

These warnings are based on the Fifth and Sixth Amendments to the U.S. Constitution. The arrested person can, however, knowingly and intelligently waive these rights and agree to answer questions and make a statement. For evidence gained through an interrogation to be admitted into evidence against an accused, the prosecution must introduce proof at the trial that the warnings were given and the suspect responded with a voluntary waiver.

An arrested person must be taken before a magistrate in the

county where the arrest took place. The magistrate must then inform the arrested person of the accusation and of any affidavit filed in support of the accusation. In keeping with the *Miranda* requirements, as noted earlier, the magistrate must further inform the suspect of the right to choose a lawyer, the right to silence, the right to have counsel present during questioning, the right to appointed counsel if the suspect cannot afford to employ one, and the right to call an end to questioning at any time. The magistrate must further inform the arrested person of her or his right to an examining trial. Finally, the magistrate must tell the arrested person that she or he cannot be compelled to make any statement and that any statement made may be used in evidence later on. The magistrate must then allow the arrested person reasonable time and opportunity to consult an attorney, either appointed or retained, and to post bail if allowed by law.

A statement the accused makes can be allowed in evidence if it appears that the statement was freely and voluntarily given without compulsion or persuasion. To qualify as a written statement from the accused, the accused must sign the statement, or it must be in the accused's own handwriting. If the accused cannot write, he or she must place his or her mark on the statement. This must be witnessed by a person who is not a law enforcement officer. No written statement from the accused made during custodial interrogation will be admissible in court unless the face of the statement shows that all the warnings by the magistrate, discussed above, were administered to the suspect before any statement was made.

An oral statement by the accused made as a result of custodial interrogation can be used as evidence in a trial only for the purpose of impeachment. When officers make electronic recordings of the statements, which can include motion pictures, videotape, or other visual recording, these are accepted as evidence if, prior to the statement and during the recording, the accused is advised that a recording is being made. Further, before the statement, but also during the recording, an officer must warn the accused of her or his rights, discussed earlier, and the accused must waive those rights in accordance with the legal requirements, also discussed. The electronic device must be capable of making an accurate recording, the operator must be competent, and the recording must be accurate and without alteration. Two people must witness the statement, and all voices on the recording must be identified.

Every electronic recording of any statement an accused made

during custodial interrogation must be preserved until its destruction is permitted by order of a district court. It is not necessary for oral statements to meet these requirements in order to be admissible if they are found to be true and lead to the fruits or instruments of the crime.

A statement made by the accused is generally admissible when made willingly in open court at the trial, before a grand jury, at an examining trial, or when the statement is part of the *res gestae* of the offense or the arrest. Literally the term *res gestae* means "things done," and in practice it includes every relevant act or circumstance comprising an event. A *res gestae* declaration is a spontaneous exclamation and covers a situation that presents: (1) an unusual occurrence, (2) sufficient to produce a spontaneous and instinctive reaction, (3) under the shock of which certain words are uttered, and (4) without the intervention of conscious forethought, reflection, or deliberate design.

Oral statements not products of custodial interrogation are usually admissible in evidence. Voluntary statements—whether or not the result of custodial interrogation—that bear on the credibility of the accused as a witness or of any other statement may be admissible under law. Evidence an officer or other person obtains in violation of any provisions of the state or national constitutions or statutes will not be admitted in evidence against the accused on the trial of any criminal offense.

Conducting the Interrogation

The interrogation should be conducted as soon as possible after the commission of the crime. Question each person individually, and allow none of the suspects to hear the questioning of the others. If possible, officers should interview the principal witnesses, especially the most trustworthy ones, before they interrogate the suspect, so that the interrogating officer can be adequately informed and prepared. The method of questioning varies widely according to the mentality of the questioned individual, the suspect's age and race, sex, religious and political views, social status, and education. The effective interrogator has a keen understanding of human behavior and so can comprehend the psychology of the questioned person.

Questioning should be fair, legitimate, and unprejudiced. The interrogator should be equally concerned about facts that work to the benefit of the suspect and those that serve to incriminate. The ability to be impartial and unbiased characterizes a skillful interrogator.

Before the suspect is questioned, officers should complete the preliminary investigation. They should examine the crime scene, collect and preserve the evidence, search the residence and office of the suspect, and gather as much information as possible. Before starting, the interrogator must know all the available facts thoroughly and be able to keep them together, an art that can be developed only through experience.

Whenever possible conduct the interrogation at the police station. Officers interrogating on their home ground have everything in their favor. In doing this, you will be in familiar surroundings, and you can plan the seating arrangement, the lighting, and other considerations ahead of time to your advantage. Regardless of whether the suspect was brought to the station or came in response to an "invitation," once there the suspect has already yielded, and you have technically taken command. The opposite is true if you go to the suspect's home or office.

In interesting cases, fellow officers, commanding officers, or even the chief may want to sit in on the interrogation. Although there might be some valid exceptions, this is not a good practice and should be discouraged. As much as possible interrogations should be uninterrupted, with no telephone calls or curiosity seekers. In general, conduct the interrogation in complete privacy, have the written statement typed, and then call in witnesses to hear the statement read.

In many cases mental notes are very important, particularly in "hot" cases when the officer interrogates right at the crime scene. Write these notes down as soon as possible afterward. Also make mental notes during the preliminary interrogations. Even though as the interrogating officer you are well prepared with full knowledge of the case and the suspect, it is generally desirable to lead the suspect into easy conversation. Allow the suspect to tell a complete story first in detail with no contradiction from you. Of course, it may be necessary to lead an unwilling talker along by suggestions, but it should be the suspect's story exclusively at the beginning. During this initial phase, refrain from making written notes. Often when seeing a record being made during this first statement, the witness tends to become wary and will not talk freely. It is generally desirable to assume an interested attitude during this first telling of the story and to make sharp mental notes. If sound recording is available or a concealed stenographer can be used, that is fine, but ordinarily you should not take notes during the preliminary discussion with the suspect.

The officer can then follow the first story with a comment such as, "Now let me get this straight," and then write up the statement in detail. If you have been alert during the first telling of the story, discrepancies in its second telling will pop out, but you should not, as a general rule, point them out until the full second story is finished.

At this point, the officer is in a position to go back and challenge the suspect on contradictory statements, using mental notes, written notes, and whatever additional knowledge of the case and the suspect is available.

Technical Support

Sound recordings of conversations have many advantages over shorthand notes. To begin with, they are likely to be more accurate, and they are less likely to be challenged in court. By their very nature, they clearly refute any implications that involved officers used "third-degree" tactics.

Law enforcement professionals use the polygraph as a psychological wedge in interrogation. It should not be used by an officer unskilled in interrogation. Of the several varieties of polygraph instruments, the most widely used is the instrument that traces and records blood pressure, respiration, and pulse rate. The principle this instrument operates on is that under emotional strain, a person's blood pressure and pulse rate will increase.

Opinions or results of polygraph examinations themselves are not admissible in court; however, confessions obtained through the use of the polygraph are admissible. If properly used, the polygraph can be very helpful in securing confessions and in eliminating suspects. Best used as an investigative aid, it must still be supported by good interrogation techniques.

The only way officers learn to interrogate is by practicing the art. The new officer will have many opportunities to test methods on complainants, witnesses, and citizens. Cultivating the ability to strike a response from the average citizen helps develop your ability to do interrogation.

When an interview or interrogation is concluded, review the case with a view to learning something from the experience, whether it was good or bad. If successful, what made it work? If unsuccessful, what were the reasons? What might have worked that you did not try? It is a good idea to maintain a list of procedures that have been successful and constantly review and add to this list.

Confessions and the *Corpus Delicti* Rule

The signed confession is a strong piece of evidence that will be admissible at a court of law *if* the statement can be supported by independent evidence. This rule of law, called the *corpus delicti* rule, prevents a confession alone from becoming evidence beyond a reasonable doubt without supporting evidence. Whenever a confession is given, the suspect's statements must be verified. If the suspect's confession states that tools used to commit the crime are hidden in a particular place, obtain a search warrant and look in the area the confession indicates. Finding the tools where the suspect stated they would be tends to corroborate the suspect's statement, and thus the tools become independent evidence that the confession is a true statement. Once admitted as evidence, the confession and supporting evidence will weigh heavily with the jury that is making a deliberation in a criminal case.

KEY TERMS

Confession
Corpus delicti rule
Custody arrest
Field inquiry contact
Interrogation
Interview
Miranda warning
Nondirective interview
Open-ended questions
Res gestae statements

STUDY QUESTIONS

1. What is the difference between an interview and an interrogation?

2. List eight different types of people whom you might interview for the purpose of gathering information.

3. When is the best and most appropriate time to conduct an interview? Justify your answer.

4. Why should you avoid interviewing someone who has just awakened from sleeping?

5. Why should you avoid interviewing potential witnesses in a hallway at police headquarters?

6. If you intend to use an office to conduct an interview, should you ask other officers to leave or remain in the room while gathering information? Justify your answer.

7. Describe how you would conduct an interview with a juvenile.

8. Where should a follow-up interview be conducted? Why?

9. Describe the necessary preparation for conducting an interview or follow-up interview.

10. Describe the proper method to start an interview. What should you attempt to accomplish at this stage?

11. What is the significance of sudden silence while conducting a witness interview. What should you do if this happens?

12. What should you understand and do if a person shifts topics (changes the subject) during an interview?

13. What nonverbal signs or signals should tip you off that a person being interviewed is under emotional stress?

14. What kind of body language signs can tell you if a person is lying to you during an interview or interrogation?

15. Should you take notes while a witness is giving you a statement? Justify your answer.

16. Describe when the yes-or-no type of question should be used during an interview.

17. What are leading questions and when, if ever, should they be used in an interview?

18. Should you ask numerous questions at the beginning of an interview? Justify your answer.

19. What is an open-ended question, and how is it used in the interview?

20. Describe the nondirective interview.

21. Describe the best way to close an interview.

22. In order to obtain a legally admissible confession, what requirements must first be completed?

23. Outline the basic elements or rights in the *Miranda* warnings given to suspect(s) before interrogation.

24. Are the *Miranda* warnings required in every situation when a suspect is arrested? Justify your answer.

25. If a suspect tells you that he or she wants to talk with a lawyer before an interrogation or interview, what actions should you take? Justify your answer.

26. What does the term *res gestae* mean, and how does this concept apply to admissible statements?

27. What preliminary work should you do before conducting an interrogation?

28. When and how should note taking be used during an interrogation?

29. Where should interrogations take place? Justify your answer.

30. Can a tape recorder be used during an interrogation? Describe how and when this device should be effectively used.

31. If a suspect is showing signs (verbal or nonverbal) of lying during an interrogation, what should you do as the investigating officer? Justify your answer.

32. When and how should the polygraph be used when conducting an interrogation?

33. How does a polygraph work, and what can you do with information obtained from this instrument?

34. Why should you critique your actions after an interview or interrogation? What can you learn from this critique?

35. What is the *corpus delicti* rule, and how does it pertain to confessions?

ACTIVITIES

1. In a classroom situation, conduct both a poor interview and a good

interview. Members of the class can critique the interviews and replay the roles.

2. Role-play both a good and poor interrogation session, and have students critique the players.

7

Routine Patrol — Anything *but* Routine

Professional law enforcement officers know that routine patrol, per se, is anything *but* routine. Do not become predictable, complacent, or take chances that can lead to disaster. Professional patrol officers use patrol tactics and techniques designed to avert predictability and implement sound practices to effectively accomplish patrol responsibilities.

In time of trouble, the community looks to law enforcement officers for help. Whenever a person is threatened, afraid, lost, injured, or just unsure about safety, that person wants someone with ability, authority, knowledge, and skills to alleviate the crisis and restore peace and tranquility. The citizen looks for a person whom he or she can trust to be prompt, thorough, competent, and concerned; the citizen in trouble calls for a law enforcement officer. This chapter discusses procedures for responding to a wide variety of day-to-day "routine" service calls. We caution you *never* to treat any call as routine. Preliminary suggestions are outlined as a beginning point for tactics that may be employed by patrol officers for safety and efficiency.

Specifically, this chapter outlines patrol responsibilities in traffic direction and control; requests for services; handling sick, injured, and lost people; repossessions; landlord-tenant disputes; labor disputes; disputes over services; animal cases; and miscellaneous services. Other chapters in this text expand topics in special cases related to other aspects of "routine" patrol.

TRAFFIC CONTROL

Directing pedestrian and vehicular traffic safely and properly is a precise and demanding task for any patrol officer. At no other time are your communication skills so tested. While controlling the movements of pedestrians and vehicular traffic, you must be able to convey directions not only verbally but also through hand signals and proper use of the police whistle.

In today's highly mobile society, the circulation of vehicular traffic creates hazards that cause injury and death to many, not to mention property damage from accidents. Encouraging the smooth flow of all types of traffic greatly reduces chances of accidents and injuries. Officers assigned the job of traffic direction must be able to think clearly and react quickly to changing traffic situations. You must be able to control and assist a turning vehicle to avoid collisions as well as control pedestrians crossing in traffic. In addition, traffic control officers assist various forms of emergency traffic to move them quickly and safely through heavy traffic areas. As a traffic controller, your skills in communications and patience will be tested; your positive performance at this demanding task will reflect an ability to promote good community relations and prevent accidents.

The Uniform and Equipment

As with most other types of work, the traffic controller has tools to learn about in order to perform effectively. And the department will require certain standards of dress that could vary with the times of day and night.

Daylight. When directing traffic during the day, the uniform readily identifies the officer to the motorists and pedestrians. Always wear the complete uniform, including the police hat, while directing traffic, in order to be conspicuous to the public. During rainy weather, wear a distinctive raincoat and hat cover that are a bright color, such as yellow or orange, so that everyone can see you easily as the light level dims. Rain gear should provide protection and comfort. Distractions such as rain running down the back of the neck or a wet uniform can prevent you from concentrating on legitimate duties. For the same reasons, wear a distinctive coat or jacket during cold weather.

The officer should have other items of equipment readily available, and one of the most useful tools is the police whistle. In addition, carry a means of communication—a portable two-way radio—at all times. You might also carry flares or traffic cones in the patrol vehicle; though not normally used to direct traffic during the daytime, these items will be needed at accident scenes and under exceptional circumstances.

Nighttime Circulation Control. During nighttime traffic control operations, the traffic control officer's major concern is being visible to the motoring public. Just as with daytime operations, the officer should wear all the items of the standard police uniform; however, most police uniforms are dark, and you should do everything within department regulations to make yourself more visible when controlling traffic circulation at night. For example, wear a reflective vest and hat cover; these uniform items should be bright orange or yellow, with strips of reflective material that form a distinctive pattern. Also use white gloves at night to make hand signals more visible.

A traffic wand (a colored cone that attaches to the flashlight) is a must for directing traffic during darkness. The cone should be a color that the motoring public can distinguish easily. Use this "wand" as an extension of your hand when giving traffic directions during adverse light conditions.

Stationary traffic cones and flares can greatly aid the traffic control officer working at night because they warn motorists in advance that they are approaching an unusual traffic situation. You can also use cones and flares to divert traffic and/or create traffic patterns that facilitate the job while maintaining a safe flow of traffic.

During inclement weather, be prepared to adapt appropriate uniform items as needed. In each instance, your visibility to the motoring public is of prime importance when selecting uniform items.

Protective gloves (with attached reflective material), additional batteries, replacement bulbs for the flashlight, and a spare whistle are all
items that you would want readily available.

Roadway Position

Generally there are two acceptable positions an officer can take at an
intersection when directing traffic: the center position and the corner
position. The decision is then based on which position permits the
officer to best see and be seen by all motorists approaching the
intersection. Furthermore, you should consider the types of manual
control devices available to operate an official traffic control signal,
the layout of the intersection, and the amount of traffic direction
needed.

Center Position. The center position affords the officer the most
visibility to approaching traffic, but it is also the most dangerous
position, because vehicles pass close by on both sides. Be very careful
to keep in an area where vehicles should not be driving. The center
position does, however, limit your ability to communicate with pedestrians on the nearby sidewalks.

Corner Position. The corner position offers a better margin of
personal safety, but this position does not permit the officer to control
circulation effectively unless the intersection's construction dictates
that the corner position is best suited to this control point—such as a
T-intersection. In another situation, you would assume the corner
position if using a manual control device as an operational official
traffic control device to assist peak-hour traffic.

In dealing with pedestrian circulation, the corner position provides the officer better opportunities to communicate with nearby
individuals. The safety of each person, whether in a vehicle or not,
should be your first concern. In some instances, you will need to
modify these positions to effectively control the flow of traffic.

Traffic Controls and Hand Signals

Once positioned in the intersection, the officer communicates with
motorists and pedestrians through hand signals, the whistle, and
occasional verbal commands. Concentrate on the traffic flow, use

good judgment, think clearly, and use precise signals that do not confuse the motorists. At the same time, maintain a calm, professional attitude in dealing with passersby. All your skills in community relations will be challenged during these operations, and your training, patience, and professionalism will help develop the department's positive public image.

Stopping Vehicular Traffic. When preparing to stop vehicular traffic, the officer must select which vehicle to stop. Try to find a natural break in the traffic flow. You would be wise to avoid stopping trucks or buses that then become the first vehicles in the line of traffic. Such vehicles take longer to stop and more time to get under way once allowed to continue through the intersection .In addition, these vehicles can block the view of other vehicles or pedestrians in the immediate vicinity and cause additional problems to the traffic director.

Having determined which vehicle in the lane of traffic to stop, point and look at that vehicle. After gaining the driver's attention, raise a hand with the palm facing this driver (see Figure 7-1). Simultaneously, blow one long blast with the whistle to command the driver to bring the vehicle to a stop. Maintain the hand position until the vehicle stops. To give cross-street traffic the right of way, stop both directions of traffic; however, because you cannot look both ways at once, stop the traffic coming from one direction first, then the other. Having halted traffic with one hand, hold that hand in the "stop position" and turn your attention to the other side and repeat the process. Do *not* lower either arm until cars coming from both directions are stopped.

Figure 7-1
The correct position and actions to stop a vehicle

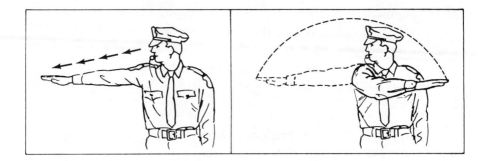

Figure 7-2
The correct position and arm action for starting a lane of traffic

Starting Traffic. To start a lane of traffic moving forward involves hand-and-eye coordination along with proper use of the police whistle. The same traffic direction tactics will also keep traffic moving through the intersection or traffic control area.

To start traffic, stand parallel to the lanes of vehicular traffic to be controlled and look at the motorists and at the same time point at the lead driver. Then turn palm inward and bend your arm at the elbow, bringing your hand to in front of your face and across the chin (see Figure 7-2). Simultaneous with the hand movement, blow two short blasts on the police whistle. To start traffic in the opposite direction moving, use the same technique except that, when bending the elbow, direct the palm of your hand behind you head and terminate the movement by touching the top of your shoulder. Repeat these movements as needed to keep traffic flowing through the traffic point.

Vehicles Turning Left and Right. Vehicles turning left and right at intersections create special problems for the traffic control officer. To avoid misunderstandings between the officer and the vehicle's driver, the officer's signals must be clear and precise. As vehicles approach the intersection, be alert for any turn signal indications the vehicle operator makes; the signal for intent to turn may be a mechanically operated signal light or hand signal. On observing the turn indication, make sure that the requested change of direction can be made safely before motioning the vehicle to turn. If the turn cannot be executed safely, either stop the vehicle—by displaying the hand, palm out, toward the operator with the arm extended—or direct the operator to proceed on through the intersection with the proper signal

Figure 7-3
The correct position and arm actions to signal a safe turn

for through traffic. Use the police whistle to reinforce the direction given: that is, one long blast of the whistle to stop, or two short blasts for the motorist to proceed straight through the intersection.

If the turning movement is permissible and safe, first point to the driver seeking to turn and allow enough time for the driver to recognize the gesture. Then swing your pointing arm to the direction that the turn is to be made and repeat the movement as often as needed to make the traffic flow smoothly (see Figure 7-3a).

Vehicles turning left at intersections can create especially hazardous situations since they must cross in front of opposing lines of traffic. Vehicles that are already stopped and awaiting directions offer the safest opportunities for controlling traffic turning left. Display a stop signal to one direction of traffic. Then, while holding the stop signal in place, motion the opposing vehicles to make the left turn (see Figure 7-3b). If appropriate, you might want to hold the through traffic on both sides of the roadway while permitting left turns from both sides.

The Police Whistle. The police whistle is an invaluable tool when controlling vehicular or pedestrian traffic. As discussed, the whistle can reinforce directions to stop (one long blast) or to start moving (two short blasts). To get the attention of traffic approaching the intersection, blow a series of three or more short blasts. The whistle should not be used alone, though, as it is intended to bring attention of all traffic to bear on you and your hand signals and directions. When the whistle and hand signals are used together correctly, they are effective and easily understood.

Voice Commands. Officers do not usually use voice commands to direct traffic because they can be misunderstood; and also, the wrong person could react to the command. Using voice commands makes it more difficult to direct a specific person or driver in areas of heavy circulation. Frequently you would have to shout to be heard, and shouting easily angers most people. When it becomes necessary to use a voice command, get as close as possible to the relevant person or driver and deliver the verbal message in a polite and professional way, seeking the voluntary cooperation of the individual.

Traffic control situations offer opportunities to either improve or destroy community relations. The frustrations and anxiety of the traffic control duty tax the officer's patience, yet to gain motorist and pedestrian support the officer must avoid profanity or abusive tones and language. Most citizens will try to cooperate with an officer in an intersection because they can clearly see how demanding and confusing the situation could become, but motorists will quickly become resentful toward a traffic controller who refuses to handle an intersection in a polite and professional way. Capitalize on this unique opportunity to promote good public relations as a respected public servant. Do not shout or lose your temper, even though provoked. A *polite* and *brief* explanation of the command will gain the citizen's cooperation.

Using a Traffic Wand. The only difference between directing traffic with a traffic wand at night and using hand signals during the day is the way in which the officer directs motorists to stop their vehicles. To stop traffic with the wand, face the direction of the flow and hold the traffic wand at about chest level in front of your body. Then begin to wave the wand from side to side with slow, deliberate movements. Avoid any rapid back-and-forth motions with the wand, as such actions can confuse motorists. In addition, do not stand in the flow of traffic or directly in front of approaching traffic. Use the police whistle along with the wand, as described earlier.

Controlling Traffic with More Than One Officer

It is easy for drivers who see more than one officer at an intersection to become confused if the officers do not work the intersection properly. Before assuming the traffic control spot in the intersection, the officers should decide which one is the "commanding" officer. Once designated, the commanding officer becomes responsible for making decisions about which lanes of traffic are to start, stop, or turn. It is also the commanding officer's responsibility to decide when traffic stops.

The assisting traffic controller takes order from the commanding officer at the traffic control point. The second officer might help keep opposing lanes of traffic either stopped or moving as the situation dictates. The assisting officer could also inform the commanding officer of special situations and/or dangers that might not have come to the attention of the controlling officer. When two officers are controlling circulation flow, each officer must work as part of a coordinated effort to ensure safe, expedient movement of the traffic through the intersection.

Traffic Flow Priorities

When directing traffic flow at an intersection, be aware of the types of traffic approaching the intersection as well as of special situations that could affect control. Emergency traffic of any kind should always be given first priority. Whenever possible, try to clear the approach for the emergency vehicle by directing vehicles in the same traffic lane to positions of safety out of the way. Then make all other traffic halt while signalling the emergency vehicle to proceed through the intersection.

The next highest priority of traffic flow is the traffic lane with the most vehicles awaiting direction. Direct this lane of traffic to proceed, using the techniques already discussed in turning and/or starting. Keep these lanes moving as much as possible to avoid spillbacks into other intersections and to avoid traffic jams. Once these heavier lanes of traffic have thinned out, move the remainder of the traffic lanes. If the amount of traffic is about the same for each direction, allow each traffic lane to move in turn, giving each direction about the same amount of running time. Such movements and interchanges of traffic flow should keep traffic moving in a sane and orderly way, which encourages maximum cooperation from motorists.

Highway Flares

When used efficiently and safely, highway flares alert motorists to a hazardous collision scene or special traffic control situation. Flares can greatly help the traffic controller to slow traffic and prevent other collisions. Seek professional training in safely lighting and extinguishing flares. It is absolutely necessary to learn and understand special hazards associated with the use of flares. For example, using flares around combustible materials can easily result in an explosion or start an uncontrolled fire. In addition, use of flares in a high-risk area such as brush and forest can easily expand into major fire incidents. In such cases, ropes, barricades, traffic triangles, or other devices may be implemented in a safer manner. Ultimately, common sense and good judgment must prevail. The professional officer understands when, where, and how to use special equipment to expedite and safely control all traffic situations.

REQUESTS FOR SERVICES

By virtue of its mission the law enforcement agency is organized for community service, and the agency needs to be cognizant of its community service requirements in planning delivery of services. During planning, the agency attempts to define and categorize specific ongoing services inherent to that community; then it specifies departmental policy to standardize police action.

A cry for help carries a high priority for law enforcement. Whenever a person is sick, injured, or disabled to the point that he or she can no longer care for him- or herself, the police are frequently called to render aid and assistance. The responding patrol officer must be prompt, capable, compassionate, and reassuring in dealing with such cases.

Patrol officers are usually the first emergency responders to arrive at the scene of a violent accident or crime. For this reason, patrol beats are designed to fit the needs of specific geographical areas conducive to prompt response. The officers' ability to help the injured can be a matter of life or death. So professional officers must gain a vast knowledge of first-aid techniques and must be able to use life-saving methods when the need arises.

Law Enforcement Activities

Officers on patrol are constantly aware that every minute of the duty day holds potential for excitement; however, veteran officers also know that not every minute is "action packed." Law enforcement patrol involves many varied activities, ranging from calls for service, traffic direction and control, and information services, to developing contacts, conducting preliminary investigations, collecting and preserving evidence, arresting offenders, and testifying in court. The officer is a "reporter" who must prepare a clear, concise, detailed record of what transpires.

Requests for Aid

In time of crisis, the community looks to the law enforcement officer for help. Whenever a person is threatened, afraid, injured, or just unsure about safety, that person wants someone with ability, authority, knowledge, and skills to alleviate the crisis and restore peace and tranquility. The citizen looks for a person whom he or she can trust to be prompt, thorough, competent, and concerned; the citizen in trouble calls for a peace officer.

A cry for help carries a high priority for a police agency. Whenever a person is so sick, injured, or disabled that he or she can no longer care for him- or herself, a peace officer is frequently called to render aid and assistance. The call may relate to an individual who threatens suicide, a woman who is about to have a baby, an assault, or criminal homicide. The responding patrol officer must be prompt, capable, compassionate, and reassuring in dealing with such cases.

For most people, picking up a telephone, dialing the police department, and asking for assistance is a traumatic experience. To that person, the call for help is the most important—and sometimes the most embarrassing—event of that day. The responding law enforcement officer must handle the call with dispatch, professionalism, and empathy for the person in trouble. Any indication of lack of concern for the complainant's problem on the officer's behalf can result in the citizen's losing respect for the police department and its ability to carry out the police mission.

You must take special care in handling the elderly and children. Elderly people may no longer be able to help themselves due to age or physical disabilities; an elderly person who falls from a bed and is not able to get back into bed without help might call a peace officer. A child may be injured or hurt and not know what to do or how to get help. You must know how to handle each situation and be able to restore calm and offer reassurance. The manner in which you respond to such situations not only will save lives but also will allow each person to retain personal dignity and reinforce the public's faith in the police department's ability to handle emergencies.

Law enforcement officers frequently handle medical emergencies as a routine part of the job, and they should have a thorough knowledge of practical first aid methods. General procedures designed to start the breathing, stop the bleeding, prevent shock, and cardio-pulmonary resuscitation (CPR) are basic techniques that each officer should become extremely familiar with.

Some calls you may respond to can involve a death. Never just assume that death has occurred; some conditions, such as electric shock and poisoning, can simulate death. Always check the victim for life signs and summon emergency medical assistance if even the slightest chance exists that the victim is alive. Some of the more common signs to check in determining or establishing death are (1) lack of breathing, (2) absence of a heartbeat, (3) loss of flushing in the fingernails, (4) no reaction of pupil to light, (5) lack of tension or dull appearance of the eyeball, and (6) other obvious signs of death such as decapitation, postmortem lividity (a dark blue discoloring of body parts that are nearest the ground), rigor mortis (a stiffening of muscles of the body after death due to chemical changes that take place within the muscle tissue), or bloating (putrefaction) associated with the dead person.

Escort Services

During the tour of duty, you may provide many types of escort services. Such services may include ambulance escorts, emergency cases, fire equipment, money escorts, parades, funeral escorts, over-sized equipment and vehicles, and many others as needed. The police administration establishes local policies and procedures to limit and control the extent of such services. You may be called on to provide the actual escort or to provide support for other officers engaged in the escort. It is important to distinguish between emergency and routine escort services.

Emergency escort service requires the officer to provide a safe corridor for ambulances, emergency cases, and fire equipment that must travel in excess of the normal speed limit or execute unusual traffic maneuvers. The patrol unit, with its emergency audible and visual equipment turned on, becomes the vanguard for the emergency vehicles that follow. In this capacity, the patrol unit may not only serve to warn other motorists and alert them to the approaching danger, but also controls the speed and routes that the emergency vehicle can use on the roadway. On approaching an intersection or other hazardous situation, the patrol unit must slow down and ensure that all vehicles approaching the intersection area are aware of the emergency in progress. Other peace officers in the area can also help by establishing a temporary traffic control point at the intersection in advance of the approaching escort. Once the escort is safely past the hazardous area, the assisting officer returns to active patrol.

The officer providing emergency services has a serious responsibility to ensure that all highway users are not endangered by the escort. You must use due care and take proper precautions in each instance; failure to do so can lead to civil litigation against both you and your agency.

In some instances, you may observe a traffic violation and stop the violator only to discover that the driver is attempting to deliver an ill person or a woman in labor to the hospital. You must use discretion to determine whether to provide an escort or call for an ambulance. Realize that the driver may be feeling highly excitable and emotional and may not be able to rationally operate a motor vehicle. If you decide to provide an escort, explain the proposed route and speed to travel, instructing the driver to maintain a safe following distance as well as to slow down for intersections. Once the escort is in progress, proceed to the *nearest* hospital emergency room.

Generally speaking, do not carry a sick or injured person in the patrol vehicle to the hospital, because of the liability risk involved. In addition, if you decide to call for an ambulance, prevent the driver of the vehicle from following the ambulance to the hospital at an emergency speed. In such instances, the driver should be instructed to proceed at a normal speed, obeying all rules of the road; you might wish to proceed to the hospital with the driver at a normal speed, to ensure that he or she will arrive safely and not create a hazard on the roadway.

Once at the hospital, verify the nature of the emergency and the condition of the injured, sick, or pregnant person. Determine whether the injury or illness is from natural causes or from criminal behavior. If criminal activity is suspected, begin an investigation and properly report the incident. Occasionally you may determine that the alleged emergency was fabricated to cover up a traffic violation or other criminal behavior. In such an instance, take enforcement action regarding all violations, make an incident report, and consider whether to press criminal charges for making a "false official report" to a peace officer.

Nonemergency escorts such as money escorts, parades, oversized equipment, and funeral escorts are subject to departmental policy. The agency provides guidelines for the proper use of emergency visual equipment in such cases. Generally speaking, money escorts do not require emergency equipment. You normally follow the person requesting the escort to a bank or night depository, and that person must obey all traffic rules and regulations and should take the most direct route available to the destination. Be aware of any suspicious people nearby and wait until the bank depositor is safely inside the bank, or has completed the action of placing the bank bag in a night depository, before terminating the escort.

Parades, funeral escorts, and oversized vehicle escorts present special problems for the escorting officer. In such cases you normally use the emergency visual signal only, unless the audible equipment is needed to gain the attention of the operators of other motor vehicles on the roadway or at an intersection. In such situations, you control the speed of the escort as well as providing a safe corridor. Since many of these escorts travel slower than the normal flow of traffic, the lead officer should ascertain a safe speed. The officer should also determine the need for additional officers if it appears that the escort will involve a number of vehicles or if special hazards are anticipated.

Handling Sick and Injured People

A call for medical assistance may concern anything from an accidental cut on the hand, to a homicide. The nature and extent of the illness or injury are usually not known until officers arrive on the scene. Of extreme importance is the responding officer's conduct. If you are competent and knowledgeable, you may well save a life. But if you are indecisive or careless, fail to control the situation, or—due to lack of training—fail to render proper first aid, serious consequences could result.

Before arriving at the scene, prepare mentally for the call—the situation may not be what you expect. Like most people, officers can be shocked and sickened by the sight of a mutilated or dismembered body. Prepare yourself beforehand to reduce any initial shock.

Citizens look to peace officers for leadership and expect officers to take decisive action. You cannot afford to become temporarily incapacitated by the shock of an unpleasant occurrence. Instead, prepare yourself by understanding

1. Your agency's policy on rendering aid to an injured or sick person
2. The agency's policy on transporting an injured or sick person
3. Locations of hospitals or emergency centers in the area
4. The extent of first aid that officers should give to the injured or sick
5. The agency's procedures for obtaining an ambulance in emergency situations

Generally speaking, all peace officers receive a course in first aid and CPR during training. These skills and techniques should be refreshed every three years. Officers should take care to learn lifesaving techniques well and keep abreast of these specialized tactics designed to save lives.

DAY-TO-DAY "ROUTINE" ACTIVITIES

One of the most interesting aspects of patrol duty is that you never know what will happen next. Although not every minute is filled with excitement, the *anticipation* of what might occur next keeps officers "on their toes." Unusual occurrences and "crimes in progress" (see Chapters 11 and 9) play a part in unexpected patrol activities. However, officers more frequently deal with a variety of "routine" activities that must be given full consideration and attention. Many of these assignments fall under the role of "service" to the community. Lost people (including children), repossessions, landlord-tenant disputes, labor disputes, alleged theft of services, news media relations, handling animal cases, and a wide variety of miscellaneous services are examples of such routine services. Although it's not exhaustive, this section helps you begin to develop a useful approach to *routine patrol*.

Lost People

Many people are "lost" each day, according to someone's definition. Many adults are absent from their homes voluntarily for personal reasons, though such an absence is not a law enforcement concern. Whenever a person seventeen years old or older is reported missing, law enforcement can conduct an inquiry to establish the circumstances of the incident. If an abduction or other criminal activity is not apparent, the police agency is not justified in conducting an investigation into the whereabouts of the missing person. Should an officer locate such a person who is voluntarily absent, the officer cannot make the person go home. The officer would be justified only in passing on the inquiry of the complainant and asking the "missing person" to make contact with the concerned party.

Lost people become a police matter when criminal abductions are involved. Law enforcement also becomes involved when children, the elderly, and incompetent people become lost. Kidnapping is the most frequent type of criminal abduction, and criminal investigations in such cases can become involved and difficult. In some cases of alleged kidnapping, civil custody suits of separated parents fighting over custody of children can result in one parent taking the child and fleeing.

Law enforcement agencies do become involved in looking for lost children, elderly people, or incompetent individuals soon after receiving a complaint. In such situations, the possibility of injury or harm to the lost person is the critical concern. Most police agencies give high priority to finding a lost child, and the child's age has a bearing on the depth of the investigation. In the event that a very young child is the object of the search, several peace officers may be immediately assigned to aid in looking for the child. The search for "lost" teenagers may be delegated to officers in the juvenile division as important but of lesser priority than that assigned to very young children.

Incompetent and elderly people may wander away from their homes or places of residence; such people may become truly lost and not know how to find their way back home. The peace officer's concern, compassion, and empathy in such inquiries is imperative in serving the police mission.

Repossessions

A repossession usually results because someone has defaulted on a conditional sales contract. For example, a person may purchase a vehicle by making time payments. While the buyer has possession of the automobile, the seller retains title to the unit until the contract is paid in full. Be extremely careful when handling requests for services when the seller is attempting to regain possession of the property because the buyer did not make payment. Your involvement is limited to keeping the peace in such instances. People who call for peace officers will probably want to use the officers as a lever on the other party involved—such a role must be avoided.

Civil law generally gives the seller, under a conditional or installment contract, the right to retake property in the event of the buyer's default. The sales contract usually contains specific clauses giving the seller the right to repossess under certain conditions. The U.S. Supreme Court has ruled that a notice and hearing are required before a seller can repossess property (*Fuentes v. Shevin*, 1972 407 U.S. 72). The usual practice of the seller is to have the buyer waive the right of notice and hearing in the contract of sale. The courts have held that these waivers are valid (*Overmeyer v. Frick*, 1972 405 U.S. 174, and *Swarb v. Lennox*, 1972 405 U.S. 191). Because of such practices, officers are likely to encounter irate buyers who have had no notice of any repossession proceedings prior to losing the vehicle.

The buyer has a right to object to the repossessor taking the property in question. This objection must be made before the repossessor has possession. For example, if the repossessor gets into an automobile, but does not move it, and the buyer objects, the repossessor does not have possession and cannot take possession. One court stated, "if the buyer is in personal possession of the automobile and protests against such repossession and attempts to obstruct the seller in doing so, under such circumstances, it becomes the duty of the seller to proceed no further . . . and to resort to legal process" (*Burgin v. Universal Credit Co.*, 1940 2 Wash. 2d 364, 98 P. 2d 29). Under ciivl law, the buyer's spouse has the same privilege as do other people entrusted with the property. In the event that repossession is complete and there is other personal property involved, the buyer has the right to retain the personal property, provided that the property is not an integral part of the repossessed property. Such items that may be reclaimed involve clothing, tools, and so on; however, the buyer has no right to remove an automobile radio or other item attached to the vehicle even if the item was purchased separately (known as *fixture law*).

In the event that the repossessor takes unattached property contained in a repossessed item, the repossessor is responsible for that property. The buyer has the right to recover his or her private property on demand. If the repossessor later refuses to return or disclaims knowledge of the existence of such personal property, the buyer may maintain a civil action to recover the value of such property (*Varela v. Wells Fargo Bank*, 1970, 15 Ca. App. 3d 741). In addition to separate private property, the buyer has the right to demand and get a receipt for attached personal property from the repossessor and may likewise recover such property or value at a later time.

When a third person has dominion and control over property in question, this person may exercise the same rights and privileges as the buyer against the repossessor. If the property, when discovered, is in a commercial parking lot where an attendant is on duty or in a checkstand, the repossessor has no right to take possession of the property. Under this circumstance, the third person has and keeps possession rights until redeemed by the buyer.

Peace officers responding to repossession calls should remember several points:

1. It is not the officer's responsibility to determine if there has been a notice and hearing or a waiver of notice and hearing.
2. Officers should not try to interpret the contract or get involved in any manner in private repossessions, except to keep the peace.
3. A person who makes a good faith repossession without complying with the notice and hearing requirements is subject to civil liability but not to criminal liability.
4. Assuming that there has been a waiver, the repossessor may retake property wherever he or she finds it, within limits:
   a. A repossessor has the right to go on private property to retake; however, in no event is he or she authorized to enter any building or enclosure without permission.
   b. The repossessor *may* retake an automobile from a driveway or furniture from an open porch.
5. The repossession act "has a tendency to excite a breach of the peace and invite violent resistance" (36 *ALR* [*American Law Review*] 853). The officer's presence should serve to maintain peace. As a rule, repossession is complete if the buyer has to pursue the repossessor in order to object.
6. Peace officers may be called on to exercise their good judgment as to whether movement of the property has been sufficient to give possession to the repossessor.

a. In order for the repossessor to have complete possession, the repossessor must exercise complete dominion and control over the property. For example, if the repossessor has moved an automobile from a driveway and into the street, the repossessor has possession and a right to retain possession against the buyer's objections.

b. If the repossessor does not have control and dominion over the property, and the buyer objects to removal of property, peace officers should advise the repossessor to seek civil remedy.

7. Repossessors are required to conduct themselves in a peaceful manner at all times. They may not commit an assault or cause a breach of the peace.

Repossessors are generally required to make immediate notification to the police by the most expeditious means available, announcing the repossession.

When a peace officer is called to settle a dispute involving repossession, the officer's primary goal is to prevent a breach of peace. Remember that the incident is strictly a civil matter, and in no event is an officer authorized to give legal advice. The parties involved should be directed to contact their respective attorneys for such advice.

At the scene of a repossession dispute, first ascertain the identity of the repossessor. The person usually has a company identification card, a private license, a copy of the contract, or a document describing the property to be repossessed. Then identify the other disputing party. If this person is the buyer, the buyer's spouse, or a third person in lawful possession, inquire whether or not this person objects to repossession. If he or she objects, the repossessor cannot take the property.

Occasionally, officers must take some positive action if a crime is committed in their presence during the dispute. The most common crimes arising at such times are assault, battery, disturbing the peace, and malicious mischief. Even though a repossessor breaks a lock on a garage to retake property, an officer would probably be incorrect in attempting to charge burglary, since the intent to steal or commit a felony is normally not present. In this case, a lesser included offense such as malicious mischief may be more applicable.

Buyers often want to report repossessed property as stolen—this frequently happens in the case of automobiles. For this reason, carefully inquire as to who has title and whether or not the buyer is delinquent in the payments before initiating a "stolen" report. Also, check through records and communications. If you reasonably conclude that the property has been repossessed, refer the buyer to the title holder.

In situations where the repossessor has not gained possession, advise the repossessor to seek civil remedy. This remedy consists of a "claim and delivery" action and the issuance of a writ of possession by the court; this writ is served by an officer of the court. A peace officer may be called to help a court officer. In such instances, the peace officer gives only such assistance as needed to prevent the commission of a crime.

Landlord-Tenant Disputes

In general, landlords and tenants enter into a rental contract agreement, which may be oral or written. The agreement gives the tenant temporary possession and use of the landlord's property for a specified amount of money for a specific period of time. In turn, the tenant agrees to return the property to the landlord at a future time. Generally, rents are paid in advance, and the landlord gives the tenant a receipt for the covered period of rental time. If a tenant contemplates moving, he or she usually gives the landlord advance notice of the intention to move. This notice is usually based on the period of time in which the tenant pays rent—day, week, or month.

In order for peace officers to effectively handle landlord-tenant disputes, officers must understand the applicable provisions governing these cases. Generally, try to avoid arrests and achieve a lasting solution to the dispute by explaining what conduct is not lawful and by suggesting alternative solutions that are lawful.

Unlawful Conduct by Landlord. A landlord's unlawful conduct may include tenant lockout, seizure of tenant's property, removal of doors and windows, and trespass. Even though the landlord may have proper legal grounds for evicting a tenant, it is unlawful for the landlord to use any of these methods in attempting to force a tenant to vacate the premises. The law regarding each act is presented briefly as follows.

When the tenant is behind in rent, a landlord may not jam or change the tenant's door lock in order to prevent the tenant's further use of the dwelling unit until the rent is paid.

It is not unusual for a landlord to seize a tenant's possessions in payment for past-due rent. It is also a seizure when the landlord locks the tenant out of the dwelling, since the tenant's possessions are thereby locked in. Generally, a landlord may not take possession of a tenant's property without first obtaining a court order allowing the landlord to do so in accordance with civil law.

Statutes clearly require that landlords obtain a lien (court order) prior to seizing the property of a tenant. Even with a lien, a landlord generally cannot seize any property necessary to the tenant's livelihood or any necessary household items (e.g., stove, refrigerator, tables, chairs, beds, or washing machines). If the landlord removes the doors or windows to the tenant's dwelling in an attempt to evict the tenant, or in any other way destroys the tenant's property, the landlord may be guilty of vandalism. Even though a landlord may thereby be destroying his or her own property, the courts have held that, since a tenant has a property interest in the premises, any such acts of destruction by the landlord constitute malicious mischief against the tenant.

In some instances, a landlord may enter a tenant's premises without permission from the tenant. If the entry is reasonable to effect repairs or for some other lawful purposes (to investigate smoke, etc.), the entry is not considered a trespass. In addition, if the tenant has consented by lease to the landlord's entry at will, then such entry is not a trespass. However, landlords often enter a tenant's premises without prior permission in order to harass the tenant or to snoop around. Such conduct is considered to be a trespass.

Peace officers can often help resolve a landlord-tenant dispute if they understand some basic legal principles and can inform the parties of their legal rights and obligations. If a permanent solution to the dispute can be found, officers may eliminate repeated calls and the possibility of a subsequent dispute leading to violence. The best legal way for a landlord to evict a tenant is by bringing an unlawful detainer action in court. There are several steps in this proceeding, involving "notice." If the tenant has violated any of the conditions of the lease or rental agreement (such as failing to pay the rent when due, keeping a pet when this is specifically prohibited, etc.), the landlord must generally give the tenant a three-day written notice to either correct the condition or move, before bringing an action in court to evict. In effect, this means that, if the tenant who is behind in the rent pays the total due within the three-day period, the landlord cannot evict.

To be on solid ground under the law, the landlord must give a copy of the notice to every adult to whom the premises were rented. In addition, the landlord must serve the tenant with a legally correct notice. Such forms are available at most large stationery stores.

A landlord has the right to terminate a month-to-month tenancy for almost any reason, even if the tenants have *not* violated any provisions of the rental agreement. To do this, the landlord must first serve the tenants with a written notice instructing them to vacate the premises in thirty days. If the tenants fail to move within the specified time period, the landlord must then bring an unlawful detainer action against them.

The landlord, however, is not without legal obligations. Landlords must keep the rental premises in a condition fit for human occupancy and must repair all defects that make the premises uninhabitable. This means that the landlord must provide

1. A structure that is weatherproof, water-proof, and rodent-proof
2. A workable plumbing system
3. One working toilet, bathtub, and bathroom sink
4. One working kitchen sink
5. Adequate heating facilities
6. Safe electrical wiring
7. Adequate garbage and trash storage and removal facilities

The landlord cannot waive these requirements by placing a burden to repair these facilities on the tenant as part of the condition of the lease.

The tenant has rights when the landlord fails to perform his or her responsibilities. If the landlord fails or refuses to correct the problem after being notified of the defect, the tenant has several alternative recourses. If the defective condition is a violation, the tenant should consider reporting the violation to the proper agency. Such an agency will investigate the defect and compel the landlord to correct the condition. If the problem is not handled by the housing authorities, the tenant should consider calling the local public health department for help. If all else fails, the tenant should seek advice and help from an attorney.

The peace officer's objective, when confronted with a typical landlord-tenant dispute, is not to make or encourage an arrest but rather to try to achieve a lasting solution to the conflict. By explaining what conduct is not lawful and by suggesting alternative solutions that are lawful, you can bring about a positive result. If you have responded to tenants' complaints that the landlord has locked them out, seized their property, removed the doors or windows to the premises, interfered with the use of their utilities, or unreasonably trespassed on the premises, you can often bring about a successful resolution to the dispute either by informing the landlord that he or she has committed a crime or by briefly explaining procedures for the landlord to bring an unlawful detainer action against the tenant. In some cases, the landlord may be unaware that his or her conduct is unlawful. First simply explain that the landlord's self-help measures are unlawful. If, however, the landlord is uncooperative (e.g., refusing to replace the tenant's doors and windows), you can explain that criminal proceedings can be initiated by the tenant.

If the tenant has a defective condition in the apartment, advise the tenant to explore the various *legal* alternatives that are open. Although you should not normally encourage an arrest, you should ultimately take whatever enforcement action is necessary under the circumstances. However, since most offenses are misdemeanors, you cannot arrest unless the offense occurred in your presence. If an on-the-spot arrest is warranted (such as for assaults), advise the appropriate party of requirements and procedures for a private person's or "citizen's" arrest.

Labor Disputes

Labor disputes are volatile situations that can evolve into major group problems (such as riots) if mishandled. Most group activities are noncriminal in nature. However, such situations can be difficult to handle, since intense emotions may be involved, and the parties can make unreasonable demands for law enforcement action. At such times, officers must remain cool-headed in the face of chaos and unreasonableness.

In responding to a labor dispute, get as much information as possible from communications or other reasonable sources. On arriving at the location, use a conservatie approach, listening for disturbances or other disorderly conduct. When contacting the participants, try to calm the situation. Frequently, the command presence of responding officers, along with assurances that officers will listen to both sides of the dispute and be objective, will help to keep the peace.

In dealing with the parties involved in the dispute, officers determine the facts, evaluate the situation, and take proper action. By talking to the parties individually, you can begin gathering facts. Although the idea is to keep the parties separated, you must not become isolated from your partner. Evaluation of the situation should determine the physical and emotional state of the participants, the condition of the property, the problem (criminal or civil), and what law enforcement action may be required.

Most labor disputes can be settled without arrests. As temper cools, so does the desire for prosecution. However, if an arrest is in order, you should determine proper probable cause for action. If the problem is criminal in nature, advise the victim of available courses of action. If civil remedies are in order, you can advise the parties to contact a private attorney, or to bring the matter up at the bargaining table, as appropriate.

Always use extreme caution in handling labor disputes. This type of call can be very dangerous, and many officers have been injured or killed. Since emotions are involved and actions are unpredictable, either party may attempt to use you to his or her own advantage. From your point of view, it is highly desirbale to settle the dispute as quickly as possible. The following typical legal provisions may be considered in applicable situations; however, check specific laws in your jurisdiction.

1. *"Trespassing."* This section may be applicable when trespassing or loitering is alleged near posted industrial property. However, understand that it is *not* considered trespassing for a labor union official to engage in *lawful* activities of a labor union, or to investigate working conditions with due *authorization.*

2. *"Loitering in Vicinity of Posted Property."* In accordance with the law, it is generally unlawful to loiter in the vicinity of another's property. However, this provision does not prohibit picketing in such immediate vicinity or any lawful activity by which the public is informed of the existence of an alleged labor dispute.

3. Investigate allegations by either management or union members that the other party is not abiding by a lawful court order.

4. Be alert for any activities that interfere with the operations of a business establishment. Illegal strike activity includes actions de-

signed to block entrances and exits to a business and forceful efforts to keep personnel or customers from entering the business.

5. Activities that interfere with orderly picketing by union members are likewise unlawful. Such actions may involve outside agitation, blocking off strike areas, and harassing picketers. Document each such allegation and seek to determine the validity of such allegations.

Disputes over Services

Occasionally, officers receive a call of a business dispute, petty theft, or disturbance that turns out to be an argument over payment for goods or services. These kinds of disputes are typically between a cab driver and the fare, a service station attendant and a customer, or a restaurant employee and a patron, but can involve any business-related enterprise. Typically, one party refuses to pay all or part of a bill for goods or services rendered or, conversely, one party is claiming to have made payment for goods or services not rendered or not rendered as promised. Frequently, one or both parties want the other party arrested (usually for theft) and want the officer to force payment or rendering of goods.

Investigating officers seek to determine whether refusal or inability to pay amounts to a "civil matter" only or whether a criminal violation has occurred. In many cases, the crime could not be called theft; however, some states, have a specific law for theft of service or "Defrauding Innkeeper." This is a public offense when any person deals unlawfully with a hotel, inn, restaurant, and so on. An act may consist of obtaining food, fuel, services, or accommodations without paying required fees; intent to defraud; obtaining credit and then absconding; or surreptitiously (or by force, menace, or threat) removing any part of one's baggage from such places with intent not to pay for the accommodations. Punishments for this offense vary with the value of the services or accommodations involved.

Responding officers should first be concerned with keeping the peace. After thoroughly investigating the allegations on both sides, determine if a violation of the penal code has occurred. However, it is extremely important not to take sides. You can explain what the law requires in order for a crime to occur. However, do not let a disputant use you to compel payments or similar action by any party. In addition, do not use the threat of arrest or other police action to compel civil action by either party. If the parties cannot or will not informally resolve their dispute, advise them to exchange identifying information and to contact their attorneys, or file a small-claims suit, or other appropriate action.

If you feel that a criminal action *might* be involved, but a definite crime cannot be established, contact a supervisor. Before leaving the scene, ensure that the dispute is sufficiently settled to preclude further confrontation between the parties.

Handling Animal Cases

A law enforcement officer is usually the first public official called whenever a person has been injured by an animal bite. This condition can be extremely serious, because the animal may be rabid. The officer must determine what action can be taken.

The officer's primary responsibility is the safety of the public. Once you have determined that a specific animal has bitten a person, the animal should be confined if possible in a manner that will keep the animal from further injuring people. If an animal is held for observation, try to identify and notify the animal's owner of the disposition and observation period. Many animals are valuable to their owners (even if the value is strictly sentimental), and you should seek to protect the property when possible.

A decision to destroy an animal, if necessary, is governed by *departmental policy*. Each agency establishes its own departmental policy concerning sick, injured, or vicious animals. Before taking the drastic measure of destroying such an animal, you must understand and abide by your agency's guidelines. Although guidelines do vary in specific language, generally a few provisions are common for handling animal cases:

1. If the animal poses no immediate threat to people, property, or its own well-being, contact an agency that specifically deals with animal cases, such as the Humane Society, department of animal control, or health department.
2. If the animal *does* present an immediate threat, try to isolate the animal until a representative from the proper department arrives.
3. If all possible alternatives have been exhausted, and a decision to destroy an animal is reached in accordance with departmen-

tal policy, seek the most humane method of handling the situation that will not anger public sentiment.

Officers can contact various groups to help remove animals from a location. The department of animal control will handle all types and sizes of animals in distress, including those that endanger people or property. The Society for the Prevention of Cruelty to Animals (SPCA) can assist when the department of animal control cannot be contacted, or when requested by the owner. Some cities and counties operate local Humane Societies, in addition to the SPCA, which can be called on when needed.

Victims of animal bites should seek treatment. Officers at the scene should apply first aid if the situation warrants. If the animal in question is wild, try to locate and confine the animal (or keep it within sight) and notify animal control personnel immediately. Since rabies is the chief danger from wild and undomesticated animals, the victim should seek immediate medical attention.

Patrol Services

It is impossible to discuss all instances where an officer renders assistance. However, in addition to the situations already covered in this chapter, you may also be called on to provide many miscellaneous services during your tour of duty. The following items are examples of such services.

Inspections. The officer continually conducts security inspections of buildings, places, and people. The veteran officer has a well-developed sense of perception. While conducting security surveys, look over the exterior and interior of homes and buildings, watching for hazards, weakened security areas, and the "unusual." At times you may "feel" that something is not right; this sixth sense—developed through experience and perception—leads you to investigate. Many times the investigation reveals circumstances that are easily explained and are not abnormal. You frequently discover, however, that the unusual situation indicates a crime or problem that has gone unnoticed.

In checking the exteriors of buildings, be primarily concerned with points of entry at night or other times when the building is not open to the public. At nighttime the light from spotlights or flashlights will reflect back when pointed toward glass windows and doors. Light that does not reflect back may indicate the absence of glass—an open or broken window—and the possibility of a burglary in progress. Some burglars are crafty and may attempt to replace the broken glass to conceal their point of entry. At such times your sixth sense should reveal that the light did not reflect off the broken glass in the same way it reflects off smooth, unbroken glass, and this should prompt an investigation.

Doors should be examined for pry marks of broken locks. Many veteran officers can distinguish between old and recent pry marks. In some instances you may have seen the old pry marks for years, in which case these marks become the normal condition for that door; new or fresh pry marks would then be obvious. In some instances, you could be required to physically check a door to determine that it is, in fact, locked. In such situations, maintain a degree of stealth since the door could also be either unlocked or pried open. If the door is open, do not go into the building or residence alone, but wait for backup assistance while assuming a position of watchful surveillance from cover and concealment.

Assistance. Officers are called on to provide assistance in a number of noncriminal situations. For example, you might come on a stranded motorist, be asked to provide directions for out-of-town visitors, and listen to complaints from local citizens regarding city services. In each instance, be aware that you are an ambassador for the city, county, or state. Show empathy for each citizen contacted and provide as much reasonable assistance as possible in the given situation. Also be aware of city, county, or state agencies that provide emergency services. Organizations such as the Red Cross, Salvation Army, and United Way Services can render valuable assistance to stranded and needy people. Know where to contact such agencies and how to put the needy person in touch with people who can help.

When dealing with complaints regarding local services, the officer should first listen to the complainant and understand the nature of the problem. In some instances, you may be able to communicate the problem to the proper official; in many other cases, you should be able to direct the complainant to the best agency to handle the matter. In all cases, listen and be responsive to the complainant's problem. In many situations, the problem can be solved easily when someone in charge of a particular city service learns of the complaint. Certainly the complainant will know that an officer who tries to help solve the problem cares. In cases where you inform the city agency of the problem, recontact the complainant and advise the citizen of the action taken.

Reporting Hazards. While conducting preventive patrol, the officer must observe and report those things that may be conducive to crime. Such items can include poor or no lighting, broken windows, or improperly secured or unlocked doors and entrances. In taking action to notify business owners or the occupants of the discrepancy, you are involved in aggressive preventive patrol by making it more difficult for the criminal to achieve an objective. The ability to observe, recognize, and become aware of such out-of-the-ordinary elements can be learned and improved with practice.

Security Surveys. Many police departments offer help to community members by providing security surveys and guidance for neighborhood watch programs. Not only do such visits help the owner to secure his or her property, but the visits also serve to open lines of communication between the community and the law enforcement agency. The survey should be conducted from a checklist or other document that covers security barriers, building exteriors, and interior controls.

Security Barriers. Security barriers are designed to reduce criminal opportunity through "target hardening." Such barriers include fences, landscaping, and lighting. Advise the occupant if any such item is missing or deteriorated to the point that it is not a deterrent to criminal activity. You may advise the occupant to increase or add outside lighting equipment in areas where the property is especially vulnerable.

Building Exteriors. Moving from the curtilage (the area around a building) to the building itself, examine doors, windows, and other points of entry. An examination should include accessibility to the building through such entry points and security locks and deadbolts. In some instances, recommend that target-hardening hardware be installed to make entry more difficult for the criminal. You might suggest iron grating for windows that are easy targets for burglars because of the windows' accessibility or vulnerability. (*Note:* Do not recommend grating for bedrooms where the occupants might have to flee in the event of a fire; in these areas, suggest additional window locks.) Doors in buildings should be equipped with deadbolts; an additional safety device might include a small "peeper" viewing port installed in the door that permits the occupant to see outside before opening the door. Other entry points that might need examining are air-conditioning window or roof units, ladders that make the roof easily accessible, and patio doors. Each area should be checked for locking devices and vulnerabilities, with follow-up recommendations provided.

Interior Controls. Inside the building or residence, the officer should be concerned with locks, alarms, and other defense mechanisms. In a business establishment, inquire about methods the owner uses in setting alarms, locking safes, and securing the building before leaving. Try to find out how many people are involved in such procedures and if each such person is complying with the guidelines set up to secure the building. Make certain that the combination to the safe is not readily available to others and that the owner follows strict closing procedures each and every time.

Operation Identification. "Operation identification" has been a highly successful police program designed to identify property. The police department frequently makes available to the public engravers or other devices citizens can use to engrave or mark valuable property with the owner's driver's license number. In the event such items are lost or stolen, the identifying number can be quickly and easily traced to the owner.

Note that the owner's driver's license number is used, rather than a Social Security or other number. The driver's license number is quickly and easily identified through license records. Since the Social Security number is protected under the right-to-privacy laws, it is much more difficult to use for locating the owner.

Once the owner's property has been marked, the police department may provide the owner with window stickers alerting potential burglars that the property in that residence is protected by Operation Identification. The deterrent effect of this operation could prevent thousands of burglary attempts each day.

VEHICLE THEFTS

People who steal vehicles do so for a variety of reasons. Many automobile thefts are for pleasure. In fact, pleasure thefts account for the highest percentage of reported vehicle thefts—the vast majority being perpetrated by young people for "joy-riding." Vehicles stolen for pleasure are frequently abandoned after a few hours, normally before a theft report has been filed with the local law enforcement agency. Generally speaking, the thief who steals a vehicle for pleasure does not intend to keep the vehicle and may leave it either near the scene of the theft, close to the victim's home, or at the location where the fuel supply is exhausted. In some cases, the subject may leave the vehicle at the scene of an accident or where the vehicle breaks down. The thief who abandons the vehicle may replace it with another stolen vehicle for a return trip.

Some vehicles are stolen with the intent of committing other criminal acts. The thief's purpose may be to use the stolen vehicle in committing another crime and to subsequently abandon the vehicle. In this case, the vehicle is usually recovered within a short distance from the scene of the robbery, burglary, or other crime. The thief either transfers to another vehicle close by or simply walks away from the scene. However, some criminals may change the identity of the vehicle and use it as a "work car" for extended periods of time.

Most thefts for profit involve vehicle resale, stripping ("chop-shop") operations, and sale of component parts. Occasionally, the thief may alter the vehicle identification number (VIN) and repaint the automobile or truck. However, the VIN is more frequently replaced with a VIN from another vehicle, because altered VINs are easily discovered under close examination. If the vehicle is to be resold, the thief must provide apparently legitimate papers for the stolen vehicle. Figure 7-4 depicts the vehicle theft cycle.

Functions of the Beat Officer

Preventing vehicle thefts and recovering stolen vehicles are important functions of the beat patrol officer. Officers use aggresive patrol techniques to identify stolen vehicles and arrest thieves. An alert officer will note conditions indicating that a vehicle may be stolen. For example, new tags on a used vehicle, or old tags on a new vehicle, should arouse an officer's suspicion. Likewise, new tag bolts on an

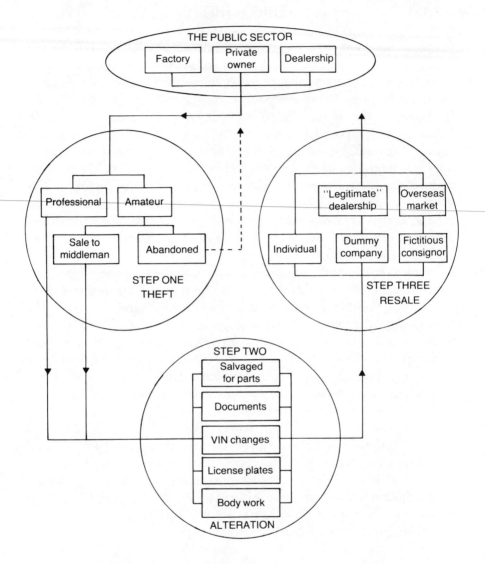

Figure 7-4
The vehicle theft cycle

older vehicle, or *vice versa*, may also indicate a need for further investigation. Other indications that a vehicle may be stolen include "dirty plates" on a clean car (or vice versa), license plates that are *wired* onto the vehicle, ignition wires hanging down from the dashboard, and recent registration of a used car advertised for sale. Occasionally, an officer may spot an abandoned vehicle that has not as yet been entered into the "wants" system. While the report may initially be negative, an officer may get a "hit" (indicating a stolen vehicle) by checking back at a later time. Even though the initial report is negative, a suspicious officer may wish to obtain registration information and contact the registered owner to determine if he or she is aware of the vehicle's location. Aggressive patrol officers should understand the vehicle theft cycle (see Figure 7-4) to learn other inventive ways of discovering stolen vehicles.

Patrol Observation Techniques

Patrol officers use many observation techniques to locate stolen vehicles. The following items are only a few indicators of a stolen vehicle:

1. Is the vehicle on the "hot" or "wanted" sheet?
2. Does the vehicle display license plates that have been reported stolen?
3. Are the plates for the right vehicle?
4. Does the vehicle have door or trunk locks missing?
5. Is the trunk wired shut, or is the wind wing broken?
6. Does the vehicle license plate sticker number match registration information and number?
7. Do the vehicle occupants have a youthful appearance, or otherwise just not "fit" the vehicle?
8. Are the side vent windows cracked or broken?
9. Are the license plates bent down or covered with tape or cloth, or do the letters or numerals appear to be altered?
10. Does the vehicle display the wrong license plates, such as commercial plates on a passenger vehicle (or vice versa), or is the license an old series plate on a new vehicle? (One note of caution is appropriate here; some plates are transferable with the owner—such as personalized plates—this transfer *does not* necessarily indicate a theft.)

11. Do the front and rear plates display the same numerals and letters?

12. Check vehicles being pushed or towed with or without lights at night. This is a common MO of the thief who may be stealing a vehicle.

13. Does the vehicle have a new or used car lot identification number or sticker on the wind wing or front area of the vehicle, usually near the windshield? (These identification numbers are often made of Dymotape.)

14. Does the vehicle VIN match the registration papers, or does the VIN appear to have been altered?

15. Is the glove box empty and clean? Are the floor mats clean or painted? Are the tires painted? These are steps taken in "detailing" a used vehicle for sale and may be a tip to the officer that the vehicle was just taken from a car lot.

If you decide that any of the conditions just listed indicate a stolen vehicle, use great care in stopping and/or approaching the vehicle occupants(s). Keep in mind that some vehicle recoveries are made before the owner's report of theft and the stopped vehicle may have just been stolen for use in other felony crimes such as robbery and burglary. Since the vehicle occupant(s) may be armed, approach the vehicle with caution and only after the arrival of a cover officer.

After cautiously approaching the vehicle, ask the driver to shut off the engine. Observe whether or not there is a key in the ignition or if the vehicle is "hot-wired." (Some "hot-wired" vehicles may have a broken key jammed into the ignition as a decoy.) Following correct vehicle stop techniques, determine whether or not the suspect has all the necessary identification of ownership documents for the automobile. If so, can the driver recite the name and address shown on the registration or other identifying data? In some instances, the fact that a suspect volunteers more information than requested may be a "tip-off" that something is wrong. Be alert to determine if the suspect appears to be nervous or whether he or she is able to answer all questions with a degree of ease. The following list of observations may also indicate that further investigation is warranted.

1. Did the driver jump from the vehicle and run back to the officer as soon as the stop was made?

2. Did the driver try to hold conversation away from his or her vehicle?

3. Does the direcion of travel agree with where the suspect states that he or she is coming from or going to?
4. Can the driver provide specific information about the vehicle such as the approximate mileage of the vehicle, the type of engine, battery make and location, type and make of tires?
5. Can the suspect identify the contents of the glove compartment?
6. Does the driver have the trunk key or know outright which key goes to the trunk?
7. Does the driver know the contents of the trunk? Does he or she know where the spare tire and jack are located?
8. Is the driver familiar with the vehicle's controls and accessories?

An alert patrol officer will understand that the way a suspect answers these inquiries may result in the thief giving him- or herself away and the officer making a vehicle theft arrest. An effective and alert patrol officer will make good "on view" and "in progress" auto theft arrests. Such arrests are satisfying to the alert officer and to his or her supervisors. Figure 7-5 illustrates eight points to remember in auto theft investigation.

Modus Operandi (MO) of the Vehicle Thief

Vehicle thieves use a variety of tools such as coat hangers, hot-wiring, slam hammers, screw drivers, alternate ignition or false ignition keys, and "slim jims" to enter vehicles and steal automobiles. The thief's method of entering the vehicle and starting the engine (*modus operandi,* MO, or method of operating) may be used to identify the offender if he or she has been handled in prior theft cases. Vehicle entry may be made through side wind wings that are forced, pried, or broken open; in addition, the thief may pull locks from doors or defeat the door lock(s) with specialized tools. Constantly watch for license plates that are bent, altered, or missing.

The VIN System

In 1954 the Automobile Manufacturers Association designated the vehicle identification number (VIN) as the only number to be used for identification of vehicles. However, the state motor vehicle depart-

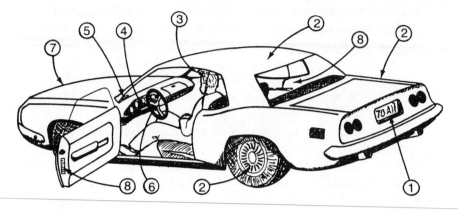

1. *License plates*: (a) front and rear, (b) condition of plates, (c) how mounted.
2. *General exterior*: (a) distinctive characteristics; (b) evidence of forced entry, pry and tool marks; (c) license numbers on hub caps.
3. *ID of driver and passengers*: (a) compare signature, address, etc., on operator's license, registration slip, and other ID; (b) when requested, search for evidence.
4. *Registration slip*: compare with information on operator's license, license plates, serial plate, engine number.
5. *Serial plate*: compare with information on registration slip and look for possible tampering.
6. *Ignition*: (a) does the key belong to that vehicle? (b) check for tampering and hot-wiring under dash.
7. *Engine compartment*: (a) compare engine and serial numbers with registration slip; (b) check for tampering.
8. *General interior*: (a) search glove compartment, behind sun visors, ash trays, under seats, dash and floor mat, all personal articles; (b) check lubrication stickers; (c) note the mileage.

Figure 7-5
Eight points to remember in auto theft investigation:

ments did not fully accept the VIN as the only number to be used for registration purposes until the late 1950s. Thus, any number appearing on the engine of an older-model vehicle may also be the identification number shown on the registration certificate. Check older records when the ownership of such vehicles is being traced. Vehicles manufactured after January 1, 1970, repeat the VIN on the Department of Transportation (DOT) sticker.

Although manufacturers differ in assigning numbers to the VIN, an investigating officer can identify the following information when it is cross-referenced to the manufacturer's guide reference to VINs:

1. Manufacturer
2. Series and body style
3. Transmission and body type
4. Model year and assembly plant
5. Sequential production number

On all U.S. passenger cars produced from 1969 until present, the VIN is visible from the front window and on top of the dashboard. If any VIN plate appears scratched or altered, have it checked by an auto theft investigator. In some cases, you may see embossing tape placed over the true VIN; this obvious deception quickly alerts the curious officer.

On General Motors (GM) vehicles made before 1964, the VIN was spot-welded on door hinge posts. A common method of detecting replaced or fraudulent plates is to pull on the VIN with a knife or fingernail; if the plate pulls off in this test, it is probably fraudulent. In Chrysler and GM products from 1965 to 1967, the VIN was secured with round-head rivets; late 1965 models used the rosette rivet. Engine and transmission numbers are always "stamped" and never "raised."

KEY TERMS

"Chop-shop" (stripping vehicle) operation
Departmental policy
Inspections
"Joy-riding"
Labor disputes
Landlord-tenant disputes
Operation Identification
Repossession (property)
"Routine" patrol
Security barriers
Security surveys

Traffic control
Traffic "wand"
V. I. N. (vehicle identification number)

STUDY QUESTIONS

1. Why is daily patrol "anything but routine"?

2. Why is it important for officers to wear all uniform items when directing traffic circulation?

3. Describe the two acceptable positions an officer can take at an intersection when directing traffic.

4. Describe the proper technique to stop vehicular traffic when directing traffic at an intersection. Which vehicles should you avoid stopping if such a vehicle will become the first vehicle in the line of traffic? Why?

5. Describe the proper method of starting traffic to move forward.

6. Describe the proper traffic direction control needed in order to permit one lane of traffic to turn left at an intersection.

7. How do you use the police whistle to stop, start, or gain attention of approaching traffic while controlling vehicle or pedestrian circulation?

8. Explain when voice commands are used in directing traffic. Why is it necessary to maintain polite and brief explanations of commands?

9. Describe when and how to use a traffic wand when directing traffic.

10. Outline priorities for traffic flow, and give a brief explanation for these priorities.

11. When should highway flares be used to assist traffic control? Under what circumstances should flares not be used to alert the motoring public of a hazardous situation?

12. Why should responding officers treat every call as the most important call of their tour of duty?

13. How do officers prepare themselves to handle cases involving unpleasant occurrences? Why is it important for responding officers to maintain calm and take decisive action in such cases?

14. Describe the appropriate law enforcement responses to missing adults, missing teenagers, and missing children under 5 years old.

15. What are the patrol officer's responsibilities in handling repossessions?

16. When can a seller repossess property from a buyer? Can the person repossessing property enter private property to make a repossession? If the property is in a locked garage, can the repossessor legally regain control of the property?

17. Describe what conduct by a landlord is considered unlawful in a landlord-tenant dispute.

18. In order to effect an eviction of a tenant, what procedures must a landlord follow?

19. Describe an officer's actions in handling a labor dispute.

20. Describe an officer's responsibility in handling disputes over goods and services.

21. How should professional officers handle news media representatives at a crime scene?

22. How should patrol officers conduct exterior building inspections during "routine" patrol?

23. List at least five instances in which a patrol officer may provide assistance to the public in noncriminal situations. What actions should you take in each such instance?

ACTIVITY

Under supervision of a law enforcement officer or instructor, set up a traffic direction and control point. The location may be a lightly traveled intersection or a driving pad or other simulated intersection. The student stands in front of the law enforcement officer or instructor to direct traffic at the intersection. Other students in the class use their vehicles to provide "traffic" at the intersection. (*Caution*: Ensure that permission is obtained to use local streets or intersections and that local law enforcement officers are advised of the training situation.)

8

Vehicle Pullovers

The traffic stop is a necessary part of the patrol officer's job. It is a potentially dangerous task that must always be guided by common sense. Officer safety is the paramount consideration in any action. General guidelines outline safety precautions that have proven to be commonsense approaches to traffic stops. However, you may find it necessary to vary the procedures from time to time, in order to adjust to particular situations.

The first rule is "Think before you act!" The alert officer is aware that every stop, no matter how minor, can instantly escalate into a tragedy. Generally, traffic stops can be divided into the following categories: (1) traffic violation, (2) investigation, and (3) felony or high risk.

The second principle is establishing "probable cause" to stop the suspect. An officer's actions to stop a vehicle must always be based on reasonable and probable cause. The specific actions and approach will depend on whether the stop involves a misdemeanor or felony activity. The following procedures outline guidelines applicable to most traffic stops.

GENERAL PRINCIPLES

Officers should *know* the reason for making a stop *before* turning on the emergency lights; that is, they should establish probable cause for the stop. By writing down the license number and a short description of the vehicle during the initial stages of the stop, mistakes may be avoided. Furthermore, check the vehicle license number against the "hot sheet" and/or have communications check the license through the automated wants and warrants system.

After closing the distance between the violator's vehicle and the patrol unit, activate the emergency lights when an appropriate stopping location is decided on. During the daytime, you may need to use the vehicle horn, or even the police siren, to gain the driver's attention. At night, the patrol unit's headlights can be alternated between high and low beams to get the driver's attention. If you use a spotlight, it should not impair the violator's vision while the vehicle is moving. The siren is used as a last resort or in any circumstances where officers deem it appropriate to alert other traffic to an emergency circumstance.

A stopping site should be in a legal location, out of the traffic flow, and should take into consideration potential avenues of escape, such as intersections or alleys. Avoid stopping a vehicle in front of unruly groups or near other hostile environments. The ideal stopping place is one that is familiar to the officer(s) and that provides surrounding cover and concealment. At all times, be alert for vehicle occupants discarding contraband or making other furtive actions.

Traffic Stop Hazards

Carelessness is one of the biggest killers of law enforcement officers today. The so-called "routine" traffic stop is the cause for this carelessness. *Any* approach to a vehicle stop is potentially dangerous; the officer never knows what the violator is thinking or what he or she has done. You may be stopping the violator for an expired license plate, but the driver may have just pulled a bank robbery or be carrying drugs. In such cases, the violator may already be predisposed to violence. By staying alert, you can stay alive!

The hazards of a traffic stop generally relate to four areas: the stop, the approach, the contact with the violator, and termination of the stop. Each area has its own dangers for the officer.

The Stop. Safety is a prime consideration during the stop. The law enforcement officer should *not* pull alongside a moving vehicle in order to get the driver's attention or direct the driver to the curb. Any sudden movement by the violator's vehicle under these conditions could result in damage to the patrol unit and injury to the officer. Furthermore, innocent citizens on the street, as well as the violator, might be injured or killed. In addition, suspects have been known to shoot at officers who pull alongside the suspect's vehicle. The correct procedure is to follow to the rear of any vehicle to be stopped.

During the pullover itself, be alert for "quick stops" or some other unusual driving movement. You can eliminate this hazard by maintaining a safe distance between vehicles during the pullover. It is extremely important to observe the vehicle occupants and to be aware of any evasive, hostile, or distracting actions.

The Approach. The approach to a stopped vehicle is the most dangerous time of the traffic stop. Be alert for any furtive movements or any indications of more than a vehicle code infraction or violation. Be especially alert for the following hazards during the approach:

1. *Physical attack by the occupant of the vehicle.* By watching the occupant's hands, officers can be alert for weapons or attempts to conceal contraband or evidence.
2. *Danger of being struck by passing traffic.*
3. *Interference by people asking directions, hostile onlookers, or associates of the violator.*

These hazards can be reduced greatly by

1. *Checking the vehicle thoroughly during the approach.* Don't overlook the vehicle's trunk, back seat area, and front seat area.
2. *Positioning the patrol vehicle in an offset position,* to the left or right of the violator's vehicle. The proper position of the vehicle provides a "safe corridor" for the officer's approach to the violator's vehicle.
3. *Being aware of surroundings and possible distractions.* Call for backup assistance if needed.

The Initial Contact. Proper positioning to contact the violator is crucial to officer safety. If there are occupants in the front seat only, take up a position slightly behind the front seat. At your discretion, you may move forward of the door when you deem such action safe. However, under no circumstances should you stand next to the door—should the driver suddenly decide to swing the door open, you would be at a grave disadvantage. If passengers are in both the front and rear seats, stand slightly behind the rear seat during the initial contact. However, you may again move forward of the front door when you feel that the forward position is safe. At all times, never forget to watch the occupants' hands.

Termination of Contact with Violator. Remain in a safe location until the violator is safely back in the traffic lane. In some instances, you may need to help by directing traffic on the highway to slow or stop.

THE "ROUTINE" TRAFFIC STOP

There is no such thing as a routine traffic stop! Any traffic stop, either for a traffic violation (including alcohol violations) or a suspected felony, represents great risk to the law enforcement officer. The officer is always more vulnerable once out of the patrol unit while the suspect remains inside a vehicle, partially or completely concealed from view. Although it is true that the officer takes additional special precautions when stopping suspected felons and suspected drunken drivers, there are certain practical procedures common to each situation.

The Seven-Step Violator Contact Method

There is no such thing as a "routine" traffic stop; nevertheless, most officers follow the seven-step violator contact method:

1. Polite greeting
2. Introduction
3. Explain reason for stop
4. Listen to violator's excuse (if any)
5. Take appropriate enforcement action, as required
6. Explain alternatives or driver's responsibility
7. Safe departure

Initial Violator Contact

The law enforcement officer will have many occasions to stop traffic violators on each tour of duty. If you see a violation, quickly begin pursuing the suspect vehicle, noting the color, make, and any distinguishing features of the violator's vehicle to eliminate stopping the wrong vehicle. If unorthodox traffic maneuvers (U-turns, lane changes, and so on) are required in the pursuit of a suspected violator, be aware of the other drivers and take care not to confuse or alarm them.

Once the patrol unit is safely behind the violator's vehicle, look ahead and try to anticipate a good place to make a safe stop. In stopping a traffic violator, engineer the stop as soon as possible, or the violator could fail to connect the stop with the infraction. This rule does not apply, however, when following a wanted felon; in such a case do not stop the felony suspect until one or more backup units have arrived to assist in the stop. In either situation, choose an area to stop in that is free of possible escape routes, is well lighted, and has enough room to park both vehicles off the main portion of the roadway.

After selecting the desired place, notify the radio dispatcher that you are stopping the suspected violator, giving a description of the violator's vehicle and the license number as well as the location of the stop. Normally, emergency lights will cause the violator to pull to the right and stop. In cases where the lights do not gain the attention of the violator, use several short blasts of the vehicle horn. Use the siren or emergency audible equipment only as a last resort. Should the violator stop in a lane of traffic or other hazardous location, direct the operator to drive to a safe location and stop.

A traffic stop at night differs slightly from the daytime traffic pullover. At night, after turning on the emergency lights, you can gain the attention of the motor vehicle driver by flashing the high-beam and low-beam headlights. Once the vehicle is stopped, leave the high-beam headlights on and aim the spotlight toward the driver's inside rear-view mirror. The cloak of darkness behind the lights provides good initial concealment until you can determine that it is safe to approach the vehicle.

The pullover site in either day or night should terminate at the right-hand curb. If there is no curb, park on an improved shoulder of the roadway or off the street or highway. With the violator's car

Figure 8-1
Correct position for the offset traffic violator stop

stopped, the officer's patrol unit should be stopped approximately 12 to 15 feet behind the violator's vehicle. The patrol unit should be stopped in an offset position from the contact vehicle so that the officer can see the left side of the violator's vehicle and the license plate (see Figure 8-1).

From the beginning of the pursuit to the moment of contact, watch the occupants of the vehicle for any unusual actions or conditions. Occupants of the violator's vehicle have been known to change places while the car is still moving because the original driver did not have an operator's permit. In other situations occupants have hurriedly tried to conceal alcohol, drugs, and other items of contraband or illegal weapons. When observing any unusual movement in the suspect vehicle, radio for backup assistance immediately.

Once the vehicles are stopped, place the transmission of the patrol unit in park and set the emergency brake. Before leaving the patrol vehicle, write down the license plate number and a brief description of the suspect violator's car on a notepad to be left inside the patrol unit. If the patrol is a two-person unit, the officer in the passenger (front-right) position of the vehicle will operate the radio and make written notes while the driver concentrates on the suspect vehicle.

Approach to Violator Vehicle

On leaving the patrol vehicle, stand momentarily behind the door of the patrol unit and continue to observe the actions of the occupants in the violator's vehicle. If any offensive actions occur, take immediate defensive action and use the patrol vehicle as cover.

On a two-person patrol unit, the officer in the passenger seat leaves the right side of the unit and remains there to provide cover for the partner. Under no circumstances should the cover officer remain in the patrol unit while the other officer is approaching the violator's vehicle or during the contact. The second officer has a responsibility to provide immediate backup assistance in the event of any offensive actions by the violator. In addition, the presence of two officers is a psychological deterrent for the occupant(s) of the violator vehicle.

In approaching the violator vehicle, use the patrol vehicle as protection from other traffic on the highway by moving slightly to the right when approaching the left side of the violator's vehicle. While watching the driver and occupants of the vehicle, place a hand on the trunk of the vehicle to make sure it is closed or locked. If the vehicle trunk lock is missing, immediately suspect that someone could be hiding in the trunk. When approaching the rear window of the violator vehicle, make a quick visual check to ensure that no one is hiding in the rear seat or on the floorboard of the vehicle.

Approaching the driver, assume a position behind the driver's door; do not stand adjacent to the driver's door because the driver can use the door as a weapon against you by swinging it open quickly. At *all times* you must be aware of the driver's hands; if the driver's hands are concealed or if they are not readily visible to you, ask the driver to place his or her hands on the steering wheel. During this time, your gun hand must be free of clipboards and/or ticket books; carry such items in the nongun hand. If the violator threatens an aggressive move toward you, immediately retreat and seek cover.

Violator Contact

After making your approach in an erect, businesslike manner and assuming a correct position, set the mood for the entire interview. Maintain a confident, courteous manner, without appearing apologetic or belligerent, by offering a polite greeting that generally includes a personal and agency identification. Provide a brief explanation of the violation, which helps the violator to accept the fact that he or she *has* committed a violation and *will* receive a citation. Do not put the violator on the defensive by requiring him or her to defend the action; however, remarks such as "Do you know there's a signal at Main Street?" may be appropriate. An interview introduction might proceed as follows:

> Good morning, Sir (or Madam). I am Officer Smith, Zee City Police Department. I have stopped you for exceeding the speed limit. May I see your driver's license, please?

(*Note*: Your jurisdiction may also require proof of insurance or registration.)

Obtain the driver's license and other required documents immediately to take initial control and to identify the driver. Be patient and professional during this contact but always mindful of safety as well. The driver may not be able to readily locate a driver's license or may try to argue or dissuade you from writing a traffic citation. *Never* argue with the violator about the violation. If the violator asks for a full explanation of the nature of the offense, give it as clearly as possible. However, take care not to be drawn into an argument about whether the violator actually violated the law or not. The violator *did* commit the violation in your mind, or else you would not have made the stop! If you issue a citation, the place to argue the point is in *court*, not while making the initial contact. In general, the violator *is* entitled to an explanation of the nature of the violation. If you handle this task satisfactorily, you will reduce the likelihood of having to argue—or explain—the case in court. Your ability to be professional and to establish good community relations will be put to the test. Keep in mind, however, that you should have decided to write or not to write a traffic ticket before leaving the patrol unit. This decision should not be changed unless special circumstances warrant such a change.

While the driver is locating the requested documents, remain alert at all times and watch the violator's hands. If the driver has to look in the glove compartment for other documents, be aware of the possibility that a weapon may be readily available to the vehicle occupant(s). At night, ask the driver to turn on the interior compartment light; in addition, you can use a flashlight in your nongun hand to observe and follow the violator's hands.

During the initial contact, be clearly aware of the condition of both the driver and the vehicle. The driver might show signs of being under the influence of an alcoholic beverage or other intoxicating substances. The vehicle could have defective lights or exhaust or some other dangerous condition that requires immediate corrective action. The ability to perceive and recognize these symptoms and hazards is paramount to your safety and the safety of others.

When asked for the driver's license, violators often start to hand over the entire wallet or card holder; *never accept it*! Courteously ask the violator to remove the license and hand over *only* the driver's license. By not accepting the wallet or card holder, you avoid the possibility that the violator will later allege that you took money, credit cards, or other items from the wallet. By not handling the item, you eliminate suspicion of wrongdoing.

Once you have obtained the documents, state the intended action—a warning, the issuance of a traffic citation, or other corrective action deemed appropriate. If it is a citation, ask the violator to remain seated in the vehicle. You might choose a standing position behind the right rear fender of the patrol unit or a seated position in the patrol unit (passenger side) to write the citation. Either of these positions provides cover for you while allowing you to continue to observe the violator's vehicle.

Frequently, a violator will want to get out of his or her vehicle to meet the officer. From a standpoint of officer safety, you also might want the violator out of the vehicle during the interview. There are both advantages and disadvantages to the violator being out of the vehicle. On the advantage side, the fact that the violator leaves the vehicle (on the initial stop) eliminates a hazardous element of a traffic stop—the *approach*. By having the violator leave the vehicle, you can direct the person over to the curb while you maintain a position of safety. The second advantage is that you can constantly observe the violator's actions—especially the *hands*! During the interview and resulting citation, the violator is constantly in your direct or peripheral field of vision. The next advantage is your position in relationship to other vehicle occupants. When the violator is between you and other vehicle occupants, assaults on you may be discouraged. The fourth advantage presumes that you will not be as vulnerable to passing traffic. Instead of conducting the interview in the street, you speak with the violator from the relative safety of the curb.

The disadvantages of the violator leaving the vehicle, however, cannot be overlooked. By leaving the vehicle, the violator is subject to the hazards of passing traffic, especially if the violator is under the influence of alcohol or other intoxicating substances. In addition, when the violator is standing, it may be easier for the subject to attempt to use either bodily force or deadly force against you. Furthermore, after the initial contact, the violator may wish to return to his or her vehicle to obtain the driver's license and/or other documents. During this time, you may be at a great disadvantage in position. The violator's back will be turned, you may not be able to watch the violator's hands, and/or the violator may block your view of the glove box or other vehicle areas from which the subject may obtain a weapon. In addition, by returning to the vehicle the violator can rejoin other vehicle occupants, who may then decide to assault you.

Ultimately, each officer makes up his or her mind how the stop should be handled. You must ensure that the contact is made as safely as is reasonably possible. The activities of the driver and occupants must be controlled to the extent that safety is maintained. This may require changing from an obviously hazardous location to a safer place, if practical. Always avoid certain locations, if possible, such as the down side of a hill crest, on a curve, alongside bridge abutments and culverts, on narrow streets (or streets without shoulders or parking lanes), in the traffic lane (or within an intersection), and in the center divider of freeways or divided highways. Generally, caution the driver and occupants to remain in the vehicle unless their exit is desired. If an occupant is out of the vehicle, you might caution the person to stay out of the path of oncoming traffic and not to stand between stopped vehicles.

Axioms

Several *don'ts* are axioms in writing a traffic citation:

Don't berate the violator.

Don't argue with a violator. The place to settle disputes over traffic tickets is in a court of law.

Don't place your foot on the violator's vehicle or the patrol vehicle while writing the ticket.

Don't use the fender and hood of either vehicle as a writing surface.

Don't stand between the violator's vehicle and the patrol unit.

Don't be in a hurry; take your time and make sure that all the information on the ticket is correct.

Don't suggest to the driver what the fine may be; this is a matter for the courts and not within your discretion.

Don't make concessions to lower the seriousness of the violation observed, such as lowering the speed for which you are writing the traffic ticket in a speeding violation. Too frequently the violator will go to court and plead not guilty because you wrote a ticket for a speed that you did not stop him for.

Don't smoke or chew gum while engaged in a traffic stop.

Don't accept gratuities or favors in lieu of writing the traffic citation.

Don't get careless! Keep your attention focused on the violator and occupants of the motor vehicle. Many officers are killed each year during *routine* traffic stops.

In addition, there are several *do* axioms:

Do be alert and aware of the actions of the suspect and the vehicle's occupants at all times.

Do be courteous and respectful; remember that the majority of people you stop will not be intentional criminals but usually law-abiding citizens who made an error in judgment.

Do be professional at all times and follow departmental rules and procedural guidelines.

Subject Identification

One objective of the field interview is to detect deception on the part of the subject. Therefore, it is important that patrol officers spend time in examining documents presented by a subject or violator who is being interviewed. Although it takes only a short period of time to properly check out an item of identification, many officers just briefly glance at a license or other identification document. Experienced officers are acutely aware that many items of identification may be false. Good officers quickly learn to distinguish and recognize the documents used for identification.

Driver's License. The driver's license is one of the most common types of documents used for identification. It may vary depending on the state of issue. The license may have various restrictions depending on the type of vehicle operated and the purpose for which the driver is operating the vehicle. Some restrictions may be typed or printed on the license. Alert officers always examine both the front and back of the license for restriction codes. A "driver's license guide" for all states is generally available within the law enforcement agency.

In examining a license for alterations, check for any additions or deletions to the license. For example, a common addition is lamination, which is generally prohibited since the lamination can hide a change of photograph, obliterate the safety seal, or disguise a typed addition. Since all license photos are generally part of the license data blank itself, you should not be able to feel an "edge" around the photograph on the license. In addition many state drivers' licenses contain a reflectorized seal on the front of the license. Be sure to examine the license for possible erasure, cutting out of data, or overlapping of new data. When any doubt exists as to the authenticity of the license, ask the violator for further, supportive identification. If the license is forged, supportive identification will probably not be available.

Keep in mind that an expired driver's license can still provide good identification. If the license is presented for purposes of identification, compare the license description to the violator and check for forgery. A temporary license is generally worthless as a means of identification because it is easily obtained. Subjects can apply for a temporary license and use it immediately. In some cases, people with suspended licenses or warrants keep applying for a temporary license in order to continue driving. If a temporary license is provided as identification, thoroughly check it out.

Immigration Identification. Resident and other aliens may have in their possession an alien registration card, which contains the bearer's photograph and other information. These cards are usually a reliable form of identification. However, since some cards may be forged, check for possible alterations, additions, or deletions when examining the document(s).

State Identification Card. Most states issue identification cards for use as official personal identification. In fact, some people may have both a driver's license and a state identification card, which will contain the same identification number. The card is issued through local department of motor vehicle offices and has an appearance similar to the driver's license.

Social Security Card. A law enforcement officer can find a Social Security card on most subjects. However, the Social Security card is not a reliable form of identification. The card is reasonably easy to apply for, and some criminals have applied for dozens of the cards, usually under different names. In some cases, phony check passers may use different Social Security cards to back up other fraudulent identification that they carry. In addition, it is quite common for the cards to be stolen or borrowed.

Armed Forces Identification. Identification from the armed forces is usually a valid form of identification; however, the photograph (especially one taken during basic training) may or may not resemble the subject. Ask the subject to repeat back his or her service number and compare it to the identification card. Anyone who is on active duty in the armed forces will be able to *quickly* recite his or her service number without hesitation. However, recently service numbers are the same as Social Security numbers. The color of the card indicates the identification status of the person:

Green: Active duty
Red: Reserve
Gray or Blue: Retired
Tan: Dependent

Issuing Citations and Warnings

The majority of the motoring public favors traffic law enforcement if it is fair and impartially applied with reasonable methods. The decision to issue a citation should be based on the facts surrounding the violation. Occasionally, you may decide to issue a warning or explanation in lieu of a citation; do so when a warning is more beneficial to the public interest than issuing a citation. Local agency policy usually dictates whether a warning or citation is issued in varied situations. Extenuating circumstances present at the time of a violation may influence a decision to give a warning instead of the traffic ticket. For example, the violator may not have seen an obscured official traffic control device and inadvertently drove through the control without incident. In another case, the person may have driven onto the divider area of a divided highway to avoid an accident. In either of these examples, good officer discretion to issue a warning solicits the driver's support for safety rather than punishes for inadvertent behavior. In the final analysis, each enforcement contact must be evaluated on the basis of sound and professional judgment.

In situations where a citation is warranted, the officer is required to give the violator detailed and complete information concerning when and where to appear for trial or settlement of the citation. The specific appearance date and time for which the violator is to appear in court should be pointed out to the violator. The time period varies from state to state. For example, in the state of California the violator has 21 days after the ticket was issued to appear in court; however, the state of Texas requires appearance in 10 days. Determine the specific time period in your jurisdiction. In directing the violator to appear in response to the citation, inform the violator of the specific court and its location. Most frequently, appearance is scheduled before a magistrate within the county in which the offense charged is alleged to have been committed and who has jurisdiction over the offense. Each agency will inform the officer of the correct magistrate in the jurisdiction.

A person arrested for a traffic violation has the *right* to demand an immediate appearance before a magistrate.[1] This is the violator's right under state law and should be complied with if the court is in session. In such cases, the officer should store, or otherwise provide for the safekeeping of, the violator's vehicle. Understand that the violator's right to an immediate appearance before a magistrate is absolute and *not* up to your discretion. If a magistrate is not in session when the offender is taken into costudy, the offender is detained until the magistrate's court commences, or is allowed bail, if applicable.

During the interview with the violator, do *not* provide any estimate of the amount of bail or fine, since each court has different procedures for determining the amount of bail or fine. If the violator states that he or she cannot appear at the cited time and date, tell the person to call, or write, the respective court for information regarding a continuance. Usually, any further information should be obtained by contacting the court by mail.

Terminating the Traffic Stop

Once the stop has been completed, terminate the meeting with a polite parting comment, such as "Thank you for your time and

---

[1] Peace officers describe this action as "instanter." Every state specifies certain situations that require officers to bring a violator "instantly" before a magistrate.

courtesy," after giving the violator his or her copy of the citation. Also take care to return all documents belonging to the violator.

After terminating the contact, remain attentive until the driver has started the car in motion. Then turn off your emergency visual equipment and notify communications that the vehicle pullover has been completed.

NONRESIDENT VIOLATOR COMPACT ACT

Various states found that in most instances, a motorist cited for a traffic violation in a jurisdiction other than the person's home jurisdiction must post collateral or bond to secure appearance for trial at a later date; or, if unable to post collateral or bond, the person would be taken into custody until the collateral or bond was posted. In many instances, the person would be taken directly to court for trial to be held in accordance with the laws within the separate jurisdiction. In some instances, the motorist's driver's license was held as collateral to be returned after the violator complied with the terms of the citation.

Recognizing the problems inherent in these practices, for both traveling motorists and law enforcement agencies, the member states agreed to ensure compliance with the terms of a traffic citation by the motorist who, if permitted to continue traveling after receiving the traffic citation, could return to her or his home jurisdiction and disregard her or his duty under the terms of the traffic citation. A motorist receiving a traffic citation in his or her home jurisdiction can by the compact agreement accept the citation—except for certain violations— and immediately continue on his or her way after promising or being instructed to comply with the terms of the citation. The participating jurisdictions agree to a reciprocal program in order to effectuate the policies and provide for the fair and impartial treatment of the traffic violator while extending cooperation among the jurisdictions to obtain compliance with the terms of the traffic citation.

The end result of these reciprocal practices relieves the motorists of unnecessary inconvenience and at times the hardship of having to post collateral, furnish a bond, stand trial, or pay the fine, and otherwise be compelled to remain in custody until some arrangements can be made. For the jurisdiction involved in issuing the citation, the reciprocal practices eliminate the necessity of expending undue law-enforcement time. In addition, each member of the compact seeks compliance with the laws, ordinances, and administrative rules and regulations relating to the operation of motor vehicles in each of the jurisdictions. Such practices result not only in smoother administrative practices, but also in safer operation of motor vehicles in each of the jurisdictions. Under the terms of the compact, the state may request suspension of the driver's license from any resident of a compact state or jurisdiction who receives a citation for a traffic violation and fails to respond.

Currently thirty-eight states and the District of Columbia are involved in the reciprocal compact agreement. Update your records as new information becomes available, however. Current members of the compact are

Alabama	Louisiana	Ohio
Arkansas	Maine	Oklahoma
Colorado	Maryland	Pennsylvania
Connecticut	Minnesota	Rhode Island
Delaware	Mississippi	South Carolina
Dist. of Columbia	Missouri	South Dakota
Florida	Nebraska	Tennessee
Georgia	New Hampshire	Texas
Illinois	New Jersey	Utah
Indiana	New Mexico	Vermont
Iowa	New York	Virginia
Kansas	North Carolina	West Virginia
Kentucky	North Dakota	Wyoming

FELONY AND HIGH-RISK PULLOVERS

Felony and high-risk pullovers differ greatly from the routine traffic stop at the point of violator contact. These types of pullovers should be made *only* when a backup unit has arrived. The location of the stop should also limit the escape routes available to the suspect and provide as much light as possible under current conditions; however, avoid the hazard of silhouetting, discussed in Chapter 2.

The key words in handling felony and high-risk pullovers are always *safety* and *caution*. Be poised, alert, and professional, and follow safe techniques. Officer survival is vital. It is of paramount importance that you work as a team member and not as an independent "hero." Independent heroes rarely make it to retirement.

An Investigative Stop

When sufficient probable cause exists that leads an officer to believe that a crime has been or is about to be committed, an investigative stop may be justified. Many legal guidelines authorize investigative stops of suspects in vehicles. Such stops are handled precisely like "routine" traffic stops. The seriousness of the investigation, number of suspects present, and type of vehicle involved are all factors that must guide your actions in requesting cover for this type of stop. Patrol officers' actions are controlled by the type of crime suspected and by the degree of probable cause.

After all prestop procedures are complete and the patrol unit is properly parked behind the suspect's vehicle, the cover officer *immediately* leaves the unit and assumes a guarding position of safety. The contact officer exits the patrol vehicle and takes a position of either approach or cover, depending on the nature of the stop (misdemeanor or felony). When circumstances indicate, use caution in removing suspects from the vehicle. The driver remains at the cover position and directs the suspect to leave the vehicle where he or she can be covered. Remove the other vehicle occupants one at a time, beginning with front seat passengers, who leave the driver's side of the vehicle. If sufficient probable cause exists, direct the suspects to leave the vehicle with their hands up, elbows locked, and fingers spread.

Both officers watch the suspect(s) very closely—especially the hands! At nighttime, the interior of the suspect's vehicle is illuminated with spotlights from the primary and backup patrol units. The additional concealment of darkness behind the patrol units' lights should be used to your advantage. However, command the suspects to walk to you slowly—do not move into the lighted area recklessly. As the last suspect leaves the vehicle, cautiously check the interior of the suspect's vehicle. The initial approach to the vehicle may be made with the handcuffed driver-suspect placed in front of you. If the driver is unwilling to return to the vehicle with you, that may indicate that additional suspects are hiding there.

The Felony High-Risk Stop

Patrol officers handle the felony stop similarly to the investigative stop. When conducting any felony arrest stop, officers exercise *extreme caution* and key their actions to the seriousness of the crime. Make a backup request and delay the stop until the backup unit arrives, if possible. A felony stop *should not* be initiated with fewer than two officers.

The cover officer may either use a door for cover or, if available, he or she can move to cover. As soon as the vehicle has been placed in "park" and the emergency brake has been set, the driver officer takes cover behind the left door post with his or her handgun drawn and properly positioned. From this point, one officer takes control.

The officer's first objective is to establish verbal control by

1. Identifying his or her authority and purpose for the stop
2. Ordering the suspects' hands to be kept visible
3. Ordering the driver to turn off the ignition, and to remove the keys

After each order to secure the vehicle has been carried out, the directing officer orders the driver and/or other suspects to keep their hands visible.

Consider known felons to be armed and dangerous. Direct vehicle occupants over the patrol vehicle's public address system to place their hands where you can see them. In addition, maintain cover and concealment at all times while directing the vehicle occupants to dismount one at a time and placing each person in a disadvantageous position. Remove the suspects from the front seat first, starting with the driver.

Have each suspect, with hands in the air, back slowly to the patrol vehicle where the officers can handcuff and secure the suspect. You may use a standing, kneeling, or prone search position once the suspect is under control. Your decision on which search position to use may be based on existing conditions. Each occupant of the vehicle can be secured in this manner until all occupants have been removed from the vehicle. The specific safety tactics employed in any situation will depend on

1. "Freshness" of the information
2. Probable cause
3. Nature of offense and possibility of a weapon
4. Citizen and officer safety

Always suspect that one or more people may be hiding in the

vehicle. If a verbal challenge does not make such people get out, you might approach the vehicle using one of the arrested suspects as a cover. If there is another person in the vehicle, the suspect accompanying you is likely to become afraid and alert you to the presence of the other offender. If the vehicle has been cleared, the presence of the suspect facilitates securing the vehicle and eliminates allegations that officers unlawfully removed property from the vehicle.

Whether the stop is a traffic stop, an investigative stop, or a felony high-risk stop, stay constantly alert for danger. In all stops, the suspect must be properly identified by a driver's license, immigration identification card, a state identification card, or an armed forces card. By following proper procedures and taking special precautions, you can survive traffic stop hazards.

UNCONVENTIONAL VEHICLE STOPS

Some vehicle stops involve unusual circumstances.

Motorcycle Pullovers

The motorcycle presents special problems for officers during vehicle stops. The motorcycle's maneuverability, speed, and vulnerability should be taken into consideration. Since a motorcycle can slide or slip, especially going onto a road shoulder, do not follow such vehicles too closely. However, be aware that motorcycles can pull away quickly and take off to areas where your patrol vehicle cannot go. Therefore, whenever possible, write down the license number as soon as possible while announcing the stop to communications. Have the motorcycle driver shut off the engine immediately after the stop, and obtain a valid identification when the motorcycle is stopped. Generally, it is best to have the cycle rider move away from the vehicle, off the highway, once the cycle is stopped. Furthermore, be aware of potential weapons (such as firearms in the handlebars) on the motorcycle.

Campers and Van Stops

Vans provide a unique set of circumstances for the officer because of the shape and concealment possibilities of such vehicles. Pullover procedures may vary with vans and campers as far as position, pullover techniques, use of lights, and approach are concerned. Furthermore, the removal of suspects from vans and campers varies considerably from passenger car procedures.

The following examples are general guidelines for most van and camper pullovers:

1. *Traffic stop.* The patrol vehicle should, within reason, be stopped back far enough to afford the officer(s) a view of all potential exits. You may decide on an approach to the vehicle or the removal of the driver, based on the circumstances of the stop.

2. *Investigative stops.* Investigative stops should be conducted with at least two officers present. The cover officer takes a position of cover as far forward and to the right as possible. In some cases, the officers may remain behind the passenger door of the patrol unit if cover is not otherwise available.

   a. The contact officer directs the driver of the van to turn off the ignition key, leave the van, and bring the keys to the rear of the van.

   b. The contact officer directs the driver to open the rear door of the van and/or the side door.

   c. The contact officer directs the driver to stand to the passenger side of the vehicle.

   d. While the contact officer is performing this task, the cover officer's main responsibility is to cover his or her partner and watch the passengers. Once the driver is positioned on the passenger side of the van, the cover officer also watches this suspect.

   e. The contact officer checks for other occupants, then directs the passengers out of the vehicle.

   f. The contact officer may move to the passenger side of the van during this procedure in order to achieve greater safety and to obtain a better position of observation.

   g. If other suspects are in the rear of the van, they should be removed one at a time by the contact officer, through either the rear or side door.

   h. The contact officer conducts the investigation.

   i. Officers should be mindful that an investigative stop can escalate into a felony arrest situation at any time.

2. *High-risk and felony stops.* The procedures in removing suspects

from a van or camper are different from procedures for removing suspects from a regular vehicle. As in other high-risk and felony stops, at least two officers should always be present and communications should be alerted as soon as possible.

a. In most van stops, the contact officer of the primary unit is in control of the stop at the beginning. The first suspect to be removed from the van is the driver by the contact officer; however, in some situations this responsibility may be shifted to the cover officer.

b. The removal of the driver suspect should begin only after the van or camper is secured, which is done in the same manner as a regular vehicle stop, except that the suspect driver is never told to throw the keys to the van out onto the ground. The cover officer, again, is positioned behind the patrol unit door or behind available cover; an acceptable alternate position may be taken at the right rear of the van.

c. The contact officer directs the van or camper driver to hold the vehicle keys in his or her right hand and place both hands out the van driver's side window.

d. When you are satisfied that the keys are the only objects in the suspect's hand, direct the suspect to open his or her door, using the *outside* handle, and step from the van or camper.

e. The driver should be directed to roll up the window and close the door.

f. The suspect should be directed to move away from the vehicle, extend his or her arms over the head, lock out the elbows, and spread the fingers. You might ask the suspect how many other people are in the vehicle.

g. Then direct the suspect to the rear of the van and ask the person to open the rear doors of the van (if the vehicle has rear doors). Be careful to maintain sight of the suspect's hands at all times.

h. If the van or camper has a side door (but no back door), direct the van driver to the rear of the van, where the cover officer directs the suspect to open the side door. In this case, the cover officer should remove all other suspects *after* the driver suspect has been secured.

i. When a van with a back door has been opened and the driver suspect properly secured, either officer may be responsible for removing the rest of the suspects, depending on which officer has better visibility and control. The officer not removing the suspects becomes the cover officer.

j. After all suspects have been removed from the van or camper, the officer makes sure the vehicle is empty.

k. The suspect's vehicle is searched by one officer.

Stopping a Bus

Stopping a bus presents special problems for officers. You may face public relations problems with the passengers, who do not want to be delayed. In addition, you must consider not only your safety and the safety of the driver, but also the safety of the bus riders. Furthermore, since the bus is much larger than the patrol unit, the bus driver may not be able to see the patrol unit as easily as other drivers.

The bus pullover is initiated by using the primary pullover techniques—use of lights, horn, and so on. Approach the front bus door from the curb side. Request the bus driver to set the brake, turn off the motor, and leave the vehicle. If the driver is to be arrested, call communications and have them ask the bus organization or firm to send out a new driver. Stay with the bus until the driver replacement arrives.

Pullover procedures for the investigative stop and felony or high-risk stops must be adapted to confront the situation. Backup support is needed to remove passengers and search the bus. Here again, all precautions should be taken for officer safety.

Semitruck Pullover

In a semitruck pullover, officers are faced with a situation similar to that of a bus; that is, the vehicle's size and weight. In dealing with such vehicles, be aware that the driver should not be *routinely* told to turn off the ignition, because of potential engine damage. Furthermore, semitrucks should not be stopped on a grade, since many cannot be restarted there if loaded.

Since visibility is still a major problem during the approach, instruct the driver to set the brake and leave the vehicle. If the vehicle has a passenger, he or she should also be directed to leave the vehicle during an investigative stop. During a search of the vehicle, do not overlook the cab and sleeper areas for additional suspects.

DRIVING UNDER THE INFLUENCE OR WHILE INTOXICATED

Every year, over half the fatal driving accidents involve at least one intoxicated driver. Since one law enforcement goal is to protect life and property, you will spend a great amount of time trying to identify, locate, arrest, and report intoxicated drivers.

Many jurisdictions refer to the offense of "driving under the influence" of alcoholic beverage or any drug as "DUI," while other jurisdictions refer to the offense as "DWI," or "driving while intoxicated." Regardless of the reference used, the elements of the offense are essentially the same for all jurisdictions: "A person commits an offense if he or she is intoxicated while driving or operating a motor vehicle in a public place." Whether the intoxication results from ingesting or using alcoholic beverages, drugs, or other controlled substances, a driver who does not have the normal use of his or her mental or physical faculties because of any substance is a danger to him- or herself and to other people in the area. Officers primarily base a DUI or DWI arrest on observable driving performance indicating that a vehicle operator does not have full control of his or her capacity to safely operate a motor vehicle (or, in some jurisdictions, a vessel on water). DUI or DWI can be measured by chemical examination that corroborates such observations.

Percentage by weight of alcohol is based on grams of alcohol per 100 milliliters of blood. If a chemical blood test is administered within three hours after a person is arrested for DUI or DWI, a concentration of 0.10[1] or more of alcohol in the blood is proof that the driver had such a concentration at the time he or she was driving the vehicle, and it is sufficient proof that a person was under the influence of alcoholic beverage. In simple terms, a 0.10 blood alcohol concentration means one drop of alcohol per one thousand drops of blood. In addition, chemical analysis of blood can determine the presence of other chemical substances.

In addition to blood tests, alcohol concentration can be measured by breath analysis and urine analysis. Generally speaking, instruments designed to measure alcoholic concentrations of breath analysis determine the number of grams of alcohol per 210 liters of breath. If urine is used for analysis, the instruments determine the number of

---

[1] Blood alcohol concentration of 0.08 is prima facie proof of DUI in California.

grams of alcohol per 67 milliliters of urine. The use of a urine analysis test is generally at the discretion and voluntary request of the accused person and not a discretionary examination available to the investigating officer.

Observing and Identifying the Intoxicated Driver

An officer can encounter a drunk driver at any time of the day or night. While patrolling an assigned district or "beat," be aware of any unusual activities that occur, including minor traffic violations that could indicate an intoxicated driver. These observations tend to be especially meaningful within two hours of the closing times of the bars and nightclubs in the patrol area.

Alert officers understand that traffic violations can be symptoms of poor judgment executed by a person under the influence of some intoxicating substance. Since the first portion of the brain affected by alcohol or drugs is the area that governs a person's judgment, the intoxicated driver will exhibit poor driving performance. Constantly be watchful for the unusual. Certain behaviors indicate an intoxicated driver. Some common indicators of the intoxicated offender can include, but are not limited to

- Inability to drive at a constant speed—going either too fast or too slow
- Inability to drive in a single marked lane of traffic
- Driving down the middle of the road (the driver is probably using the center lane dividing line as a guide in order to stay on the roadway)
- Improper wide turns to left or right
- Being asleep at the wheel while parked at an intersection awaiting the change of lights or slumped over steering wheel at any time
- Driving with the window down in winter
- Driving without headlights at night or driving with headlights on during the day
- Driving the wrong way on a one-way street or highway
- Driving on wrong side of road—not passing
- Driving alternately on and off the roadway
- Failure to dim headlights or obvious hesitation to dim headlights
- Following too closely

- Being overly anxious to pass—pulling out from behind vehicle being followed—or passing with insufficient clearance
- Pulling off roadway and stopping to check car, or turning off onto side road when he or she sees a patrol unit
- Vehicle occupants attempting to switch drivers on observing patrol unit
- Exhibiting a "straightforward stare" and/or a firm grip on steering wheel with both hands
- Slowing down and refusing to pass patrol unit when overtaking from behind (*note*: patrol officers generally drive 5 miles per hour below speed limit, and most normal drivers will pass)
- Being overly cautious and may veer away from oncoming traffic
- Driving without lights when lights should be used
- Improper start from parked position—especially from a night-club or other place serving alcoholic beverages
- Wide, slow turns when unnecessary
- Jerky passing or jerky steering
- Driving on shoulder of highway when roadway is open for traffic
- Cutting corners on curves
- Having trouble judging distance, and having to use brakes hard to keep from hitting vehicle he or she is overtaking
- Lack of stability when negotiating a curve
- A slow-moving vehicle disregarding a red light or stop sign
- Stopping on a green light
- Applying brakes when meeting traffic, especially at night
- Driving on extreme right side of roadway—vehicle tires occasionally drop off roadway shoulder
- Excessive use of horn
- Traffic stacking up behind a car on a two-lane roadway or other road
- Inappropriately using vehicle equipment—such as windshield wipers working when it is not raining
- Keeping headlight on "bright" when following
- Driver seems attracted to the headlights of oncoming cars
- Stopping at uncontrolled intersection for no apparent reason
- Passing other vehicles, then slows down
- Hitting or running over a curb when turning
- Returning to right side of road too slowly after passing
- Using poor judgment on lane changes

Although this list is not exhaustive, it presents a starting point for the officer to recognize intoxicated drivers. It should also be noted that any of the above actions could be committed by people "not" under the influence of alcoholic beverages or controlled substances. However, understand that such actions are not good driving behavior and may indicate a DUI or DWI person. Once such a driver has been observed, take immediate action to stop the violator. Take special precautions during the vehicle pullover to have the violator's vehicle put in park and the motor turned off. Since the intoxicated driver may unknowingly place the vehicle in reverse instead of park, extend the distance between the vehicles when parking the patrol unit.

Making the DUI/DWI Violator Stop

Having decided to stop the suspected intoxicated violator, the officer begins to make mental notes of all observations during the time that the officer is in contact with the suspect. When you are in this situation, note all the driver's actions while taking care to follow all the normal precautions of a "routine" traffic stop. For example, note how long it takes the driver to react to the overhead emergency lights or the patrol vehicle's horn or siren. Frequently the intoxicated driver has to concentrate so hard on steering the vehicle straight that he or she misses paying attention to the surroundings. Also be alert to how quickly the suspect violator stops the vehicle in response to the red lights and siren. Should the violator commit any other traffic violations while you are attempting to stop the suspect, include these violations in the filed report.

Once the violator begins to stop, observe how safely the violator stops. Does the violator run over the curbs in trying to stop? Did the operator cause any other vehicles to take evasive action to avoid a collision while stopping? Always look out for any unpredictable actions the suspect commits. Many times an intoxicated driver will pull to the curb on the wrong side of the road or stop in the middle of an active traffic lane and make no other attempt to move from the roadway. Some violators lock the brakes of their vehicle while attempting to stop too quickly, trying to please an officer.

In parking behind the suspect's vehicle, park offset from (not directly behind) the violator's vehicle, approximately 25 to 30 feet back. At night, use high-beam headlights and spotlights to illuminate the interior of the suspect's vehicle. Before leaving the patrol vehicle, use the car public address system to command the suspect to turn off the motor. In a situation such as this, you should realize that an intoxicated driver can believe he or she has put the gear selector in park when in reality he or she has put the vehicle into reverse. Be prepared to leave the area if the suspect's vehicle begins rolling backward. Also be alert for any unusual movements and "expect the unexpected." Keep in mind that the intoxicated driver is impaired, and in most cases will not act, or react, in a predictable way.

Before exiting the patrol unit, begin making mental notes of how the suspect acts. This observation period also permits you to alert communications of the location and nature of the stop. Also report to communication the license number and description of the stopped vehicle.

Contacting the DUI or DWI Suspect

On approaching the suspect's vehicle, use the same precautions as in making a "routine" vehicle stop. Check to see if the trunk is shut; in addition, check the back seat and/or other passenger compartments for other occupants, weapons, or contraband. On approaching the driver, assume a protected position behind the point where the driver's door opens; and at all times, watch the driver's hands.

At the first contact with the suspect, ask for the operator's driver's license. Be alert to the operator's response to the request and observe any unusual conditions such as the smell of alcohol, slurred speech, or the suspect showing any signs of difficulty in following requests or directions. Also note the condition of the driver's clothing and appearance, such as having bloodshot eyes, or the inability to perform simple tasks such as taking a driver's license from a wallet. These symptoms do not necessarily mean that the person stopped is, in fact, under the influence of intoxicants; however, these observations can be indicators leading to probable cause.

On obtaining the suspect's driver's license and other required documents, if any, ask the suspect to step from the vehicle after making sure that the vehicle's motor has been turned off. It is also a good idea to have the suspect remove the keys from the ignition to prevent the suspect from driving off. As the suspect steps from the vehicle, watch the method and manner of the suspect's movements. Did the driver show any signs of difficulty in getting out? Did he or she require any support to remain standing? Is the operator able to stand without assistance, or must he or she lean against the vehicle? Once the suspect has left the vehicle, ask him or her to step to the rear of the vehicle away from the threat of traffic. As the suspect turns and walks, observe his or her movements for signs of imbalance or staggering. Be prepared to stop the suspect who swerves into the lane of traffic; it is your job to keep the subject from being injured. If the suspect can stand, also watch for signs that the violator sways or is unable to maintain balance.

The peace officer handling a suspected intoxicated driver should remember to stay patient with the suspect and act professionally during the contact. If, based on all observations, the officer believes that the suspect driver is under the influence of an intoxicant, the officer would then place the suspect under arrest for "driving under the influence"; the officer should then handcuff and search the suspect prior to transporting him (or her) to the appropriate facility for detention. At this point the officer advises the suspect of his constitutional rights in accordance with the *Miranda* warnings. It is desirable to read the suspect these warnings from a preprinted card; this rights card may be admissible into evidence at the suspect's trial. It is always desirable to have another officer or person witness the fact that the officer warned the suspect in accordance with law whenever possible. Then these facts should be recorded in the officer's report.

Once the suspect is secured, the officer conducts an investigation of the suspect's vehicle; the officer is permitted to look into the passenger compartment for any evidence that is in plain view and corroborates the offense for which the suspect was arrested. The very mobility of motor vehicles often constitutes exigent circumstances authorizing a warrantless search (*Chambers v. Maroney*, 399 U.S. 50–51, 1970). In accordance with *Harris v. United States* (390 U.S. 234, 236, 1968), "objects falling in the plain view of an officer who has a right to be in the position to have the view are subject to seizure and may be introduced as evidence."

Seizure of Vehicle and Inventory

The U.S. Supreme Court has held that "the authority of police to seize and remove from the streets vehicles impeding traffic or threatening public safety and convenience is beyond challenge" (*South Dakota v. Opperman*, 428 U.S. 364, 369, 1976).

Once the intoxicated suspect has been placed under arrest, the arresting officer is responsible for the vehicle and its contents and should summon a tow truck in accordance with department policy. Many departments have a policy of first conducting an inventory search to fulfill the law enforcement caretaking function of securing the vehicle's contents. If your department has such a policy, which generally follows a routine practice of securing and inventorying the automobile contents for the protection of the owner's property as well as protection of the police against claims or disputes over lost or stolen property, you may look into places of the vehicle not within plain view such as its trunk (*South Dakota v. Opperman*). The courts have held that during such inventory searches if "the car was lawfully in police custody, and the police were responsible for protecting the car," any evidence of an incriminating nature the police found "while engaged in the performance of their duty to protect the car" would be admissible in a court of law against the vehicle's occupant (*Harris v. United States*, 390 U.S. 234, 1968).

In investigating the suspected DUI or DWI case, seize as evidence any alcoholic beverages seen during the inventory search and mark these as evidence in the same way evidence of other criminal investigations is marked. In marking an open container of an alcoholic beverage, make a line on the outside of the container to indicate the level of liquid contained in the bottle or other container. Since alcohol can evaporate or dissipate, the actual level discovered is an item of the on-scene investigation. As with other evidence, once it is taken into custody, the officer must establish and maintain a chain of custody to ensure that the evidence will meet the requirements of being relevant, material, and competent.

The Implied Consent Rule

The majority of states have an implied consent law. For example, California Vehicle Code Section 23157 is typical of such a law:

> Any person who drives a motor vehicle is deemed to have given his or her consent to chemical testing of his or her blood, breath, or urine for the purpose of determining the alcoholic content of his or her blood and to have given his or her consent to chemical testing of his or her blood or urine for the purpose of determining the drug content of his or her blood, if lawfully arrested for any offense allegedly committed in violation of DUI statutes. The testing shall

be incidental to a lawful arrest and administered at the direction of, and when ordered by, a peace officer having reasonable cause to believe the person was driving a motor vehicle in violation of DUI statutes.

This implied consent rule specifies that any person arrested for DUI or DWI while driving a motor vehicle has *already* given consent to chemical tests. The mere operation of the vehicle is *consent*. However, vehicle codes require that an officer must inform a person accused of DUI or DWI of the consequences of refusing such chemical testing. Refusal of a chemical test can result in loss of driving privileges, and in some states mandatory incarceration, if the person is convicted of DUI or DWI.

If you lawfully arrest a person for driving under the influence of an alcoholic beverage or drug, the person has the choice of whether the test will be of his or her blood, breath, or urine, and you must advise the person of that choice. If the person arrested is either incapable, or states that he or she is incapable, of completing any specific test, the arrested person may submit to his or her choice of the remaining tests. You must advise the arrested person that he or she can choose from the remaining choices. You may order a person who chooses to submit to a breath test to also submit to a blood test if you have reasonable cause to believe that the person was driving under the influence of any drug or the combined influence of an alcoholic beverage and any drug and if you have a clear indication that a blood (or urine—if requested) test will reveal evidence of the substances. You must state in your report the facts on which that belief was held and the clear indications that your conclusion was based on.

In the event a person lawfully arrested for a DUI or DWI offense is in need of medical treatment and the person is first transported to a medical facility where it is not feasible to administer a particular test, the person has the choice of those tests that are available at the facility to which that person has been transported. In such an event, tell the person which tests are available.

In administering the tests, advise the suspect that he or she does *not* have the right to have an attorney present before stating whether he or she will submit to a test or tests or before deciding which test or tests to take. Furthermore, the person does *not* have the right to have an attorney present during the administration of the test or tests. However, the officer is correct in advising the suspect that, in the event of refusal to submit to a test or tests, the refusal may be used against him or her in a court of law.

Any person who is unconscious or otherwise in a condition rendering him or her incapable of refusal shall be deemed not to have withdrawn his or her consent and a test or tests may be administered whether or not the person is told that his or her failure to submit to, or the noncompletion of, the test or tests will result in the suspension of his or her privilege to operate a motor vehicle. Any person who is dead is deemed not to have withdrawn his or her consent, and a test or tests may be administered at the direction of a peace officer.

Be aware that certain people are exempt under the law from blood tests. Any person who is afflicted with hemophilia (a blood disorder characterized by immoderate bleeding, even from a slight injury), or any person afficted with a heart condition and using an anticoagulant under the direction of a licensed physician, is exempt from the blood test required by the code.

Chemical Testing Advice

In addition to advising an intoxicated suspect of the implied consent rule, you should tell the suspect who chooses to submit to a breath test that the breath-testing equipment does not retain any sample of the breath and that no breath sample will be available after the test that could be analyzed later by that person or any other person. Because no breath sample is retained, the suspect may wish to provide a blood or urine sample—even though he or she completed the breath test— that can be retained and subsequently analyzed for alcoholic content. Collect and retain the sample as evidence in accordance with local policy. In such an event, the suspect should also be advised that the blood or urine sample may be tested by either party in any criminal prosecution.

Chemical Testing Procedure

Most jurisdictions stipulate that only a licensed physician and surgeon, registered nurse, licensed vocational nurse, or other qualified person, acting at the request of a peace officer, may withdraw blood for the purpose of determining the alcoholic content therein. This limitation does not apply to the taking of breath specimens.

The person tested may, at his or her own expense, have an

authorized person or any other person of his or her own choosing administer a test in addition to any test administered at the direction of a peace officer, for the purpose of determining the amount of alcohol in the person's blood at the time alleged, as shown by chemical analysis of his or her blood, breath, or urine. The failure or inability to obtain an additional test by a person does not preclude the admissibility in evidence of the test taken at the direction of a peace officer.

Numerous vehicle codes provide that the person tested may request and must be informed of full information concerning the test taken at the direction of the peace officer. In addition, codes protect the person taking the blood specimen from civil or criminal liability when the test(s) were taken in a reasonable manner according to accepted medical practices, without violence by the person administering the test, and when requested in writing by a peace officer.

If the test given in accordance with statutes is a chemical test of urine, the person tested should be given such privacy in the taking of the urine specimen as will ensure the accuracy of the specimen and, at the same time, maintain the dignity of the individual involved.

Breath Test

A certified breath test operator administers the intoxilyzer test procedures in accordance with department regulations. Before the test is given, the suspect is given the admonition prescribed by law. The suspect is told that the breath-testing equipment does not retain any breath samples for later analysis and advises the suspect of his or her right to provide a blood or urine sample that can be retained. The person administering the admonition records his or her name on the appropriate record and the defendant's response, if any, using the exact words (if possible) the defendant utters. The intoxilyzer operator must follow exact procedures in preparing and using the intoxilyzer instruments in order to obtain legally admissible samples.

Refusal or Failure to Complete Chemical Tests

In most cases, a person charged with DUI or DWI may refuse to take a breath test or give a blood specimen. General exceptions to this rule are cases involving a person who is charged with an offense while DUI or DWI resulting in the death or critical condition of another person; in such cases, the state may require the suspect to provide a blood sample for analysis—even against the person's will. Each state requires specific documentation to document that an individual refused to complete a chemical test in accordance with the implied consent rule. Additional documents are required if a mandatory blood sample is to be taken. Learn what documents you are required to complete in your jurisdiction.

Tests on Dead or Unconscious People

Occasionally the peace officer will be involved in the investigation of a fatality accident or other accident where the officer believes that a deceased or other injured or unconscious person was or is intoxicated. Procedural law has ruled that a dead or unconscious person is not deemed to have withdrawn consent from the specimen (*Breithaupt v. Abram*, 352 U.S. 432, 1957; *Schmerber v. California*, 384 U.S. 757, 1965). If the person is dead, the county medical examiner or the examiner-designated agent may withdraw a specimen. If the county does not have a medical examiner, a licensed mortician may draw the blood. If the person arrested is not dead but is not capable of refusal, a qualified person may draw a specimen.

DUI or DWI Investigative Reports

Each state establishes investigative reports when a DUI or DWI arrest is made. Although the forms are different, generic similarities frequently appear within various state reports. For example, every report requires information regarding the arresting agency, case number, time, date of the incident, location of incident, and required booking information. Completely identify the suspect, and complete his or her vehicle information in appropriate blocks on the form. Record names of any witnesses, including vehicle passengers and officers as applicable.

Most forms contain a narrative and remarks section. Begin with probable cause for the stop or contact, along with the manner in which the suspect can be "placed behind the wheel" of the vehicle (if not directly observed). Describe (1) the distance you observed the operator driving and (2) the suspect's actions while operating the motor vehicle. Complete the narrative section with your statement of facts surrounding the incident in the same manner as other incident reports are filed. During the narrative report, record all observations relevant and material to the case in a chronological order to relate the events in their time sequence. Be specific in reporting any observations or other facts relevant to the case. For example, it is not specific enough to report that "The suspect appeared to be drunk." Instead, report specific observations apparent at the scene and let the reader of the report draw any conclusions based on these observations. It is specific to report that "The suspect had a strong odor of alcoholic beverage on his breath; his eyes were bloodshot; his walk was staggered; and he could not maintain his balance while turning around." In this example, the officer has drawn a word picture to establish the reasons for making an arrest and its follow-up action.

In the appropriate section of the investigative report, record your admonition to the suspect. Inform the suspect of his or her constitutional (*Miranda*) rights before carrying out an interview; it is also advisable to give the suspect the *Miranda* warnings at this point even though the arresting officer or any other officer involved in the investigation may have already given them once. If the suspect waives rights and answers your questions, this interview should be done in a location—such as an office—that precludes interruptions. If possible, conduct the interview in the presence of another officer who can witness the reading of the rights and the interview itself. Read each question as it is written on the interview section of the form; neither paraphrase the question nor offer explanation. Then write down the exact words the suspect says even though the response may not answer the question or express sarcasm or something else not relevant to the question.

Example:
Officer: "Were you driving the vehicle?"
Suspect: "No, my dog was."
Officer: "Where were you going?"
Suspect: "Dog pound."
Officer: "Time started?"
Suspect: "Dinner time."
Officer: "Where did you start driving?"
Suspect: "In the back seat."

While such responses help strengthen your case, be fair and also report correct responses that the subject may provide in response to your questions.

During the interview, the suspect may decline to answer any specific question or may wish to discontinue the interview altogether. At this point write the word *refused* in the appropriate box or section. The suspect's answers to the questions asked can constitute an admission of guilt; however, in addition to the specific answers, the "responses" themselves and the way the suspect perceives and reacts to the questions are important to the case. Direct, polite, and accurate responses benefit the suspect in the investigation; sarcastic, nonsensical, or nonresponsive answers tend to impeach the suspect's credibility and support the prosecution's case.

Record the sobriety tests given at the scene of the arrest and at the booking, or other facility. Complete each section, including observation, finger dexterity, balancing on one foot, and line-walking descriptions. A space is usually provided for observations made at the scene of the arrest separate from those made at the facility.

In the appropriate section, record the chemical test given and results. If the breath test is refused, record what the suspect said in his or her statement. Additional blocks provide a space for location where the test was conducted; disposition of samples; name and title of person giving tests or taking sample; arresting officer's name, rank, identification number; and time and date that the report was completed.

KEY TERMS

Blood/alcohol concentration
Breath test
Driving under the influence (or while intoxicated)
Emergency audio and visual equipment
High-risk or "felony" pullovers
Immediate appearance (before magistrate)
Implied Consent Rule (vehicle operations)
Instanter (traffic ticket)
Inventory search
Investigative stop

Nonresident Violator Compact
Probable cause
"Routine" traffic stop
Seven-step violator contact method
State identification cards
Traffic citation or ticket
Traffic stop "hazards"
Unconventional vehicle stops
Violator contact
Warning ticket

STUDY QUESTIONS

1. What is the paramount consideration an officer should weigh in making a traffic stop? Justify your answer.

2. What is the first rule of any traffic stop? What is the second principle?

3. Describe the correct method used to stop a driver who has violated a traffic law.

4. Outline hazards associated with "the traffic stop."

5. Outline hazards an officer may encounter during "the approach" to a violator. How can you reduce these hazards?

6. What are the procedures used in the "seven-step violator contact method"?

7. In a two-person patrol unit, discuss the role of each officer during a traffic stop.

8. What are the safest locations in which to write a traffic ticket? Why?

9. What should you do if the violator wants to get out of his or her vehicle?

10. During a traffic stop, you must constantly be aware of the subject's actions. What parts of the subject's body must you continually watch? Why?

11. Why do you want the violator to remain in his or her vehicle during a traffic stop?

12. Discuss the "do and don't" axioms of the traffic stop, and indicate the potential problems associated with violating these axioms.

13. List documents that you may use to identify the driver or occupants of a vehicle. Which documents are not considered valid proofs of identification?

14. When a traffic ticket is issued, how many days does the driver have in order to appear in court in your state? What happens if the violator does not appear, thus violating his or her written "promise to appear"?

15. When you issue a traffic ticket, when should you immediately take a driver before a magistrate?

16. Why should you avoid telling a driver what the fine may be for a specific violation?

17. Why should you avoid "giving the driver a break" by writing a traffic citation for 65 mph (in a 55-mph zone) when the driver was actually clocked at driving 70 mph?

18. Is your state included in the states that recognize the Nonresident Violator Compact Act? If so, outline the procedures for writing a traffic citation for a violator who lives in another state associated with the compact.

19. What is an "investigative traffic stop"? Explain what additional precautions you should take in making such a stop.

20. How are felony and high-risk traffic stops different from "routine" traffic stops? What are two key words in handling such stops?

21. Should you attempt a felony traffic stop alone? Explain.

22. Describe the method you use to establish verbal control in dealing with a felony high-risk stop.

23. How should the suspected felon be removed from a vehicle during the traffic stop?

24. Describe the proper procedure to conduct a motorcycle pullover.

25. Describe correct actions to stop a camper or van for a traffic stop, an investigative stop, or high-risk felony stop.

26. What procedures should you use to stop and interview the driver of a bus?

27. Define the word "instanter."

28. What additional considerations should you use in stopping a semi truck for a traffic violation?

29. Discuss the proper way to search a vehicle? What specific areas should you search inside and outside the vehicle?

30. What blood alcohol concentration is sufficient to determine that a person is DUI (or DWI) in your state? In general terms, what does this percentage mean?

31. What driver actions may alert you to the fact that the driver is under the influence of alcoholic beverage or drugs? (List at least fifteen different actions.)

32. Describe additional precautions you must take in stopping an intoxicated driver.

33. What authority did the Supreme Court case *South Dakota v. Opperman* provide to patrol officers making traffic stops?

34. What is the implied consent rule in your state?

35. What happens to a person who declines to take a breath or blood test after being arrested for DUI or DWI?

36. If the suspected intoxicated person is unconscious, can you still obtain a blood specimen for analysis? Explain.

37. Which people are exempt from giving a blood specimen for analysis? Are there any other tests that such a person may provide? Explain.

38. Can a blood specimen be obtained from the victim of a fatality accident? Justify your answer.

39. What documentation is required in your state if a person declines to give a breath or blood specimen? How do you complete these reports?

40. Are there any circumstances under which a person "must" give a blood test in your state? Explain.

41. Why is it necessary to "quote" the suspected DUI or DWI suspect during an interview following arrest? How should such an interview be conducted?

ACTIVITIES

1. Using role-playing tactics, conduct a routine traffic stop.
2. Using role-playing tactics, conduct a felony or high-risk traffic stop.
3. Research the statutes in your state that require officers to "instanter" a

traffic citation and bring a violator before a magistrate. What happens if the magistrate is not in court (such as late at night or on weekends)?

4. Obtain a copy of report forms required in your state for DUI or DWI investigation; complete the report form using personal information.

9

Crimes in Progress

At any moment, a patrol officer may receive a radio call or observe an action involving a crime in progress. A call regarding a silent "alarm down" may begin a sequence of events that leads to an arrest of a burglar in the building. Officers performing *routine* preventive patrol may observe unusual events in a local convenience store, indicating that a robbery is in progress, demanding quick, immediate attention. Citizen informants may lead you to investigate a suspected narcotics transaction that results in an apprehension. A "man with gun" report might result in a criminal homicide investigation. Any of these situations put the patrol officer in the vanguard of a police response situation that requires a person who can think on his or her feet and favorably resolve the situation. The response must be immediate and must implement precise tactics designed to protect both the officer and the public. During such events, time is of the essence. Officer response must ensure a safe approach to the scene to eliminate potential harm for the officer and victims or others in the area, as well as seek to apprehend the perpetrator(s).

Successful patrol response to a crime in progress is directly related to sound preparation and planning. Patrol officers constantly seek to learn their patrol beat and gauge the risk threat to various businesses in the area. Knowing which stores, businesses, banks, or other targets are high risks for criminal attack, the professional patrol officer can begin to plan for potential crimes in progress.

If you have learned your beat thoroughly, you can quickly review the streets, alleys, and other pertinent details about high-risk sites and the surrounding area. In your mind, determine the best location for observation and surveillance. Where are the best possible locations to provide you with cover, position, and advantage? Where are the doors and windows located in the building? Can perpetrators use the roof to attempt a possible escape? What are the relevant lighting conditions that you could use to your advantage or that might adversely affect your ability to gain control of an area? By asking these and other questions, you begin to create a basic plan that ensures appropriate response to crimes-in-progress calls.

This chapter looks at the patrol officer response and offers suggestions that permit law enforcement officers to successfully handle numerous types of crimes in progress, including crimes of robbery and burglary, as well as prowler calls. Close examination of these details will give you a beginning point for correct officer response resulting in criminal apprehension. Once a suspect is in custody, you must follow correct procedures for prisoner restraint, search, and transportation. During your tour of duty, you will no doubt receive many other types of calls that require similar response techniques. With a basic understanding of correct tactics for such calls, you will begin developing suitable strategies for effective action.

INTRODUCTION—PATROL UNIT RESPONSE

Many different circumstances can confront an officer at the scene of a crime in progress. No hard-and-fast rules cover all incidents. However, most calls can be adequately handled by using common sense, certain basic principles, and some simple techniques. Extreme caution should be used in approaching and deploying at the scene of crimes in progress.

When in-progress crimes are reported, apprehension of offenders depends on quick law enforcement response. The objective of officers is to arrive as quickly as possible, consistent with safety. Normally, the regular beat car is used as the primary or first unit to respond to a call unless another unit is closer and advises communications. The primary unit is responsible for the in-progress call unless relieved by a ranking officer. Other units will be assigned or stationed in positions where they might intercept a fleeing suspect.

The first basic principle of any call is to arrive safely. The decision to use siren and flashing lights must be made on the basis of the following factors:

1. Distance from scene
2. Amount of traffic
3. Adequacy of horn and an occasional red light to clear the immediate route
4. Need to halt ongoing physical assault by warning assailant of police approach
5. Consistency with agency policy

The response route should be the most direct line of travel that facilitates the quickest response. In some instances, a crowded highway that is the most direct route of travel may not permit as quick a response as will an alternate road that may be a couple of miles longer. In choosing how to respond, consider how far you are from the scene (distance in time) and how far are assisting units from the scene. Furthermore, consider how much time has elapsed since the crime occurred, the geographic environment (streets' configuration, freeway ramps, etc.), and the agency policy regarding use of authorized emergency vehicles. In addition, the traffic situation in the area, the time of day, condition of the route to be taken, the best approach direction, and how critical the situation is, must all be considered.

The primary function of the first radio car arriving at the scene is to evaluate and manage the incident. Generally, command responsibilities rest with the unit that first receives and responds to the call, until relieved by an officer of higher authority. This unit develops a flexible plan and implements the plan to control the incident. In addition, the primary unit directs and coordinates other units responding to assist. To avoid confusion, one officer issues commands to execute a given plan properly. It is the duty of this officer to advise suspects what is expected of them and to coordinate the investigation. Emergency conditions may, however, change the actual implementation of general guidelines.

Although deployment at a crime scene may vary due to physical limitations, personnel generally cover opposite diagonal corners, for containment. In this manner, two radio-controlled units can establish a cordon around a building and observe most doors, windows, and other building areas, to secure the area. The need for assistance of additional equipment and personnel should be determined as quickly as possible and the dispatcher notified.

When all units are in place, officers begin approaching the location, taking advantage of all cover and concealment. During the approach, stay alert for possible suspects leaving or hiding in the area. In addition, be aware of vehicles leaving the area, pedestrians in the vicinity, and any other unusual condition. If it is necessary to stop a potential suspect during the approach, notify communications immediately, in order that other responding units may provide backup assistance and/or replace you at the scene. If a suspicious vehicle is spotted and circumstances do not justify a stop, jot down the license number and description for follow-up investigation at a later time. If time permits, notify the communications of the suspect vehicle description.

BURGLARY-IN-PROGRESS CALLS

In approaching the location of a burglary in progress, officers must have a flexible plan of operation that coordinates partners and other units. Arrive quickly, quietly, and safely. Unless a specific hazard exists, *do not* use red lights or siren near the location. When safe to do so, turn off headlights before the final approach and use a slow speed to eliminate tire squeal and engine noise. Turn radio volume down, and secure loose keys and objects to prevent unnecessary noise. On leaving the patrol unit, turn off the dome or other interior lights so they will not illuminate the car when the doors open. On leaving the unit, turn off the ignition and take the key to avoid allowing burglars to use the patrol car as an escape vehicle. Finally, be cautious not to slam the vehicle doors after exiting the car.

The first officer at the scene takes a position of observation and control. Advise other units of the arrival and communicate the specific location of your vantage point. It is *most* important to communicate and coordinate responses, in order to contain suspects and prevent their escape.

An exterior search of the area should include vehicles parked at or near the location. A warm engine may indicate the suspect's vehicle and thus a potential direction for escape. Other places of possible concealment should also be checked; boxes, trash bins, stockpiles, trees, hedges, and shrubbery are all possible hiding places for escaping burglars or their lookouts. Don't forget to look upward for possible hiding places. Many burglars climb to a high vantage point to avoid detection.

At the scene of the burglary, search for the point of entry. Use extreme caution, and never walk or stand in front of windows. Also, take care to avoid the hazard of being silhouetted—use effective light control. Two officers search: one officer covers while the other officer searches. Use the walls for protection when looking into windows or trying doors. After checking the interior from the window, cross under the window and check from the other side. If used at all, the flashlight should be used properly and cautiously. Once the point of entry is located, notify communications and other units. In addition, be aware of and preserve physical evidence. The following items might be present on doors, transoms, windows, and roofs:

- Pry marks
- Cut or broken glass (burglars also attempt to replace broken glass to disguise the entry point)
- Cobwebs or disturbed dust on window ledges

In some instances, the entry point may be a tunnel or roof. Access to search a roof may be difficult, and a ladder may be needed. In extreme circumstances, call the fire department to provide necessary equipment for a roof search. In addition, officers may need air support for roof searches and/or cover. Remember, helicopters using infrared devices can quickly check for persons on roof tops or in the immediate area.

If one officer climbs to the roof on a ladder, the second officer provides cover. Advise other officers in the area that an officer is on the roof. The searching officer should check adjacent roofs, sign boards, air vents, and any other areas that may provide places of concealment. Furthermore, the searching officer should keep ground officers advised of conditions, should use extreme caution, and should use natural cover. If you discover an entry hole, don't approach it! Instead, advise other officers and watch the hole from a safe vantage spot.

Once the perimeter is secured, officers may decide to make an interior search. Perimeter units may be redeployed, to cover the entering officers and to avoid crossfire hazards if weapons are needed. Spotlights can be used to illuminate the interior of the building in some cases. When all units are in correct position, command officers use loud speakers (or voice) to tell the suspect(s) to come out of the building hands high or fingers tightly interlaced behind the head. Several commands should be given before officers consider entering the building to search if suspects do not comply with the orders. If available, dogs can be effectively used in building searches, to reduce hazards for investigating officers.

The building owner should be called and requested to respond to the scene. Owners can provide information on interior plans, location of light switches, and keys to doors. However, don't let the owner approach the building or unlock doors because of inherent dangers and the possibility that he or she may be taken hostage.

If possible, searching officers should wait to unlock a door rather than climb through a broken window, holes in the roof, and so on. At the moment of entry, all responding officers should be alerted that searching officers are commencing operations.

Searching officers take a position of cover outside the entry point and avoid standing directly in front of the door. When the door is opened, remain in position and listen for noise or unusual sounds from inside the building. At the right moment, enter the building quickly in a low position, to avoid offering yourself as an easy target. Move quickly away from the entrance, and use any available object for cover and concealment. Allow your eyes to adjust to the ambient light. With your duty weapon ready, properly use available light (flashlight, room lights, spotlights, etc.) to familiarize yourself with the area and to locate the suspects, if possible. Turn on all building lights if possible rather than search in darkness or low light. During the operation, one officer searches and the other officer covers; these roles change as officers advance to different cover areas.

Several axioms for searching should be followed, or modified to fit changing conditions:

1. A search should never be conducted by one officer alone! The actual number of personnel needed will be determined by the type and size of the building, the arrangement of furniture, display counters, partitions, and/or stacks of merchandise.

2. Use only one opening to enter the building. Officers entering from several directions can mistake each other for burglars, which might result in shooting a fellow officer.
3. Doors should be fully opened to the adjacent wall, to preclude this area as the hiding place for suspects. If the door will not open fully, look between hinged edges of the door and the door jamb before entering, to determine the cause of the blockage.
4. The search for suspects should include all places large enough to conceal a person. Check the area thoroughly before moving to another location.
5. Thoroughly search each room before searching another room. Close the doors of rooms that have already been searched.
6. At all times, be aware of potential crossfire situations and avoid shooting your partner officer!
7. In multistory buildings, confine the search to one floor at a time. When possible, conduct the search from the top and work down. This type of search requires enough personnel to provide one officer for each stairway.
   a. All elevators in the building should be put out of service on the ground floor.
   b. Once a floor has been searched, the area is sealed off by the stairway officer, to prevent suspects from escaping by moving up where officers have already searched.
8. All possible exterior exists should be guarded until the interior is completely searched.
9. Do not abandon the search just because several suspects have been found.

When a suspect is encountered during the search, officers properly challenge the perpetrator from a position of cover. The challenge commands the suspect to drop any weapons and surrender, and notes the superior position of officers in the area. Stay alert at all times! The suspect is now on the defensive and must decide how to respond to the officers' challenge. Respond appropriately to the suspect's actions, and remain alert for the possibility of multiple suspects and attack. Arresting officers seek to control all suspects and secure them. When possible, arrested suspects should be removed from the location while searching officers look for other suspects.

Secured suspects should be questioned about the possibility of other suspects in the area and about the weapons such suspects have.

By framing questions positively, officers may gain needed information to protect searching officers. Arrested suspects usually do know the desired information. However, in asking for the requested information, avoid making promises that cannot be fulfilled.

Once the building has been completely searched, owners and/or employees can resume access to the area. Remember to return keys or other property that were not seized as evidence of the crime in progress. If the owner's property was seized as evidence, advise the owner of the disposition of the evidence and provide the owner with a receipt for the property. Once the building is returned to the owner's control, patrol officers make frequent checks of the area during routine patrol coverage in the district.

Robbery in Progress

On receipt of a robbery-in-progress call, officers begin to implement a flexible plan of operation that takes into consideration coordination between partners and other units. Generally, the following tactical considerations are important:

1. Determination of response method
2. Plan for deployment
3. Containment of the scene
4. Apprehension of suspect(s)
5. Initiation of crime broadcasts

Robbery is the "felonious taking of personal property in the possession of another . . . accomplished by means of force or fear." This situation is complicated, because a victim is directly involved and his or her safety is in jeopardy. Get to the crime scene quickly, quietly, and safely. As a rule, do *not* use red lights or siren near the location of the robbery: at nighttime, turn off headlights before the final approach when it is safe to do so. A slow speed on final approach will eliminate tire squeal and engine noise that might alert the suspect that peace officers are at, or near, the scene. In all stealth approaches, control extraneous noise (keys, objects, doors, etc.) and interior, as well as exterior, vehicle lighting.

The first officer at the scene establishes a protected observation position to control the scene. Once in place, making maximum use of cover and concealment without being detected by people inside the building or structure, advise the communications center and subsequently coordinate the response of other officers to contain the suspect(s). Look for getaway vehicles and for accomplices who may act as lookouts.

One of the primary officer's first responsibilities is to determine if a robbery is in fact in progress. By waiting and observing the area, or by phoning the location, you can quickly determine the status of the robbery-in-progress investigation. If a robbery is in progress, stay concealed and report observed actions to communications and to arriving units. It is imperative at this point to *avoid entry* and to wait for suspects to exit; the last thing that officers want is to create a hostage situation.

All people who leave the location should be treated as suspects until determined otherwise. Suspects should be allowed to exit the building or structure far enough to prevent reentry. Officers at the scene then challenge, control, and secure suspects in a manner similar to challenging burglary suspects. Once apprehended, suspects should be questioned about additional suspects, accomplices, and weapons.

If suspects have fled the area before the officer's arrival, only the primary officer should be at the crime scene. Other officers assigned to assist in the investigation cover the escape routes and search for suspects. The primary officer protects the crime scene and obtains necessary information for quick initial or supplemental broadcasts of the suspects' description, mode of transportation, direction of travel, and so on.

Backup officers search the area for suspects who have left the scene. If the suspects are believed to be using a vehicle, officers estimate the distance that suspects might be able to travel in a given time after the crime occurred. In that time period, suspects in vehicles will generally travel the same distance from the scene that the officer will drive toward the scene. As a rough rule of thumb, suspects can drive a mile per minute; therefore, suspects should be within a 5-mile radius from the crime scene during a five-minute period after leaving the robbery.

Some departments require units not close to the scene to remain in their assigned beats while close-in units respond to the scene directly. The units away from the scene might figure out where the most strategic location (intersections, major traffic arteries, alleys, parking lots, etc.) for intercepting suspects is, and calculate arrival time based on the preceding time-distance rule.

The most natural tendency for units close to the scene is to rush to the area. Support units watch for suspects trying to evade arrest and check out suspicious vehicles and people in the area. Once the decision has been made to enter the building, officers must be alert. Even though it may appear that suspects have fled the scene, the building should be checked thoroughly for other suspects that may be hiding or trapped inside. Keep in mind that the safety of all parties is of paramount importance.

Prowler Calls

Prowler calls are among the most common complaints received by law enforcement agencies. The reporting party is usually very frightened and often arms him- or herself for protection. Suspects can range from burglars, sexual psychopaths, "peeping toms," jealous suitors, and ex-husbands to completely innocent neighborhood boys who are taking a shortcut, animals roaming the area, or tree limbs rubbing against the side of the home. Even though this type of call results in few arrests, officers must guard against becoming complacent and assuming the call to be insignificant.

A good knowledge of the area is of great value in responding to a prowler call. Approach the residence at right angles, by turning at the last intersection nearest the scene. A stealth approach is appropriate, if it can be accomplished safely. When necessary, check house numbers by using a flashlight to view numbers on the opposite side of the street or by checking for curb numbers where the light may be less conspicuous.

When nearing the scene, reduce speeds to eliminate tire squeal and motor noise. In some cases, coasting to a stop may be appropriate; if you roll past the address, do not back up. Investigating officers should control all other noises (radio, doors, keys, etc.) to avoid detection at the scene. Other units in the area should be deployed to cut off natural escape routes and contain the area.

The primary officer at the residence should contact the reporting party as soon as possible. Keep in mind that this person may be armed. Take care not to mistake the complainant for the subject; admittedly, it's not always easy to be sure. The complainant should be advised of your presence in the area and requested to provide details, information, descriptions, direction of flight, and so on, relative to the suspect prowler. Then move quickly and quietly to search the area. By stopping, listening, and watching for activity (such as barking dogs), you may locate the suspect.

During the search, officers might look for footprints or signs of attempted entry. The search should be slow and cautious. Walk in shadows and avoid being silhouetted in the light. If the flashlight is needed, use it cautiously. For example, a flashlight used at an oblique angle on a grassy area wet with dew may reveal footprints, exits, or hiding places of suspects. Favorite hiding places include trees, shrubs, large garbage bins, and parked vehicles. Officers should check vehicles in the area for warm engines, which may indicate which vehicle belongs to the suspect.

A note of caution, however, should be considered. While checking the area for "things out of place" or the "unusual," watch out for clotheslines, garbage cans, and dogs—to mention but a few hazards. During the search, you may also encounter curious neighbors and onlookers anxious to see "what's going on."

After the yard search is completed, the backup or second officer searches the neighborhood and surrounding area for possible suspects. The primary officer interviews the complainant in order to gain additional information; this officer then alerts other units regarding relative data that may aid in the search.

As noted, the complaint may turn out to be "unfounded"— perhaps as in the case of tree limbs brushing the house. In such instances, take care not to ridicule the complainant, but rather assure the citizen that officers are concerned about the well-being of people in the community. If there is reason to believe the complaint may be valid, reassure the resident of continued police surveillance and advise the complainant of procedures to follow if the prowler returns. For example, tell the complainant the following:

1. Do not alert the prowler that you are aware of the suspect's presence.
2. Illuminated lights in the house should be left on.
3. Telephone the law enforcement agency out of view of the prowler, if possible.
4. Be certain to clearly repeat the address, and so on, when calling the police desk.
5. Do not leave the house to search for the prowler alone.

After the initial search, officers in the area make frequent checks on the complainant's home. A searching spotlight in the area will reassure citizens that officers are concerned about safeguarding the neighborhood. The community relations aspects of this courtesy cannot be overemphasized.

KEY TERMS

Building cordon
Burglary
Crime-in-progress
Mile-a-minute rule
Prowler calls
Response to crimes-in-progress
Robbery

STUDY QUESTIONS

1. Discuss your responsibility in responding to crimes in progress.

2. Why might you choose to travel a route that is two miles longer, when responding to a crime in progress, rather than use the shorter route?

3. What considerations may affect your decision to use emergency lights and siren when responding to a crime in progress?

4. What is the primary function of the first radio car arriving at the scene of a crime in progress?

5. How should a vehicle be placed to establish an effective building cordon, in order to secure all exit points?

6. Discuss the proper way to respond to a burglary-in-progress call.

7. Outline the rules for searching a building. How should you search a building when you suspect that a burglar may still be in the area?

8. What should you do when you find a burglar in a building?

9. What is the difference between "burglary" and "robbery"?

10. How would the response to a robbery-in-progress call differ from a burglary-in-progress call?

11. What is the primary officer's responsibility in handling a robbery in progress?

12. In conducting an area search for a criminal's parked vehicle, what indicators can you use to locate such a vehicle?

13. What actions should other units that are not assigned to directly investigate a robbery in progress, take to locate a fleeing suspect?

14. Describe the patrol officer's response to a prowler call.

15. List the various "hazards" you should be aware of in responding to a prowler call.

16. How do you make a stealth approach to any crime-in-progress call?

17. If you are unable to locate a prowler, what directions should you give to the resident in case the prowler returns at a later time?

18. What should you do if you find that the "prowler" is really just the branch of a tree brushing the complainant's house?

19. What actions should the patrol officer take following an unsuccessful search for a prowler?

ACTIVITIES

1. Interview a law enforcement officer who has responded to various crimes in progress, and write a report about his or her experiences and contributions to your knowledge about handling such events.

2. From a list of movies provided by the instructor, critique the actor patrol officer's response to crimes in progress. Note what they do correctly or incorrectly, for a class discussion.

10

Preliminary Patrol Investigations

Basic law enforcement functions include protecting life and property and maintaining peace. When these fundamental tasks are not fully accomplished, the third basic task must be undertaken—crime repression directed toward identifying the suspect and bringing the perpetrator before a court of law. The success or failure of this effort is closely related to the actions initiated by officers immediately following the report of the crime.

Law enforcement patrol officers frequently are the first units to arrive at crime and accident scenes. Each officer must know and follow departmental policy and good procedures in order to protect the crime scene, secure evidence, identify witnesses, and care for the injured. This chapter outlines basic patrol responsibility in handling preliminary investigations to ensure that crime and accident scenes will be protected from contamination and that evidence will be preserved. The importance of immediate first-responder techniques to aid the injured is emphasized. In addition, follow-up techniques of reporting, sketching, and photography are discussed as important aspects of the preliminary investigation.

PRELIMINARY INVESTIGATION

A preliminary investigation is an observation or inquiry into allegations, circumstances, or relationships in order to obtain factual information. Criminal investigation has four major objectives, First, it must be determined if a crime has in fact been committed, and, if so, what crime. This is usually accomplished by visual inspection of the scene and interviews with victims and witnesses. Second, the investigating officer attempts to identify the perpetrator. Investigative activity at this point includes further interviews of victims and witnesses and examination and study of physical evidence, as well as a review of the *modus operandi*.

The next step is to apprehend the suspect at the scene if he or she is present and if probable cause exists to believe that a felony has been committed. Where the suspect has already fled the area and the strong likelihood of arrest is indicated, hot pursuit would be part of the initial immediate action. Of course, if neither condition exists, immediately relay descriptive information to headquarters and other patrol units to help bring about the suspect's arrest. Additional and supplemental broadcasts of information, as it is discovered and developed, are disseminated whenever pertinent.

The fourth phase or objective of the preliminary investigation involves gathering and preserving evidence. This state of the process usually involves the technical assistance and facilities of the crime laboratory. The crime scene must be cleared of all unauthorized people and protected until it has been thoroughly examined for evidence. Before physical evidence is gathered, the crime scene should be photographed and sketched, a fingerprint search conducted, and casts made of tracks, footprints, and tool marks, if such traces can be located. Make complete field notes, including all events and conditions.

SECURING THE CRIME SCENE

What the officer does or fails to do in the first phase of any investigation often determines whether the criminal is identified and arrested or goes free and undetected. A criminal investigation rests firmly or dissolves based on the thoroughness and immediacy of the preliminary investigation. This means that protecting and preserving the crime scene and the subsequent search are prime factors in the outcome of a trial.

The crime scene is the place where a crime occurred. It is the location of a crime, and any overt act associated with the crime is subsequently investigated, beginning with the crime scene. Since the crime scene is the most productive source of evidence, the officer must arrive there as soon as possible. Physical evidence in the form of weapons, fingerprints, tool marks, and tire tracks could be obvious, awaiting your discovery. This evidence can change very quickly, though, and even a few minutes' delay can mean the difference between gathering substantial direct evidence or a frustrating and fruitless effort.

Protection and Preservation: First Steps

The protection and preservation of the crime scene is the responsibility of the first officer on the scene. Quick action could prevent the destruction or contamination of the scene by rain, snow, or wind or damage by other people. Early arrival could also allow you to prevent loss of witnesses, further injury, or even loss of life.

Preserving the crime scene involves all activities necessary to maintain the site in exactly the same physical condition as it was left by the perpetrator. Prevent damage or destruction of all tangible clues. Touching objects or walking over stains, footprints, or tire tracks will destroy the value or reliability of otherwise good evidence.

The first phase of protection allows the officer responsible for collecting evidence to arrive and begin work. Continuing preservation serves to protect against the destruction or contamination of evidence by either authorized or unauthorized people. This second stage also gives the investigative team the freedom to move about examining the various aspects of the crime scene.

The first concern of the officer at the scene must be to protect, and prevent the removal and destruction of, any evidence present at the scene of a crime. Proper treatment is essential at this point if the evidence is to have any value. Failure to obtain reliable evidence often results from faulty crime scene protection at the start of an investigation.

Normally, the patrol officer is the first to arrive at the scene. That officer should first secure the focal point of the scene and then extend the protected area outward to the perimeter. For example, once the officer has secured the room in which the crime was committed, he or she must extend protection to cover the entire building or yard.

The criminal leaves traces of actions, which are part of the crime scene and can easily be destroyed or rearranged if people are allowed to wander all over the crime scene before the investigators have completed their work. If any contamination has occurred, investigators could be led to false conclusions, or they could develop blind leads that would prevent them from reaching a successful conclusion to the investigation. For all these reasons, the patrol officer must preserve the crime scene in its original condition.

The first officer continues to protect and preserve the crime scene while investigators and technicians sketch, photograph, and search the area. Utmost security at this time ensures obtaining a sketch or photograph accurately representing the crime scene's original condition. Only such evidence will be acceptable in court. Should the defense be able to show that a piece of evidence was altered or otherwise tampered with before the sketching or photographing or that persons or things are present that were not there originally, the court will question the reliability of the testimony and other evidence, and its value will be diminished.

Extending Protection

The officer must keep all unauthorized people out of the crime scene area and must also prevent anyone, including him- or herself, from moving or picking up objects that are in disorder. Sometimes if the crime takes place in a store or a home, the owner will want to "clean up the mess." This urge is understandable, but cleanup must be delayed until experts have processed the entire scene for evidence.

Individuals at a crime scene before, during, or immediately after an offense often leave fingerprints. When fingerprints are discovered, developed, and photographed, they firmly establish the presence of certain people at the scene of the crime. Thus, the officer guarding the scene must be especially careful to avoid handling a weapon found lying about the premises and also avoid touching any smooth surfaces the suspect might have touched. If, as the officer in charge, you do have to handle any objects, immediately inform the personnel who are processing the scene of the incident. Careful investigators often develop clear fingerprints from windows, glasses, bottles, and other surfaces only to discover that the fingerprints were left by the officers assigned to protect the scene.

The officer needs to extend strict security to the outer fringes of the actual location of the offense. These measures should include protecting the adjacent area of buildings or hallways leading to an apartment or room where a crime has occurred. This greatly increases the possibility of locating, photographing, and making plaster casts of tire tracks or other impressions. In addition, rubber soles and heels can also leave individual imprints on virtually all types of smooth floor coverings, on dust-covered surfaces, or on the ground itself. Investigators might find evidence that the criminal used a vehicle of some type based on clues in the immediate vicinity of the incident. Tire prints left in soft earth can be photographed and preserved by plaster casts, and such evidence could provide the vital link between the suspect and the scene of the crime.

Other possible signs include tool markings at points of entry into buildings, rooms, safes, or vehicles. Seek and diligently protect evidence of such markings. Any tool leaves identifying markings on any substance softer than the tool itself. Such markings, found at the crime scene, can later be matched against test markings made by the suspect's tool. This matching is done with the same high degree of accuracy found in matching a suspect's fingerprints with those found at a crime scene.

An officer protecting a crime scene must always be mindful that nothing within the crime area should be overlooked or too quickly considered insignificant and unnecessary to protect. Seemingly unimportant objects such as a scrap of paper, a matchbook cover, a piece of cloth, or a glass fragment—properly guarded and handled—have often become the key to success in resolving a case.

Investigative Techniques

As noted, on arriving at the crime scene, determine if a crime has, in fact, been committed, and if so, establish the *corpus delicti* of the offense. Since the court will want to know where specific items of evidence were found, the identity of the finder, and the condition of the evidence, be extremely careful to protect the scene and allow no one except authorized personnel to enter the crime scene area. Individuals who may have legitimate access to the scene include investigators, coroner, and laboratory technicians. Once witnesses have been located and identified, separate them to help ensure that their statements are their own observations and accounts, and are not influenced by what others saw and heard. Identifying and interviewing the person who discovered the crime may provide valuable information, and even hearsay information may help.

The responding officers should prepare an initial broadcast of the suspect's description, including vehicle, if one was used, and the direction of the suspect's flight. The broadcast should include the (1) type of the crime, (2) nature of the business attacked, if applicable, (3) location of the offense, (4) time of the offense, (5) number and description of suspect(s), (6) direction of flight, (7) mode of travel, (8) description of weapon used (if applicable), and (9) description of property taken, if such was the case.

Initial information should be gathered and broadcast as soon as possible because a suspect's vehicle will cover nearly a mile in one minute. A supplemental broadcast should include additional information such as a detailed description of the suspect and his or her clothing and vehicle.

Of course, the officer should administer first aid or secure medical assistance for the victim if needed. If a victim has sustained a potentially fatal injury, a brief statement from him or her may be very valuable. Furthermore, no unauthorized person should be allowed to touch or move the victim's body, whether the victim is dead or alive.

The responding officer should carefully observe the crime scene. It may disclose obvious items such as the weapon used, broken articles, blood, scuff marks, overturned furniture, trampled ground, or smaller physical evidence including buttons, pieces of fabric, skin, hair, and so forth, where the victim fought with the assailant.

Officers should begin interviewing the victim and witnesses, starting with the suspect's first known act, and record successive actions and words used before, during, and after the crime, including what was said, by whom, and the relative positions of the victim and the suspect. As the preliminary investigation progresses, photograph, sketch, make notes, and measure before moving or collecting items of evidence. If possible, photograph injuries; color photographs are preferable.

The victim's and suspect's reputations for peacefulness or quarrelsomeness may be useful in refuting a possible self-defense plea. Also

determine whether there have been any previous threats, prior difficulties, and quarrels between the suspect and the victim, including
details of such encounters.

If the offense is one against the person, secure a professional evaluation of any injuries from the attending physician, and request a copy of
the medical report. Obtain the victim's clothing (if applicable) for
laboratory examination, particularly where there was physical contact
between the suspect and the victim. Also, if the suspect is apprehended,
obtain his or her clothing for examination and comparison.

INFORMATION GATHERING

In the investigation of any crime, an officer must use all possible
sources of information available. To use information resources, you
must first be aware of the kinds of resources available. Information
may be obtained from three basic sources: (1) people, (2) physical
objects, and (3) records, documents, and other public and private
written sources. Officers who conduct preliminary investigations contact numerous individuals who can provide information to them,
including victims, suspects, witnesses, juveniles, and people from all
areas of the community representing diverse backgrounds, occupations, and motives.

Informants

Information provided by informants often plays an essential part in
successful investigations. Such information may lead to evidence of
crime or provide the necessary probable cause for a search warrant or
a legal arrest. Since informants come from virtually all walks of life,
you may find it useful to determine their motivations.

The general informant furnishes information openly and without
concern that his or her identity remain confidential. Often this "good
citizen" informant simply possesses information that may be helpful
in the law enforcement effort and is willing to share it.

Other informants wish to remain anonymous or, if known to the
officer, do not want their identity known to others. When dealing with
a confidential informant, you must take care not to reveal the subject's
identity. Once a confidential informant's identity is revealed, his or

her potential value as an information source is seriously weakened or entirely lost.

Most informants have a particular reason or motivation for their willingness to provide information. Some, as mentioned, feel a sense of civic responsibility or duty, while others expect money payment for their information. Still others desire to win favor, present or future, with peace officers; or they may fear impending arrest or personal harm by a criminal element. Jealousy is a strong motivation and is often the basis for providing information that will affect someone of whom the informant is jealous. Sometimes information is given to officers with the hope and expectation that it will eliminate criminal competition. Finally, revenge against another informant or someone who has taken advantage of the subject now willing to offer information is sometimes a reason for giving officers information. Evaluate information in light of the motivation of the person providing it, if you can discern the motivation.

An effective field officer usually has many sources of information that have been developed in the course of routine contacts over a period of time. Potential sources of information represent a cross-section of the population; however, some of those typically mentioned as possible sources include bartenders, bank and lending company employees, service delivery personnel, cab drivers, store clerks, hotel and motel employees, insurance and private investigators, newspaper delivery people, prostitutes, public utility employees, those who associate with known criminal elements, and fellow officers who have cultivated other sources of information.

An informant, to be effective, must be treated properly. Proper treatment of informants should minimally include fair treatment, maintaining reliability, and remaining in control of the informant. Irrespective of the informant's character, background, or status, the subject should be treated fairly. Always be truthful and fulfill all ethical promises made to the informant; distrust will negatively affect an officer-informant relationship. An informant should never be allowed to take charge of any phase of an investigation, and never tolerate an informant's breaking the law.

In dealing with criminals and other less respectable individuals, be fully familiar with your department's policies concerning such matters, and seek agency approval before entering into an officer-informant relationship. The district attorney should always be contacted in cases of doubt when making a deal with an informant. This action safeguards against allegations of misconduct or inappropriate behavior on the officer's part.

Other Sources of Information

Information may also come from things. A crime or an accident is generally a starting point for an investigation, and physical evidence may help identify or connect those involved in the crime or incident. Valuable information may be gained from clothing, body fluids, hair, tissue, glass, paint chips, soil, tools, weapons, and other physical objects. Physical objects must be identified, collected, and properly preserved.

Many private organizations are valuable sources of information, and—if tactfully approached and assured that their identity will remain confidential—most organizations will cooperate with officers conducting official investigations. If the information is to be used in court, seek a subpoena for the needed records rather than compromise any private source of information. The number of private organizations and business records capable of providing information are as numerous as the individual officer will permit them to be.

Auto rental and leasing companies can provide the identity of individuals leasing automobiles, driver's license information, make and model of the car used, and the mileage traveled. Better Business Bureaus can provide identities of local businesses, reputations of businesses and firms, and information about rackets and confidence games. Banks and loan companies have records on bank accounts and deposits, loan information, and credit records—a search warrant will probably be necessary in light of recent increased concern by the courts in the area of privacy. City directories and telephone books contain lists of names, addresses, telephone numbers, occupational listings, and street addresses with occupant names. School and college records can provide biographical data, handwriting samples and student signatures, educational achievements, and school yearbooks.

The ease or difficulty with which information from these sources can be obtained depends largely on the relationship of the law enforcement agency with the company or agency whose assistance is being sought. Usually, if the law enforcement agency and its individual officers enjoy a good reputation and the community's respect, gaining information from public and private agencies is less difficult, especially when all concerned are satisfied that the need is valid and the information is useful in helping the community as a whole deal with the crime problem.

CRIME SCENE SKETCHES

Sketching is one of the three methods of recording that should be used at the crime scene (the others being note taking and photography). A sketch is a drawing that represents the crime scene and supplements photography by providing accurate information concerning the distance between various points in the scene. Sketches make a permanent record of conditions not easily recorded otherwise. They are helpful in reconstructing the crime scene, and they help correlate witness testimony. A sketch can be enlarged by an artist for courtroom presentation, and is especially useful in eliminating unnecessary and confusing detail. Sketches record the exact locations and relationships of pieces of evidence and surroundings.

Sketches are prepared at the crime scene to demonstrate the spatial relationship between and the location of significant items of evidence. Sketching provides a means of illustrating items that are difficult to adequately describe verbally. It also supplements notes and coordinates photographs. (Photography, being a two-dimensional representation of the crime scene, does not provide accurate information concerning distances between various points. In a photograph, for example, objects in the foreground are often distorted as compared to those in the background.)

Adequate materials must be kept on hand if sketches are to be made properly. These materials include a compass (engineering type), a sketchboard, graph paper, soft lead pencils, good erasers, a triangle, a 20-foot-long × 3/4-inch-wide flexible rule, and a 100-foot tape measure. More elaborate drafting equipment should be maintained if finished drawings are to be produced by agency personnel.

Types of Sketches

The rough sketch is generally the one made at the crime scene, although in some instances, a finished drawing may be prepared there. A rough sketch is generally the basis for the finished drawing that is primarily prepared for courtroom use, and, as prepared at the scene, must stand alone. In other words, some measurements may be obtained at a later time, but those that serve to locate movable objects must be taken when the scene is processed. Memory must not be relied on to later fill in holes and gaps in the sketch prepared at the crime scene. All measurements must be written down.

A sketch of the scene of the crime and its environs should include other buildings, roadways, or the presence of miscellaneous materials nearby. An arson scene, for example, might require this type of sketch in order to illustrate the nearness of combustible materials. This type of sketch would be particularly useful in locating the position of evidence removed from the immediate crime scene.

A sketch of the grounds includes the crime scene and the nearest physical surroundings. For example, the entire floor plan may be drawn, even though the crime scene, as such, may have involved only several rooms. The actions of other people who may have been present but not actually involved in the crime may clearly be indicated through the use of this type of sketch. This type of sketch, as well as the one described above, may also be used to illustrate the routes of approach to and departure from the crime scene taken by the suspect. The presence of footprints and the trajectory of bullets may also be shown.

A sketch of the immediate crime scene is restricted to that area where the actual crime occurred. The following four methods may be employed, singly or in combination, to sketch not only the immediate scene but the general locality and the grounds as well.

1. In the *perspective sketch*, objects are drawn in such a way as to show them as they appear to the eye with reference to relative distance or depth. This sketch is useful when no camera is available, or when the condition of the scene is such that a photograph would not be illustrative.

2. The *projection sketch* is the most frequently used. It is employed when it becomes desirable to portray three dimensions, to allow better correlation of the evidential facts of the scene. All places and objects are drawn in one plane, as seen from above.

3. A *cross-projection drawing* is one where the walls and ceiling of a room are seen as folded out into the same plane as the floor. This type of drawing is employed to illustrate interrelationships between objects in different planes, such as bullet holes and bloodstains.

4. The *schematic sketch* is employed to describe a small area that is not illustrated due to the scale chosen for the rough or finished

drawing. Examples of such areas would be bullet holes, toolmarks, blood spots or patterns, and the location or orientation of a latent fingerprint. Another example would be a drawing of the placement of ammunition in a revolver cylinder. It is also useful when small items of evidence must be illustrated before being removed from immovable objects.

The Finished Sketch. The finished drawing is usually made for courtroom presentation, but it is based on the information recorded in the rough sketch. The finished drawing—unlike the rough original—is drawn to scale and includes standard techniques of drafting. This finished drawing can be as simple or as complex as needed to convey the information. The artist can add specific items relating to the investigation to the drawing using transparent overlays. Using heavy inking or different colored inks calls attention to specific locations, such as points of entry and exit.

The finished drawing helps the judge and jury better understand the crime scene and the testimony of the investigator and witnesses. An accurate and professional drawing that creates a positive impression greatly enhances the presentation of the case. A well-done drawing instills respect for the work and competence of the police.

PHYSICAL EVIDENCE

The admissibility of an exhibit introduced into evidence depends in part on how the evidence was collected and the precautions followed to ensure its integrity. Testimony must also show that officers found the item of evidence at the scene of the crime or in the possession or control of the defendant or that it is in some way connected to the crime scene. You must also satisfy the court as well that the evidence has not been changed and that it can be positively identified and distinguished from similar items.

Although various guidelines can aid an officer in assessing the value of crime scene evidence, the final choice in collecting these articles is still a matter of individual judgment. The personalized approach to identifying and collecting evidence often leads to the common mistake of overlooking or disregarding the significance of less apparent physical traces the criminal has left behind.

Once the officer in charge has decided an item is relevant to the case, the item should remain undisturbed until it is photographed, measurements are made, its position recorded on the crime scene sketch, its description entered in the officer's notebook, and the article is processed for latent fingerprints if the case calls for it. When all such preliminary tasks have been accomplished, very carefully collect the evidence so that it is not damaged or destroyed.

Laboratory Testing

At times officers will submit evidence for scientific examination. Such evidence includes paint scrapings, fibers, hairs, blood, semen, soil, liquids, and so forth. In these instances, collect a liberal sample of the substance whenever possible. This ensures that the laboratory analyst will have enough to conduct a thorough and complete examination without worrying about destroying or contaminating the entire amount of evidence available. Furthermore, too small an amount of any substance used as evidence reduces the extent of the scientific evaluation that can be done because chemical analysis generally consumes part of the evidence. When some of the evidence is still available and can be introduced in its natural state, it is easier to show the judge or jury the significance of the evidence to the question at issue. Still the lack of generous samples—though it limits the extent of the examination—should not discourage you from having a laboratory examination done.

In all major investigations, evidentiary matter (standards) that may be used for comparison purposes at a later date should be collected. A standard can be an identified fingerprint or a torn shirt from the suspect's clothes. A standard whose source is known can be compared to a sample, such as a latent fingerprint or a torn piece of cloth found at the crime scene, whose source is unknown when it is found. Serious crimes against the person or property and serious traffic offenses are examples of instances in which evidentiary matter is important. The significance of such standards rests on the possibility that they will be compared with other physical characteristics found on the body, the clothing, the shoes, the automobile, or in the home of the suspect, thus connecting him or her to the crime or placing him or her or his or her vehicle at the scene.

Labeling Evidence

The officer must immediately and properly mark and label all recovered evidence to ensure its proper identification at some future time. One major reason for these precautions is that police officers involved in the investigation must testify and identify exhibits introduced as evidence in a trial held several months after the investigation has ended. In such instances, the accuracy and scope of the officers' testimony will reflect the manner in which they have placed identifying marks on the evidence and recorded the data in their notebooks.

The officer on the scene must mark each item of evidence when it is removed from its original position. A personal marking, such as initials, badge number, or serial number, should accompany the date of discovery, case number, and other identifying data on the evidence where space permits.

A stylus, scribe, or electric marking tool all work to mark metal objects. Pen and ink are fine for absorbent items such as clothing or documents. Seal small-caliber bullets or shell casings, jewelry, and other objects too small for marking in a small container and identify the contents by writing the necessary information on a label or the container's sides. Keep liquids and pastes in their original containers whenever possible, sealed and labeled.

An identification mark should never be placed where it might damage or alter possible traces such as on the side of a spent bullet. If evidence consists of several similar objects, the identification mark should be put in the same general location on each object. If an exhibit has removable parts, each part should be properly marked.

Envelopes, pillboxes, vials, jars, bottles, and cartons are all suitable containers for packaging evidence. Place each piece of evidence in an individual container. Then seal these so that they cannot be opened without breaking the seal. Having sealed the container, write your name and number on the seal or across the sealed flap of an envelope.

Once an article has been marked for identification, placed in a container, and sealed, attach a label or tag to it. The label or tag should list the case, inventory or property number, and other data concerning who found it, where it was found, when it was found, and so forth.

Integrity of the evidence can be further ensured by choosing a container that will protect the specimen against damage or contamination. Each item should be placed in its own container or paper wrapping. This is especially true if the evidence contains foreign matter such as stains, metal filings, or dust. This precaution is particularly necessary when the evidence is to be scientifically analyzed; contamination can lead to incorrect conclusions.

The Chain of Possession

Using proper methods to collect, mark, and package all evidence can be negated if the people who have handled, examined, or stored the evidence cannot be accounted for and a clear chain of possession established. This chain, marking who possessed or held the evidence, begins when the evidence is first discovered and continues until the time it is presented in court.

The testifying officer must know about and be able to establish possession at all times. If the officer on the stand cannot account for a signature or any phase in the handling of the evidence, the defense attorney will quickly challenge the integrity and admissibility of the exhibit, and most often the evidence will not be admitted into the trial.

THE SEARCH

After the officer has firmly secured the crime scene, it must be searched. The purpose of this part of the investigation is to obtain all physical evidence—a weapon, clothing, fingerprints, footprints, tire prints, or other investigative leads—that might help achieve a successful conclusion to the case.

Knowing how to properly conduct this crime scene search is as much an essential police skill as photography, fingerprinting, plaster casting, and other skills are. The officer who does not know how to conduct a systematic and thorough crime scene search is not fully equipped to discharge professional police duties.

The officer should approach the search of a crime scene by realizing that the solution to the crime could very well depend on what is found at the scene. Teamwork and thoroughness are essential. Everyone participating in the search should have the proper attitude and work with willingness, recognizing that the work of all the other participants could be invalidated by a half-hearted effort on one officer's part.

Physical Evidence

Criminal investigation is concerned with people and things. It is *people* who commit crimes, but invariably they do so using *things*. In almost every crime, the perpetrator either takes something identifiable or leaves something identifiable at the scene. This is also part of the physical evidence. The purpose of the crime scene search is to collect all physical evidence. The investigator should understand what physical evidence is and how to collect, identify, and preserve it. Then the investigator must also know how to pull out the information the evidence carries and how to interpret the information found there.

One of the major objectives of the search is to obtain legally admissible evidence that will establish the fact that a crime was committed and that the department had jurisdiction over the crime. Further objectives are to identify the person(s) who committed the crime and to locate and identify supporting evidence. Finally, the search is conducted to determine the who, what, when, where, how, and why of the crime.

In many instances, a successful search of the crime scene depends on the efficiency of the person who receives the complaint. Keep a record of the complaint, including the date, time, name, address, and phone number of the complainant, and where officers can locate her or him. Second, obtain the specific address and location of the site of the crime and also gather details as to who discovered the crime, when it was discovered, and the general type of crime.

Search Organization

The proper organization of the initial search depends on a great many things, including, for example, the type of scene—whether it is indoors or outdoors, upstairs or downstairs, wet or dry weather, a crowded hotel lobby or a private living room, and so forth. It is impossible to establish rules that will cover every situation. A proper search could involve one officer or many, depending on the nature of the locale and the crime committed. Nevertheless, it is possible to point out certain essential principles of organizing a search.

For an efficient operation, one officer should be in charge of the search. If you are in charge, you must be tactful and possess the ability to manage others. You should not take part in the actual search but rather assess the needs of the situation and assign tasks to other personnel. Do not allow other officers, witnesses, or unauthorized people to enter the crime scene until you have personally examined it to establish the logical areas and sequences of the search. Then designate a sufficient number of personnel to guard and protect the crime scene as the primary responsibility. In addition, you must maintain contact with headquarters and news media representatives who are either present or interested in the search. Although the nature of the offense will provide some degree of direction in the search, you must organize the search and determine the area to be searched. Make specific assignments to ensure complete coverage and to establish the responsibility each participant has.

It is imperative to make definite plans for searching the scene before actually undertaking the task. Someone who is knowledgeable must instruct searching officers about what to look for and within what area. Once adopted, the search plan is carried out. As stated, any careless walking about can destroy evidence. The searchers should always proceed with caution, and their movements should not be haphazard but should follow a predetermined course.

Search Strategies

Figure 10-1 shows four effective methods for conducting a search. One type, the point-to-point search, cannot be pictured, as it varies with each setting. In the point-to-point search, the searching officer enters the crime scene from the point of entrance and goes to the first apparent item of evidence. After viewing the item, move to the next closest item and continue this process until the room or area has been systematically scrutinized. Never wander aimlessly from point to point but carry out a precise and methodical search.

Another search method, the sector or zone search, involves dividing the scene into specific areas or sectors. The officer in charge assigns each officer a specific search area. This method of searching is a good choice when a large area such as an open field has to be covered.

The concentric circle or spiral search method involves personnel starting at the focal point of the crime scene and searching in an unfolding spiral. This search is useful when the officer suspects that evidence has been moved or hidden some distance from the actual scene of the crime. This tactic requires searching the central area first,

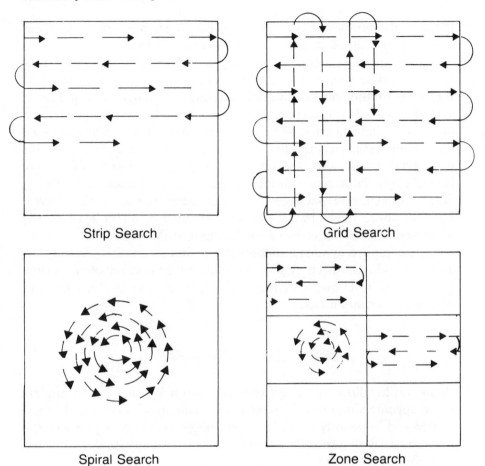

Strip Search   Grid Search

Spiral Search   Zone Search

Figure 10-1
Four different methods of searching a crime scene

and once this location has been thoroughly searched, the officer in charge draws a new and larger circle.

Another effective method of searching is the grid. This relatively thorough approach involves blocking off an area in the form of a rectangle or square. The searchers then proceed along a parallel path from one end to the other. This method has a number of useful variations, such as the double grid or strip.

The strip method, similar to the grid, is less detailed and is effective when officers must cover a large, relatively open area. Although any number of personnel can do the strip search, one officer can also do it alone in a limited area such as a room.

Sometimes chances of uncovering any physical traces of a criminal can appear remote if not totally impossible. Appearances aside, the officer on the scene must undertake the search with determination and alertness. The search is serious police work, with no place for a defeatist or light-hearted attitude. On occasion, the search can be an unpleasant task. Nevertheless, time after time alert police work has uncovered small and seemingly unimportant objects that have brought new hope to a criminal case. A piece of glass, a button, a crumpled cigarette package can seem meaningless by themselves. Each of these items has, however, provided a direct lead to the identity of a criminal or has added weight to the amount of evidence already compiled against a suspect at one time or another. A complete and methodical search is like the efficient protection of the crime scene. Each in its own way plays its important role in the successful course of a criminal case.

CRIME SCENE PHOTOGRAPHS

Photographs allow the judge and jury to quickly and clearly understand specific situations. Photographic evidence can be stored indefinitely and be readily available when necessary. It also provides the investigator with a record of the crime scene and any items connected with the investigation.

The trial court determines the admissibility of all evidence, including photographs. This judgment—to decide what is and is not admissible—is based on legal precedents that have established certain points of law. The first of these is that the object portrayed in the photograph must be material and relevant to the question at issue. Further, the photograph must not appeal to the emotions of, or tend to prejudice, the court or jury. Finally, the photograph must be free of distortion and not misrepresent the scene or the object it purports to reproduce.

Although a photograph makes a clear reproduction of a scene, it has certain limitations. Pictures by nature are two-dimensional; thus they lack depth and do not accurately represent the distances between important items. Furthermore, the angle and distance of the photographer from the object can promote false interpretations of critical relationships between objects. A photograph's value is further reduced when no one can clearly identify the items in it. A camera, lacking selectiveness, reproduces all objects within its range. This lack of discrimination can detract from a photograph's effectiveness.

FINGERPRINTS

Fingerprints can be both valuable and conclusive evidence in a criminal investigation. When a person touches anything, that individual's fingertips transfer oily matter and perspiration onto the surface, which is quite likely to produce images of the skin pattern. Each person has his or her own unique pattern of fingerprints, which makes them an accurate identifying mark.

There are three types of fingerprints: latent, visible, and plastic or molded impressions. Latent prints are seldom visible and must be developed by dusting, fuming, or chemical treatment in order to be collected. Latent prints include any fingerprints, visible or not, that officers find at a crime scene and on articles connected with a crime. Visible prints are formed when a finger is covered with some substance that is transferred to a surface, such as oil, newsprint, grease, blood, ink, dirt, or some other substances. Plastic or molded prints are formed when the fingers come into contact with a soft, pliable surface that takes an impression of the skin patterns. Such patterns are usually found in fresh putty, wax, butter, soap, hard grease, and on any surface that forms an actual mold of the fingerprint pattern.

Fingerprint marks and smudges should not be mistaken for fingerprints. These are highly visible and mistakenly called "fingerprints" by the inexperienced officer. They have little value, however, as investigative aids or evidence because the ridge lines are either not distinct enough or have been destroyed.

When handled properly, fingerprint evidence is meaningful, but it does have certain limitations. Due to its delicate and fragmentary nature, a latent fingerprint rarely has enough of the detail and information necessary for classification and subsequent file search. Such a print can still contain enough characteristics for identification purposes, though, when compared to the inked impressions of a suspect.

The investigating officer should carefully search for latent fingerprints at the crime scene or on any recovered evidence. This means handling suspected articles and surfaces carefully to avoid contaminating or damaging any latent prints. Most surfaces the human hand touches will retain prints, but you will find the best prints on hard, smooth surfaces, such as glass and metal and painted, polished, or varnished woods.

When you find latent prints, make every effort to determine if they were made by someone having legitimate access to the crime scene. This can be accomplished by taking inked fingertip impressions of any household members, employees, other peace officers, or anyone else present at the crime scene. Of course, be certain to indicate the correct name on each set. The availability of these prints makes possible rapid comparison of test and latent prints. This quickly determines if latent prints should be regarded as evidence or are simply traces of a household member or a careless officer or other person.

PRELIMINARY INVESTIGATION OF THE ACCIDENT SCENE

Obtaining the facts at the accident scene is the foundation of an officer's investigation—without facts, there *is no* investigation. The primary source of information is your own observations. The accident investigator is charged with the responsibility of determining the violation or other factors that directly caused the accident. In addition, you record conditions of the weather, light, roadway surface, right-of-way controls, and related factors to determine how each contributed to the accident. The investigating officer obtains information from drivers, passengers, and witnesses to draw conclusions on how and why the accident occurred and who was responsible.

On receiving notification of an accident, the responding officer begins to plan the accident scene priorities. A safe response is of paramount importance: plan the route of approach to arrive at the scene quickly, taking into consideration roads, traffic, time of day, and obstructions. When approaching the scene, look for any vehicle(s) that may be leaving the accident scene. Hit-and-run vehicles may show vehicle damage, be dragging loose parts, emit steam from a broken radiator, or be violating various traffic laws in order to leave the area quickly and avoid getting caught.

At the accident site, the responding officer surveys the scene for hazards. Evaluate the scene to determine the severity of the crash by considering the number of injuries, extent of injuries, whether or not the situation is hazardous, and whether or not utilities are damaged. The position of the colliding vehicles in the roadway, the presence of other traffic, damaged power lines, inoperative traffic control devices, and the presence of pedestrians at the scene are examples of inherent hazards associated with accidents. Other hazards that must be considered include glass, bits of metal, sharp objects, and other debris, which are often scattered around the roadway.

The arriving officer begins protecting the accident scene by properly positioning the patrol vehicle to protect the crash scene and prevent further damage or injury. The position of the patrol vehicle should not create a greater hazard to the scene—do not incorrectly park just inside a blind curve, so that approaching traffic cannot see the vehicle until it is too late to avoid a collision. Generally, the primary responding officer should park his or her vehicle across the road, in plain view of approaching traffic, far enough away from the collision site to protect the scene. Secure the vehicle with the parking brake, and exhibit operating emergency lights. An assisting patrol unit may park across the road at the other end of the accident scene (depending on the road and other inherent hazards) to cordon off the accident area. As a rule, the location of the protecting patrol units should emphatically alert other users of the roadway that no one is to cross the path of those two vehicles except for a law enforcement officer, doctor, nurse, or other emergency worker. If the scene is stretched out over quite a distance, request additional assistance.

Once the patrol vehicle is properly positioned, immediately evaluate the need for emergency medical assistance. Your primary concern is for the injured! On ascertaining the extent and severity of injuries during a cursory inspection, notify communications and request appropriate assistance. Emergency responders may include, but are not limited to (1) an ambulance and paramedics, (2) fire department and rescue teams, and (3) additional law enforcement units.

Care for Injured or Dead

While awaiting medical assistance, begin necessary first-aid treatment. Do not remove seriously injured people from any vehicle unless there is danger of fire. If a person is trapped inside a vehicle, rescue teams experienced in using the "Jaws of Life" (equipment designed to enter a damaged vehicle) may be required to get people out of crumpled wreckage.

Never place an injured person in the patrol vehicle that is positioned to protect the accident scene. Too frequently, other drivers fail to recognize the emergency situation or are unable to stop their vehicles before colliding with the parked emergency police unit. If an injured person is sitting inside the law enforcement unit at such a time, the individual may receive additional injuries. In addition, the officer and the department may be liable for civil damages for negligence in handling the care of injured people.

An officer is generally the first official on the accident scene who determines whether an ambulance or coroner is needed. Although you are not qualified to determine that a person is dead, some situations obviously indicate death. In addition, medical personnel on the scene may tell you that a death has occurred. In any case involving a death, a coroner or Justice of the Peace (depending on the jurisdiction) is summoned to the scene and this official assumes responsibility for the body and its property.

Traffic Control

Subsequent requests for assistance may involve traffic control, tow trucks, and hazardous material removal teams. In some instances, hazards from downed electrical wires or other utilities may require other specialists trained in handling emergencies. Specific needs should be determined as quickly as possible and communications notified.

One of the peace officer's priorities is to restore traffic flow. This task may include the use of alternate routes, alleviating congestion, dealing with hazards in the roadway, and obtaining assistance to correct inoperative traffic control devices. Traffic accident investigators must be constantly aware that other traffic on the roadway is a continuing threat to all people at the accident scene.

The emergency lights of the patrol unit are the first visible alert to other users of the street or highway that an unusual condition exists. An officer can use other appropriate traffic control devices, including highway emergency triangles, traffic cones (if available), and in some cases flares, if flammable or hazardous materials are not a threat. Assisting officers can be positioned to direct traffic around the accident location. In some cases, officers may be needed to divert traffic to detour routes around a major accident scene. At night, a flashlight with a colored cone is a valuable aid in directing traffic at an accident scene.

Traffic control officers at an accident scene should help expedite the arrival and departure of responding emergency vehicles. This job may include creating a path or area through which such a vehicle can quickly reach the problem area. In some cases, law enforcement units away from the scene may block intersections or otherwise help responding emergency vehicles get through traffic. Cooperation and teamwork are essential elements in accomplishing all police tasks and objectives.

Spectator Control

Large crowds can gather quickly at accident scenes. Bystanders complicate accident investigation, and they can inadvertently move or remove evidence or property. A spectator's safety is at risk any time that he or she is in the roadway or at the accident scene. In addition, spectators may interfere with efforts of emergency personnel to accomplish their jobs.

All nonessential people should be requested to move away from the accident scene. In some cases, you may obtain a rope from a patrol unit and ask two or three bystanders to help hold the rope at the limit established for spectator control in a safe area off the street or roadway. Then make it clear to those present that they are not authorized to cross the rope into the accident area. At such times, tact and diplomacy can be used effectively to solicit voluntary compliance. You can emphasize your concern for the spectators' safety and request that they not interfere with emergency efforts to aid the injured or investigate the accident scene. Spectators should be specifically asked not to move or remove any evidence or property from the accident scene.

Hit-and-Run Accidents

Once it has been determined that a vehicle involved in the accident has left the scene, get a description of the vehicle, driver, and occupants (if applicable) and broadcast the information as quickly as practical. Law enforcement officers near or around the scene can begin to search for the hit-and-run vehicle. If the hit-and-run unit is found on a highway or on private property that is open to the general public, a peace officer is authorized to remove the vehicle for investigation.

Investigating officers at the accident scene collect and preserve evidence unique to hit-and-run investigations. For example, gather paint samples and measurements of damaged areas on the vehicle, for future reference. If a pedestrian was involved in the collision, collect the victim's clothing as evidence (be sure to allow clothing to dry before storing). Laboratory analysis may be able to match the victim's clothing to cloth imprints in the hit-and-run vehicle's damaged parts.

TRAFFIC ACCIDENT INVESTIGATION

The goal of an accident investigation is to determine how and why the accident occurred. The investigating officer's conclusion must be based on all facts gathered through observation, interview, and physical evidence obtained at the scene of the accident. In arriving at a sound conclusion, officers frequently use a method of accident reconstruction. This technique of putting together a puzzle may be executed as a mental exercise or done as a physical map-to-scale model of the accident scene. Using either reconstruction technique, you can determine who caused the collision, if anyone, and take follow-up enforcement action.

Sources of factual evidence are people, vehicle(s), and the highway itself. Ask drivers, passengers, and other witnesses to provide written statements. Describe the condition of the vehicle(s), including damage to the exterior and interior as well as the mechanical components. Invaluable evidence can be gathered from investigating the highway to locate marks left by involved vehicles, debris, location of the point of impact (POI), and the presence of contributing factors such as traffic conditions, weather, lighting, and the presence (or absence) of control devices, to mention but a few. The following sections analyze each of these areas in more detail.

Interviews with Participants and Witnesses

The investigating officer must locate and identify the drivers of the involved vehicles. Unless the driver has already been identified, you can place a hand on the vehicle and ask, "Who was driving this vehicle at the time of the crash?" Another acceptable alternative would be to point at a particular vehicle and ask, "Who was driving that (color) (car, truck, motorcycle) at the time of the crash?" The resulting answer will be a *res gestae* statement (a spontaneous exclamation) and is admissible in court. If this procedure is followed on each and every crash investigated, you should have no problems in court "wheeling" ("putting the driver behind the wheel") the suspect.

Obtaining information from drivers and witnesses is important for several reasons. First, these statements will add to the total information obtained; second, the statements can verify or disprove opinions based on observation of physical evidence.[1] A primary technique of any investigator is to be a good listener, which means being receptive to the information others give. In obtaining statements, interview witnesses first and participants second; conduct each such interview privately and, if possible, free of interruptions. For most minor accidents, this interview will take place at the accident scene. Fatality collisions and other serious accidents may require interviews at various locations, including the hospital, the law enforcement officer's office or place of work, or the homes of the victim(s), of witnesses, and of the responsible party.

In speaking with each person, keep in mind that each person saw the accident from his or her own perspective. By interviewing the parties separately and privately, you get each person's perspective of the accident and the factors that were operating, based on how that particular witness or driver interpreted the events. In many situations, private interviews facilitate the exchange and permit a witness to disclose information without being intimidated or influenced by others who were present at the accident scene.

During the interview, listen to the witness's *complete* statement. Too frequently an investigator obtains only partial information and forms conclusions without hearing all the facts. Each driver, passenger, and witness should provide a written statement, which becomes part of the accident report.

The officer's friendly and courteous attitude during such interviews greatly aids in soliciting a statement. It is extremely important to accurately clarify any information obtained during such interviews. If you are unsure of a person's statement, do not repeat the statement

---

[1] *Traffic Accident Investigator's Manual for Police*, 2nd ed. (Evanston, Ill.: Traffic Institute, Northwestern University, 1973), p. 141, Sec. 31.020.

to the person; rather, ask the individual to repeat the statement or later ask him or her a question about what was said at an earlier time.

Getting statements from all individuals at the accident scene is imperative to the investigation. However, do not consider these statements conclusive in themselves; rather, they are useful only to the extent that they help you and other people form opinions about what acutally took place. Keep in mind that witnesses tend to leave the crash scene very quickly. They may not think their observations are important, may be in a hurry, or may have something to hide. A witness may not like law enforcement officers. Some people want to act important and impress friends with their knowledge, and thus volunteer erroneous information. Each of these conditions creates problems for the investigation. Only by listening attentively to each person, without jumping to conclusions, can you obtain all data necessary to draw a professional conclusion on how and why the accident occurred.

In interviewing participants, first obtain each person's driver's license, registration certificate, and proof of insurance (as applicable in your jurisdiction). These documents contain information that is required in completing the accident report, and you should verify that the information is currently correct. Ask each driver to recount the events of the accident as she or he perceived it to have happened. This interview should include all the circumstances leading up to the accident, as well as what happened during and after the collision took place. Although not conclusive, answers to the following questions give a basic idea of how, and often why, an accident occurred (the questions assume that you have already taken care of any injury questions before the interview):

1. Were you driving the vehicle? What direction were you going?
2. What were you doing just before the accident happened?
3. Who owns the vehicle?
4. Where were you going? Were you late?
5. Where was the other vehicle?
6. Where were you when you first saw the other vehicle?
7. Who was driving the other vehicle? (or:) Can you identify the driver of the other vehicle?
8. What in your opinion caused the accident?
9. Was your vehicle in good shape?
10. Have you taken any medicine or drugs in the last few hours?

11. Have you been drinking alcoholic beverages? (if so:) How much?
12. Can your vehicle be driven?
13. Do you need a tow truck? (*Note*: If a tow truck is needed, call one as soon as possible, to save time at the accident scene.)
14. Where did the accident take place?
15. Where did you stop after the accident?
16. Did you notice any other people in the area at the time the accident happened?
17. What else can you tell me about the accident?
18. Were you wearing a safety belt and/or shoulder strap?
19. Were there any passengers in your vehicle?

You might ask the following questions of passengers in either vehicle:

1. Where were you sitting in the vehicle?
2. Who was driving the vehicle?
3. What direction were you going?
4. Did you see the other vehicle before the accident?
5. Can you identify the driver of the other vehicle?
6. What did the driver or other passengers say just before the accident?
7. Did the vehicle appear to be in good shape?
8. Where did the accident happen?
9. What did you do after the accident?
10. Did you see any other people near the accident scene prior to, during, or after the accident who may have witnessed the accident?
11. Were you wearing a safety belt and/or shoulder strap?

When interviewing a witness, you might ask the following types of questions:

1. Where were you when the accident occurred?
2. What were you doing?
3. What brought your attention to the collision?
4. Did you see the accident occur?
5. What direction were the vehicles traveling?
6. Did you hear any noises (tire squeal or other) before the crash? If so, what and where?

7. (If the accident occurred at an intersection controlled by an official traffic control device, the officer can ask,) Did you notice the color of the traffic lights before, during, or after the crash?
8. In your opinion, who caused the accident?
9. Did you notice any other unusual conditions?
10. Can you identify the drivers of the vehicles involved in the accident?
11. Did you see any other witness to the collision?
12. What did you do after the accident occurred?
13. What else can you tell me about the accident?

After interviewing each participant, passenger, and witness, ask each person to complete a written statement, including all details of the interview. You may suggest that the witness write the story in chronological order (what happened first, second, etc.) in order to avoid leaving out an important detail. After obtaining the statement, review it to make sure if the witness included all details of the oral interview and to determine if any new information was included in the statement.

Vehicle Condition

One of the variables that can contribute to an accident is the condition of the vehicle(s) involved in the collision. The condition of the vehicle can easily be overlooked, especially when road and driver conditions seem to explain the accident sufficiently.

In determining the condition of the vehicle and establishing if there was any contributory negligence on the part of the vehicle owner or operator, examine the following:

1. *Speedometer reading.* The speedometer frequently indicates the speed of the vehicle at the time the accident happened.
2. *Tires.* Examine for excessive wear, underinflation, defects, or extensive sidewall cracks or splits.
3. *Brakes.* Look for brake fluid on the ground, depress brake pedal to determine condition of brake action, etc.
4. *Steering gear, wheels, and springs.* Check the action and suspension; be alert for broken parts and determine how much play is in the steering mechanism.

5. *Load of vehicle* (in addition to passengers). Determine how vehicle was loaded and if weight shifts contributed to control of vehicle at the time of the accident.
6. *Wipers.* Worn or inoperative?
7. *Lights.* Tail lights, brake lights, headlights, etc; are they all in good operating order? What was the position of the light switch? Were the high-beam headlights or the low-beam headlights in operation?
8. *Safety belts.* Is the vehicle properly equipped with safety belts, and were the vehicle occupants wearing them?
9. *Accelerator pedal.* Determine if the pedal was stuck down or otherwise inoperative.
10. *Other safety equipment.* Was the vehicle equipped with "safety air bags" or other safety equipment, and did the equipment operate correctly?
11. *Visors.* What was the position of the sun visor, and did it obstruct the driver's view of the roadway?
12. *Other obstructions.* Was the driver's view obstructed by objects in the vehicle or coverings on the windows?
13. *Loose objects in vehicle.* Were there loose objects in the vehicle that collided with the driver or passengers? Did any object distract the driver's attention?

In each instance, the officer should look for damaged or defective parts. In some instances, an examination of the vehicle could determine that other factors—such as items in the vehicle interfering with observation or with the driver's movements—could have contributed to the collision.

While investigating the condition of the vehicle, inspect and note the vehicle identification number (VIN) of each vehicle. In most modern models, the VIN is located on top of the dashboard on the driver's side of the vehicle. In some pickup trucks and other vehicles, the VIN is located on the driver's door or on a plate fixed to the frame near the driver's door. In each instance, check to see that the VIN plate is, or is not, firmly attached to the vehicle; in some cases, a vehicle could be stolen. If in doubt about the correct VIN, or if a vehicle is so damaged that the VIN is not obtainable, compare the VIN with the registration certificate and/or check the license plate number and request a registration check.

The Highway and Other Conditions

The accident investigator can gain valuable information from marks left by involved vehicles (skids, gouges, etc.) on the road surface. In addition, the road type and surface, location of debris (solids and liquids), the presence or absence of control devices (and their operational condition) significantly affect the findings of the investigation. Along with information about traffic, weather, and lighting conditions, begin gathering evidence necessary to complete the investigation and to draw professional conclusions as to how and why the accident occurred.

The Road. Road and surface conditions can vary widely. Consider how the road twists and turns. In some instances, the road may be straight or curved, at the crest of a hill, or rolling. The road may have an improved shoulder, or the shoulder could drop off abruptly at the edge of the street or highway. When considering the roadway, also note whether the road surface is asphalt, concrete, gravel, brick, or dirt. The road surface may be new or used; it may be free of defects or under construction. Coupled with the weather, the surface may be wet, dry, icy, or snowy. Each factor has a bearing on the amount of friction relative to the tire-road contact.

Be particularly concerned with skid marks and gouges left by involved vehicles and the location of debris from the vehicle(s). The experienced investigator will be able to locate and identify skid marks (including skip or bounce skid marks, yaw marks, and gap skid), which are made by the tire sliding without rolling or by both rolling and sliding (scuff marks, including acceleration scuffs) of one or more wheels. Accident investigators receive special training in skid mark evidence.

While investigating the roadway, identify fixed reference points near the accident scene. These are points that you could return to several years later. Primary reference points might include utility poles, fire hydrants, underground utility casings, corners of buildings, traffic signs or signal posts (permanent), mile marker signs, manhole covers, bridge abutments, or other signs of a permanent nature. In some locations, primary reference points may not be present; at such times an investigator may need to locate secondary reference points, such as minor culverts, signs of a nonpermanent nature, trees, or guard rails. Because of recently passed legislation, the life of highway billboards is limited, and these should not be used for measuring purposes. However, the presence of such fixtures should be noted in the reports and diagrams if relevant to the investigation. The key to choosing reference points is to identify fixed objects that will be easily identifiable at a future date. When several reference points are available, choose the most identifiable and fixed points that will help in recording the scene.

In checking for roadway conditions, be aware of holes or deep ruts in the roadway surface. Furthermore, loose material on the roadway, obstruction on the roadway, construction (repair zone), reduced roadway width, or other unusual conditions (such as flooding, ice, snow, etc.) should be indicated in the appropriate section of the accident report. It is relevant to the investigation to indicate whether the roadway is an intersection, driveway, access road, freeway, or other special roadway type.

Location of Debris and POI. Of particular interest to the accident investigator is the location of debris—both solid and liquid—left on the roadway by the colliding vehicles. The physical location of debris can be used to locate the point of impact (POI) or the approximate point of impact (API). Look for the area where the maximum engagement of the collision occurred. To determine such a point, look to see where the majority of underbody debris is located. Underbody debris is the mud, dust, rust, paint, liquids, road tar, and metals knocked loose from the underside of the body, fender, frame, and other parts by crumpling, shock, or violent shaking of these parts in collision.

The center of the area where most of the underbody debris is located will be the POI. However, keep in mind that the debris does not drop straight to the ground if the vehicle it comes from is moving when the debris is loosened. Having determined the POI (or API), note it on the rough sketch and make relevant measurements.

Traffic Control Devices. The accident report generally requires the investigating officer to indicate the type of right of way or other control devices present at the accident location. You are responsible for determining not only what traffic controls are present—if any—but also the working condition of such controls. You may have to watch the cycling of the red, green, and amber lights of an official traffic control signal to make sure that the device is operating correctly. Also make sure that speed limit signs or other regulatory and/or warning signs are properly posted and legible. Check street and lane markings to determine their visibility under the prevailing conditions. Each of these elements could have had a bearing on the conditions that contributed to the accident. If a determination involving faulty traffic signals or signs is made at the scene, notify traffic engineers as soon as possible in order to correct the signs, markings, or signals before another accident occurs.

Traffic Conditions. Determine the traffic condition at the moment the accident occurred. The presence of other vehicles and pedestrians may have had a direct or indirect effect on the collision. In some instances, a noncontact vehicle may have been involved in the traffic situation preceding the accident. For example, Vehicle A may swerve to avoid hitting Vehicle B, which failed to yield the right of way, only to hit Vehicle C or a fixed object. Too frequently, the noncontact vehicle leaves the area before the officer arrives on the scene.

Pedestrians' actions at the scene of the accident are reported on the accident report. The pedestrian may be crossing the roadway (with or without a crosswalk), walking along the roadway, approaching or leaving a school bus, or otherwise contributing to the traffic condition. Even if the pedestrian is not physically involved in the accident, he or she may be a valuable witness to the accident and may provide helpful information to the accident investigator.

Weather and Lighting. Understandably, the weather and light conditions prevalent at the time of an accident are important to the investigator. Although these factors are not generally considered the cause of an accident, the professional investigator realizes that such elements can combine with other conditions—such as driver, road, and vehicle conditions—to explain how and why a collision occurred.

In describing the weather, consider the conditions occurring at the time of the accident. Many conditions, such as rain, snow, ice, sleet, fog, and blowing dust, can reduce visibility and obscure the driver's view by coating the car windows. Such conditions can be so bad as to make it difficult to see road signs and markings. During the interview with the driver(s) involved in the collision, determine how the operator(s) coped with the adverse conditions. Where adverse weather existed, find out whether the vehicle headlights were on and whether the upper or lower beam was in use. Keep in mind that in fog, falling rain or snow, and dust storms, high-beam headlights will reflect back into the driver's eye, making it more difficult for the driver to see the road ahead.

The prevailing light conditions also contribute to an understanding of whether or not the driver's view was limited or obstructed. While the terms *daytime* and *nighttime* indicate the presence or absence of natural light, many conditions can alter the actual amount of light present at any given time. For example, sunrise and sunset create special light problems for the driver. Adverse weather conditions can dramatically affect light conditions even during daytime, requiring drivers to use headlights when visibility is limited to less than 1,000 feet. During time of reduced visibility, always consider the possibility that the operator was overdriving the vehicle's headlights (driving faster than the safe stopping speed allowed by poor visibility). In some instances, the adverse light condition could result when one driver failed to dim her or his headlights, thus blinding the other driver. During daytime, adverse light conditions can be due to sun glare or reflections off glass or metal objects such as buildings, other vehicles, or other objects. Each of these factors can contribute to the accident and can help explain how and why the accident occurred.

Physical Evidence and Protection Against Infectious Disease

Officers at accident scenes are required to identify, locate, collect, and preserve physical evidence. Take all necessary precautions, however, in handling body fluids, such as semen and blood. Infectious diseases such as AIDS and hepatitis are caused by communicable viruses. Recent studies by the U.S. Department of Health and Human Services and the Bureau of National Affairs, Inc. (Washington, D.C. 20037) indicate that the AIDS virus is transmitted from infected people through the exchange of body fluids during intimate sexual contact. Transmission also occurs by sharing contaminated needles, or less frequently, through blood or blood product transfusions. In some cases, people have contracted the disease by exchange of bodily fluids through open wounds and sores.

Many police agencies throughout the nation provide officers with plastic gloves to wear during investigations. While the risk of actually contracting the disease thus is small, take every precaution, and wear gloves before handling any physical evidence involving bodily fluids or assisting bleeding victims in vehicle collisions.

ACCIDENT INVESTIGATION PROCEDURES

The basic principles of traffic accident investigation generally follow the following procedures:

1. Statement taking
2. Evidence collecting
3. Diagramming
4. Determining primary collision factor
5. Completing accident report

Begin by obtaining information from people, vehicles, the highway, and the environment. These tasks start immediately on your arrival at the accident scene. This information is vital to allow the investigating officer to reconstruct the accident.

In order to reconstruct the accident, the investigator begins by working from the results back to the cause of the accident. The sequence of reconstructing generally follows the following pattern:

1. Vehicle's point of rest
2. Path from point of impact
3. Point of impact (or approximate point of impact)
4. Evasive route to avoid collision
5. Direction and path leading up to collision
6. Primary and associated factors causing accident

The investigating officer's ultimate task is to determine the primary and associated factors causing the accident. Often more than one cause contributes, depending on how the variables of people, vehicles, and highway environment interrelated at the moment of the accident. To determine the cause, the investigator relies on physical evidence, statements of involved persons and witnesses, and corroboration of physical evidence and statements.

A primary collision factor is the one element or driving action that best describes the *main or primary cause* of the accident. Professional investigators know that most automobile collisions will have more than one cause. Through effective investigative techniques, an officer must look at *all* the causes of the collision and decide which one driving action or element contributed most and was the *main* cause of the accident. Once the main cause is identified, the other causes may be listed on the accident report. Since the primary collision factor may not always be apparent, the investigating officer will have to examine carefully the contributing causes to arrive at the correct primary collision factor.

Many conditions or actions can contribute to causing a traffic accident. For example, driving actions, physical conditions, emotional condition(s) of the driver(s), visibility, roadway conditions, mechanical conditions of the vehicle(s), and weather or light are but a few main variables. Keep an open mind and look for each condition before deciding which condition may be the primary cause of the accident.

Report Writing

Accident investigators complete statistical information as required by local agency forms. The accident narrative documentation should be clear, concise, and complete, and should answer the questions *who*, *what*, *when*, *where*, *why*, and *how*. Many "fender-bender" accident investigations can be handled and completed in a relatively short period of time. In the event of a fatal collision, however, or in cases involving a hit-and-run, or in cases where not all the information is readily available, you may have to conduct a follow-up investigation. Such a task is handled in much the same manner as any criminal investigation. Seek additional witnesses, evidence, and information from as many sources as are available. In the case of a hit-and-run accident, paint scrapings and debris might be analyzed in a criminal laboratory to determine the type and age of particles. Such forensic evidence could help determine who the perpetrator of the accident was and where to find the suspect, especially if a suspect vehicle is found in a repair garage. In every instance, all such evidence, statements, and information must be accurately and correctly documented and recorded in order to be legally admissible in a court of law.

If the investigating officer determines that one or more drivers were in violation of the law in causing an accident, the officer must then decide on the appropriate enforcement action. In determining driver error, decide either to issue a traffic citation or to make an arrest. For example, an arrest is necessary if either driver was under the influence of an intoxicating substance. When a traffic citation is issued to the driver in violation, a citation should always show the accident report number, along with the specific violation resulting in the collision. Additional citations (such as "no driver's license," "expired license," and so on) should be issued to any party in the accident when such violations are evident.

KEY TERMS

Chain of possession (or custody)
Cross-projection drawing
Hit-and-run accident
Informants
"Jaws of Life"
Latent fingerprints
Mile-per-minute distance rule
Perspective sketch
Physical evidence
Plastic (or molded) fingerprints
Preliminary investigations
Preserving evidence
Projection sketch
Protecting and preserving crime/accident scene
Rough sketch
Scale drawing
Spiral search pattern
Strip search pattern
Visible fingerprints
"Wheeling" the driver
Zone search pattern

STUDY QUESTIONS

1. Define a "preliminary investigation."

2. What is the primary patrol unit's responsibility when arriving at the scene of a crime or incident?

3. Outline the various steps in conducting a preliminary investigation.

4. Why is it so important to protect and preserve a crime scene?

5. Discuss the various types of evidence that may be found at a crime scene and how to collect such evidence.

6. Define *corpus delicti*, and state how this term relates to a crime scene.

7. What information must you give in alerting surrounding units to watch for a crime suspect?

8. Discuss the role of the informant in gathering information. List five people who might be able to provide you with useful information to help in investigating a crime.

9. What are the purposes and techniques used in completing a crime scene sketch? List and describe four types of sketches.

10. Describe two measuring techniques used at crime scenes to complete a formal sketch.

11. What is the "chain of possession" of evidence, and why is it so important to a criminal investigation?

12. Discuss the proper method to photograph a crime scene.

13. Describe the investigative officer's role in collecting and preserving fingerprints at a crime scene. How can fingerprints aid in the investigation?

14. How are the preliminary investigations of a crime scene and an accident scene similar? What major difference can you outline?

15. Outline the patrol officer's responsibility in managing an accident scene.

16. Discuss tactics you may use to "wheel" (put the driver behind the wheel) the operator of a motor vehicle at an accident scene.

17. On a 5 × 8-inch card suitable for carrying in your traffic accident investigation kit, make a personal checklist of questions to ask drivers and witnesses at an accident scene.

18. Outline at least twelve elements to investigate in determining the condition of a vehicle involved in a collision, to establish if there was any contributory negligence on the part of the vehicle owner or operator.

19. How can you determine the point of impact (POI) at an accident scene?

20. How can you guard against infectious diseases when conducting a traffic or crime investigation?

21. How does an accident investigator reconstruct the sequence of events that lead up to a collision?

22. Discuss the proper use of photographs at an accident scene and the types of photographs you should take.

ACTIVITIES

1. Obtain a copy of accident report forms used in your state, and complete a "mock" accident using personal information.

2. Interview a police investigator and obtain information to write a report about the officer's investigation of a crime scene.

11

Unusual Occurrences

Peace officers are expected to display a great deal of control, patience, and understanding under circumstances that can cause other people to lose control. The public looks to peace officers to bring order to chaos, calm to disorder, and resolution to problems under circumstances that generate stress and confusion. A great deal of the law enforcement officer's duties and responsibilities revolve around service to the public and handling a variety of crisis situations. This chapter surveys (1) different types of calls for service, and (2) methods of handling these situations.

HANDLING UNUSUAL OCCURRENCES

An "unusual occurrence" is an unscheduled event involving potential or actual personal injury or property damage arising from fire, flood, storm, earthquake, wreck, enemy action, civil disturbance, or other natural or human-caused incident. In addition to many other local possibilities, these occurrences may involve

- Electrical wires down and/or surface transformers damaged
- Malfunctioning traffic signals
- Hazardous road conditions
- Damage to fire hydrants
- Gas leaks

Officers responding to an unusual occurrence should inform communications of the need for helping officers and traffic control. By observing and evaluating the situation quickly and efficiently, you can help to prevent or reduce injuries and deaths due to the unusual occurrence. Follow certain general guidelines in handling the unusual occurrences just noted.

For example, in handling electrical wires that are down or in handling surface transformer damage, isolate the area and remove all unauthorized people. Barricade the area from pedestrian and vehicular traffic. Treat any fluids leaking from a transformer as hazardous material. Notify communications of the *exact* situation and request assistance from the fire department, gas and/or electric company, additional law enforcement units (if necessary), and the phone or television cable companies if appropriate. Remain in the area, establishing crowd and traffic control until the situation is handled.

A malfunctioning traffic signal can cause a serious accident. Notify (or have communications notify) city utilities of the specific location and problem; for example, lights inoperable, lights burned out, or delay in phase. Direct traffic until repairs are complete. If additional officers are needed because of the size of the intersection or due to the amount of traffic, request this assistance as soon as possible. You may place the traffic lights on "flash" if the duration of an inoperable condition may be lengthy. If you do not have a signal box key, you may request help from a traffic officer who has a key. Leave the scene only when

1. The lights are repaired.
2. The lights have been placed on flash (leave a note describing the nature of the malfunction inside the control box if a repairperson is not on the scene).
3. Temporary stop signs or other controls have been set in place.

Hazardous road conditions can result from inclement weather, such as rain or fog, major highway construction, road disrepair (chuck holes, inadequate lighting, street sign down, etc.), or other unusual occurrences. Advise communications and other appropriate agencies (construction company, city utilities unit, etc.) and take appropriate action to prevent injuries. Direct traffic, barricade the roadway, request a signal repair (where appropriate), or verify compliance with construction permit restrictions.

The water utility agency and fire department should be notified of damage to fire hydrants. Officers on the scene should establish vehicular and pedestrian traffic control. In some instances, you may need to reroute traffic. Be alert for flooding conditions, which could result in erosion of streets, flooding of an intersection, or flooding of private property. Alert communications to any special condition that could cause damage to property and/or injury to people, and seek assistance to repair the problem.

The gas company should be immediately notified when a gas leak is found. Evacuate the area, and establish a security perimeter at a safe distance. Avoid activating sources of ignition including, but not limited to, smoking, flares, and starting cars. On scene, observe and report any changes in conditions.

RESPONSIBILITY OF FIRST OFFICER AT THE SCENE

The first officer at the scene of an air crash, major vehicle accident, or other disaster should request needed assistance and equipment. Additional patrol units (including a supervisor), emergency medical services (EMS), tow trucks, and notification of other agencies (state police, sheriff, harbor police, fire department, etc.) should be requested as the situation warrants. In the event that an aircraft is involved, communications should request special investigators of the Federal Aviation Agency (FAA), the military, or hazardous materials specialists to assist at the scene.

The first arriving officer establishes a security perimeter to isolate the area. With help of other officers (when needed), traffic and crowd control should be established. In some cases, it may be necessary to barricade a roadway; the patrol unit may be used at such times if departmental policy permits such use. The first officer at the scene may establish a command post until relieved by a superior officer. Entrance and exit corridors to the affected area generally use routes that are easily located and that are most efficient. These routes must be kept free from unnecessary traffic.

Determine who and where the most seriously injured persons are, and solicit qualified assistance. Local hospitals and EMS personnel may be needed in serious cases of injury or disaster. Officers on the scene may provide emergency first-aid treatment until professional medical help arrives.

AIRCRAFT PROCEDURES

Civilian or military aircraft crashes are major disasters. When a civilian aircraft is involved, the FAA and/or the National Transportation Safety Board (NTSB) will investigate the crash. Responding law enforcement officers follow normal procedures to help casualties, cordon off the area, prevent looting, and gain as much information as possible for investigators. When reporting the crash to communications, the following information should be obtained:

- Aircraft tail number
- Color of aircraft
- Type of aircraft
- Number of people on board

Military authorities are in charge of investigating crashes involving military aircraft—even though the plane may crash in a civilian area. Cooperation is the key to successfully completing such operations. Peace officers provide logistical support and perimeter control during the incident. Since classified materials or dangerous weapons (which most patrol officers are not qualified to properly handle) may be involved at the crash site, professional experts manage the actual crash scene investigation.

Peace officers at the scene only protect the area and keep out unauthorized personnel. Law enforcement officers *cannot* authorize news media representatives to enter the scene of a crash involving a military plane. Media personnel should be referred to the military person in charge of the disaster. Tactfully explaining problems involving national security and/or dangerous materials will help to gain the cooperation of news media personnel who may be overzealous in reporting the current events.

HAZARDOUS MATERIAL INCIDENT

Whenever a railroad accident, traffic accident, shipping accident, or aircraft crash occurs, officers should recognize that potentially hazardous materials may be involved at the scene. At any such crash site, discarded and abandoned materials (such as manufacturing waste products) could endanger public health if contaminators pollute the environment. The officers' health, as well as the general public's welfare, should be the prime consideration in protecting the area. Therefore, as the first responder to a hazardous material incident, you should be able to

- Recognize potentially hazardous materials incidents
- Prevent contamination to yourself and the public
- Notify proper agencies

The Department of Transportation (DOT) *Emergency Response Guidebook* provides guidelines for the initial actions of first responders to a hazardous materials incident. In addition, the book aids in identifying hazardous materials, including—but not limited to—explosives, poison gas, flammable solids, radioactive materials, and corrosives. This publication can be ordered from the Materials Transportation Bureau, Research and Special Programs Administration, U.S. Department of Transportation, Washington, DC 20590.

Any vehicle transporting explosive, blasting agent, flammable poison, radioactive material, or other hazardous materials is required to display placards and markings on the vehicle exterior. Eighteen different types of placards are in use, each of which is $10\frac{3}{4}$ inches square in size, in a diamond shape. Each placard must indicate the symbol, the name (or ID number), and the color assigned for the appropriate hazardous material being transported. The placard is placed on all four sides of the transporting vehicle, and each sign must be visible from a distance of at least 50 feet away. With the exception of a 600-cubic-foot or larger container, a placard is not required on the material being transported. Once the hazardous material has been removed from a vehicle, the vehicle's placards must be removed also.

Officers at the scene of an accident involving hazardous materials should recognize potential danger immediately. If the hazardous materials are not inside the vehicle, the material can be identified by a 4 × 4-inch label that is similar in color and identically numbered as the vehicle placard. These labels are placed on the packages rather than on the vehicle. In addition to the labeling system, officers can use other methods of identifying the contents of a vehicle. The most obvious method is to ask the vehicle driver or to observe his or her actions. For example, if a driver is running away from the vehicle, he or she probably is attempting to escape from a potentially dangerous area. Observe the types of containers used to transport the cargo. For example, 55-gallon drums often contain flammable liquids, pesticides, fumigants, and corrosives; a 5-gallon container often contains flammables such as paint and solvents; and plastic and paper bags may contain pesticides or fertilizer.

Do not walk into or touch any hazardous and/or spilled materials. If gases, fumes, and smoke are present, avoid inhaling them even if no hazardous materials are involved. Never assume that gases or vapors are harmless just because there is no smell. At such times, identify the wind direction first, and avoid approaching the area from a "downwind" direction.

The first responder's action at a hazardous material scene is to isolate the area and deny entry until specialized people arrive to handle the incident. An officer may use the patrol vehicle and a public address system to manage and isolate the scene. Notify communications of the incident or spill as soon as possible, so that proper assistance can be dispatched without delay. Maintain a position "upwind" from the area and continue to monitor the wind direction. Attempt rescue only if it does not compromise safety and/or risk contamination. When people do become contaminated, they should be kept isolated. Contaminated people should remove all clothing, which should be placed in plastic bags and left at the scene.

While waiting for assistance and/or rescue teams, officers at the scene should look for placards, shipping manifests, or people who can aid in identification of the hazardous material, *if* such action does not endanger personnel at the scene. Peace officers may close the area of the disaster scene and prevent unauthorized personnel entry. Depending on the magnitude of the incident or spill, an "inner" and "outer" perimeter can be established. Generally, the "inner" perimeter should be at least 2,000 feet from the incident; only people wearing protective clothing and self-contained breathing apparatus should be allowed to enter the closed area. All unauthorized individuals should be kept outside the "outer" perimeter, which can be established at the most convenient location. The command post is established "up-wind" between the "inner" and "outer" perimeters.

Officers at the scene can help identify aspects of the incident or spill that could damage the environment. For example, storm drains, sewers, ponds, and streams may be affected by contamination. Take appropriate action to alert cooperating agencies organized to handle these problems. During such times, you might prohibit eating, drinking, and smoking in and around the hazardous material area. Since contamination can be accomplished by inhalation (fumes and vapors), ingestion, and absorption, affected personnel should seek first aid as soon as possible. Usually water is used in cleanup and decontamination. However, understand that such use of water can pollute and spread contamination to sewers and storm drains and you should avoid this problem. Contaminated victims should be transported to appropriate decontamination facilities. If an ambulance is used, it must be decontaminated before being used for other emergency calls.

The overall objective in handling hazardous materials is *containment*. Efforts to stop, slow, or redirect the flow of hazardous materials to prevent environmental damage is of paramount importance. In making choices, realize that "environmental damage" is more severe than "property damage." First responders should evaluate methods to minimize environmental damage. Some methods to accomplish this goal include damming, diking, absorbing, isolating, diverting, containerizing, plugging, or covering.

Many agencies become involved during disasters. Coordination between local (city or county) responders, fire department, county OES, county health (product and material identification), emergency medical systems, public works, flood control (material in sewer or storm drain), air management (monitor air pollution), and the agriculture commissioner (information on pesticides or their use) can result in successful conclusion of the crisis situation. In addition, in specific instances state agencies such as the state police, fish and game department, state health services, water resources control board, parks and recreation, and the department of forestry can assist. Federal agencies such as the U.S. Coast Guard (as scene managers on coastal zones and waterways) and the Environmental Protection Agency (EPA) can likewise provide appropriate assistance. In some cases, private organizations and agencies are available to help in emergency situations. For example, some chemical manufacturers maintain 24-hour telephone numbers to provide information about their products; the Chemical Transportation Emergency Center or CHEMTREC—(800) 424-9300—is one such agency.

The authority for the management of the scene of an on-highway hazardous substance spill or disaster is vested in the appropriate law enforcement agency having primary traffic investigative authority on the highway where the spill occurs. This authority remains in effect until all emergency operations at the scene have been completed and order has been restored. In some cases, however, the agency having primary traffic investigative authority may enter into written agreements with other public agencies to facilitate management at the scene on streets and roadways other than freeways, which are under authority of the state police. For the purposes of this section, "management of the scene of an on-highway hazardous substance spill or disaster" means coordination of operations that occur at the location of the incident. However, this coordination does not include how the specialized functions provided by the various other responding agencies are to be performed. In all instances, all functions should be performed in a manner designed to minimize the risk of death or injury to other people.

BOMB THREATS, BOMBINGS, OR FOUND BOMBS

Bombs, or the threat of bombs, should be taken seriously. Officers must be aware of several hazards to avoid injury and death. For example, radio transmissions can activate electrical explosive devices, so all police radios, including hand-held portables, must be turned *off* before arriving at the scene. During such times, telephones are the only way to obtain assistance or give information. The most obvious hazard is the device suspected of being a bomb. Never open, lift, or move any suspected device, or disturb any switches or wires, until experts are at the scene to take charge of the device.

Responding officers should immediately isolate the object and effect reasonable evacuation of the area. In a bomb threat where a device has not been located, the decision to evacuate is the responsibility of the person in charge of the premises. Conduct a systematic search, using people familiar with the location. If a device, or suspected device, is located, isolate the device and help with evacuating the building. At such times, traffic and crowd control techniques are implemented and officers maintain perimeter security.

Various professional agencies are organized to handle bomb threats. When it has been determined that a specialized agency is needed, communications may notify the following:

- Explosive ordnance division or bomb squad
- Fire department
- FBI; Alcohol, Tobacco, and Firearms; U.S. Treasury Department—when applicable
- Military installations

FIRE CONDITIONS

In the course of their duties in the field, law enforcement officers should be prepared to take appropriate action when confronted by an uncontrolled fire condition. Swift reaction can minimize unnecessary loss of life and property. Major groups of fire types have been established for easy recognition. You should be able to recognize the following three types readily:

- *Class A fires*: common combustibles such as wood, paper, and cloth
- *Class B fires*: petroleum-based fires such as gasoline, oil, solvents, flammable gases, plastics, and vinyls
- *Class C fires*: electrical fires created by generators, electrical panels, appliances, or wiring

Dry combustibles (Class A) fires can be extinguished by cooling with water or a Class A extinguisher. Hoses, buckets, or a fireline might be implemented to put out the fire; in addition, the object can be physically removed or smothered with dirt or other acceptable objects or substances. Petroleum product fires (Class B) can be smothered with a nonflammable blanket, soil, and so on. In addition, carbon dioxide (CO_2), foam, or a Class B fire extinguisher can be used. For electrical fires (Class C), first attempt to turn off the power source (if possible), and then smother with nonflammable material or use a Class C fire extinguisher. Under *no circumstances* should water be used in handling electrical fires. Learn to quickly recognize fire extinguishers and understand which kind can be used with which class of fires.

Type of Fire Extinguisher	Classification of Fires
Water	A
Carbon dioxide (CO_2)	B, C
Dry chemical	B, C
Tri-class dry chemical	A, B, C

As an officer, you may confront a fire condition in which people are trapped and rescue may be necessary. You can prepare for this type of situation by learning some techniques used to survive this hazardous condition. Before approaching the fire, determine the kind of fire; the color of the smoke can be a clue. For example, yellow smoke indicates a chemical fire; white smoke normally identifies combustibles (usually nonchemical and nonpetroleum-based); and black smoke identifies petroleum-based fires. Notify communications and request fire fighting units and medical assistance if needed. Also indicate the kind of structure involved in the fire.

If a rescue is necessary, officers should estimate the time of arrival of firefighters. Since firefighters are better trained and equipped to enter the fire area, do not attempt rescue unless absolutely necessary. If you are committed to a rescue, determine the safest route of entry; it is imperative that an escape route must remain available. Once entry is made, stay low and close to the floor. Crawl and feel your way through the burning structure to avoid falls down stairways and through floors into elevator shafts and other openings. In addition, the low crawl minimizes exposure to toxic gases and fumes (such as burning plastics) when they are present. Victims in fires can be anywhere. Inspect closets, areas under beds, behind furniture, and in shower stalls. During the search, listen for sounds of coughing, crying, or moaning.

Feel (touch) a closed door before opening it to determine the extent of heat on the other side of the door. If the door is extremely hot, exercise extreme caution, since oxygen-starved fires may violently explode outwardly if the door is opened. At all times, avoid becoming trapped! Maintain an escape route constantly!

If you become trapped in a room, close the door(s) and open or break the windows. Remain calm and work at a measured pace. If smoke prevents outside rescue personnel from seeing you, you might throw out your uniform hat or some piece of personal equipment to the ground, to get attention. During such times, avoid stairways above a fire, because this area acts like a chimney flue. At such times, a portable radio can be your lifeline. By remaining calm and using good logic, you increase your chances of rescue.

Officers should be alert at all times to life-endangering situations. For example, superheated smoke and gases in a tightly sealed building or room explode violently if a door is improperly opened. This occurrence is referred to as a "backdraft explosion." Other danger signs to consider are

- Presence of any highly combustible material or explosives
- Toxic chemical gases or fumes
- Firestorms in wildland fires (may trap officers and others)
- Type of clothing worn

The absence of flames within a burning structure, accompanied by dense smoke pulsating from cracks in the structure, should also indicate caution. In this situation, the roof may also be pulsating if it is poorly reinforced. This condition should alert the officer to the extremely dangerous "breather" fire. This is the most dangerous kind of fire. It is oxygen starved and can literally explode when a door or window is opened. Carbon monoxide ignites at temperatures of 1004°F; a normal house fire generates temperatures between 1004° and 1800°F.

HOSTAGES OR BARRICADED SUSPECTS

Officers responding to the scene of a hostage or barricaded-suspect situation have the responsibility of containing the scene and protecting the life of the hostages, which is the primary concern. A second, but also important, responsibility is to apprehend the suspect, if possible. The general procedures include (1) a safe approach, (2) containment, (3) requesting appropriate assistance, (4) evacuation, and (5) communication and negotiation with the suspect.

Responding officers should be aware of the type of call, and caution should be used during the approach to maintain cover. Contain the scene, evaluate the circumstances, and provide information to other responding officers, communications, and supervisors. Once the scene has been identified and notifications have been made, all efforts should be made to safely contain the scene. This effort includes keeping all foot and vehicular traffic out of the area. For the immediate safety of responding officers, a perimeter should be identified and officers assigned to temporary posts until a superior officer arrives and makes necessary adjustments.

A special weapons and tactics (SWAT) team and a hostage negotiator should be called as soon as it is determined that a hostage or barricaded-suspect situation is occurring. Normally, this request for assistance comes from a supervising officer. In the event an evacuation must be made, the safety of officers and citizens is of paramount concern. Evacuations should be systematically conducted as safely as possible.

Negotiations with the suspect(s) should be conducted by a qualified negotiator if possible. Any contact made with the suspect(s) should be as nonthreatening to the suspect(s) as possible. During such negotiations, the policy of the negotiating department must be considered. Problems can arise with the media and with how the department handles negotiation considerations. Regardless of the situation, the techniques of hostage negotiation involve

1. Establishing communications
2. Identifying the type of subject(s)
3. Using suggestibility
4. Evaluating the subject's motives and demands
5. Keeping subject(s) in a decision-making status
6. Keeping a detached viewpoint
7. Buying time
8. Never trusting subject(s) or hostage(s)
9. Keeping the subject(s) talking
10. Being a good listener

A number of different types of individuals may create the hostage situation. Criminals may be trapped while committing a crime and may seek a way to escape the consequences of capture. Prisoners revolting in a prison may be seeking improved conditions and treatment in facilities and services. Mentally disturbed people may display antisocial or inadequate personality traits that present difficult situations for responding officers. Political terrorists may attempt to produce social change through their actions. Each situation presents monumental challenges for responding officers. The incident can be the result of a crime, domestic dispute, or a carefully planned political terrorism situation. Officers on the scene should attempt to quickly identify the type of situation present and alert negotiators and other officers as quickly as possible.

Officers at the scene should be aware of a condition called the Stockholm syndrome, which affects prisoners in a hostage situation. When a period of time exists and interaction between hostages and hostage-takers develops, empathy begins to develop between the closed-in parties. Because of the common area and problems shared by the two groups, hostages may begin to have positive feelings toward their captors. In many cases, the hostages may be "grateful" to the subject(s) and may feel that their captors have "given" the hostages another chance to live. While the empathy strengthens between the hostages and subjects, hostages may begin to have negative feelings toward the authorities. The hostages may feel that they are in danger from the authorities, who may attempt to "rush" the location and capture the terrorists. These feelings can endure long after the situation has been handled. Officers who encounter such people should understand that the victim has been through a traumatic experience. If the Stockholm syndrome is apparent in the victim, do not attempt to dissuade him or her. Officers should not expect the victim(s) to lavish praise and thanks on their rescuers, whom they may view with distrust and hate. Time is the best cure for this condition.

CRISIS INTERVENTION

One of the most difficult and hazardous jobs the peace officer faces on a day-to-day basis arises when the officer is called on to settle disputes and handle domestic crises. Society looks to the peace officer to maintain order and bring resolution to problems when the individual family loses control and can no longer handle its own problems. Such incidents have become so violent that one of the individuals reaches out for police assistance to control and mitigate the crisis. The other person involved in the argument frequently is opposed to having law enforcement intrude in a "personal" matter, and such opposition can lead to an attack on the officer by the opposing party or others involved in the dispute.

Domestic Violence

Historically, one-third of all homicides and a larger percentage of assaults have taken place within the family. The violence, however, is not limited to the family itself. Nationally, 18 percent of all law enforcement officers who were killed and about 33 percent of officers who were injured were intervening in cases of domestic violence, domestic disputes, and other disturbance calls. Public awareness of the number of homicides and assaults to both officers and citizens led to the development of police crisis intervention training in the 1960s and the years following. More recently, emphasis on the criminal and lethal nature of domestic violence has created legislation that mandates a proper law enforcement response to domestic violence.

Generally speaking, *domestic violence* is *abuse* committed against an adult or fully emancipated minor who is a spouse, former spouse, cohabitant, former cohabitant, *or* a person with whom the suspect has had a child or has (or had) a dating or engagement relationship. The word *abuse* means intentionally or recklessly causing or attempting to cause bodily injury, or placing another person in reasonable apprehension of imminent serious bodily injury to him- or herself or another.

By contrast, a *family dispute* involves issues of disagreement within the family that do *not* involve violence, threats of violence, or court order violations. It is important for officers to distinguish between domestic violence and family disputes in order to properly apply the legislative intent to control illegal behavior.

By implementing domestic violence statutes legislatures have sought to address specific acts as serious crimes against society. The official response to domestic violence stresses the enforcement of laws to protect victims. In addition, legislatures want to give notice to potential violators that an attitude of violent behavior in the home is criminal behavior that will not be tolerated by society.

Historically, the criminal justice system has not been consistent in its response to domestic violence. Until recently, domestic violence was more or less accepted and condoned by society. Such behavior, which was learned and perpetuated in the home, was viewed as a private "family matter," rather than criminal behavior. The victims of such behavior faced assaults, permanent injuries, and death. Lack of assistance and intervention by public and private agencies led victims to be reluctant to ask for help or call law enforcement.

However, recent public attention and community education in the area of domestic violence has resulted in the recognition that victims need effective criminal and civil remedies to help break the cycle of violence.

In prior years, mediation was used in situations where an arrest is now the appropriate response. With the implementation of specific statutes, law enforcement agencies now have guidelines to provide maximum protection to the victim from abuse:

1. Address domestic violence as a serious crime against society.
2. Enforce laws to provide the victim maximum protection from abuse.
3. Violent behavior in the home is criminal behavior and will not be tolerated.
4. A peace officer has the right to use discretion in handling domestic violence.
5. A peace officer will not be held liable for exercising discretion in handling domestic violence.

Today's society expects victims to be protected as well as the violator to be arrested and prosecuted. Because of the frequency of occurrence and the escalating nature of the crime, state legislatures know that intervention in domestic violence is necessary to prevent permanent injury or death to victims of this offense. In addition, studies reveal that such crimes also have an adverse effect on children within the family as well as on other victims. Not only may children be injured (either accidentally, intentionally, or while intervening), but the children also often thus learn that violence is an acceptable and expected part of relationships. In some instances, children may blame themselves for the problems or may become emotionally or physically neglected.

Profile of Batterer and Victim. A profile of the "batterers" reveals some interesting facts. In numerous studies, a large percentage of batterers (who are usually men) saw their mothers abused or had themselves been abused as children. Almost all such offenders have a history of assaultive behavior, and a high percentage assaulted their partners in previous relationships. Without intervention, batterers continue their patterns of violence; in fact, nonintervention reinforces perceptions that violent behavior is appropriate. The batterer uses violence as a tool to feel powerful and to have control over others. In many cases, the person blames others and uses violence and aggression in reaction to conflict or anger. The person is afraid, jealous, or obsessed with controlling the mate's activities. The person may also become desperate for fear of living without a mate. Such fear escalates at the time of separation or divorce, leading to increased potential for homicide or suicide.

Interestingly enough, the violator may not be violent or aggressive outside the home. However, many violators have low self-esteem and may experience remorse after committing acts of violence against family members. Although many offenders state that they will not repeat the violence, they often use intimidation and reprisal against victims and witnesses. This pattern is evident in the three phases of the "cycle of violence" (see Figure 11-1):

1. Tension-building phase
2. Acute battering phase
3. Remorseful (asking for forgiveness, "loving") phase

The victim of this crime may be immobilized by fear and may believe any or all of the following myths:

Myth 1. Violence is a traditional aspect of relationships.
Myth 2. The victim is responsible for the violence.
Myth 3. The victim *should* and *can* solve the problem alone.
Myth 4. There are no alternatives.
Myth 5. If the victim complies with the batterer's demands, the violence will stop.
Myth 6. Violence is caused by poor relationships, substance abuse, and stress.

These myths too frequently reenforce the victim's belief that the family should be kept together at all costs. The victim may remain in the violent relationship because she fears retaliation for leaving her partner, economic poverty, problems with children, or lack of support from family and friends. Frequently, the victim does not have the resources or options to resolve the problem. Low self-esteem, emotional dependence, fear of the unknown, and loss of faith in the criminal justice system to resolve the problem cause the victim to accept the limitations and controls set by the batterer.

Phase 1
Increased tension, anger,
blaming and arguing.

Phase 2
Battering—hitting, slapping,
kicking, choking, use of objects
or weapons. Sexual abuse.
Verbal threats and abuse.

Phase 3
Calm stage (this stage may
decrease over time). Man may
deny violence, say he was
drunk, say he's sorry and
promise it will never happen
again.

Effects of battering, over time

Women

- Isolation from others
- Low self-esteem, depression
- Increased alcohol or drug
  abuse
- Emotional problems, illness
- Pain and injuries
- Permanent physical
  damage
- Death

Men

- Increased belief that power
  and control are achieved by
  violence
- Increase in violent behavior
- Increased contact with law
  enforcement
- Increased emotional
  problems
- Decreased self-esteem

Children

- Emotional problems, illness
- Increased fears, anger
- Increased risk of abuse,
  injuries, and death
- Repetition of abuse behavior

Society

- Increase in crime
- Increase in legal, police,
  medical and counseling
  costs
- Cost of prison
- Perpetuation of cycle
  of violence
- Perpetuation of myths
  of inequality of women
  and men
- Decrease in quality of life

Figure 11-1
Battering cycle of violence

Law Enforcement Response. Domestic violence happens at all cultural, economic, and educational levels. Research shows that violent behavior crosses all sociological divisions regardless of economic status or ethnic background. The traditional social response is to keep the family together. This approach traps the victim in a relationship and inhibits the individual from seeking professional help. However, since family violence is *not* a private family matter, but serious criminal behavior, proper law enforcement response can have a positive influence on the family unit.

Positive law enforcement action can have an effective impact on both the victim and the violator. Victims begin to believe that something can be done, that someone is willing to help. In addition, the victims realize that they have legal rights and they do not need to feel guilty or ashamed. And the batterers learn that no matter what the motivation, domestic violence is not acceptable, and their actions are classified as criminal. Contrary to traditional responses, the violator now faces the fact that negative consequences follow violent behavior—arrest, jail, fines, etc. Ultimately, the violator will find out that violence is not a private, family, or civil matter, but is criminal behavior that will not be condoned by society. Many experts believe that this response will stop the cycle of violence and deter continuing violent behavior in the family.

Positive law enforcement response can also affect children in the family environment. Correct response may prevent further violence, abuse, and emotional trauma. Certainly children will get the message that violence is wrong. The long-range results may show that the violent parent is the responsible party, not the victim nor the child.

Finally, peace officers who respond correctly benefit. Early action and proper documentation can have a positive impact on both an immediate and a long-range basis. Good law enforcement action increases the chance of successful prosecution. Once such actions have been accomplished, repeat calls in the same families decrease, and allow officers to concentrate efforts in other crime areas. Even in situations where no arrest is made, you can positively affect the victim, offender, and children by what you say and how you speak to the parties involved. Current laws give officers additional tools that can reduce frustration as well as relieve officers' exposure to violence and liabilities. Certainly officers' public image is enhanced by effective protection of victims and families from destructive behavior.

The Nature of the Crisis Call

In responding to a family violence or disturbance crisis, obtain as much information as possible before arriving at the location. Since many civil disputes also involve criminal assaults, attempt to determine whether a crime has already been committed. You should also be informed if a gun, knife, or other deadly weapon has been alleged in the complaint. When a criminal action has taken place, you are justified in making a complete investigation. In matters concerning only civil law disputes, your jurisdiction and authority are limited to restoring peace and preventing disorderly conduct from developing. In either instance, the intense emotions of the encounter at home can be turned against the officer who tries to bring a temporary solution to the problem

In such actions, the officer's first concern is for personal safety and the safety of others. An officer approaching the location of the dispute may not wish to park the patrol unit directly in front of the residence or building. Instead, park the patrol vehicle down the street from the problem area and approach the location on foot; a backup unit might approach the area from the other direction. During the approach, be aware of possible cover and concealment areas near or adjacent to the building or nearby structures. Be constantly aware of inherent dangers involved in the approach without provoking anxiety in either the disputants or other citizens watching the episode.

When making the final approach to the residence or structure, listen for arguments and other noises to determine the nature of the confrontation. Since a dispute can be between married people, landlord and tenants, and/or neighbors, never assume the nature of the argument until you have taken the opportunity to investigate. When making the final approach, never stand in front of the door when knocking or using the door bell. Once the complainant has been contacted, continue to take safety precautions while interviewing the individuals involved. Occasionally the person who *did not* call the law enforcement can become angry and violent when faced with intervention in a "private" matter. Providing that the complainant has a legal right to the premises and the complainant has invited you onto the premises, you have a legal right to remain at the location until the crisis is resolved or until the invitation has been revoked by the complainant.

Elements of the Crisis

Obtain as many facts regarding the dispute as can quickly be gathered. In some instances, the dispute might involve only civil matters over which you have no direct authority or control. In such situations, you serve as a directory to inform the disputants where they might obtain assistance and legal advice. Never give legal advice. Without the benefit of law school and the legal right to act as a practicing attorney, you are not equipped to settle disputes involving contracts or torts.

In such cases the officer's main concern is to bring a temporary resolution toward some peace and harmony. Your positive outlook and calming presence might restore communications between the disputants, who are ultimately responsible for regaining control of themselves and the situation. You might use the opportunity to promote good community relations and obtain the respect of the parties involved in the dispute. The officer who becomes angry will lose self-control as well as the ability to control the situation at hand.

How to Intervene in a Crisis

First and foremost in any crisis intervention, the officer must continually adhere to safety precautions. Every year officers are killed or injured seriously in handling domestic disputes. Your first concern is to prevent the disputants from causing harm to yourself and backup officers at the scene. The second most important factor is to prevent the disputants from injuring themselves, each other, or others.

After gaining legal entry to the premises, the officers face the problem of defusing the immediate crisis. The purpose of such defusing is to remove the immediate hostility and allow disputants to regain their rationality. Defusing techniques are limited to the immediate crisis and are not considered long-term resolutions to the problem. In dealing with the people involved, you must be able to size up the personalities and mental states of the subjects in a few moments and then relate to an individual to help that person regain control. These requirements demand that you be able to communicate well with the individual and be sympathetic in helping the disturbed person return to a rational state of mind.

Whenever possible, separate the individuals involved in the argument and interview them separately. The approach to either person must bolster that person's self-control while permitting the person to explain his or her side of the story. You can use a number of defusing techniques, depending on the personality of the individual involved. In some instances, you might calm a person down by taking notes; in this instance, you can change the subject from the dispute to another subject—such as a person's job or hobby—to allow the individual time to relax and calm down. In some instances, you may sympathize with the problem without taking sides and suggest outside agencies and/or counseling organizations that specialize in civil disputes. If the individuals are members of a particular church, you might summon the priest or pastor to counsel with the parties. The objective of this interview is to allow time for the parties to regain their proper sense of self-control and good judgment. Frequently one party will agree to spend the night away from the residence to permit tempers and emotions to cool down before attempting further communications at some later time. In any event, a report must be made.

In handling domestic disputes, it is important for officers to impress on the parties involved that violent behavior is a crime. Special interview techniques can help overcome a victim's reluctance to report a violent incident. When you learn that a domestic dispute involves violence, focus on the criminal aspects of the dispute. In a separate and private interview, reassure the victim and eliminate fear for self, children, and possibly for the suspect. The compassionate officer deals with the victim's feelings of guilt, shame, embarrassment, or helplessness to stop the violence. A victim often feels responsible for any violence and may have socially isolated him- or herself. In such cases, the victim may appear unresponsive or even impaired.

During such interviews, officers frequently use tape recorders, which can be useful in successful prosecutions. In dealing with the victim, reassure the person, to solicit the victim's willingness to reveal specifics of the crime. Emphasize that the victim is not responsible, nor to blame, for the violence. Reinforce the concept that the officers' presence is a positive way for the victim to receive help. During the interview, victims may tend to deny or minimize the extent of their injuries. Ask specific questions designed to gather factual information that clearly identifies the extent of injuries and the violence that took place. The interview should also elicit any past history of violence in addition to the current attack.

The victim may also be reluctant to provide specific information, for fear of what may happen to the perpetrator. If appropriate, you might advise the victim that an arrest may help prevent future violence and can lead to "forced help" for the batterer. The law specifies that a court may order detoxification, specialized counseling, and domestic violence diversion programs to prevent future violence. You can also explain to the victim the impact of violence on children in the home. When appropriate, law enforcement personnel on the scene should advise both the victim and the suspect that *the officer* (not the victim) is initiating the arrest and what police action will follow.

If a crime involving domestic violence has occurred, conduct a crime scene investigation. Obtain statements from the victim, witnesses, and the suspect in accordance with proper procedure. At the scene, collect evidence and establish proper chain of custody. When firearms are discovered at the scene of a domestic violence incident involving a threat to human life or physical assault, you may take temporary custody of such weapons discovered in plain sight or discovered pursuant to a consensual search as necessary for the protection of yourself or other people present.

Several factors should *not* be used to avoid making an arrest. The decision to make an arrest is *not* affected by

1. The marital relationship of suspect and victim
2. Whether or not the suspect lives on the premises with the victim
3. Existence or lack of temporary restraining order
4. Potential financial consequences of arrest
5. Complainant's history or prior complaints
6. Verbal assurances that violence will cease
7. Complainant's emotional state
8. Nonvisible (internal) injuries
9. Location of the incident (public versus private)
10. Speculation that complainant may not follow through with the prosecution, or that the case may not result in a conviction

An arrest for domestic violence may be justified under many penal code sections. The specific charge and language used will depend on specific state statutes. In general terms, the following common violations may be applicable in various jurisdictions.

1. Aggravated assault or lesser included offenses of assault

2. Corporal injury to spouse or cohabitant
3. Battery
4. Rape or sexual assault
5. Intimidating or dissuading a witness, or interfering with a witness (if threats of force are implied)
6. Various statutes involving brandishing or displaying a weapon in an obviously offensive manner
7. Deadly assault with weapons
8. Contempt of court order or violation of a civil court order to prevent domestic violence
9. Criminal trespass or unauthorized entry of property
10. Disturbing the peace or disorderly conduct
11. Unlawfully exhibiting or using a firearm

Other associated penal code sections that may be involved in a criminal investigation are burglary and kidnapping or false imprisonment. The investigation should include a report on the extent of the injury, to determine the seriousness of the crime.

Documenting Cases of Domestic Violence. Investigating officers report all cases of domestic violence regardless of whether or not an arrest was made. The reports must include information on weapons involved in the case, such as guns, knives, or other weapons (belts, baseball bats, etc.). The reports should include detailed description of any injuries and the nature of the crime(s) committed. For example, include the number of times that the suspect allegedly hit the victim. In addition, include the following information, if available:

- Statement of prior domestic violence (from the victim, the officer's knowledge, or documented reports)
- Medical records and/or victim's statements of past medical treatment received for past injuries
- Existence of restraining order or stay-away orders
- Notes on the victim's emotional condition

Investigating officers should preserve all evidence and take both initial and delayed photographs. Each incident should be fully documented for use in future prosecutions, or for use in civil courts (e.g., to obtain restraining orders). Give the victim the report number, if available, or tell the person how to obtain it at a later time. In addition, explain the criminal complaint procedure and other necessary information to help the victim.

Assistance to Victims of Domestic Violence. Officers have a positive responsibility to help victims of domestic violence. Such assistance may be in the form of obtaining appropriate medical attention, transportation to alternate shelter, standing by while individuals remove personal property, and explaining options for follow-up procedures. Each department develops its own policy for officers to follow in giving such help. Therefore, you must seek out specific guidelines relative to such issues.

Generally, department policy will govern how and when to render assistance to complainants who claim injury. The injury may, or may not, be visible. Keep in mind that shock can mask the extent of an injury; an apparent minor injury can be much more serious than it appears on the surface. Based on department policy, arrange transportation for the victim to obtain medical attention or to arrive at an alternate shelter. Such transportation may be needed if a victim expresses concern for safety or if you determine that a need exists. A concerned officer should know how to contact shelters for battered women and children pursuant to departmental policy.

Officers are frequently asked to stand by while victims of domestic violence remove personal property from a potentially violent home. This is another area where departmental policy should guide your actions. Generally speaking, however, your presence is designed to prevent violence while the individual removes essential items of personal property at the time of the incident or at some later time on request. During such operations, personal safety is the prime concern.

Give the victim of domestic violence as much information as possible to help her (or him) make wise decisions to secure safety. If the suspect was arrested, tell the victim approximately how soon the suspect's release may occur. You might also encourage the victim to take steps to avoid future violence—such as changing locks, staying with friends or relatives, and changing routines and travel routes. As noted, you should be aware of alternate shelters and be able to properly advise victims how to contact such facilities. Finally, encourage victims to call the police if needed. The victims of family violence must know that peace officers are willing and available to render assistance and support. Victims must believe in peace officers' ability to protect the family from violence and to generate positive reenforcement to prevent repetition of violence.

When advising victims about criminal justice system procedures, provide emotional support for them. Inform victims about follow-up procedures (statements, photographs, court appearances, etc.) when a subject is arrested. In addition, provide information about local victim and witness programs designed to create support systems. If the suspect is not apprehended, officers still conduct complete investigations (collect evidence, take photographs, write reports) and explain the warrant process to the complainant. In such instances, encourage victims to follow through with criminal prosecution. If provided with information about domestic violence diversion (counseling, alcohol treatment programs, etc.), victims can gain insight into how to obtain restraining orders from courts and how to get public and private aid (legal aid, family law, custody, tenancy, etc.).

Court Protective Orders. Courts may issue restraining orders to prevent family violence. When the court has reasonable proof of past acts of abuse and/or threats of violence that place another person in reasonable apprehension of imminent serious bodily injury, courts may issue an *ex parte restraining order*. This writ is a restraining order issued without prior notice or hearing and is usually valid until the "order to show cause" hearing. The document is signed under penalty of perjury that a suspect or defendant has been served a copy of the court order. A hearing is held to determine if the *ex parte* order is justified and should be extended. If the court determines that a permanent injunction (order requiring a person to refrain from a particular act) is justified, the order is enforced under "contempt of court" proceedings.

The court orders restrain violent behavior or threats of violence. The order can provide for a "kickout" provision when victims show "colorable" (demonstrative) right to possession, even though the victim may not own the house or pay any rent. Furthermore, the court order can require subjects to "stay away" from complainants. Such orders may require the suspect not to contact the victim or even to come within so many feet of the victim, the victim's home, work, school, or the victim's children or relatives who may be harassed or threatened. Such orders provide for temporary custody and temporary support, and can provide for restitution or court-ordered counseling for the suspect. Generally, restraining orders effectively prevent violence if peace officers enforce them.

Law enforcement agencies are required to maintain a complete and systematic record of all protection orders with respect to domestic violence incidents, restraining orders, and proofs of service in effect. Officers should determine the actual location where their respective department maintains restraining orders for verification, since record-keeping procedures vary from agency to agency. Such records are maintained to inform law enforcement officers responding to domestic violence calls of the existence, terms, and effective dates of protection orders in effect. Whenever a complainant advises an officer of the existence of a restraining or protective order, the officer should ascertain

1. Whether a restraining order is on file with the department or whether complainant has a copy of the restraining order in possession
2. Whether a restraining order is still valid as to duration or time
3. Whether the proof of service or prior notice exists or whether the suspect was in court when the order was made
4. The terms of the restraining order

By law, the terms of a restraining order are effective when the document is issued and must be enforced by peace officers. Law enforcement officers arrest when there is reasonable cause to believe that a suspect has violated the court order in the presence of the officers and when any one of the following conditions is met:

1. The existence of the order and proof of service on the suspect has been verified by the officer.
2. The complainant produces a valid copy of the order bearing a file stamp of a court and a proof of service on the subject.
3. The existence of the order has been verified by the officer; no proof of service is required if the order reflects that the suspect was personally present in court when the order was made.
4. The existence of the order has been verified, and there is proof that the suspect has previously been admonished by an officer.

A knowing and willful violation of such orders occurs if the suspect violates the terms of the order. Peace officers are limited in applying discretion in these matters. Once an arrest is made, officers should not cite and release the offender, due to the likelihood of recurrence of harm to the victim. Most courts will not issue a restraining order unless there has been evidence of abuse and imminent harm to victim if the suspect is not restrained. If an officer is not certain whether proof of service (or prior knowledge) exists, the officer should

- Inform the subject of the terms of the order.
- Admonish the subject of the order that the subject is now on notice and that violation of the order will result in arrest. If the subject continues to violate the order after being advised of the terms, an arrest should be made.

In the event a subject has left the scene of the incident, and an investigation determines that a crime has been committed or domestic violence exists, the officer completes a full report. The complainant should be advised of the follow-up criminal procedure and the report number for future reference. In the event that officers cannot verify the existence of an order, they write a report and give the victim the police report number. The victim is advised to contact the appropriate department unit for follow-up.

Arrest Criteria and Enforcement Procedures. Once a restraining order has been verified, officers are required to make an arrest if the suspect has violated any terms of the order. The subsequent report filed by arresting officers should note the specific violations of the court order. The victim should be given the police report number for follow-up action.

In addition to any charges resulting from the subject's actions (assault, unlawfully using a weapon, etc.), officers should also charge a violation of the court order. An act of victim intimidation relating to the court proceedings is a violation of the penal code. For example, an act of intimidation may include

- An attempt to prevent or dissuade a victim from attending or giving testimony at any proceeding
- Using force, or expressing or implying threat of force or violence related to the court proceeding

Other Disputes. Other types of disputes may involve anything from an unknown trouble call to a neighbor's complaint. Such requests for service can be either a criminal violation or a civil dispute —depending on the elements of the call. Frequently, all that is required at such times is the calming influence of the investigating officer to resolve the dispute.

The officer's prime responsibility in handling nonviolent disputes is to keep or restore order rather than enforce the law. However, seek to determine if a crime has been committed before pursuing other alternative actions. As in violent disputes, provide safety to individuals and property and seek to calm the participants in order to resolve the immediate difficulties. In addition, help the parties to find solutions to their problems In some instances, the proper course of action may involve civil courts when the participants cannot find other solutions. Your image is enhanced by being tactful and using good reasoning powers to persuade the disputants to seek nonviolent remedies for the problem in question. However, keep in mind that you are not in a position to give legal advice or recommend private counsel. You may, however, inform people of the procedures to contact the district attorney, public defender, city attorney, or legal aid foundations. People certainly have the right to seek their own attorneys for advice.

Be careful of the words you choose when trying to help individuals in civil disputes. The public often takes an officer's opinion as law— and the law enforcement officer is not qualified to give legal advice. Advise the disputants that your role is to *keep the peace*. Your primary goal is individual safety and to find a solution to the problem through some kind of mediated resolution. In some instances, you might elicit suggestions from the disputants for resolving or improving the situation. Each proposal should be checked out until an agreement is reached or a compromise solution is agreed on. Once such a course of action is stipulated, make sure each person understands the commitments he or she has made according to the plan. Finally, encourage the disputants to have confidence in the agreed-on course of action and to follow through with their plan. Once a solution is acted on, you may leave the scene.

Referrals. Referring civil disputants to a community service agency for counseling is effective only if the officers know that the agency is equipped to help the people with their particular problem, and that the problem identified lends itself to a specific agency. You have a responsibility to continually familiarize yourself with the operations of referral agencies. A problem should be referred to a specific agency when a relatively specific problem exists that an agency is equipped to handle. This referral is appropriate when disputants ask for help with a continuing problem that they believe is beyond their resources. Do not make a referral when the dispute appears to be an isolated incident, or when both disputants insist that they do not have a problem or that they can solve the problem themselves.

When there is a choice between agencies that can provide similar services, make the referral to the agency closest to the home of the disputants. When the disputants or the family have more than one problem and really need the services of a number of agencies, determine the most acute problem and direct the individual to the agency that can provide appropriate help. Get a commitment from all involved parties to complete the referral—the participants must agree to try problem resolution. Write down the referral information for the convenience of the disputants and explain the nature of the services, its fees (if known), hours, location, and telephone number. General referral agencies include Alcoholics Anonymous, Legal Aid Society, Family Services Bureau, or any other referral agency specializing in working with such problems.

In some instances, a temporary separation may help solve the immediate situation while the individuals calm their emotions. In some cases, one disputant may decide to stay with a friend or relative for a night or two until the people have a chance to reflect on the problems and seek mediation. Although this is not designed to solve any deep-seated problems, it may help restore the peace until other arrangements can be made.

Suicide Intervention Procedures

Handling a suicide attempt may be one of the most difficult assignments you face. Understanding some common facts and misconceptions about suicide and support resources available within the community will make the job easier.

Facts and Myths About Suicide:

1. *Myth:* Very few people ever think about suicide.
   Fact: Thinking is different from doing. Many people *do* consider suicide at some point in their lives, although they never attempt it.
2. *Myth:* People who talk about suicide don't kill themselves.
   Fact: Eight out of ten people who commit suicide tell someone that they're thinking about hurting themselves before they actually do it.
3. *Myth:* Only certain types of people commit suicide.
   Fact: All types of people commit suicide: male and female, young and old, rich and poor, country people and city people. It happens in every racial, ethnic, and religious group.
4. *Myth:* Suicide among kids is decreasing.
   Fact: The suicide rate for young people has tripled in the last ten years.
5. *Myth:* Most people who kill themselves really want to die.
   Fact: Most people who kill themselves are confused about whether or not they want to die. Suicide is often intended as a cry for help.
6. *Myth:* When a person talks about suicide, you should change the subject and try to get his or her mind off the subject.
   Fact: Take the person seriously and listen carefully to what he or she is saying. If the person says, "Nobody cares!" respond with "I do!"

Suicidal Conditions. Suicide among young people between the ages of 15 to 25 is among the top two causes of death; the other major cause is traffic collisions. Suicide for black youths is 50 percent higher than for the national average for all ages; the male suicide rate is higher than that for females. Suicide is the second leading cause of death among college students.

The two primary situations when a person is at the greatest risk of suicide is when the individual is seriously depressed and when the person is facing a crisis situation. Recent loss of a loved one, recent loss of status (job, position of esteem, money), poor marital or family relationships, and a history of drug or alcohol abuse are all factors that signal high suicide risk. Studies indicate that warning signs of depression include sleep difficulties; depressed physical appearance;

slumping; poor personal hygiene, tiredness and fatigue; general loss of energy; sitting in fetal position; weight loss or loss of appetite; crying for no apparent reason; slow thinking and speaking; apathy and despondency; easy agitation or terse replies; not wanting to converse and appearing preoccupied or sad; and increased alcohol or drug use.

The following list suggests why a person might attempt suicide; the person may want to

1. Escape from an intolerable situation
2. End an unresolved conflict
3. Join a deceased loved one
4. Improve his or her conditions
5. Gain attention
6. Manipulate others
7. Be punished or avoid being punished
8. Control when death will occur
9. Destroy the "internalized other"
10. Become a martyr
11. Punish the survivors
12. Respond to a voice during a "command hallucination"

Other warning signs of a suicide risk include

1. Running away from home
2. Truancy
3. Hostile behavior or rebelliousness
4. Neglected personal appearance
5. Increased alcohol or drug use
6. Theft or vandalism
7. Carelessness or accident-proneness
8. An actual suicide attempt
9. Change in eating or sleeping habits
10. Giving away prized possessions
11. Loss of interest in friends
12. Long and deep depression over a significant loss
13. Significant change in school grades
14. Feeling hopeless or full of self-hate
15. Feeling constantly restless or overactive
16. Sudden interest in arranging personal estate (will, insurance, etc.)

17. Loss of interest in social activities
18. Absenteeism

SLAP Method for Assessing Risk. To assess the degree of suicidal risk, determine the

- *S*pecific details of the suicide plan
- *L*ethality of the proposed suicide method
- *A*vailability of the proposed method
- *P*roximity of helping resources

If the accumulated data suggest a high probability that an attempt at suicide is imminent, take immediate steps to intervene in the crisis.

Suicide Intervention. There are five basic steps in the suicide intervention process. Each officer should learn and practice (perhaps through role playing) how to intervene and save a life.

1. Establish a relationship with the person at risk. Do not become judgmental; remain supportive. Let the person know that you "really care." It is best to maintain contact and obtain information. Convey patience, interest, self-assurance, hope, and knowledge. Above all—*listen* to the person.

2. Identify and focus on the central problem(s). Divert the person's attention from self-destruction. Try to help the person to recognize the central problem involved in the crisis.

3. Evaluate the risk by using the SLAP method. Identify the precipitating stress or crisis, and try to uncover recent significant changes in the person's behavior that would indicate that he or she will take drastic action.

4. Get help for the person, and protect the person from the immediate possibility of self-destruction. Place the person in protective custody if reasonable cause exists. If appropriate, bring to the scene someone important to the person—friends, relatives, or the clergy. If possible, involve mental health professionals. Do not leave the person alone until medical care is available.

5. Follow up on referrals to make sure help has reached the person. Be sure that the dispatcher notifies the hospital or treatment facility of any incoming attempted suicide case. Ask the attending doctor to annotate the medical report certifying the doctor's opinion

that the person no longer presents a danger to him- or herself or others if you release the person.

Officer Safety Factors. When responding to an attempted suicide, move quickly and quietly to avoid creating additional stress for the suicidal person, but avoid rushing onto the scene. Assess your own safety and that of others in the immediate vicinity. Move away onlookers or potentially disruptive people who are at the scene. Separate the suicidal person from any weapon as a first priority.

Establish contact and begin intervention procedures if you are the first officer at the scene. Try to lead the suicidal person away from any immediate danger. Avoid placing yourself in a position where your life and safety depend on the suicidal person. Avoid situations where avenues of escape are blocked. Above all, remain alert for any sudden attack or another self-destruction attempt by the suicidal person. Remember, the suicidal person may not have the "intestinal fortitude" to do the job him- or herself and may put you in a position to use deadly force to accomplish the task.

Other officers at the scene may need to assume traffic and crowd control duties. If necessary, another officer can provide support to an intervening officer when responding as a backup to an attempted suicide call. Backup officers should provide the same supportive and encouraging attitude as the initial officer. *Do not* make the mistake of encouraging a suicidal person to "go ahead and kill yourself" as an attempt at reverse psychology. Statistics show that this person may well do it! Each officer's job is to be caring and avoid injury to everyone—especially yourself.

HANDLING THE ABNORMAL INDIVIDUAL

Mental or emotional illness is a disorder that affects the way a person thinks, acts, feels, and behaves. Officers frequently have to handle people who are mentally or emotionally ill because their abnormal behavior frequently includes illegal or disruptive conduct. The behavior can be of a mild nature, as in a person who is viewed as odd or eccentric, or it can scan the spectrum of abnormal behavior up to the psychotic individual who can take the life of another person without remorse.

Recognizing the Mentally Ill Person

The word *abnormal* is defined as "Not according to rule; different from the average; unusual; irregular" (Funk & Wagnalls Standard Desk Dictionary, 1979). In recognizing the possibility of a mentally ill person, the officer is concerned with changes in behavior, strange losses of memory, or paranoia, to mention a few types of abnormal behavior. The individual in question might have illusions of self-greatness, see visions, smell strange odors, talk to him- or herself, or hear voices. A mentally ill person can feel bodily ailments that are not possible or could be in a state of panic or be extremely frightened. Frequently such an individual acts in a way that is dangerous to him- or herself or to others. The behavior of any individual might not fit totally within a single category because frequently more than one condition is present.

Handling a Mentally Disturbed or Violent Person

An officer confronted with handling a mentally disturbed or violent person should first take time to look over the situation. Knowing that the individual might not be able to recognize the seriousness of his or her behavior, be extremely careful—the mentally ill person could strike out in a fit of paranoia. Do not abuse or threaten the person, since such actions put the abnormal person on the defensive and block efforts to gain the ill person's cooperation. In handling the individual, do not let the person's behavior disturb you; avoid excitement in order to control the person and the situation. Do not deceive the person because once the individual realizes the deception, he or she will lash out and may never trust a person in uniform again.

Occasionally physical restraints are necessary to ensure the safety of the individual or the officer. Some mentally ill people can get completely out of control, well beyond the ability to reason and make rational decisions. In such cases, you will need help in restraining the out-of-control person until physical restraints can be applied. Take care to use only whatever force is needed to control the individual and prevent that person from inflicting harm. Handcuffs are the first line of physical restraint. When applied, the handcuffs should connect the person's hands behind his or her back with the palms facing outward. The handcuffs should be double-locked to prevent them from tightening any more than is actually necessary to restrain the person. When medical personnel are at the scene, the use of straitjackets or other restraints may be more appropriate than handcuffs. The main concern in restraining the person is to prevent any harmful actions; take due care and precautions to avoid inflicting unnecessary injury to the person.

Handling Depressed People

Officers deal with many abnormal behaviors, and one of the most commonly encountered disorders is depression. A depressed person may well attempt to commit suicide, and any person who threatens to take his or her own life should be taken seriously. In handling such threats, act quickly to gain the confidence of the individual. Do not threaten or heighten the excitement of the moment but rather attempt to calm the person and rationalize the importance of life, family, and loved ones who will suffer should the person take his or her life. Be patient and have a physician called to the scene.

If custody of the depressed person is necessary to prevent self-harm, contact a family member who cares for the individual. If necessary, you might recommend professional treatment. The officer's empathy, concern, and professional manner can well make the difference between life and death for the individual. However, keep in mind that the suicidal personality can easily turn the threat from him- or herself toward you. Don't take unnecessary risks, and do not let the suicidal person push you into doing the deed for him or her.

The officer should realize that the individual could carry out a suicide threat in jail. Prisoners who commit suicide frequently do so by hanging. The officer in charge of the custodial facility must constantly supervise and watch the depressed person. As soon as feasible, officials should make arrangements to transfer the depressed person to medical facilities where the individual can be treated for the disorder.

Disorders That Look Like Mental Disorders

In dealing with abnormal behavior, the officer should be aware that some disorders can look like mental or emotional illnesses but in fact are physiologically based. Illnesses such as diabetes, severe infections, meningitis, pneumonia, brain tumors, high blood pressure, epilepsy, hardening of the arteries in the brain, and head injuries may, in many ways, appear like behavior that is due to a mental disorder. Whenever possible, look for medical bracelets, wallet cards, or other sources of information that indicate the presence of any of these physiological illnesses. Also contact a member of the person's family or the family physician whenever an illness is suspected. Under no circumstances should you administer medicine or drugs to the person unless directed to do so by a physician.

Special Mental Conditions

The officer should be able to recognize special mental conditions that lead to special law enforcement problems. These conditions include the psychopathic personality, the alcoholic, the drug addict, the sex offender, and the mentally retarded. Each of these conditions requires special attention and care.

The Psychopathic Personality. The psychopathic personality is the most dangerous type of individual. This person has a type of disorder in which the individual is totally detached from reality. The psychotic individual can exhibit traits of paranoia (delusions of persecution or of grandeur) and/or manic-depression (a psychosis in which the individual experiences periods of manic excitation alternating with melancholic depression). The psychopathic personality can take the life of another person and totally justify the act and feel no remorse. To the psychopathic person, the peace officer represents a person in authority who is a constant threat. Thus your life is constantly in danger when handling this type of person.

In dealing with the psychopathic personality, learn as much as possible about the individual's tendencies, habits, and state of mind. Whenever possible, contact the individual's personal physician to assist in controlling the abnormal behavior. If you must handle the individual without medical assistance, ensure that a backup officer is available before confronting the person. Plainclothes officers may be able to deal more effectively with the psychopathic personality, since the law enforcement uniform represents a direct threat to the subject. In any event, exercise a great deal of caution in making an arrest or otherwise taking this type of person into custody.

The Alcoholic. The alcoholic person is an ill person, and alcoholism is an illness that affects the brain and motor functions. The alcoholic individual is addicted to alcohol. If alcohol is withheld, the individual may well experience physical withdrawal called *delirium tremens* or the DTs. Ethyl alcohol (the type of alcohol used in intoxicating beverages) is a toxic substance that, when introduced into the body in relatively small quantities, produces a depressant effect on the brain and central nervous system. In substantially larger quantities, ethyl alcohol is fatal. Alcoholics not only may abuse ethyl alcohol but also drink after-shave lotion or other liquids in order to maintain and support the alcohol habit.

Drug Addicts. People addicted to drugs constitute a serious threat to the law enforcement officer. Drug abusers who are addicted will use almost any means to obtain their "fix." Users who experience symptoms of habituation, while less dangerous than addicts, still constitute a large portion of the drug abuse problem. To recognize the drug abuser, the officer must understand the effects of various types of drugs on the central nervous system:

- *Barbiturates:* depressant drugs that slow down the central nervous system
- *Amphetamines:* stimulant drugs that excite the central nervous system
- *Narcotics:* painkillers that block messages of "pain" traveling from the central nervous system to the brain
- *Hallucinogens:* drugs that excite the part of the brain controlling perception and the senses; effects are unpredictable

Each of these substances is hazardous to the abuser when used alone, but drug abusers frequently mix them in dangerous combinations to obtain the "best" effects of each while masking the "bad" side effects of the other. Abusers also combine these substances with alcohol, which makes identification of the drug abuser more difficult. For the abuser, combining the addicting substances with alcohol can be lethal.

Many signs should alert you that a person is a suspected drug abuser. Heroin abusers will have "tracks" (a series of needle marks) puncturing the skin, usually near veins such as on the inside of the arms. Cocaine users can develop sores near the nasal passage where the cocaine has been "snorted" or have sores on their face and body where the users "scratch" the skin to get at imaginary insects under their skin. Drugs should be suspected whenever there is an abrupt change in a person's behavior patterns and lifestyle, change in personality, inability to concentrate, abrupt loss of appetite, or an abnormal desire for privacy. Although these symptoms might be explained by other reasons than drug abuse, these are known characteristics of drug abusers too.

In addition to symptomatic behavior, you should be able to recognize drug paraphernalia associated with drug abuse. These items of equipment or "tools" used to administer drugs can include hypodermic needles or "spikes" used to inject drugs, spoons used as cookers for heroin, razor blades used to grind cocaine and prepare the substance to be "snorted," "roach clips" used to smoke marijuana, and a variety of other devices designed to administer the drugs.

Keep in mind that the drug abuser is desperate. The need to avoid the pains of withdrawal due to physical dependence is real to the addict, who will do whatever is necessary to obtain the next fix. Many females turn to prostitution to obtain the necessary funds to purchase drugs to which they are addicted. Other addicts will steal, rob, assault, and even murder to avoid the pains of withdrawal or to pacify the compelling psychological desire for a drug. In handling the drug abuser, take precautionary measures to ensure that the addict cannot harm him- or herself, you, or others. Whenever a suspect exhibits signs of habituation or addiction, advise a supervisor to determine if hospitalization is appropriate in the situation.

The Sex Offender. The sex offender is one of the most difficult types of individuals law enforcement officers must deal with. The typical peace officer whose attitudes toward sex are relatively normal may experience unusual emotions when dealing with the sex offender's abnormal behavior. The law enforcement problem is compounded when the public is shocked and stunned by acts of the sex offender, and the law enforcement agency is expected to protect society from the acts of deranged individuals. Media coverage surrounding sex crimes is generally exploitative and extensive, bringing the disgusting acts of the sex offender into the living rooms of community residents. The peace officer, working under the eyes of the community, is hampered in any investigations because of the heightened publicity and public interest. When the law enforcement agency successfully solves the case, public confidence in the ability of the law enforcement agency to solve crimes is reenforced. Failure to solve crimes—especially those perpetrated by the sex offender—eats away at public confidence in their police department, and the general morale of the line officers suffers.

A sex offender is anyone who breaks a law pertaining to the sexual offenses outlined in the penal code. The violator is usually involved in molesting others or creating a public nuisance by violating codes of decency. The individual is usually an emotionally immature or mentally ill person who has, either temporarily or permanently, taken on some form of abnormal sexual behavior as a symptom of a behavioral problem. Offenders in this category can be homosexuals (both male and female), voyeurs, exhibitionists, transvestites, sadists, masochists, and individuals with numerous types of fetishes.

The people involved in sadism, masochism, and child molesting are, by far, the most serious of the sex offenders. The sadist is a person who derives sexual satisfaction through cruelty, torture, or the suffering of others; the sadist might indulge in beating, slashing, cutting, or otherwise torturing a victim or sexual partner. The masochist, on the other hand, derives sexual satisfaction by being tortured or humiliated. Individuals with such abnormal behaviors are frequently involved in "piquerism" (or lust mutilation) so that the person derives sexual satisfaction from cutting, slashing, or mutilating a victim, usually before, during, or immediately after an aggravated sexual assault. The child molester is an extremely dangerous sex criminal. In most instances the individual who sexually molests children is a male who is unable to relate normally to mature women. He is a potential killer because his victim, the frightened and desperate child, will often cry out or threaten to tell her or his parents about the assault; the molester can panic and kill the child to protect himself.

To investigate such cases, follow the normal tactics of a criminal investigation. Be aware, however, that the sex offender "routinely" commits his crime, frequently in a ritualistic manner. Be conscious of the *modus operandi* (MO) or method of operation embodied in the *corpus delicti* or body of the crime. Since the sex offender is ritualistic, the offender will repeat the crime in a similar pattern each time. This "signature" of the crime is helpful in determining who perpetrated the offense.

Other criminal acts such as arson have been linked to sex offenders. A condition known as "sex pyromania" (known also as the fire-water complex) results in criminal arsonists who set fires to achieve sexual gratification. The pyromaniac, after setting the fire, usually stays to watch the fire burn and might even try to help put out the fire. Whenever several fires occur within a short period of time, the officer should suspect that a compulsive pyromaniac (or "firebug") is likely to be found at the scene of the arson. Pictures or videotapes of the crowd might reveal one person who is present at several fires in different areas.

Sex offenders can be—and usually are—extremely dangerous to society and the peace officer. If the victims of the sex offender are young children, try to reduce the possibility of mental harm to the child by limiting discussions of the incident in the presence of the child. In such cases, you are dealing with highly emotional situations and individuals and must rely on professionalism, knowledge, experience, and compassion.

The Mentally Retarded. The mentally retarded individual requires special handling. Such a person may look like a grownup but have an intelligence no greater than that of a child. The officer should be well versed in handling such people and be able to recognize possible indicators of mental retardation. In dealing with a person suspected of being mentally retarded, inquire how far he or she went in school. Possibly you can judge the mental age of the person based on behavior; the following examples might be useful as guidelines.

Retarded people are not inclined by nature to get into trouble with the law, but are easily influenced by others who are troublemakers. The manipulator believes that he or she can use the retarded person to achieve desired benefits or goals. The retarded individual generally has poor judgment, and retarded children are quite sensitive about being retarded. Retarded adults often wander aimlessly about and might stare at other people; such adults are frequently interested in children because they better understand what children are doing. Retarded people are frequent victims of robbery, theft, sexual assault, and other violations.

In dealing with the retarded person, the officer must be patient, kind, and understanding. Frequently the mentally retarded adult will not talk when asked a lot of questions one right after the other. Local policy may dictate that the mentally retarded person should be returned to his or her home or other place of care and protection. In dealing with the parents of a mentally retarded child, keep in mind that the parents or guardians have had a rough time raising the person, and be patient and understanding with the parents as well. If the parents have not already done so, you might suggest that they consult a physician or psychologist who specializes in this type of behavior.

Mental Disorders in Old Age. When a person grows older, changes can take place in the individual's brain. Blood vessels carrying nourishment to the brain can become hardened and narrow; once the vessels are not able to provide all oxygen and food the cells need, the individual's brain can begin to disintegrate.

An elderly person can hide a purse, money, or other valuables and then forget the hiding place. In such cases the person might falsely accuse others of stealing, which could result in an unfortunate arrest that turns out to be extremely embarrassing for everyone involved. The elderly person can also wander into the wrong house, thinking it is his or her own, or can think that a complete stranger is a relative. An elderly person can pick up objects in stores and forget to pay for them. The aging person might live alone and forget to eat properly and thus become physically ill.

The officer who is assigned to handle such cases must be patient, gentle, and understanding. If the elderly person needs medical attention, make the necessary arrangements and contact the elderly person's family or friends. Be aware of the local social service agencies in the community that are adept in assisting such cases, and make referrals to these agencies whenever such assistance is needed. It helps to remember that one day we all will join the ranks of the elderly.

In some cases, an officer may be required to invoke the involuntary mental health services for emergency detention. If you apprehend a mentally disturbed person without a warrant, you must make out an application for emergency admission and detention. The application must be signed by an adult, and a warrant for admission must be issued. In seeking such emergency admission and detention, the officer generally provides the facts of the case to the county judge, or other designated magistrate, who will review the case and decide whether the warrant should or should not be issued. On receipt of the warrant, transport the mentally ill person to the hospital or facility designated in the warrant. During the time that you have such a person in custody or during the transportation to a medical facility, be patient and understanding with the ill person. However, exercise a degree of caution with the mentally ill person since he or she may not understand the difference between right and wrong and could attempt to attack or injure you.

KEY TERMS

Abnormal persons
Addiction (drugs)
Alcoholic
Amphetamines
Batterer
Barbiturates
"Breather" fire
CHEMTREC—Chemical Transportation Emergency Center
Classification of fires (A, B, C)
Court protective orders
Cycle of violence (domestic violence)
Delirium tremens (DTs)
Domestic violence
Emergency medical services (EMS)
Ex parte restraining (court) order
Explosive ordnance disposal (EOD) units
Federal Aviation Agency (FAA)
Hallucinogens
Hazardous material incident
Hazardous material placard
Hostage negotiator
"Inner" and "outer" perimeters (hazardous materials incident)
Paraphernalia for drug use ("tools," "spikes," "roach clips")
Psychopathic personality
Pyromania or "sex pyromania"—"firebug"
Unusual occurrences
"Upwind" vs. "downwind" position (hazardous spills incident)
SLAP method for assessing suicide risk
"Stockholm syndrome"
Suicide intervention

STUDY QUESTIONS

1. Describe the difference between domestic violence and a civil disturbance involving family members.

2. Why should officers be especially careful when responding to a domestic violence situation?

3. Why is domestic violence considered to be a serious crime against society?

4. Outline the profile of a "batterer" in a domestic violence dispute.

5. Outline the profile of the victim in a domestic violence dispute.

6. What is considered to be the appropriate law enforcement response to domestic violence? Why?

7. How does positive law enforcement response to domestic violence affect children in the family environment?

8. Describe the proper steps law enforcement officers should take in handling a family or domestic violence crisis.

9. Why should officers separate disputants when interviewing each person involved in the family dispute?

10. If an officer makes an arrest for domestic violence, he or she should explain to the arrested person and the victim that the officer—not the victim—is the person initiating the complaint. What is the rationale behind this notification?

11. List ten factors that should *not* be used to avoid making an arrest in a domestic violence situation.

12. What actions should the responding officer take if the victim alleges that a restraining or protective order exists?

13. What is an officer's prime responsibility in handling nonviolent disputes? Explain the proper procedures for officers to follow in handling this type of complaint.

14. Describe the proper method of handling a mentally disturbed person.

15. What actions should officers take when dealing with a depressed person?

16. The psychopathic personality is the most dangerous type of individual to a peace officer. Describe this type of personality trait and why you should take great care when dealing with such people.

17. What is *delirium tremens*? Why is it important to recognize this condition in affected people?

18. Why is the sex offender one of the most difficult types of individuals law enforcement officers must deal with?

19. In investigating sex offenses, why should you be conscious of the criminal's *modus operandi* (MO)?

20. Describe the proper way to handle a mentally retarded individual.

21. What situation(s) may cause a person to consider committing suicide? List the top five reasons you believe contribute most to suicide attempts.

22. What is the SLAP method for assessing suicidal risk situations?

23. Describe the five basic steps in the suicide intervention process.

24. Describe basic safety considerations that you must take in approaching a potentially suicidal person.

25. If a suicidal person says he or she intends to kill him- or herself because "nobody cares," what should your response be? Why?

26. Should you use reverse psychology on a suicidal victim and tell him or her to "Go ahead and kill yourself"? Why or why not?

ACTIVITY

Contact a professional in one of the disciplines discussed in this chapter, and discuss a real-life experience this person has had in the field. Make a written report of the interview and schedule an oral in-class report for the class.

12

Crowd and Riot Control

A principal responsibility of local and state law enforcement is to maintain law and order. Officers can best perform this crucial role when they have the wholehearted support of all segments of the community—civil organizations, church leaders, public officials, business leaders, news media, and other responsible members of the community. Prevention and control of civil disorders are community responsibilities, not exclusively a law enforcement function. Actually, law enforcement agencies function most efficiently and effectively where there is mutual understanding of both community problems and law enforcement responsibilities. Such understanding provides the necessary basis for effective action to successfully maintain law and order. When community problems that could lead to civil disorder are encountered, give intelligence reports to appropriate officials so that remedial steps can be taken.

BASIC RIGHTS

The founders of our country recognized that human beings have inalienable rights—rights that cannot be taken away. These rights are considered so paramount that they were expressed in the Declaration of Independence as a basis for action:

> We hold these truths to be self-evident, that all men are created equal, that they are endowed by their Creator with certain inalienable Rights; among these are Life, Liberty and the pursuit or Happiness.

In order to exercise these rights, our natural needs must be satisfied. We must have food, clothing, and shelter to sustain life; the right to freely choose legitimate goals and lawful means in the exercise of liberty; and the right not to be unjustly denied, because of such considerations as our race, color, creed, or national origin, the opportunity to legitimately fulfill all our natural, physical, and mental capabilities in the pursuit of happiness. This does not mean, however, that the individual's rights or desires will always prevail; there must be at all times a balancing of one person's rights with the rights of another individual's and of society as a whole.

We are social beings who, with rare exception, desire to be secure, crave recognition and approval, and expect to be treated as possessed of human dignity. As an extension of personality, most people share certain aspirations. Various schools of thought concerning human aspirations are often mentioned, among which are independence, justice, wealth, recognition, and self-esteem.

Most people aspire to be independent in their choice of goals, objectives, and actions. They express this quest in assorted ways. Generally, people use a peaceful approach to accomplish independence; however, once emotionally motivated and organized, some may resort to drastic means to attain their objectives.

We aspire to justice. Our sense of justice expects equality before the law for all members of society regardless of wealth or position, race, color, creed, or national origin, both in protection of rights and in the punishment for wrongs.

Some people use wealth as a measure of both individual and social progress. Wealth can add to an individual's sense of security regardless of the particular environment. This aspiration for wealth is sometimes correlated with an individual's desire to obtain personal, economic, and social recognition.

We generally seek to communicate our ideas, problems, and desires. In return, most people desire to be recognized and treated as contributing members of society.

Most people realize human dignity is shared in common, and desire respect from and equal treatment with other members of society. As individuals develop self-esteem, they may collectively assert themselves in attaining objectives and goals.

Any unjust denial, actual or imagined, of our basic rights, needs, or aspirations can give rise to a feeling of frustration and desperation that can (1) be exploited by elements of a community prone toward violence and/or (2) serve as a foundation on which additional grievance can build, all of which could lead to possible violent protest action.

Every civil disorder or riot is brought about by previously existing factors. The buildup may or may not be apparent and may or may not have a legitimate beginning. Whatever the background, the atmosphere contributing to a riotous situation develops over a period of time, and many factors are often involved. In the final analysis, the most effective means of preventing riot and mob situations is to eliminate conditions that lead to friction and misunderstanding and ultimately to violence and lawlessness.

CROWD CONTROL SITUATIONS

People gather in groups for many reasons. They gather in small, spontaneous groups out of curiosity and in large, formal groups out of common interest. The group may be passive or aggressive, or a mixture of both types.

Officers who encounter a crowd control situation must appraise the situation carefully. Keep in mind that the overall objective is control of the situation. There are many factors to be considered in controlling such assemblages, including

1. The legal rights of the group to assemble
2. Right of the public to carry on business
3. Tactical ability of the law enforcement agency to handle the situation at the time of the occurrence
4. Emotional complexion of the group

The task of handling different situations is complicated by the fact that various people will view the law enforcement officers' activities differently. One of the primary considerations of the law enforcement agency is to assess the makeup of the group and the reason(s) for its gathering. Although the First Amendment of the U.S. Constitution guarantees all citizens the right to assembly, this right has parameters to ensure public safety. You must weigh the group's right to assemble against the rights of the entire community. Since your duty is to protect the rights of all people, without regard to sexual or ethnic makeup, or political, religious, or moral views, your actions and conduct must be professional and legal.

In some instances, a group may gather to protest real or imagined infringements of its rights. Officers at such scenes should comply with their agency's guidelines, which dictate each officer's actions. Assess the crowd control situation, and be prepared to advise your supervisor or agency of the changing status. At all times, your manner should be professional, unbiased, and firm in all contacts with the crowd or its representatives.

Chemical agents are not normally used against single individuals or very small groups in crowd control situations. The decision to use chemical agents to disperse, demoralize, or deny access to a crowd must be carefully weighed against tactical considerations.

The containment of riotous activity is essential to terminating the problem. A law enforcement agency must respond as rapidly as possible to curtail rioting activity and control its spread. However, officers should not respond or be sent to a riot area before sufficient personnel are on hand to effectively control the perimeter of the affected area. When a perimeter is established, ingress and egress traffic must be strictly controlled, thus preventing the spread of the riot, and preventing outsiders from entering to loot or join the riot.

Dispersal of the rioters can begin once the perimeter has been established and ingress and egress traffic has been controlled. The dispersal plan should be accomplished systematically. The affected area can be divided into sections; officers then clear one section at a time. Part of the plan to disperse must establish or create a path for rioters to flee without allowing violators an opportunity for vandalism and continued involvement. After one section has been cleared, it must be patrolled by sufficient personnel to prevent any resumption of riotous activity.

Teamwork is the key in handling a number of disturbances. Several basic formations provide flexible methods that have proven to be effective in controlling crowds and riots. However, it is relevant to note that such formations are effective only when all squad members operate as a team! In selecting the appropriate formation, the squad leader considers such factors as the size, demeanor, attitude, and intent of the crowd. In addition, attention must be given to surrounding terrain, the available dispersal routes, the objectives of the department, and other involved elements—such as tactical withdrawal. The following basic crowd and riot control formations might be used depending on various special considerations:

- *Skirmisher line* (see Figure 12-1). This formation can be used to move crowds straight back, to contain a riotous group, or to deny people access to restricted streets or areas.
- *Wedge* (see Figure 12-2). This formation can be used to penetrate and split a crowd.
- *Diagonal* (see Figure 12-3). This formation can be used to change the course of direction of groups in either open or congested areas or to move a crowd away from a structure.
- *Column* (see Figure 12-4). This formation can be used to move a group of officers from one location to another and to divide a crowd.

HUMAN BEHAVIOR IN CROWDS

Law enforcement agencies, from time to time, face dangerously explosive situations. Civil rights statutes have in some areas produced resentment, resistance, and sometimes retaliation. Resulting dissatisfactions and disagreements are sometimes so fraught with bitterness that tensions build up to the boiling point. Changes in social structure and cultural values are perceived by many misguided people as threats to their well-being and way of life. Sometimes they react violently.

The law enforcement officer is used to controlling crowds, as this is part of his or her everyday activities. However, different kinds of problems may be involved. The mere presence of a large crowd does not necessarily constitute a serious law enforcement problem. However, a relatively small group of people acting as a lawless mob can be very dangerous and can present problems of major importance.

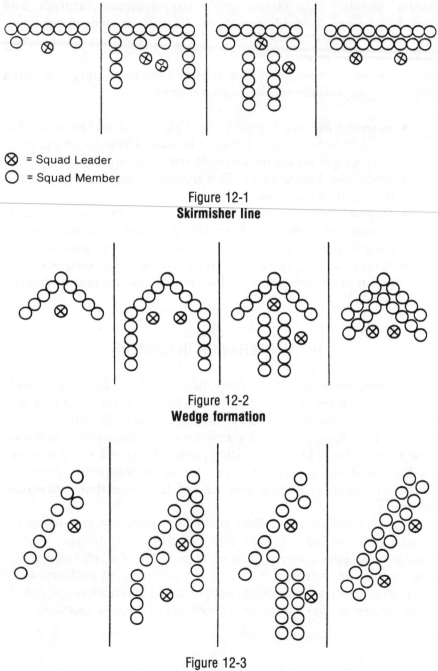

⊗ = Squad Leader
○ = Squad Member

Figure 12-1
Skirmisher line

Figure 12-2
Wedge formation

Figure 12-3
Diagonal formation

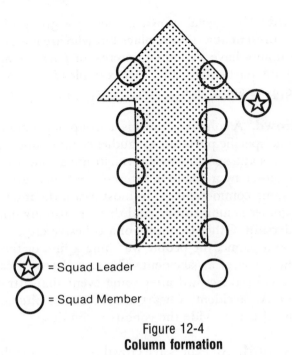

⊛ = Squad Leader

◯ = Squad Member

Figure 12-4
Column formation

Law enforcement is interested in the actions of groups of people, and a study of the nature of crowds is helpful. A crowd is composed of individuals; the person is the basic unit. The behavior of individuals, in the final analysis, is most important. If criminal charges grow out of mob violence, individuals are charged, not groups. Yet officers must understand the nature of groups because, at times, controls are most effectively applied against a group, rather than against individuals.

Nature of Crowds

Crowds may be classified in several ways. For example, they could be grouped according to size; however, size is not usually the most significant factor. They may be grouped according to sex, race, religion, political beliefs, or in many other ways, but these would not be useful classifications for purposes of this discussion. Of greatest interest to law enforcement are the behavior and motivation of the people. In other words, law enforcement is most interested in what people are doing and why. The following types of crowds may be distinguished.

Casual Crowd. The casual crowd is merely a group of people who happen to be present at a specific place but who are not unified or organized. They do not have a common interest or purpose, and they are not following any particular leader. An example of a casual crowd is a group of shoppers going from store to store.

Cohesive Crowd. A cohesive crowd is a group of people who are assembled for some specific purpose. An audience attending a play or a concert, or the fans at a sporting event, constitute a cohesive crowd. They are held together by a common interest, and their attention is directed toward some common focus. In most cases, the interest that brought them together is momentary, and they are usually not under well-defined leadership. Other examples of a cohesive crowd include the participants at a picnic, the people watching a fire, or those who are present at the scene of an accident. The casual crowd can very easily turn into a cohesive crowd after some event that attracts the people's attention. An accident, a heart attack, a sales pitch, a fight, or anything unusual can provide the cohesive stimulus.

Expressive Crowd. An expressive crowd is a group in which the people are held together by some common purpose. They usually hold more or less similar attitudes for or against something. They are ordinarily under the direction of well-defined leadership. This type of crowd displays a somewhat unified mood. Their likes and dislikes, their loyalties, their desires and intentions are normally quite easily seen. Expressive crowds are found at political rallies, picket lines, and religious revivals.

An expressive crowd is, at the same time, a cohesive crowd. Clearly, a casual crowd may turn into a cohesive or even an expressive crowd. For example, two officers may receive a call to investigate a disturbance at a tavern. On arrival at the scene, they find a group of people idly standing around on the sidewalk in front of the tavern. They are not aware of the disturbance inside the establishment. The officers enter and arrest two men who have been fighting. As soon as the officers arrive, the casual crowd becomes a cohesive group because their interest is focused toward what promises to be something exciting. When the officers bring their prisoners out of the tavern, the cohesive crowd may become expressive, hooting and jeering at the officers for making the arrest. This expression of disapproval may well be instigated by some individual who himself had been arrested under similar circumstances on a prior occasion. His reaction to the officers' performance of duty can easily stimulate bystanders to express similar sentiments. In fact, in some cases, such crowds may go a step further and turn into an aggressive crowd.

Aggressive Crowd. The aggressive crowd, under positive leadership and strong emotions, engages in some kind of aggressive action. Ordinarily, these people have come together because of strong feelings about some issue and show definite unity of purpose. Their actions may be impulsive and highly emotional and, unfortunately, may become destructive. This type of crowd is the most difficult for officers to handle. The aggressive crowd is, at the same time, both expressive and cohesive. Thus, our classification shows a progression in which the law enforcement problems increase as each step is reached.

Mob Patterns

Students of mob behavior identify several basic patterns into which the actions of the mob members fall. These classifications are not necessarily intended to be mutually exclusive or all-inclusive. There may be combinations of these patterns, including the following.

Aggressive. Aggressive tendencies show up in the actions of lynch mob members or in the violent clashes between strikers and strike breakers. Similar aggressive behavior may be seen in juvenile "rumbles." The objective of the violence differs, of course, with the situation. Often the objective of the violence is some person or group of persons, while at other times it may be property. In some cases, it is both.

Escape. The behavior tendency involving escape is seen in panic situations. Escape behavior dominates the members of a crowd of people panicking at a fire or other disaster. Individuals driven by overwhelming fear react emotionally and irrationally to avoid the source of the danger. This behavior is often maladaptive because the people act blindly and do not take time to figure out the best way to avoid the danger. In panic, escape behavior often ruthlessly disregards the welfare of others in the crowd; each individual takes a "Me first" attitude. Panic behavior occurs in a situation where the people have no prepared response with which to meet the emergency. At first, the sense of shock involves a moment of indecision, during which the people appraise the situation. This moment is quickly followed by a sense of panic during which the danger is comprehended, and great fear and terror result. If, at the onset of the panic, firm leadership springs up that brings the crowd to its senses, maladaptive and dangerous escape behavior may be avoided.

Acquisitive. In some mobs, the main purpose of the emotional and irrational behavior seems to be the acquiring of some desired object. Law enforcement officials have observed that what starts out, in some cases, as a riot soon changes into a wild and uncontrolled looting spree. Other examples of acquisitive behavior include runs on banks and hunger riots.

Expressive. The behavior of people in certain highly emotionally charged situations is not any of the foregoing, but rather, simply expressive. The behavior of people attending conventions is sometimes the expressive type. Such crowds are also seen on occasions of great revelry. This kind of behavior apparently provides a release for pent-up emotions and an escape from dull routine of the workaday world. Religious revivals, carnivals, county fairs, rock music festivals, parades, wild parties, and orgies all may contain elements of expressive behavior. With the exception of religious revival, in which the main police problem is one of traffic control, all these crowds may be difficult to control. Such expressive behavior can very easily be converted into one of the other types. A demagogue or professional agitator may whip a crowd into an expressive frenzy that he or she may capitalize on by instigating some kind of aggressive action. The law enforcement executive who makes a study of such matters takes a long step toward successful control.

The People Involved

It is obviously important to anyone concerned with crowd behavior to consider the kinds of people involved and how they may behave. One type of people that may be found at a mob scene are the *impulsive and lawless* persons whose mob behavior may be similar to the behavior they exhibit in ordinary daily life. Such people are short-tempered and hotheaded, the kind who are always spoiling for a fight. They need only a fancied insult or a slight provocation to excite them to violence. They start the riot or incite others to violence. Many of them are ignorant, bigoted, and of low social status. *Suggestible* people are those who are easily influenced to follow the lead of the more violent. They get into the action early. *Cautious* individuals are those who would like to get into the fracas but who wait for the cloak of anonymity to give them courage by hiding their identity.

Yielders are those who hang back on the sidelines and do not join the action until the large number of people participating gives the impression of universality. In other words, they may think, "Everyone's taking part, so why shouldn't I?" Another type of yielder is the person who opposes violence, but only passively or half-heartedly. When the fighting starts, he or she yields even though opposed. *Supportive* people are those who do not actively join the mob but who enjoy the show and even shout encouragement. *Resisters* are those whose values and standards of judgment are not swayed by the emotional furor of the mob, who maintain level heads, and who disagree with the actions of the majority. A mob is intolerant and meets resistance with violence. *Psychopathic* people are those with a pathological personality structure who might be part of a mob. They are angry at the world, because of frustration or mental illness, and may use the riotous situation as a means of getting even with society.

Behavior Dynamics

When a crowd becomes a mob, restraint is lost. The crowd may be boisterous and disorderly, but produce only isolated, minor violence. However, haranguing by a hothead or a demagogue, or the arrival on the scene of a hated figure, can transform belligerence into frenzy in an instant.

The various factors in determining the behavior of a mob have a tendency to reduce the behavior of the total group to that of the worst of its members. In a mob situation, the first people to express their feelings and who take definite action are likely to be the most impulsive, the most suggestible, the least self-controlled, and the least inhibited. The most ignorant and the most excitable are the ones who are likely to trigger the violence, and, once it has begun, it usually spreads quickly, engulfing even the more intelligent and self-controlled. This tendency for members of a mob to exhibit similar behavior has been referred to by various terms—*suggestion, imitation, primitiveness, sympathy, circular reaction,* and *social facility*.

Mob behavior is essentially emotional and without reason. Generally, there is an apparent dissimilarity to the behavior in the private lives of the people involved. In other words, their behavior when part of the mob is not like their behavior when they are acting individually. Moreover, mob behavior is not something that occurs only in certain sections of the country involving only certain types of people. It may occur anywhere and for a great variety of reasons.

Among the psychodynamics of human behavior, social suggestion is a phenomenon familiar to all. If, as you walk along the street, you see three or four people looking up toward the top of a building, you are almost irresistibly drawn to look up yourself. In an audience, when a person begins to clap, others follow. The conduct of people in crowds tends to be contagious. One person takes his or her cue from another. Many people readily fall in line and follow a leader, taking his or her suggestions as to their conduct. In other words, they imitate the actions of the leader or of each other. Naturally, some people are more suggestible than others. Some individuals are nonconformists, more or less independent, and not readily swayed. Most people, however, are susceptible to suggestion.

The behavior of a crowd often depends on momentary suggestion. It is, of course, not entirely dependent on things arising at that moment, but is often triggered by a momentary impulse. The behavior of a crowd of people is essentially irrational. The attention of the crowd members is directed principally to objects and symbols that excite their feelings, emotions, and impulses. The rational powers of the crowd members are in abeyance, so to speak. In other words, crowd behavior is governed not by intellect, but by impulse.

One of the psychological factors influencing behavior in crowds, and especially in mobs, is the fact that people have a tendency to believe the attitudes and emotions they are experiencing are being shared by everyone present. The mere fact that large numbers of people are present tends to discourage behavior different from that being exhibited by others. Crowd members stimulate each other, and, before long, the individual gets the impression that everyone feels as he or she does.

In a mob, Person A stimulates B, B stimulates C, C stimulates D, and so on throughout the mob; in turn, D stimulates C, C stimulates B, and A, and so forth, in a kind of circular reverberation, heightening the overall potential for emotional excitement. A wise course for law enforcement officers is to break up the mob into ever smaller groups, thus limiting the reinforcement of common excitement. Another reason for splitting the mob into ever smaller groups is that this practice destroys the protective anonymity the crowd affords. The individual who is thus isolated or shuttled off into a very small group is exposed to identification and feels a hesitancy about engaging in violence that the cover of the crowd might eliminate.

Anonymity

One factor of considerable importance in unruly crowd behavior is the anonymity of the individual. Large numbers serve as cover in which she can hide her identity. She feels that since she is one of a large number, people will not be able to point to her, to ascribe guilt to her, to single her out. She is but one of many, and the things that she does, however violent, will be but small, isolated incidents in the much larger violent picture. The overall excitement, frenzy, and passion grip her, and she becomes but a small cog in a much larger machine. At the same time, paradoxically, the mob participant frequently experiences a sense of inflated ego or exalted self-importance. A police officer with a camera taking pictures of the mob members may be a deterring influence because this action tends to destroy the feeling of anonymity and to create a feeling of anxiety.

Another factor involved in crowd behavior is the reluctance of any individual to buck the trend. The individual is generally afraid to express views contrary to those of the majority. He or she finds it easier and safer to go along with the mob. Conformity is approved; the nonconformist is in peril.

Sometimes, even though the individual may have been present at first only out of curiosity and was only a passive observer, he becomes drawn into the activity, perhaps unwillingly. He may eventually become so deeply enmeshed, even though he is not a leader, that he is unable to physically withdraw from the action. This reluctance to withdraw may stem from the same reason that he is unable to express views or sentiments contrary to those of the crowd members; that is, he lacks the courage to do so and feels that it is safer and easier to "go along."

When people have been brought together by some strong social motivation, whether it be political, racial, economic, or whatever other reason, certain factors influence the organization of the group. When a group is subjected to a common frustration, the cohesiveness of the group is increased; that is, common frustration draws the people closer together psychologically.

Some people seem to feel that hostility and conflict between groups can be eliminated by "having a good fight and getting it over with." Psychologically, this is definitely not true. Such conflicts do not eliminate the source of frustration that produced the hostility in the first place. Regardless of the outcome of intergroup violence, both sides come out of the action with increased hatred and solidified hostile attitudes. They perceive each other as greater threats than ever before. Engaging in open violence actually increases the hostility and lays the groundwork for further conflict.

THE RIOT PATTERN

When a civil disturbance or riot occurs, certain factors or developments have already prepared the way. Verbal aggression, for example, may have existed for a long time and with increasing intensity. Furthermore, economic frustration and dissatisfaction with status, coupled with gradually changing social organization, have resulted in increasing irritation. Moreover, like-minded people band together in various kinds of groups. Some of these may be formal organizations with definite programs, and others may be informal, more or less spontaneous, such as a mob. These organizations, having grown out of frustration and discontent, serve to provide the individual with courage and support. He feels that his anger and his gripes are approved, and his beliefs justified; thus, his tendencies toward violence are stimulated.

Some kind of provocation triggers the violence. This precipitating incident, even though it might have been completely imaginary, becomes exaggerated through rumor and magnified out of proportion to its actual importance. Isolated cases of violent aggression occur. A few of these, over a short period of time, may serve to increase the already existing tension and excitement.

Full-scale rioting begins when one or two of these isolated clashes take hold and instigate mob action. At this point, through social contagion or social facilitation, the destructive activity is sustained. The level of mob frenzy in various individuals participating in the rioting is reinforced and augmented by seeing others who are equally excited and also rioting.

Role of Rumor

Social violence such as race riots, lynchings, industrial violence, and the like originate in a state of mind, in a convergence of public opinion. Rumor plays a major part in crystallizing this public opinion. In fact, some authorities assert that no riot ever takes place without a buildup through rumor.

Animosity is gradually intensified, before a riot, by stories of provocations and aggressive acts on the part of the opposition, which is said to be conspiring, plotting, even saving up guns and ammunition. A rumor can often spark the explosion. It is circulated rapidly, and through distortion it grows in ugliness at each recitation. Rumors are also significant during the actual rioting by helping to sustain the excitement.

Since the participants are acting irrationally and emotionally, rumors may become firm beliefs. One of the most obvious things about the mental makeup of the rabid mob member is that he or she tends to accept unqualifiedly any and all reports that fit into certain preconceived notion about the situations.

In ordinary daily contacts among people, all sorts of rumors float around. Little or nothing comes of them. Rumors that lead to riots and other social violence such as war, for example, are generally uglier and more exciting. They are often couched in provocative language, and they become more sensational and exciting as they spread. Because of distortions that occur, one rumor tends to beget another. As feeling mounts, the rumors get nastier. Rumors may start out as stories of insults, progress to stories of impending trouble, and finally become inflammatory accounts of intolerable acts, such as beatings and so forth.

These rumors frequently provide the grist for the psychological mill that results in rationalizing (justifying) the actions of the mob. Rumors are of various types. They include tales that are partial statements of facts, to which the rumormonger frequently adds significant material from his or her own imagination. They include stories based on incorrect assumptions and conclusions. They may also be complete fabrications that are entirely unfounded and sometimes deliberately concocted and spread by vicious individuals who intend to stir up trouble.

If officers collect and analyze these rumors in a community, they will be taking advantage of a sensitive index for the state of hostility and thus they themselves can help forestall violence. Rumors, to-gether with other signs, are important to law enforcement authorities.

Pattern of Action

When the tension has built up, when the frustration has existed long enough, and when the rumor has done its work, the conditions are ripe. When irritations on both sides have become common, when the potential opponents are in close proximity, and when there is enough bad feeling, the ingredients are available. Every little clash must be regarded as a spark that can ignite the conflagration.

Obviously, not all riots and civil disturbances will follow the same precise pattern. Nevertheless, certain identifiable phenomena accompany such eruptions. We have discussed the pattern of preparation and the role played by rumor; next, we analyze the conflict.

Bristling Stage. In some cases, there may be a stage that can be referred to as the *bristling stage*. This phenomenon may be found in conjunction with certain kinds of social contentions such as labor-management difficulties involving picket lines and strike breakers. It is also found on occasion where groups of demonstrators appear before a government establishment, either local or national, or before an embassy, an ambassador's residence, a chancellery, and so forth, to register protests. In many instances, advance publicity gives opportunity for the gathering of a crowd. The more frenzied members of the crowd may engage in testing the temper of the situation. There may be half-accidental and half-intentional jostling and an excess of name calling. Unless the situation is firmly controlled by evenhanded action during this bristling stage, the action can proceed rapidly to bloodshed.

Word of the impending violence and excitement spreads rapidly through rumor. Individual members of the mob may detach themselves momentarily to enlist more recruits. Rumors fly back and forth from person to person and by telephone. More and more appear on the scene. Some of these are mere bystanders and curiosity seekers; others immediately join the activity. As the crowd grows, so do the rumors, and social facilitation encourages increasingly dangerous behavior.

The members of the mob, particularly the more active ones, move around from one small group to another, often aimlessly. There is an undercurrent of excitement, uncertainty, and testing as they contact each other. Bristling continues and increases during this stage. More individuals break off to warn friends, get recruits, pass on rumors, and generally add to the hysteria.

At some point, when the frenzy reaches fever pitch, an event of some type noted during the bristling and milling will flare up, and the riot is underway. The precipitating event is usually one of a series of similar incidents. It may be no more serious than any of the others, but it occurs at a time when everything else is ready.

It is often very difficult, if not impossible, in retrospect, to identify some specific incident as the precipitating event. In a large and unruly gathering, there will be many incidents of bristling and jostling going on at the same time, and any one of these can unpredictably spread to involve many people. It is not unusual, therefore, to have one or several somewhat serious outbreaks precede the main riot.

Now that the violence has begun, the acts of the individual mob members are without logic, completely unreasoned, and hysterical. The individual mob member tends to feel a loss of personal identity. She becomes merely an anonymous member of a large group. As she sees others engaged in the same kind of behavior and under the influence of the same excitement, she tends to believe that everyone is involved. The psychological effect of this anonymity and universality is to absolve the individual of responsibility for the brutal acts she commits.

When the mob violence "gets into high gear," the objects against which the violence is directed become more generalized. Whereas the violence may originally have been directed solely against members of another race, against management, or against school authorities (to name a few), the emotionally driven, illogical destruction may now spread to include other people or property that, no matter how remotely, symbolize to the mob members the conditions that provoked the initial frustration. They may see the police officer or other authorities as symbols of their hatred. The statehouse, police station, churches, grocery stores, pawn shops, liquor stores, and all sorts of establishments become "fair game" once the violence gets out of control. No rules apply; there is no fair play. The behavior is governed by mass hysteria, hatred, and impulse. Any attempt at remonstrance or control is met with immediate retaliation.

In mob control, the development of a good tactical plan depends in large measure on the quantity and quality of intelligence gathered by the interested law enforcement agency. Planning and preparation should, to a degree, depend on intelligence data. Police intelligence should be constantly aware of the day-to-day social, economic, racial, and other changes that may indicate the basis for unlawful assembly or riotous activity.

Every source of information must be cultivated, and the temper of the community must be known by the officers of the agency. They should be aware of every meeting, planned or otherwise, and every rumor. Every law enforcement officer should be a listening post, alert to the changing attitudes in the community. Each bit of information, however insignificant, should be promptly reported to headquarters. Names and descriptions, if possible, and photographs of known leaders and agitators of riots and mobs should be on file.

Remember that there is a legitimate role for serious, peaceful citizen protest, so that preconceptions and stereotypes do not pave the way for undue police fear and hence harshness. Such harshness may appear unprovoked, and thus serve as fuel for disorder. Crowds are not homogenous, and rumor usually has a kernel of social fact that clear, full discussion can thresh out. Police must keep the peace, as a priority. Law enforcement officers are like everyone else, and have the same opinions and feelings—which they must lay aside in order to deal with emotional people, in maintaining the peace. And finally, officers must remember that citizens have both the right of free speech and the right of assembly, as guaranteed by the Constitution of our country.

In order to obtain information and intelligence data at the scene of any threatened civil disturbance, certain members of the enforcement agency may be assigned to act as observers. Their duties are to report their observations, to ensure that the proper information is furnished to the commanding officer. Their reports may greatly influence the action that will have to be taken in a given situation. Personnel assigned to this duty should be in plain clothes and dressed to fit the occasion so they can mingle with the crowd without attracting undue attention. No parts of their uniform should be worn while on this duty. The given situation will control the number of individuals assigned to this work.

Observers should be mentally and physically alert at all times. Do not consort with the factions involved, except as it may be necessary to obtain information. Do not engage in any unwarranted conversation or social activity while on duty, except in extreme necessity to

obtain information. Report all information and facts without prejudice, bias, or partiality.

The Leadership

Any situation allowed to develop to the point of riot is easy prey for a
demagogue. The catchwords and phrases, deprecating descriptive
terms, the irritating incidents, the frayed tempers, the accumulated
emotional tensions, hatred and bitternesses are ready-made to capitalize on. A demagogue does not have to be an important celebrity.
His leadership is sometimes spontaneous and sometimes calculated
and organized. Police frequently encounter self-appointed vigilantes
from the outside who have come for the express purpose of seeing that
violence is done.

The leaders who set the wheels in motion may be older people,
vicious middle-aged hoodlums, or people who see in the situation
some real or imagined danger to their interests. Very often, these
people whip up the frenzy, after which they stand back and let the
younger and more impulsive do the actual fighting. These younger
people, the vanguard of the club-wielders and fist-swingers, are the
most excited and violent of the mob.

To remove the leaders is to strike at the heart of the disorder. A
leaderless group is a bewildered and confused group that does not
function effectively. The leaders, who would ordinarily supply the
initiative, the rallying symbols, and the sustaining force of the emotional enthusiasm, should be taken in hand and restrained. And, like a
fire from which the fuel has been cut off, the violence will generally
subside.

Breaking the group up into ever smaller units has the effect of
reducing the stimulus provided by social contagion or social facilitation. It also reduces the impressions of universality and anonymity
that are so important in mob functioning. In removing the leaders,
militant agitators on both sides should be objects of police attention.
In any event, it is those creating the disturbance who should be
repressed.

In many cases, a strong stand backed up by an impressive show of
force may be all that is required. However, a false move by a poorly
trained officer may start a riot. Officers who participate in putting on
a show of force must be well disciplined, so that they will follow orders
to the letter, stand firm in the face of abuse, and not lose their heads.

The law enforcement authority, obviously, must be ready, if necessary, to apply sufficient force to promptly overcome resistance. Well-disciplined officers, properly uniformed and equipped, quickly and efficiently taking their posts in a purposeful and determined manner, will discourage many would-be rioters.

Tactics

To accomplish the removal of the leaders and the dispersal of the crowd, speed and decisiveness, coupled with an impressive show of force, are necessary in any tactical situation. The longer a crowd is permitted to mill around and commit various acts of violence, the more it gets out of hand, thus making it more difficult for officers to handle. This delay permits the crowd to develop into a mob.

In the tactical situation, several items are of extreme importance. The initial show of force by the police may well be decisive in successfully handling the situation. Thus, rapid mobilization of the force is extremely important. The law enforcement commander should not attempt any tactics until he or she has sufficient personnel available to complete the mission. He or she should, however, if the emergency demands, use the available forces at the time to contain the situation.

To use the show of force to the greatest advantage, officers should make a surprise, formidable appearance. They should assemble at some point beyond sight of the mob. This point should be as near the mob as practicable to save time and conserve energy, and yet far enough from the scene of the disturbance to ensure security. When sufficient forces arrive at the scene, they must organize into tactical formations without delay. When the forces are organized into formation, they should march smartly into view at a reasonably safe distance from the mob, showing that they are well organized and highly disciplined. With this impressive show of force behind him or her, the commanding officer may now issue over the public address system a proclamation to disperse. This proclamation should be clear and unequivocal. It should state the legal basis for the proclamation, issue a firm order to disperse, and designate the avenues of exit. This proclamation should be repeated again and again. Following the proclamation, the commander should inform the mob that it has a specific time in which to comply with the order to disperse. If the mob does not disperse within the given time, the commander should then employ whatever measures are necessary to disperse the mob.

If the personnel available permit, the police commander should usually employ his or her forces by having one-third in direct contact with the mob, one-third as support units, and one-third held in reserve. Pressure should not be placed against members of a mob if no route of exit is open to them. Routes of exit must be planned and designated. Announcements over public address systems and/or leaflets dropped from planes could be employed to direct the people to these routes. The greater the number of routes open to the people, the sooner they can be dispersed. The objectives are to remove the leaders as soon as they can be identified and to divide the mob. Some time-honored tactical formations have been designed to help accomplish these objectives. To drive a short distance into a mob to remove a leader or a prisoner, or to effect a rescue, the squad wedge formation is an excellent procedure. However, where the purpose is to divide and disperse a large mob, it may be necessary to use a platoon wedge with lateral support and a platoon in close support.

Isolated Officer(s) and Hostile Crowds

Occasionally, lone officers may encounter a hostile crowd while on routine patrol. In such instances, move to a safe position and call for backup. While awaiting help, watch the crowd's actions and notify communications of the crowd's growth, general age of people in the crowd and any weapons that might be present. Once help arrives, advise the commanding officer of the crowd's actions and take appropriate action.

If a hostile crowd surrounds your vehicle, *stay in the patrol unit*; put up the windows and lock all doors. If possible, try to escape by driving away from the crowd. You can use the PA system to try to dissuade the crowd from criminal action. Use extreme caution, and alert communications for backup assistance.

If a hostile crowd closes in on you while you are on foot, use your portable radio to request backup assistance. Stand at a location that eliminates the possibility of an attack from behind; for example, stand against a wall. Walk away from the crowd in a side-stepping fashion. Inform the crowd that backup or additional officers will arrive shortly. Direct your attention to the loudest member (agitator), and seek to render him or her ineffective. When speaking, your voice should be loud and firm; however, do not use language that aggravates or excites the crowd to anger or action. Words that are respectful and authoritative will gain the crowd's cooperation. Veteran officers will tell you that it is better to talk your way out of an adverse situation than fight your way out. What you say, and *how* you say it, can either incite the crowd to anger or cause the people to disperse.

Protective Equipment

Individual officers should have the following protective equipment when dealing with a hostile crowd:

- Baton or riot stick
- Shotgun, if necessary
- Riot control helmet with visor
- Radio
- Gloves
- Boots
- Shin guards
- Shields

Riot Baton. The police baton, a weapon traditionally a symbol of authority, should be used only in an emergency. When you strike, you should do so with the intention of stunning or temporarily disabling, rather than injuring. You must have a thorough knowledge of the vulnerable areas of the body and must avoid dealing blows that produce permanent injury or fatality. Avoid blows to the head. Deliver baton blows only to toes, ankle front, shin, side of calf, kneecap, thigh, hand, forearm, inner elbow, outer bicep, shoulder top, above the clavicle, ribs, solar plexus, behind the scapula, behind the knee, calf muscles, ankle bone, and ankle tendon. Points of the body to be avoided with baton blows include head, throat and side of neck, armpit, and chest cavity. You should train to the point where baton action is reflex action rather than a thought-extended process. Using the baton as an extension of the arm or thrust is generally more effective than using it as a bludgeon or club.

Riot Gun (Shotgun). The most extreme action a law enforcement officer can take in any situation is the use of firearms. Under no circumstances should you use firearms unless all other measures for controlling the violence have been exhausted. Never fire indiscriminately into a crowd or mob. Such extreme action may result in injury and death to citizens and may erupt into a prolonged and fatal clash between officers and the mob.

Any violent civil disturbance requires that officers approach the situation with a clear head and a steady hand. The decision to resort to the use of firearms is indeed grave. It should be made only on the basis of the most carefully considered judgment. Obviously, no set of rules can be established covering such situations. Such a decision must be based on realistic evaluation of the existing circumstances. Among the important considerations, of course, are the protection of the officer's own life and the lives of fellow officers, and the protection of innocent citizens.

A basic rule in police firearms training is that a firearm is used only in self-defense or to protect the lives of others. This rule applies to any situation, and particularly where a large crowd is involved and hence the possibility of an innocent bystander being injured or killed is greater. A firearm in the hands of a well-trained law enforcement officer is an instrument of defense, not of destruction, and the officer's role as public defender is unchanged whether he or she faces one individual or a thousand.

Riot Helmets. The head is one of the most vulnerable areas of the body. Headgear that affords maximum protection is essential. It must consist of a hard outer substance capable of withstanding or diverting tremendous force; at the same time, it must have a firm, but padded and absorbent, inner surface to protect the head from the force encountered. The helmet worn by motorcycle officers makes an excellent riot helmet. It meets the necessary requirements of withstanding great pressure while affording maximum inner protection. These helmets usually have a plastic or fiberglass outer surface and are lined with leather or foam rubber.

Construction helmets also afford excellent protection, for they are engineered to offer maximum protection. They have a brim that affords greater protection for the neck area. This advantage protects against thrown missiles. These helmets are usually made of metal and are lined with leather or foam rubber.

Gas and Masks. Law enforcement agencies have two objectives when using tear gas in riot control situations. The first is to prevent violence by the rioting group, and the second is to disperse the crowd with minimum hazard to the people in the mob and to the officers attempting to quell the disturbance.

Members of the riot control squad should be wearing gas masks as they move into position so there will be no delay or confusion when the order to deliver the chemical agents is given.

If at all possible, the squad should take a position upwind (the wind at their backs) from the mob and move up close enough to effectively use grenade cannisters. The ideal distance from the mob in the use of grenades is about 150 feet.

The intensity of the wind is an important factor. With a very strong wind blowing, more of the chemical agent should be used, since the gas will dissipate quicker. If there is any uncertainty as to the direction of the wind, use a smoke canister to test for wind direction. Often the wind direction on the ground is different from the wind direction overhead. This is especially true in metropolitan areas, where buildings alter the flow of air currents.

Before using chemical agents, provide an avenue of escape for the mob. Dispersing the mob with a minimum of hazard to the members of the mob is one of the essential goals. Again, following this basic principle, the mob should be repeatedly called on to disperse and given an opportunity to break up before chemical agents are used.

The riot control squad should not throw all the canisters at one time. To ensure that a solid line of gas reaches the mob, every other officer in the squad could toss canisters; then the remaining half can fill in the gaps in the gas cloud being generated. The officer in charge should make certain that sufficient gas is used to accomplish the task.

Officers without adequate protection are no more immune to the effects of gas than the mob they intend to incapacitate. When the use of chemical agents is anticipated, officers should always be outfitted with properly functioning gas masks. Many different designs are available to law enforcement agencies and afford excellent protection from the effects of tear gas and DM gas (diphenylaminechlorarsine), also called "sickening," "nauseating," or "knockout" gas.

USE OF CHEMICAL AGENTS[1]

The research and development of a nonoffensive chemical agent by the U.S. Army during World War I (1914–1918) resulted in the discovery of chloroacetophenone (CN), which (when exposed in proper concentration) produces an abundance of uncontrollable tears and a temporary incapacitating effect with no harmful aftereffects on persons exposed to the agent. Following the war, law enforcement agencies around the world eagerly welcomed the new humane chemical agents for use in combatting violent offenders. In the 1960s, the U.S. Army adopted a new chemical agent for use in suppressing riots; orthochlorbenzalmalononitrile, or CS, was produced to meet the demand for an agent more potent than CN.

Generally speaking, there are four basic fields in which riot control chemical munitions and projectiles are used by law enforcement agencies: (1) riot control and mob dispersion; (2) barricaded criminals and insane persons; (3) control and discipline in prisons and mental institutions; and (4) individual protective devices, such as chemical mace, which contains a CN formula that is both fast acting and safe.

Control of riot situations and mobs is one of the most serious problems facing law enforcement officers today. In such situations, the use of lethal firearms is not justified under normal conditions. Society expects the law enforcement agency to disperse the crowd without using excessive force. Any law enforcement agency's failure to successfully combat a mob usually leads to increased mob violence, loss of lives, and destruction of property. The use of riot control chemical munitions by small, well-trained riot units can give the domestic police the ability to control and disperse all dangerous mobs.

Criminals and insane people who barricade themselves in a protective area, room, or building present one of the most frequent and hazardous combat situations peace officers face. The situation is frequently complicated by the fact that assailants take hostages. Before the development of chemical agents like CN, law enforcement

---

[1] A great deal of the technical information for this section is summarized from Smith & Wesson Company, *Police Chemical Agent Training Manual* (Springfield, Mass.: no date).

officers had to physically assault and use gunfire to attack the perpetrator's position; the loss of life among the police and innocent people was often very high. In 1934, the Smith & Wesson Company developed and introduced a 37-mm chemical projectile that could be fired from a distance toward the armed, barricaded individual, forcing the criminal to vacate his or her position and greatly facilitating subsequent capture.

Riots frequently occur in prison. Whenever a prison riot happens, guards and prisoners alike are in danger. The use of chemical agents and fog machine devices can be of particular benefit in a situation where the prisoners must be moved or driven from a yard area. Chemical agents can likewise be used to control inmates of mental institutions; however, this situation should be handled with great care and skill because some chemical agents may have a delayed reaction on psychotic individuals.

The most common chemical agent carried by law enforcement officers is chemical mace (which contains a CN agent). It will incapacitate the suspect in approximately 2–5 seconds without harmful aftereffects. For everyday law enforcement use, the chemical agent CN is considered superior to CS. Although CS produces immediate incapacitation if sprayed directly into an assailant's eyes, extensive eye damage and injuries could result from such use (the legal implications of such results are obvious). If the CS agent is sprayed somewhere other than directly into the eyes, it takes approximately 20–30 seconds to incapacitate the suspect.

Tactical Use of Chemical Agents

Before a chemical agent is employed, several factors must be weighed. First, the situation must be examined. The decision to use a chemical, and the exact type of agent, will vary, depending on whether you are dealing with a single individual or a crowd. Weigh the amount of hazard inherent in using the chemical agent against the amount of hazard inherent in the kinds of conduct the chemical agent is designed to control. The environment, avenues of escape, and preparedness (as well as capabilities) of the control force must be considered.

Once the decision is made to use a chemical agent, decide which type of product will produce the most desirable effect: a grenade, a projectile, a fogger, or an aerosol. Each has a particular application in a civil disturbance or hostage situation, owing to its characteristics and capabilities. Armed with knowledge of the potential of each chemical device under your control, evaluate the tactical environment to determine which agent will be of the greatest benefit.

Wind. The prevailing wind at any location must be taken into consideration when using chemical agents. Whenever possible, take a tactical position that gives you full advantage of any wind currents. If you are in a position with rear wind, it can carry the chemical agent into the crowd. With a flank wind, the officers must release the grenades or projectiles so that the wind will carry the agent across the crowd's path. With a direct wind (wind blowing directly at the officers from behind the crowd), long-range projectiles or grenades launched from a 12-gauge shotgun might be fired over the heads of the crowd, to hit behind the crowd. Care should be taken to use rubber projectiles or rubber ball grenades if there is a danger that someone might be hit by a projectile in this situation. Special care should be taken to evaluate what is near the scene of the confrontation. If the wind conditions may carry the chemical agent toward retirement homes, orphanages, hospitals, and such, officers may be well advised to avoid using chemical agents because they may cause considerable problems. Officers should always evaluate the wind in terms of this possibility.

Size and Temper of the Crowd. The area occupied by rioters will determine the line of release of the chemical agent and the quantity required to cover it adequately. The temperament of the crowd will determine the best tactics to be used and will also influence the decision on the quantity of the chemical agents to be employed. Violent mobs require heavy initial and continuous concentrations of the chemical agents.

Escape Routes for the Crowd. The use of chemical agents will create a desire for rioters to escape. Streets or fields over which they can flee must always be left open to them. If the escape routes are blocked, crowd members have no choice but to remain and fight the police. The basic purpose of using chemical agents is to break up the group and destroy its sense of unity and purpose. Exits must be provided to achieve this desired result.

First-Aid Treatment for Chemical Agent Exposure

The symptoms associated with CS and CN exposure are largely the result of irritation produced by tiny particles that contact moist areas of the skin or are inhaled into the mouth, nose, and lungs. The severity of the symptoms is generally related to the concentration of the chemical agent, the duration of exposure, and to some extent the physiology of the victim. The person who is exposed to a chemical agent should consider first-aid care for both eyes and skin and be aware that some of the chemical agent will also be embedded in clothing. Table 12-1 lists first aid for various symptoms of chemical agent exposure.

Table 12-1
First Aid for Symptoms of Exposure to CN and CS.
For severe or prolonged effects, complications, and contamination of wounds, obtain medical aid as soon as possible.
Note: Always remove contact lenses before flushing the eyes!

Area Affected	Symptoms	First Aid
General	Complete incapacitation.	Remove affected person from the contaminated area to an open, up-wind position. Remain calm, restrict activity. Major discomfort should disappear within 10 to 20 minutes.
Eyes	Burning sensation, heavy flow of tears. Involuntary closing of eyes.	Keep eyes open facing wind. Do not rub eyes. Tearing helps clear the eyes. If particles of agent are lodged in eyes, wash out with lots of cool water. Tears can be blotted away.
Skin	Stinging or burning sensation on moist skin areas. Blisters from very heavy concentrations.	Sit and remain quiet to reduce sweating. Expose the affected areas to the air. Gross contamination can be relieved by flushing with clear water for at least 10 minutes. For CS, a solution of 5 or 10% sodium

Area Affected	Symptoms	First Aid
		bicarbonate ($NaHCO_3$ or sodium carbonate (Na_2CO_3) or a specially prepared skin wash solution (6.7% $NaHCO_3$, 3.3% Na_2CO_3, and 0.1% benzalkonium chloride in water) is superior to water and need be used only in small amounts.
Nose	Irritation, burning sensation. Nasal discharge.	Breathe normally. Blow nose to remove discharge. Nose drops should help if discomfort is severe.
Chest	Irritation, burning sensation. Coughing, feeling of suffocation. Tightness in chest, often accompanied by a feeling of panic.	The victim should relax and keep calm. Talking reassuringly to the victim will help to relieve his or her discomfort and prevent panic.

Source: International Association of Chiefs of Police, Professional Standards Division, *Police Chemical Agents Manual* (Washington, D.C.: IACP), p. 7.

In addition to first aid, there are several actions you should avoid if you come into contact with a chemical agent:

1. Avoid rubbing the eyes or scratching irritated skin areas. This action will only rub the particles deeper into the skin, prolonging the effects.
2. Avoid using only small amounts of water on contaminated areas. When flushing away gross contamination, use *copious* amounts (lots) of cool running water for at least 10 minutes, or use one of the wash solutions recommended for CS contamination.
3. Avoid using any first-aid creams, salves, Vaseline, or greases to cover irritated skin. These dressings may trap particles of the chemical agent, creating severe discomfort, chemical burns, and increased absorption into the skin.

Table 12-2
Identifying Colors of Chemical Agents

Color	Chemical Agent
Red	CN
Blue	CS
Yellow	HC or Smoke
Green	DM (also called Adamite in the United States). This agent makes people feel very ill; effects are both dangerous and extremely painful.
Violet	CR (a new chemical agent not presently available in the United States). CR is a very stable chemical that is not affected by the presence of water and therefore cannot be flushed away.
Gray	Practice items ("dud" projectiles)

4. Avoid touching contaminated clothing or equipment with bare hands. The chemical agent is easily transferred to unprotected skin once the hands are contaminated.
5. Take off wet clothing that has been contaminated by chemical agents. Severe chemical burns and blistering can result.

Chemical Agent Identification Color Coding

In order to facilitate identification of chemical agents, all manufacturers of such products use the same colors to designate the presence of a specific agent. These colors are listed in Table 12-2.

Protective Equipment and Training

Peace officers must learn the correct way to put on, clear, and remove a gas mask, which is the only protection against CS, CN, or other chemical agents. In using the gas mask, make sure the canister (which contains the filters) is not damaged. In addition, the elastic straps of the gas mask must be pulled tight to prevent leaks.

Before attempting to quell a riot or handle a violent individual, officers must be able to recognize both the advantages and hazards of using chemical agents. Employed correctly, these agents can save lives and permit peace officers to perform their jobs more efficiently. Used incorrectly, they can injure innocent people as well as law enforcement officers. The questions of amount and type of force authorized in any situation require the most serious consideration and training. The basic rule—whether in the use of physical force, firearms, or chemical agents—is that only the *minimum* amount of force to achieve the legal objective of law enforcement is justified in any given situation.

KEY TERMS

Acquisitive mob
Aggressive mob
Anonymity in mob behavior
Baton or "riot" stick
Casual crowd
Chemical agents
Civil disorder
CN (chemical agent)
Cohesive crowd
Column formation (riot control)
Crowd control
Escape mob
Expressive crowd
Gas mask
Riot

STUDY QUESTIONS

1. Discuss the constitutional safeguards guaranteed to citizens for peaceable assembly.

2. Outline the characteristics of the different types of crowds that may gather for different purposes. Which of these constitute the greatest hazard for patrol officers?

3. Discuss when the various types of basic crowd and riot control formations may be used to control a violent situation.

4. Outline the difference between an *expressive* crowd and a *mob*.

5. What role does *anonymity* play in the dynamics of mob behavior?

6. Outline the progression of the "riot pattern" in mob behavior.

7. Why is it so important to determine who the mob leaders are in handling a riot situation?

8. Discuss the tactics officers use to quell a riot.

9. What should you do if a hostile crowd surrounds your patrol vehicle?

10. List the protective gear you should have in a riot situation.

11. Outline the types of chemical agents available for riot control situations.

12. Discuss when and how chemical agents should be used in varying wind conditions.

13. What other tactical considerations should be discussed before deciding to use chemical agents to disperse hostile crowds or riots?

14. If you should come in contact with a chemical agent, what first-aid treatment procedures should you instinctively follow?

15. Record the identifying colors of chemical agents.

ACTIVITIES

1. Using members of the class, organize squads to move from a column formation to various riot control formations discussed in the chapter.

2. Using flash cards indicating various parts of the body affected by chemical agents, have class members orally report correct first-aid measures to decontaminate and prevent severe or prolonged effects of chemical agents.

13

Arrest and Apprehension Techniques

Law enforcement officers must have the ability to properly and safely apply practical considerations for effective arrest techniques. Planning for safety and control includes knowledge of arrest tactics to defend against elements of an attack, defensive tactics, disarming an assailant, and defense against various weapons. Once the arrest has been accomplished, law enforcement officers must be able to properly handcuff and search the arrested person to ensure safety as well as seize weapons and contraband that the arrested person may have on his or her person. This chapter outlines important aspects involved in the mechanics of arrest, including use of personal weapons, defensive tactics, restraint holds for violent offenders, weapon takeaway techniques, weapons retention, and baton techniques.

AUTHORITY FOR ARREST

Laws of arrest are based on the U.S. Constitution, state constitutions, state codes of criminal procedure, and case law. Every peace officer must understand the relationships among the Constitution, statutory law, and the authority to make an arrest. Officers must also know the limitations placed on them in order to protect the freedom of the individual citizen.

Although several provisions of the U.S. Constitution relate to controlling the government in the area of arrest, two amendments in particular guide the behavior of all peace officers. The Fourth Amendment to the Constitution states,

> The right of the people to be *secure in their persons*, houses, papers, and effects, *against unreasonable* searches and *seizures*, shall not be violated, and no warrants shall issue, but upon *probable cause*, supported by oath or affirmation, and particularly describing the place to be searched, and the *persons* or things *to be seized*. [Emphasis added.]

The phrases, "secure in their persons," "against unreasonable . . . seizures," and "persons . . . to be seized" all refer to arrest. An arrest means the seizure of a person by a peace officer or another citizen.

Amendment Fourteen of the U.S. Constitution states,

> Section 1 . . . No state shall make or enforce any law which shall abridge the privileges or immunities of citizens of the United States; *nor shall any state deprive any person of* life, *liberty*, or property, without due process of law; nor deny to any person within its jurisdiction the equal protection of the laws. [Emphasis added.]

The phrase "nor shall any state deprive any person of . . . liberty . . . without due process of law" refers to the act of arrest. The U.S. Constitution clearly ensures that every citizen has protection against government oppression. However, the letter of the law stipulates that if "due process of law"—or correct procedure—is followed, then arrests are lawful.

The Ninth and Tenth Amendments of the U.S. Constitution give individual states authority to make laws for respective jurisdictions. State constitutions and subsequent codes of criminal procedures mirror the U.S. Constitution in language regarding authority for and limitations of government in making arrests.

ELEMENTS OF ARREST

A person is arrested when he or she has actually been placed under restraint or taken into custody by a law enforcement officer, a person executes a warrant of arrest, or other people act under "citizen right of arrest." The important words are *under restraint or taken into custody*. These words refer to depriving the arrested person of liberty and freedom of movement. An arrest binds the person arrested to the will and control of the person making the arrest.

For an arrest to be lawful, certain elements must be present. These elements are

1. The intent of the person making the arrest
2. Arrest authority
3. An actual or constructive seizure and detention of the person arrested
4. An understanding by the person arrested that the arrest occurred

On a variety of occasions, a peace officer can stop a person, deprive him or her of liberty, and restrict the person's movements without the detention constituting an arrest. These occasions include crowd control, driver's license checks, field interrogations, traffic stops, and many others that are not arrest situations. To constitute a valid arrest, law enforcement officers must *intend* to take the person into custody and detain him or her.

For an arrest to be lawful, the officer must have authority to make the arrest. This authority to arrest is controlled by the type of offense and the jurisdiction.

A seizure occurs when the arresting officer actually controls the arrested person's movements—either by actually laying hands on the person arrested or verbally controlling the subject who submits to authority. Seizure is often accompanied by detention in the patrol car and/or the use of handcuffs. An actual seizure also occurs when an officer points a handgun or other weapon at a person, orders the person to stop, and takes the detained person into custody.

Seizure and detention do not always require force or actual contact. Many times peace officers simply inform a person that he or she is under arrest, and the arrested person submits without any further action. This is called *constructive* seizure and detention, and it meets the requirements for arrest. For example, a law enforcement officer might inform the driver of a vehicle that she is under arrest and direct her to move the vehicle to a safer location, and she complies. This is constructive restraint and detention.

To constitute a viable arrest, the arrested party must understand that he or she is in custody. The arresting officer must say or do something to ensure that the arrested person knows he or she is being seized and detained. The officer can reach this point of understanding by using words such as "Police—don't move" or "You are under arrest." The circumstances of the arrest itself can also impart understanding. For example, an officer might chase a fleeing person following a burglary in progress, tackle him, place him under restraint with handcuffs, and never say a word. The person placed under such restraint readily understands that his freedom of movement is restricted and that he is under arrest.

There are several exceptions to the rule requiring understanding. The officer can place unconscious, intoxicated, insane, and other incapacitated people under arrest without their awareness or understanding that an arrest has occurred.

Probable Cause

The constitutional standard for the degree of proof to arrest and seize is *probable cause*. One of the most frequently cited definitions of probable cause is in *Draper v. U.S.*, 358 U.S. 307 (1959); paraphrased, the U.S. Supreme Court stated that probable cause amounts to facts and circumstances in the peace officer's knowledge that would lead a reasonable and prudent person to believe that a crime has been or is about to be committed. This definition notes that an arrest may not be based on *mere suspicion alone*. It also notes that four elements are necessary to develop probable cause:

1. *Facts or apparent facts.* These are the circumstances surrounding the incident. People running after a burglar alarm goes off at night, and a person driving a reportedly stolen vehicle, are examples of apparent facts that a peace officer might view as probable cause. An arrest would be lawful even though it was later found that the apparent facts did not hold true.

2. *Viewed by a law enforcement officer.* Officers can arrest on probable cause based on the evidence of any senses. An officer could actually see what looks like a criminal offense but could also develop probable

cause based on hearing or smell. For example, an experienced narcotics officer can easily recognize the smell of certain controlled substances.

3. *Prudent or reasonable caution.* There must be a logical and reasonable connection between (a) the facts and circumstances the law enforcement officer sees and (b) the person to be arrested. A reasonable and prudent person is one who acts wisely and does not make rash decisions. Ultimately, however, the officer will have to convince other *reasonable people*—a magistrate or possibly a jury—that the facts and circumstances reasonably lead other prudent people to come to the same conclusion that led the officer to make the arrest.

4. *That a crime has been or is being committed.* Many situations can lead the officer to believe a crime has been or is being committed. These include—but are not limited to—time of day or night, location, furtive actions, abnormal behavior, tools of a crime, contraband, and the suspect's dress and physical condition.

It is important for the peace officer who has arrested a person without a warrant, on probable cause, to properly note and record all the facts and circumstances that led the officer to believe an arrest was necessary. The officer may need to relate this information under oath at subsequent judicial proceedings.

Arrest Situations

A warrant protects an arresting officer from one of the defendant's most frequent challenges to lawful arrest—lack of probable cause. A warrant of arrest is a written order from a magistrate commanding that the person named in the warrant be arrested and brought before the court.

Under exigent circumstances, officers generally have authority to make an arrest without a warrant. However, these types of arrest require more than mere suspicion or a "hunch" on the officer's part. Most jurisdictions permit arrest without a warrant under specifically defined situations. Check the laws in your jurisdiction for the specific language of the law. Generally, most states follow the following criteria for arrests without a warrant:

1. *Offenses committed within an officer's view.* A peace officer may arrest an offender without a warrant for any offense—felony or misdemeanor—that occurs within the officer's presence or view.

2. *Offenses committed within a magistrate's view and the magistrate orders*

a peace officer to make an arrest. The verbal order of a magistrate who has personally seen a felony or a breach of the peace justifies a lawful arrest in most jurisdictions. In this case, the responsibility of probable cause is on the magistrate, not the officer.

3. *Suspicious people and circumstances that reasonably lead a peace officer to believe that a felony or breach of the peace has occurred or is about to occur, justify an arrest without a warrant.* Under this exception, the officer must be able to show that the circumstances were suspicious in nature and would lead a reasonable person to believe that a felony or breach of the peace had occurred or was about to occur. The officer must further show that probable cause existed to believe that the person arrested is in fact the person who committed the offense.

4. *A felony offense is committed in the presence of a credible person, and the offender is about to escape.* To justify an arrest under this exception, the officer must believe that the complainant is a *credible*—or believable— person who will be available at a later time to make a statement or testify against the accused. Admittedly, this aspect requires that a law enforcement officer must readily make a value judgment regarding the complainant. In addition, the surrounding situation and actions of others—such as the apparent escape efforts of a suspect—will have a bearing on the officer's judgment in making this type of felony arrest without a warrant.

5. *Assaults.* When a peace officer has probable cause to believe (a) that a person has committed an assault resulting in bodily injury to another person and (b) that there is danger of further bodily harm to the victim, the officer is generally authorized to make an arrest without a warrant. This frequently occurs in relation to domestic violence situations where violent acts have occurred or are indicated by the facts and circumstances at the scene.

6. *Violations of protective court orders.* Most jurisdictions have adopted laws that authorize peace officers to arrest people who violate the provisions of a court protective order (frequently resulting from a domestic violence situation). The officer must know that the order exists and have reasonably good reason to believe that the restricted person is aware of the "stay away" order. An officer should not leave the scene of the investigation while confirming that the order exists.

PRINCIPLES OF WEAPONLESS DEFENSE

The basic principles of weaponless defense are balance, awareness, and self-control. Just about everything a person does in life begins and ends with balance. For example, you cannot walk, sit, or stand if you cannot keep balance. By maintaining good balance, you establish a safe position that affords both mobility and safety. Conversely, by keeping a suspect off balance, you can minimize his or her mobility or the ability to fight back. Through awareness of your own position (and that of a suspect) and through self-control, you enhance your safety.

It is important to understand that weaponless defense and its principles are just one part of the overall concept of self-defense. The first principle of self-defense is prevention. The best method of defending against an assault is to avoid getting into that situation. Think ahead and be prepared *before* you are required to act. By being aware of potential dangers, you can mentally and physically prepare for the inevitable confrontation. In addition, avoid overextending to a point of no return; do not commit yourself to an act that you cannot reasonably carry out. Furthermore, maintain the proper distance from a suspect, which will allow you adequate reaction time.

The second principle of weaponless defense is that it is better to move out of the line of force than to try to stop the force when attacked by an assailant. An officer might side-step and allow the force to pass by and dissipate before applying a control technique. At this point, you must function at a high performance level of self-control, balance, and awareness to survive the attack.

Self-Control

Self-control alone will bring the officer more success in dealing physically with law violators than all the defense and control methods ever taught. If you cannot control yourself in a stressful situation, then any skill techniques you attempt will be neutralized. Self-control is attained through confidence, and confidence is gained through knowledge and ability. Self-control is enhanced through practice and perfected through understanding the theory and principles behind the technique. When you apply a control technique on a law violator, your body does not do the job itself; your mind and body operate in unison to complete the task. Principles explain "why" things work and why you should stand or move in a certain way to accomplish the purpose. A student understands better and retains training longer when he or she not only knows how to perform, but also the "why" of the performance. The following principles are an important training aid in self-defense and weaponless control.

1. The law enforcement officer's role in physical arrests is essentially defensive. Your job is to defend the public and to take the violator safely into custody. The word *defend* means "to repel danger or harm, and to serve to protect." An officer's actions are neither offensive (which means "committing the first act of hostility") nor passive (which means "enduring without resistance").

2. An arrest is an emotional problem as well as a physical problem. Both the officer and the arrested person undergo emotional stress. Your stress is based on prior experience in other arrest situations and on attitudes developed through training and violator contact. Furthermore, you can never be sure of the danger level of any given situation. The violator feels emotions and stress because he or she is about to be arrested and taken into custody.

3. The mind and body are one, are a whole. This is physiologically true, as well as being true in self-defense and weaponless control training. The body sends messages to the brain through the five senses, and responses to those stimuli are sent back to the body. Usually, this communication is a routine, everyday act of the body; however, the function becomes increasingly important to understand when dealing with stressful situations. Understanding the need to improve this coordination and cooperation is essential to successful training in self-control and weaponless defense.

Balance

Balance consists of two different areas: mental balance and physical balance. Mental balance is being prepared through training and practice to control the emotional and physical self and then being prepared to control the violator and, ultimately, the situation. In each situation, it is necessary to think the problem all the way through to its successful completion and not allow the emotional level of the violator or situation to overcome the officer's self-control and balance.

Interrogation Position

The "interrogation position" was developed to allow officers to establish a position of balance while protecting their sidearm and parts of the body that are vulnerable to physical attack. The position is assumed by approaching a suspect at a 45-degree angle with the sidearm away from the subject. Therefore, the right-handed officer will approach the suspect's right side, and a left-handed officer will approach the suspect's left side. In a position just outside the suspect's reach, assume a stance with the front foot pointing toward the suspect and the rear foot perpendicular to the front foot; the open stance distributes your weight equally between your legs, providing a good center-of-gravity balance. By bending your knees, you can prevent being pushed or pulled off balance if the suspect initiates an attack.

The 45-degree angle interrogation position is far superior to a straight-on approach to the suspect because it allows officers to protect areas of the body that are vulnerable to physical attack; in some instances, such attacks may be potentially fatal. If a male officer is in a straight-on position, the suspect may kick the genital area, which will render even the strongest man helpless against the attacker's assault; female officers can also receive serious injury from such an attack. If the suspect then decides to take the officer's sidearm, the officer, as well as innocent bystanders, will be in danger. With proper initial position, the officer both avoids being in an unbalanced position and protects vulnerable body areas.

Proper interrogation positioning allows the officer to be able to see the suspect from head to foot (and everything in between). Do not stare into the suspect's eyes: rather, watch the suspect's *shoulders*. Any movement that the suspect attempts to execute will be "telegraphed" by movement of the shoulders. At this point you are already using the third main principle—awareness.

Awareness

Awareness is basically observing the entire situation and being specifically aware of hazards when approaching suspects. There are five major concerns to analyze when approaching a suspect:

1. *The suspect's hands.* Where are the suspect's hands? If they are in his or her pockets, do not tell the suspect to remove them. In

fact, do not draw attention to this concern until you are in a position to remove the hands safely.

2. *Weapons.* Visually frisk a suspect, paying particular attention to the waistline area of the suspect's body. Be alert to anything in the immediate proximity to the suspect that could be used as a weapon in its natural state.

3. *Associates, relatives.* Anyone who may come to the suspect's aid or assistance may be a threat to you.

4. *Escape routes.* Be aware of any possible escape routes the suspect may take when confronted. Remember that the suspect may be more familiar with an area than you are, especially in his or her own home, neighborhood, or area.

5. *Your footing.* Understand the terrain where the contact is being made. Roadway curb, staircase, front porch, obstacles (such as furniture, water, or shrubs) and sloping ground each present different balance and positioning problems.

Personal Weapons

In unarmed defense, an officer uses numerous body parts to overcome resistance. For example, a fully flexed elbow blow may be the most powerful delivery of force that the average person can make. The meaty portion of your forearm might be used to block punches or similar attacks and/or strike the subject if warranted. The fleshy edge of your hand can be used to "chop" or strike the resisting suspect. The edge of your hand (or fist) might be used to strike the attacker's head, shoulder, chest, arm, rib, stomach, abdominal area, or joint areas. The palm of your hand can likewise be effectively used. Your fingers can grasp the person's body or be thrust into the adversary's eyes to temporarily blind him or her so you can escape an attack or use an appropriate defensive movement. You can use your head butting a suspect. Your knee (just above the knee joint—do not use the front or the hinged section of your knee, because it may break) and foot can be used to force a suspect to release a grip.

These movements are used only in self-defense, and the officer may never use more than necessary force. Personal weapons are generally used when a firearm, a baton, or a chemical agent cannot be used or are not appropriate. You must learn to distinguish the difference and apply the correct amount of force in any given situation.

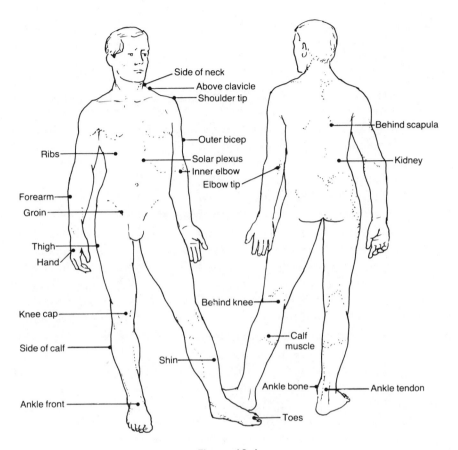

Figure 13-1
Impact points of the human body

The human body has many vulnerable areas. Some nerve centers and organs are unprotected or only lightly protected by bone or muscle tissue. A well-timed blow to any of these areas can incapacitate an opponent quickly. Such spots include the testicles, eyes, neck area, back and kidney area, abdominal area, chin, nose, and temples (see Figure 13-1).[1]

A knee blow to the testicles usually terminates any resistance; the strongest of holds can be broken if the testicles can be grasped or hit.

---

[1] Much of this information is summarized from Donald O. Schultz, *Police Unarmed Defense Tactics* (Costa Mesa, Calif.: Custom Publishing, 1985).

The eyes are very delicate and easy to reach; people instinctively retreat when their eyes are attacked. A blow with the edge of the hand across the windpipe in the "Adam's apple" can be fatal and should be avoided; however, blows delivered by the edge of the hand to the sides of the throat and back of the neck (at the base of the skull) can knock an assailant out. A blow to the small of the back can effectively disable an opponent, and a blow to the kidneys (located just above the hips on each side of the spine) can possibly knock someone out. Likewise, a hard blow delivered to the abdominal area, particularly if the opponent's muscles are relaxed, is very effective.

An officer should take care with any blows delivered to the chin, nose, or temple areas. A strike on the chin, especially with the edge of the hand directed downward at the point of the chin, can dislocate or break the lower jawbone. Blows to the nose can cause death by crushing the most fragile bones of the facial structure. A blow delivered to the temples with the knuckles or the edge of the hand will often knock the person out. A blow with the back of the fist or hand (or edge of the hand) with a snapping motion to a point behind the ears and at the base of the head can be devastating. Joints of the knee, wrist, elbow, arm, and fingers are designed to bend in only one direction; strong blows or pressure in the opposite direction will force an opponent to yield. Attacks on other sensitive areas include pulling the hair, tearing a lip, grasping and twisting the nose, kicking the Achilles tendon at the back of the heel, and gripping or pinching the thick muscles close to the neck that extend from the neck to the shoulder.

Defensive Tactics

Once you have assumed the proper position, which affords optimum balance, you depend on self-control to maintain an advantage over your assailant. The techniques of good body mechanics and leverage permit you to use your strengths against your opponent's weakness. Good body mechanics include both muscular control and breath control. The large trunk muscles of the torso play an important part in many physical movements; exercises can help you improve your upper body strength. Breath control allows you to exhale sharply, thus causing the diaphragm to become rigid, which minimizes the effectiveness of a blow to the chest or abdomen. The techniques of unarmed defense then use leverage against an opponent's weakness and maximize your strength and balance. For example, should an opponent push you, you can go with the hold or pull the subject in the direction of the push rather than resisting or bracing up against the attack. Your control of the opponent's weight and momentum by your strength and balance gives you the advantage in this situation.

The specific techniques of "come-alongs," "takedowns," and unarmed defensive manuevers should be learned under the controlled guidance of an academy instructor. The scope of this text is too narrow to explain each tactic and technique in detail, and each professional instructor uses slightly different approaches to each technique. The following list of defensive measures is the minimum of techniques officers should learn in academy-controlled situations.

Control Holds

1. *Rear wrist lock* (applied from cursory search position) can be used on either the right or left wrist.
2. *Twist lock* can be applied to a suspect in a standing, sitting, or prone position as well as from the front, side, or rear.
3. *Front wrist lock* can be applied in the same situations outlined for the twist lock.

Takedowns

1. *Hair-pull takedown* is executed from behind the suspect. If you are in front or beside the suspect, use a shuffle pivot or progressive pivot to get behind the person.
2. *Leg-sweep takedown* succeeds in taking a suspect down, but gives you no control over the person. However, this tactic can be used with the carotid control technique.
3. *Reverse wrist takedown* (front-choke escape and takedown) can be effectively used in a variety of situations, including an escape from the front-choke hold. The academy employs this takedown maneuver using distraction, escape (removing the subject's grip), and a throw-and-control hold to complete the tactic.
4. *Cross-face takedown to control* maneuver is accomplished when an officer approaches a suspect from the rear. The decision to use this maneuver depends on the suspect, positioning, control requirements, and opportunity.

Carotid Restraint Versus Trachea (Bar Arm) Choke

Law enforcement officers have a legal and moral obligation to limit the amount of force used to subdue and control offenders. Officers should follow a hierarchy of force in making quick, but accurate, decisions regarding the exact amount of force necessary in any given situation. Such force may range from verbal commands in minimal control situations to deadly force where the officer's life or another person's life is placed in jeopardy. Between these two extremes lie numerous decisions on how much force is necessary to control subjects who are under arrest. Violent offenders—especially those under the influence of alcohol and drugs (especially phencyclidine or PCP) —can exhibit unpredictable responses that threaten the arresting officer's well-being but do not warrant the use of "injuring force." Generally considered to be in the mid-range of force used by peace officers, neck restraints (upper body control holds) are more forceful and more dangerous than wrist or arm locks, but less harmful than the use of a baton or gun. The carotid control restraint may be effectively used in some situations if an officer understands its application, hazards, and first-aid techniques that are necessary if the technique is used.

An officer's primary function is to gain control over a suspect by taking command of a situation while preventing injury or death. The carotid control restraint should be used only as a last step before entry into "deadly force." Officers must understand the effects of this restraint on the body so that they can see the difference between the carotid restraint and the trachea/bar arm "choke," which is not recommended.

Trachea/Bar Arm Choke (not recommended). A number of deaths in California led to a series of lawsuits and court actions that has seriously curtailed use of "choke holds" in law enforcement. The U.S. Ninth District Court of Appeals ruled in a 1981 court case (*Lyons v. L.A.*, 656 F. 2d 417) that peace officers could no longer use the choke holds unless "someone was threatened with serious bodily harm." This decision was followed by a moratorium on the use of choke holds; the Los Angeles Police Commission imposed an outright ban on the use of the bar arm control hold and severely restricted the use of the carotid hold to situations where the officer is faced with serious bodily injury or death.

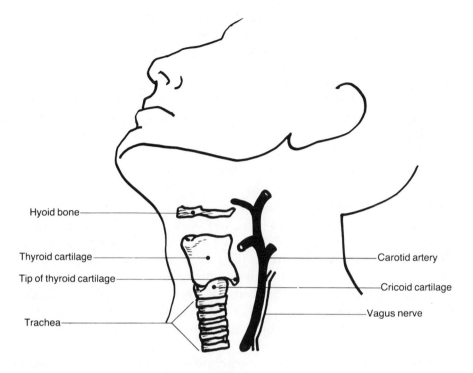

Figure 13-2
Diagram indicating location of carotid artery and other major parts of the human neck

Studies[2] show that the trachea/bar arm choke can fracture the laryngeal structures of a person's throat. This choke hold employs the officer's forearm to apply pressure on the front of the suspect's neck, thereby compressing the trachea. The closing of the trachea interrupts the flow of air to and from the lungs, thus preventing the exchange of oxygen necessary to sustain life. The level of oxygen in the blood is reduced throughout the entire body including the brain, resulting in loss of consciousness. The process may take two minutes or more until the suspect ceases to resist. During the "choke" time, the trachea is crushed with the officer's forearm, which can result in the subject's death (see Figure 13-2).

---

[2] Ronald N. Kornblum, M.D., "Medical Analysis of Police Choke Holds and General Neck Trauma," *Trauma 27*, No. 5 (February 1986), 5-7–5-60; and *28*, No. 1 (June 1986), 1-13–1-63.

Carotid Restraint. The carotid restraint (recommended when reasonable force is justified) is classified as controlling force that is used as a last resort before deadly force. The use of this tactic should be to subdue a violently resisting subject, including, but not limited to, violent mentally disturbed people and drug users when injuring force may not be effective because such people may not feel pain. Therefore, the carotid restraint may be the last step before entry into "deadly force." Your intent in using the carotid restraint should be to control the subject.

The carotid restraint applies pressure on the sides of the neck with intent to compress the carotid arteries (see Figure 13-3). Wrap your arm around the suspect's neck with your elbow pointing forward. Stand behind the suspect and place your arm around the neck in such a way that the Adam's apple is nestled in the crook of your elbow (see Figure 13-4). Apply pressure to the *sides* of the neck with the upper arm and forearm, so that the lines of force are exerted to the sides of the neck instead of against the front of the neck. The jugular veins and carotid arteries are the principal structures affected by this hold; the flow of oxygenated blood to the brain is diminished, causing the brain to lose consciousness. If properly applied, most subjects lose consciousness within 12 seconds; generally, the subjects will regain consciousness unaided within 30 seconds, although full recovery may take up to 24 hours.[3]

The amount of force required to compress or injure the various vital structures in the neck varies considerably from person to person. However, investigation conducted by Dr. Ronald N. Kornblum, M.D., indicates that only a relatively small amount of force is required to occlude the jugular veins and the carotid arteries, while more extensive force is required to cut off the trachea.[4] Officers should be aware of what is happening to the victim at the moment that the restraint is being applied. It is almost impossible for anyone to passively submit to being choked and to permit the airway to be obstructed. The subject's instinctive response is to struggle in order to free him- or herself and restore his or her breathing. If the subject has been using alcohol or drugs, his or her response may be unpredictable and violent. Many officers interpret the suspect's actions as belligerent and believe that the subject is purposefully not cooperating. So an

---

[3] Kornblum, pp. 5-32, 5-47, and 5-50.
[4] Kornblum, p. 5-45.

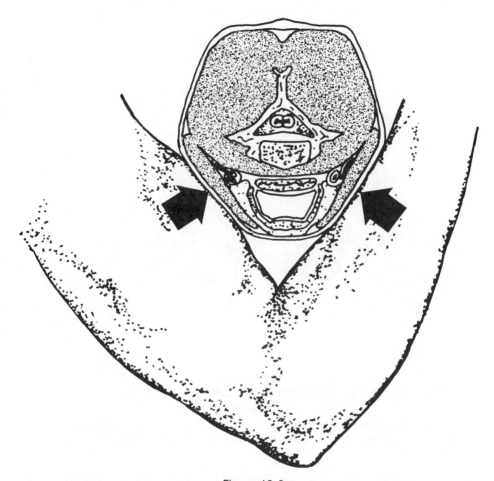

Figure 13-3
Schematic representation of lines of force during the carotid takedown hold.
The directions are oblique, against the carotid sinus on each side.
Source: Ronald N. Kornblum, M.D., "Medical Analysis of Police Choke
Holds and General Neck Trauma," *Trauma 27*, No. 5 (February 1986),
5-33.

officer may respond by applying even more force to the neck. This
combination can lead to fatal results! Maintain constant pressure,
without increasing the pressure, until the subject becomes unconscious or ceases to resist.

Using the carotid restraint is not without hazards. Once the
restraint has been used, check the subjects for vital signs of pulse and

Figure 13-4
Schematic representation of lines of force as an officer applies carotid takedown hold.
Source: Ronald N. Kornblum, M.D., "Medical Analysis of Police Choke Holds and General Neck Trauma," *Trauma 27*, No. 5 (February 1986), 5-34.

breathing. First aid can be administered on the scene if necessary. If the oxygenated blood flow to the brain cells is restricted for more than one minute, irreversible brain tissue damage can occur. Therefore, discontinue the hold as soon as you gain control of the subject. Other hazards associated with the carotid restraint are

1. Improper application of the carotid restraint could result in trachea/bar arm hold being applied to the front of the throat, damaging the larynx (voicebox) and trachea (windpipe).
2. The hyoid bone located at the base of the tongue, and the tip of the thyroid cartilage (which is located on either side of the throat) will fracture under excessive pressure and cause swell-

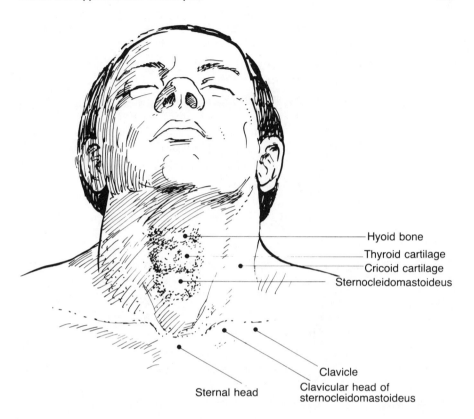

Hyoid bone
Thyroid cartilage
Cricoid cartilage
Sternocleidomastoideus

Clavicle
Clavicular head of
sternocleidomastoideus
Sternal head

Figure 13-5
Vulnerable neck structures often injured by neck trauma, including both types of choke holds.
Source: Ronald N. Kornblum, M.D., "Medical Analysis of Police Choke Holds and General Neck Trauma," *Trauma 28*, No. 1 (June 1986), 1-23.

ing. The condition could result in suffocation and death. (See Figure 13-5.)

3. Both the carotid sinus and the vagus nerves affect the heart muscle. Depression of these nerves could produce irregular respiratory and cardiac activity. The effects of drugs, alcohol, and/or medical disorders will enhance this reaction.

4. Improper application that results in jerking or twisting the subject's neck when the carotid restraint is applied, could

break the subject's neck, resulting in his or her death or
permanent paralysis.

5. The carotid restraint should not be applied while the subject is
    standing. If the person should lose consciousness while stand-
    ing, the possibility of injury or death increases drastically
    because the subject is in a vulnerable position.

6. The carotid restraint should never be applied more than twice
    in a 24-hour time frame. Application of this tactic more
    frequently than twice a day greatly increases the chance of
    serious injury to the suspect.

7. During loss of consciousness, subjects may lose control of their
    bladder and/or bowels as their body muscles contract and
    spasms occur.

Use common sense and restraint when applying any force. Any
blow, strike, kick, twisting, or tearing will be highly scrutinized by
both the police agency and the courts. Unarmed defensive tactics
should be designed to gain and maintain control over a suspect who is
resisting apprehension. Any control hold, "takedown" tactic, or
restraint tactic is justified only to meet the opponent's use of force and
permit the officer time to correctly apply handcuffs or other physical
restraints. Blows designed to cause death or permanent disability
should be used only when justified by the penal code.

First Aid for Carotid Restraint

Four major blood vessels supply the brain with blood and oxygen: two
carotid arteries in the front of the neck and two vertebral arteries
running up the protective bony canals in the neck section of the spine.
(see Figure 13-3). Certain parts of the brain depend on only a single
branch of the arteries and are especially vulnerable to any disturbance
in the flow of blood. Whenever part of the brain is damaged because
its blood supply is disturbed, a stroke occurs. As a result, the physical
or mental functions controlled by the injured area deteriorate. Unconsciousness, numbness, confusion, and dizziness are all potential
symptoms; a continued blockage of a carotid artery can result in
death. As soon as the subject discontinues resistance and is restrained,
check the subject for vital signs, pulse, and breathing. The following
first aid should be administered:

1. Establish an airway.

2. Check for breathing.
3. Check for brachial pulse.
4. Manually massage neck muscles to stimulate blood flow.
5. Obtain a verbal response from subject.

If the subject lacks any vital signs, de-handcuff the subject and render first aid immediately while waiting for medical help, if summoned. If the subject is to be transported, observe the subject closely for any signs that may be life threatening. Regardless of whether or not the subject was rendered unconscious, have the subject checked by medical personnel. Agency policy on the use of the carotid restraint may vary. Understand and follow your agency's instructions and guidelines.

PCP Intoxication. People under the influence of PCP have sensory blockade. Users lose their sense of touch and, in particular, their sense of pain. Since the subject may not comprehend what is happening, he or she may not submit to arrest without resistance. Such a person cannot be subdued by ordinary measures. Since sensory blockade leaves the person without a sense of pain, the subject will not realize he or she is in danger if a choke hold is applied and will continue to fight and increase the danger to him- or herself.

It is this lack of pain sensation that renders the PCP-intoxicated person so difficult to subdue. As a result, law enforcement officers in turn are obligated to increase the amount of force necessary to control the subject. The situation creates a dilemma of "reasonable force" under the condition. You cannot use deadly force (unless otherwise justified) because it is normally not warranted. You are restricted in using a choke hold because it is too dangerous. You cannot use persuasion because it is not effective. Theoretically, the best method would be to allow the outburst of frenzy to run its course, wait for the adrenalin to be used up, and let fatigue subdue the suspect. Unfortunately, this method is not practical because the risk of injury to the victim as well as to innocent people is too great. Doing nothing also carries risk of the suspect suddenly going into cardiac arrest and stopping breathing from the effects of the drug or following the exhaustion of adrenalin.[5] The carotid restraint may or may not be

---

[5] Kornblum, p. 1-60.

effective in controlling a PCP victim. However, officers must use only necessary force to protect themselves and others.

After Using a Carotid Restraint. After a carotid restraint has been used, allow the suspect time to recover before he or she is placed face down on the floor of a police car. Respiratory movements are restricted when lying in a prone position with handcuffs on the wrists and arms behind the subject's back. This, combined with the confined space near the floor of the vehicle (where oxygen is limited), places the suspect in extreme peril. Always be ready to administer first aid.[6]

WEAPON RETENTION AND WEAPON TAKEAWAYS

Officers must be conscious of their sidearms or other weapons at all times. Although sidearms are for self-defense and defense of other people, they can be used to cause death or serious bodily injury to you or innocent bystanders if they are permitted to fall into an assailant's hands. Whenever anyone attempts to grab your sidearm, immediately clasp the person's hand to prohibit him or her from removing the weapon from the holster; use your fingers to attack the assailant's eyes. The assailant will not be able to avoid the involuntary retraction and will turn his or her head to avoid the attack. During this time, you must use quick movements and maneuvers to retain possession of the sidearm. Then apply appropriate restraints to assume custody of the suspect.

Whenever an assailant does get an opportunity to point a weapon at an officer, the officer must choose wisely and quickly the best method to avoid injury. In the academy, officers learn how to quickly take away handguns, knives, shotguns, and rifles from suspects who initially achieve the superior position. However, the actual decision to attempt the maneuver should be considered in light of reality. You might attempt to keep suspects talking and reason with them. Every second gained during these crucial moments puts you in a better position to survive! Attempt a weapon takeaway only when you actually believe you will be killed by the suspect if you do not take immediate action. While attempting the weapon takeaway, you ac-

---

[6] Kornblum, p. 1-61.

cept certain risks of being seriously injured or killed. The maneuver thus should be chosen only as a "last resort," with total understanding that there are no alternatives in handling this critical situation. Without a doubt, the result will be a "life or death" decision.

Gun Takeaway Techniques

Before an officer tries to take away a gun pointed at him or her by an assailant, certain conditions must be considered. If the assailant has not yet fired the weapon, you have a chance. However, if there is considerable distance between you and the assailant, your chances are diminished. Therefore, to employ a disarming technique, get as close to the gun as possible. Whether you live or die will depend on a fraction of a second. Do *not* concentrate on the firearm, but rather try to observe the *type* of firearm the assailant is holding. The techniques you use to disarm the assailant will depend on whether the firearm is a handgun, rifle, or shotgun.

One of the best times to make a move is while the assailant is talking. Certainly the assailant will react to your move; however, the assailant will have to switch his or her thoughts from what he or she is saying, to what to do about your move. This "lag time," however slight, will delay the assailant from pulling the trigger. If the assailant must move the barrel of the gun to point it at you, this further increases the time and decreases accuracy. In spite of the "lag time" thus afforded, assume that the assailant will get at least one shot off. Therefore, your initial move cannot be directly for the gun, but rather to get out of the line of fire. Now is when you are rewarded for honest and diligent practice of defensive training—it will never be worth more to you than at this moment!

Any and all tactics, including situations where the officer is held hostage by the suspect, will be demonstrated under controlled conditions and should not be attempted without proper instruction. Under no circumstances should such techniques be practiced with loaded weapons! When available, simulated weapons are highly desirable for training purposes.

Weapons Retention

The FBI Uniform Crime Reports indicate that incidents of assaults against law enforcement officers have increased tremendously in recent years. In addition, the reports note that more officers are being killed with their own guns than ever before. In one recent study, reports of 129 officers killed showed that 19 were murdered with their own weapons—an increase of 111 percent in six years!

An officer must be constantly concerned with weapons retention. Holster design can affect weapons retention. The holster and straps should be able to withstand stress of someone pulling violently on the gun. You can improve the holster's ability to retain weapons by maintaining the holster in good condition and replacing worn straps and snaps. With thumb-break holsters, you should be aware that a downward grabbing action from the suspect's hand (from the front) could cause the holster to unsnap. Regardless of the holster used, it should be designed so that you can draw the gun quickly and safely, yet so that the gun can remain secure in the holster when unsnapped during vigorous body movement. Suitable techniques of weapons retention are demonstrated under defensive tactics training supervision.

The principles of handgun retention are accomplished by providing more physical stress against an attacker then he or she can withstand. The primary concern is an immediate release of the assailant's hand(s). All counterattacks should be directed against the assailant's arm, which includes the hand, wrist, forearm, elbow, and shoulder. Your initial response should always be appropriate to the situation and provide the best opportunity to safely defend the gun and yourself. The three principal objectives are

1. *To secure the weapon.* Secure the weapon in the holster and then prepare to apply the release technique.
2. *To gain position.* Move into a position that offers the greatest opportunity to exert maximum leverage and physical stress against the attacker and at the same time provides body movement that protects you against additional assault, and apply the release.
3. *To effect release.* Apply the release with the appropriate technique. The release is ensured by simply applying more leverage and physical stress against the attacker than he or she has the ability to withstand.

BATON TECHNIQUES

The police baton is a traditional symbol of authority and a weapon long associated with the military and law enforcement. The modern police baton is made of hardwood or sturdy plastic. Its width ranges from 1 to 1½ inches in diameter; its length may vary from 12 to 24 inches. The official police baton is durable and designed to meet the requirements of police service without the need of weighting or leading. The baton may be straight or coupled with a handle. Many officers prefer the side-handled baton for greater leverage and flexibility. Whichever style of baton is used, officers have a responsibility to learn to handle the weapon properly before carrying it on duty. Furthermore, the courts have recognized that municipalities and police administrators have an "affirmative duty" to train the peace officers they employ. Therefore, modern officers must understand the proper methods of using the police baton.

Officers must be trained in the use of the baton as well as in the use of unarmed defense. The baton offers an alternative to using firearms in some situations. Once officers have proper training with the baton, its systematic and scientific deployment make it a versatile control device as well as an effective deterrent to aggression. The baton is primarily an impact weapon, designed for defensive purposes. The police baton is an alternative to using lethal force.

Scope and Nature of Use

It must be remembered that the police baton "is a deadly weapon." Any officer who uses the baton against a person beyond reasonable force, can be charged with "Assault" or "Assault with deadly weapon." As a weapon, the baton can be used either defensively or offensively. In law enforcement, however, in order for the baton to be used in an authorized manner, it must be used defensively; that is, to repel or protect. Use of the police baton is proper in lawful situations requiring a degree of force greater than that readily provided by weaponless control techniques, but less than that provided by resorting to the use of other deadly weapons. Keep in mind the general requirements of most penal codes: An arrest is made by an actual restraint of the person, or by submission to the custody of an officer. The person arrested may be subjected to such restraint as is *reasonable* for his arrest and detention. However, the officer must justify the baton's use by the totality of circumstances. The factors tending to justify the baton's use are (1) the physical stature of the suspect as compared to the officer's stature, or (2) the need for immediate control of the suspect or situation due to a tactical consideration. The officer's perception of the suspect's knowledge or apparent knowledge of a martial art form may constitute such a tactical consideration. If the suspect assumes an aggressive stance or if the suspect cannot be controlled by lesser means due to the influence of alcohol and/or drugs, such facts tend to lend credibility to the officer's explanation for using the baton.

Most penal codes also grant the officer right to use reasonable force to prevent escape as well as to effect arrest; for example,

> Any peace officer who makes or attempts to make an arrest need not retreat or desist from his/her efforts by reason of the resistance or threatened resistance of the person being arrested; nor shall such officer be deemed an aggressor or lose his/her right to self-defense by the use of reasonable force to effect the arrest or to prevent escape or to overcome resistance. (California Penal Code 835a)

Penal codes also outline what amount of force may be used; for example,

> When the arrest is being made by an officer under the authority of a warrant, after information of the intention to make the arrest, if the person to be arrested either flees or forcibly resists, the officer may use all necessary means to effect the arrest. (California Penal Code 843)

Similar language appears in most penal codes; check the specific statutes in your state.

Based on these penal code guidelines, certain rules may be adopted for using the baton in appropriate situations:

1. The baton should normally be positioned between the officer and the suspect.
2. If you hold the baton in either your right or your left hand, maintain a good defensive position.
3. Do *not* intentionally use a baton to strike at the head or throat.
   a. The head is the easiest part of the body for the suspect to

defend by using hands and arms to block the movement.

b. During such movement, it is easy to lose control of the baton to the suspect.

c. If you strike the suspect's head, the blow could cause death or serious bodily injury to the suspect.

4. Do not use the baton to apply a choking technique.

Baton Target Areas

The police baton is designed to supplement normal force when a subject is resisting arrest and cannot otherwise be subdued or controlled. The primary intent of the baton is not to counter deadly force or to inflict serious injury, but rather to temporarily immobilize aggressive people or discourage them from pressing an attack. It is vital, therefore, that you understand what areas of the body are appropriate targets and which should not be struck with the baton.

Avoid striking an assailant's head with the baton. A blow delivered to this part of the body may result in a serious or fatal injury or brain tissue damage that may evolve into an incurable psychosis. Side blows to the temple, forehead, or throat can likewise be lethal.

The general target areas of the baton are portions of the body that may be struck without causing permanent or fatal injuries. These target locations are (1) highly sensitive areas such as the solar plexus and groin; (2) muscular areas such as the back of the thighs, hamstring muscles, calves, and biceps; and (3) areas where the skin is near the bone, such as the hand, wrist, arm, or shins.

The baton may be effectively used to check an onrushing assailant by a jablike thrust to the solar plexus. This sensitive area is located in the center of the abdomen about 4 inches above the waist. A thrust to the groin will accomplish similar results. Keep both hands on the baton as you jab the opponent. Gripping the baton in this fashion adds force to the thrust and reduces the possibility of the blow being blocked or the weapon being wrenched from your hands. The tactic is intended to cause discomfort and temporary shock and give you time to control an otherwise violent person.

Baton strikes to the lower limbs, such as a hard blow to the back thigh muscle (hamstring), can generally be administered without fear of serious injury. The effectiveness of such blows lies in the fact that they cause muscle spasms and temporarily immobilize a would-be assailant. Furthermore, the baton can be used to guard against an assailant's kicks. By holding the baton with two hands, the officer in a crouched position can parry a kick and follow up with an offensive measure designed to immobilize the attacker.

Before attempting to use the baton on an assailant's upper limbs, consider the possibility of a misdirected blow striking the opponent in a vital area. A blow to the upper or lower arm, the elbow, the wrist, or the back of the hand will effectively curb any opponent's desire to continue an attack. Furthermore, striking assailants on the wrist or the top of the hand will force them to release any weapon or object they may be holding. However, consider this tactic in light of the discussion surrounding "weapon takeaways," and remember that the baton was never intended to replace or combat a gun.

Training and the Baton

Officers must have professional baton training. In any technique used, three firm rules must be applied:

1. The technique must be safe for the officer.
2. The technique must be effective.
3. The technique must be socially acceptable and conform to court acceptance, state law, and departmental guidelines.

Professional training in baton use increases your ability to strike from a distance as well as provides you with greater striking power. Properly trained, with the baton you can have the same striking force as—or more than—the experienced karate black belt. Such ability provides you confidence in awareness of the baton's power and uses. Armed with this information, you are less likely to have to use the baton because you will possess both a psychological and a physical advantage that you will transmit in most confrontations by your self-confidence, demeanor, and body language. Once the assailant correctly assesses your confidence, the necessity of using the baton often disappears.

In the final analysis, survival is the name of the game. What you do, how you approach situations, and how you have prepared yourself to meet the demands of being a modern peace officer all translate into survival. Your physical habits, training, education, common sense, alertness, and self-control give you the winning edge.

KEY TERMS

Arrest warrant
Balance (weaponless defense)
Carotid restraint
Constructive seizure
Defensive tactics
Detention
Exigent circumstances
Interrogation position
Lawful arrest
Magistrate
Mere suspicion
PCP intoxication
Personal weapons
Physical restraint
Probable cause
Reasonable person
Seizure
Trachea (bar arm) choke
Under restraint
Weaponless defense
Weapons retention
Weapons takeaways

STUDY QUESTIONS

1. What is the basis of authority for making arrests in our society? Justify your answer by using exact language from the U.S. Constitution.

2. Outline the four elements necessary to create an arrest.

3. What is *constructive seizure*?

4. What is the difference between "mere suspicion" and "probable cause"?

5. Define the concept of "probable cause." Outline two hypothetical situations where a person acts in a suspicious manner that would lead

you to believe that a crime has been or is about to be committed, and that would justify an arrest.

6. Relate three reasons why an arrest with a warrant is considered more desirable than an arrest without a warrant, provided that time permits obtaining such a warrant.

7. Research your state laws, and determine the circumstances that justify an arrest without a warrant. Outline each of these authorities for reference.

8. Under what circumstance can you arrest a fleeing person based on the word of a *credible* person that a crime has just occurred? What information would you need after this type of arrest?

9. Courts in many jurisdictions issue "protective orders" to prevent domestic violence and protect the victim(s). If such an order is applicable in your state, do you have to see the actual violation of the order to make an arrest? Justify your answer.

10. What are the basic principles of weaponless defense? Define each principle.

11. An officer's role in physical restraint is essentially defensive. Define what the word *defend* means and how it applies to the law enforcement officer's role in making arrests.

12. What are the two different types of "balance" as defined by the text? Relate each to the patrol officer's duty performance.

13. Describe the "interrogation position." Why is this stance a position of strength, safety, and balance?

14. In positioning yourself to observe a person and protect yourself against attack, what specifically should you be aware of in order to defend against suspect hazards? Justify your answers.

15. List your "personal weapons," and how you might use them to protect yourself and gain control over a suspect.

16. When using personal weapons to control a suspect, what types of blows to the body should be avoided, because they may be considered as "deadly force"?

17. Outline the correct method to apply the "carotid restraint" hold. When, how often, and why would you use this tactic?

18. Why should you avoid using the trachea (bar arm) choke hold? Would any circumstances justify using this tactic?

19. If properly applied, the carotid restraint will cause a subject to lose consciousness. How long will the subject become unconscious? What actions should you take during this time?

20. When the subject resists the pressure of the carotid restraint hold, should you apply more pressure? Justify your answer.

21. What hazards may be associated with the carotid restraint?

22. Describe the tactics of first aid to use once a person has been subjected to the carotid restraint hold.

23. Why might you consider using the carotid restraint hold on a person who is under the influence of PCP?

24. Relate why weapons retention is a vital concern for the patrol officer.

25. Under what circumstances should you attempt to take a weapon away from a person who is pointing the weapon at you? Justify your answer.

26. If you are going to make a move to take a weapon away from an assailant, *when* should you attempt this tactic?

27. What are the three principal objectives of weapons retention?

28. Describe the police baton. Is this an offensive or defensive weapon? Justify your answer.

29. Under what circumstances should you decide to use the police baton?

30. Describe the target areas you should concentrate on to properly use the police baton. Are there any parts of the body you must avoid when using the baton? Justify your answer.

31. Outline the rules that should be adopted in using the baton.

32. What three rules must be applied in baton training?

33. What is the "winning edge," and how do you attain this condition?

ACTIVITIES

1. Under a proper training situation, practice various restraint holds, defensive tactics, and weapon takeaways.

2. Under proper supervision, learn to use the police baton in arresting and controlling a suspect who resists arrest.

3. Consider the following situations in determining what may be consid-

ered reasonable force if you use a baton. Write your response and compare your reaction with other members of your class.

a. You are a member of a tactical squad in a crowd or riot control formation. How should you use the baton to move, separate, disperse, or deny a person access to a structure or through an area?

b. When an officer is attacked by a suspect armed with a weapon that is not a firearm, how should you use the baton to disarm, distract, or disable the suspect, or to hold the suspect at bay until additional assistance arrives?

c. When the officer is assaulted by an unarmed suspect, how do you use the baton to disable the suspect, or to defend against an assault?

d. When the officer confronts several suspects who are threatening the officer, and the suspects are capable of carrying out the threats (and they make an overt act to carry out the threats), can you use the baton to fend off an attack or assault and make an arrest(s)? Justify your answer.

e. When the officer is confronted by a suspect or suspects who the officer has reasonable cause to believe committed a crime, and the suspect(s) refuse or fail to comply with the officer's direction prior to searching or handcuffing, may you use the baton to obtain compliance? Justify your answer.

14

Prisoner Restraint, Search, and Custody

Once an arrest has been properly executed, law enforcement officers must ensure proper restraint and searching techniques and subsequently transport the prisoner to a confinement or detention facility. This chapter outlines general approaches to prisoner restraint, including handcuff devices and application techniques. Custody responsibilities and processes are discussed, including booking procedures and predetention procedures for properly handling and disposing of prisoners and their property.

USING FORCE

The peace officer is vested with society's greatest trust—the right to use force to accomplish the police mission. However, the amount of force permitted in each situation is limited to the officer's ability to exercise good judgment and competence in accordance with the penal code and departmental policy. You must have the basic knowledge and physical ability necessary to make wise decisions in applying the correct amount of force in any given situation. Whenever you are threatened with danger, your confidence, ability, instinctive reaction, mental alertness, and concentration—coupled with self-control over emotions and body reactions—will determine whether or not you survive the crisis. In addition, you must constantly be aware that superiors will closely scrutinize any use of force to determine if it was an appropriate response to the threat. The community will be quick to judge your actions and apply sanctions for inappropriate behavior. In some instances, both you and the department will be subject to liabilities should you fail to use "reasonable force" in performing police duties.

Officers must remember the legal aspects of using force in law enforcement work. When you use force, the action can result in death or injury—or in control of the situation. Force in law enforcement is used for *protection of life* and to *enforce the law* within the "limits of the law." Whenever force is used, you must be certain at all times that your actions are necessary, justified. Courts will examine whether or not the act was *committed by necessity* in your performance of duty. Furthermore, courts will determine if you acted as a reasonable person and used the *minimum amount of force necessary* to take the suspect into custody. Failure to meet these minimum standards of justification exposes an officer and the police agency to possible litigation.

REASONABLE FORCE

The "reasonable force" doctrine is the penal code standard used to determine whether an officer's use of force in any given situation is, or is not, appropriate. One definition of the word *reasonable* notes that a state of sensible or rational behavior must exist. Reasonableness is judged on whether another prudent person—or officer—would act in the same or similar manner under the same conditions. Typical penal codes say that (for example),

> An arrest is made by an actual restraint of the person, or by submission to the custody of an officer. The person arrested may be subject to such restraint as is *reasonable* for his arrest and detention. (Section 835 of the California Penal Code [emphasis added])

The words "may be subjected to such restraint as is reasonable" are both (1) authority for the use of force and (2) a limitation on the amount of force justified. Reasonable, or sensible, restraint for both arrest and detention of offenders gives the officer the right to immobilize and control a suspect in order to bring the person before a magistrate to answer the charges made against him or her. However, it is understood that *excessive* force to accomplish the task is beyond the officer's authority under law. In addition to the reasonable restraint rule, statutory law generally authorizes reasonable force to prevent escape. For example, consider the following language of one such statute:

> Any peace officer who has reasonable cause to believe that the person to be arrested has committed a public offense may use reasonable force to effect the arrest, to prevent escape or to overcome resistance. Any peace officer who makes or attempts to make an arrest need not retreat or desist from his/her efforts by reason of the resistance or threatened resistance of the person being arrested; nor shall such officer be deemed an aggressor or lose his/her right to self-defense by the use of reasonable force to effect the arrest or to prevent escape or to overcome resistance. (Section 835a, California Penal Code)

The peace officer is clearly expected to take positive action to accomplish the police mission. In addition to using reasonable force to effect the arrest, you are authorized to use reasonable force to prevent escape and overcome any resistance to the legal arrest. Whenever a suspect is arrested, that person is required to refrain from using force or any weapon to resist such arrest. However, few violent offenders stop to read the penal code at the point of confrontation with a peace officer. If the offender uses force to resist the arrest, you are granted authority to overcome such resistance and you "shall not be deemed an aggressor or lose [your] right to self-defense by the use of reasonable force." The following examples are designed to demonstrate these principles.

Example

An officer responds to a silent alarm at a warehouse. On arriving at the building, the officer observes an individual leaving the rear door of the warehouse with some articles in her hands. The officer draws her revolver and shouts, "Police! Don't move!" The offender throws the articles in her hands at the officer and begins to run away. What should the officer do?

1. Fire the revolver to prevent the offender's escape.
2. Issue a second challenge to the offender to stop. If she does not halt after the second challenge, the officer should fire her weapon to stop the fleeing suspect.
3. Issue a second challenge for the offender to stop. If she does not respond to the challenge, the officer should alert other officers of the fleeing suspect and use reasonable physical force to prevent the offender from escaping.

In the first two choices, the officer would be exceeding her authority of "reasonable force" by using deadly force to prevent the burglar's escape. She was never placed in jeopardy of a life-threatening situation; therefore she would not be justified in using deadly force to prevent the offender's escape. In the third choice, the officer resorts to "reasonable force" and "good logic" to effect the arrest and control the offender.

Example

Officers respond to a family disturbance call. On arrival at the residence, they hear loud outcries of obscene language coming from inside the residence. The officers take a conservative approach to the residence, using cover and concealment, and assume a protective position on either side of the front door before knocking. An angry man, who is apparently one of the individuals causing the disturbance, responds to the knock and challenges the officers' right to interfere in the civil dispute between himself and his wife. The officers gain entrance to the home on the invitation of the woman involved in the dispute and succeed in separating the disputing couple inside the home. The angry man details the account of an alleged adulterous affair between his wife and their neighbor, exclaiming intent to kill the neighbor on sight. At this time, a knock is heard at the door, and a man (later identified as the neighbor accused in the affair) enters the room and immediately proceeds to comfort the woman. The angry husband reaches for a handgun from a nearby desk drawer. What should the officers do?

1. Draw their sidearms and immediately fire at the man grabbing the gun.
2. Draw their sidearms and order the resident to stop. They should fire their guns only if the resident opens the drawer.
3. The officers should never draw their handguns, because innocent bystanders are in the room.
4. Draw their handguns and order the actor to stop. They should fire their weapons only if the actor continues toward the weapon and subsequently points it at one of the individuals in the room.

If the officers react too quickly, as suggested in the first choice, they would probably be cited for excessive use of force. In the second choice, the officers must decide if it is reasonable force to fire the duty weapon when the actor merely opens the drawer. Because the actor possesses ability and opportunity, but has not as yet demonstrated the element of jeopardy, the officers' actions would probably be declared premature. The third choice could be a deadly mistake because this is an obviously violent situation in which the actor has declared his intent to use deadly force against the neighbor. In the fourth choice, the officers must decide the precise point at which the actor has ability and opportunity, and places the life of the officers or another individual in jeopardy. If the actor stops, the officers would be justified in using only physical restraint to ease the hostility of the moment. If the actor persists in his efforts to obtain the weapon and point it at the others in the room, the officers would have no other choice but to use deadly force to prevent the actor from harming another person.

The choices and timing are critical, the decisions are not easy to make, but society expects law enforcement officers to react quickly and accurately in each crisis to protect everyone involved. No one said that the officer's job is easy; indeed, it is a tough job with tough decisions in each conflict circumstance. Good, sensible reasoning power must prevail in the officer's decision-making responsibilities.

Deadly Force

Deadly force is that amount of force likely to cause death or serious bodily injury. A resulting death is called "homicide" under the law. An intentional homicide may be classified as either "justifiable" or "criminal." Justifiable homicide is generally committed in obedience to any judgment of a competent court, or when necessarily committed in overcoming actual resistance to the execution of some legal process; justifiable homicide may also occur when a peace officer is acting in the discharge of any other legal duty, including retaking felons who have escaped from legal custody. Thus, in many situations officers have a duty to use force, up to and including deadly force, when necessity dictates, when the force is in fact reasonable.

The "deadly force" statutes in various states differ in exact language. Obtain a copy of your state penal code and determine exactly when, and under what circumstances, deadly force will be justified. In general, statutes authorize peace officers to use deadly force if the officer reasonably believes the deadly force is immediately necessary

1. To protect him- or herself against another's use or attempted use of unlawful deadly force
2. To lawfully defend an innocent third person
3. To prevent the imminent commission of specific felonies (check your local jurisdiction for exact language)
4. To prevent the escape of a fleeing felon (check your local jurisdiction for exact language) for specific types of offenses
5. To protect property or prevent someone from escaping with property *if* the property cannot be recovered by any other means (check your local jurisdiction for exact language)
6. To prevent the escape of an arrested person from a penal institution

Note: The use of deadly force is generally regarded as a "last resort" when other degrees of lesser force fail to prevent the injury, harm, escape, or loss of property.

Many penal codes require that more than "bare fear" must exist to justify homicide. Courts frequently note that the circumstances must be sufficient to excite the fears of a reasonable person, and the killing party must have acted under the influence of such fears alone. In fact, there should be an "overt act" on the part of the suspect, in addition to the killer's fear, to justify the use of deadly force.

Keep in mind that the use of force, including deadly force, against another is never justified in response to verbal provocation alone. Furthermore, in making an arrest an officer may not use any more force than is immediately necessary to effect the arrest. Peace officers may use force only when and to the degree they reasonably believe the force is immediately necessary to make or assist in making an arrest or a search, or to prevent escape from custody.

Whenever peace officers face the decision to use deadly force, they must be concerned with a number of circumstances that dictate when such force is authorized. First, they must understand the type of crime and suspect(s) involved. Felons and their actions may or may not justify the use of deadly force, depending on the actions and situation at the moment of the confrontation. You must consider the present and future threat to lives of innocent people, the environment, and the law regarding the exact amount of force authorized in any given situation. To make the situation even more difficult, add your present capabilities, the threatening weapon's capabilities, and the immediacy of the threat. Each of these separate but distinct complicated contingencies must be analyzed and scrutinized, and good reasoning power must be called on to reach a wise decision on the correct amount of force, if any, to use in each situation.

How much time do you have to accomplish these difficult tasks? Usually only fractions of a second! The courts will have days, months, and even years to decide whether or not you acted correctly during those crucial seconds of encounter. The courts expect professional peace officers to understand the laws and departmental policy regarding the legal use of deadly force. Furthermore, the courts expect peace officers to be able to decide quickly and accurately—based on training and education—when deadly force is authorized.

Common Deadly Force Policies

The most common conditions stated in law enforcement agency policies regarding the use of deadly force include self-defense, defense of others when immediate threat to life exists, shooting at nonviolent fleeing felons, and warning shots. You must be constantly aware of the letter of the law and departmental policy in dealing with each of these complicated situations.

Self-defense. The right to self-defense precedes even English common law. Generally statutes state that lawful resistance to the commission of a public offense may be made (1) by the party about to be injured, and (2) by other parties. Furthermore, resistance sufficient to prevent the offense may be made by the party about to be injured to prevent an offense against his or her person, or his or her family. Undoubtedly, the legislature wants to protect the right of the individual to resist another's unlawful use of force. The affirmative defense also carries over to the use of deadly force.

Example

A peace officer is on routine patrol and observes a robbery in progress. She leaves her patrol vehicle and confronts the robber coming out of the business establishment. The robber points a handgun at the officer, who has assumed a position of cover behind the patrol vehicle. What should the officer do?

1. Maintain a position of cover behind the vehicle, but do not fire the duty weapon.
2. Get back into the patrol unit and retreat, awaiting backup units.
3. Fire her handgun with intent to wound the robber.
4. Because this is clearly a self-defense situation and the officer has no duty to retreat, she should fire her sidearm with intent to kill the robber.

The alternatives might seem tough, but there is only one clear and distinctive choice—this is a self-defense situation even though the officer has cover. Choice 1 might be a good decision, except the officer has a duty to protect the public as well as herself. Remember that penal codes generally note that officers are justified in using deadly force when necessarily committed in arresting persons charged with felony, and who are fleeing from justice or resisting such arrest. The second choice is contrary to what the public expects of peace officers in crisis situations. With a position of cover, officers should not retreat. Choice 3 supposes that the officer should "shoot to wound"; this might work well on television, but in real-life situations officers should use their duty weapons only when deadly force is actually warranted. Only in Choice 4 has the officer taken actions to protect herself as well as others in this critical situation. However, the decision to use deadly force could also depend on the presence of innocent bystanders.

Defense of Others. Peace officers carry a legal responsibility, by virtue of their office, to protect society. Many penal codes state language similar to the following: "Homicide is also justifiable when committed in the lawful defense of person(s) or when necessarily committed in attempting to apprehend any person for any felony or in lawfully keeping and preserving the peace." Society deems that peace officers have, in fact, a legal duty to protect the innocent in violent situations.

Example

A peace officer responds to a fight-in-progress call in a residential neighborhood. On arrival at the scene, he observes a man committing the act of rape with a knife at his victim's throat. The officer should

1. Retreat from the scene and call for backup assistance.
2. Voice a challenge to the offender in hopes he will run away.
3. Immediately draw his duty weapon, challenge the offender, and use deadly force if he reasonably believes it is immediately necessary to protect the victim's life.

The choice is clear! The officer has a legal, as well as a moral, responsibility to protect the victim, and this is obviously a situation in which his action is immediately necessary to do so. Retreat (Choice 1) or inaction (Choice 2) are clearly inappropriate. Positive, quick, and diligent use of force, possibly deadly force, is required of the officer in this situation.

Shooting at Nonviolent Fleeing Felons. The decision to shoot (or not) at a nonviolent fleeing felon is one of the most difficult for the peace officer. On one hand, officers may use deadly force when necessarily committed in arresting people charged with felony, and *who are fleeing from justice* or resisting such arrest. However, recent court cases have indicated that the use of deadly force to prevent the escape of a nonviolent offender will be scrutinized closely. Each department or agency issues a policy covering the use of force in such situations, although, in general, deadly force should *not* be used to prevent the escape of a nonviolent offender. In these situations, neither the officer nor any other person is in immediate danger of a life-threatening situation from the fleeing offender. Other means of force, less than deadly, are called for here.

Example

An officer receives a call in reference to a prowler in a residential area. On arrival at the home in question, she first checks the alley behind the home. Seeing the law enforcement officer in the alley, a "peeping tom" jumps off a fence and flees. The officer should

1. Immediately report the fleeing suspect to the communications and request backup assistance. Subsequently, she should pursue the offender in an attempt to arrest him.
2. Draw her duty weapon and immediately challenge the offender to stop. If he does not stop, the officer should shoot to kill.
3. Alert the communications about the fleeing suspect and request backup assistance. She should then check the residence to determine if a more serious crime has been perpetrated before pursuing the alleged offender.

Choice 2 is obviously uncalled for in this instance. The officer is neither aware of any felony having been perpetrated nor presently being threatened with a deadly force. She might choose either Choice 1 or 3, depending on additional facts and circumstances present at the scene of the disturbance. For example, the appearance of a homeowner or other person might dictate whether the officer should pursue the offender or not. In the majority of situations, most officers will probably be inclined to chase the fleeing "peeping tom" and return to the residence following the pursuit.

Warning Shots. Warning shots are *not* authorized by any organization or department. Peace officers are delegated the right to use deadly force in strictly controlled circumstances. The use of a firearm to "warn" a suspect is not authorized. If officers use their duty weapon, the intent to use deadly force must be specific. They should keep in mind that a bullet will travel in whatever direction the firearm is pointed. Even if the firearm is pointed up, the bullet will fall back to earth once its momentum is overcome by gravity.

Example

A law enforcement officer takes up a foot chase when an arrested burglary suspect is fleeing from custody. The pursuing officer yells, "Stop or I'll shoot!" The fleeing suspect continues her escape. The officer should

1. Fire a warning shot into the air as proof that the threat to shoot was not an idle threat.
2. Fire the sidearm with intent to stop the fleeing burglary suspect because the penal code authorizes the use of deadly force to prevent the escape of people charged with a felony who are fleeing from justice.
3. Never use deadly force at all, but rather pursue on foot, because the fleeing suspect is a woman.
4. Pursue the suspect and use reasonable force to recapture the offender. The officer should fire the weapon if the fleeing suspect presents a life-threatening situation during the pursuit.

Choice 1 is obviously not warranted; warning shots are not authorized. The suspect's sex has nothing to do with the decision to shoot or not to shoot; therefore, the third choice is not correct either. Choices 2 and 4, however, offer different difficult alternatives. In the second choice, the officer may appear to be justified in using deadly force to prevent the escape of the fleeing felon by the "letter of the law." However, the suspect has been arrested on suspicion of burglary and has not been formally charged with the offense. The suspect's actions in fleeing may indicate a guilty mind, and the officer's actions may be justified in certain circumstances, but the choice to shoot is not clearly justified in all circumstances. Choice 4 tends to follow a more logical and prudent resolve. In this instance, the officer is using good judgment and exercising mature decision-making procedures in using deadly force.

PRISONER RESTRAINT

All officers are subjected to the dangers of searching a suspect. Many conditions can make the officer's job not only difficult but also dangerous. The dangers may vary depending on the suspects involved and their physical, emotional, or mental state. Person search techniques are designed to provide officers a margin of safety by giving them an advantage over suspects. The general approach to prisoner restraint is as follows:

1. *Immobilize.* Assume a superior position of advantage in relationship to the suspect, and reduce avenues of escape. Remain constantly alert!

2. *Control.* When a decision is made to place a suspect under arrest, place the suspect in a position of disadvantage (standing wall position, kneeling search position, prone position, etc.) in order to establish and maintain control.

3. *Handcuff.* Experts agree that it is best to handcuff a suspect *before* searching. By controlling the suspect's hands quickly, you eliminate the most imminent hazard. Suspects should be handcuffed with their hands behind their back, the palms of the suspects' hands facing outward. Proper handcuffing techniques must be learned and practiced in hands-on simulations.

4. *Search.* Searches must be thorough. Veteran officers can tell many "horror stories" about weapons found on or near suspects after the person was supposedly searched by an arresting or transporting officer.

5. *Transport.* Officers assume control and ensure care of prisoners *en route* to confinement facilities. Even though one weapon may be found, thoroughly search the subject for additional weapons.

Even though the circumstances and techniques of each search are different, several principles underlie all effective searches. As previously noted, you must remain alert at all times and maintain control of the suspect(s). Advantageous positioning and thorough searches provide the greatest degree of safety. In addition, do the following:

1. Safeguard all weapons, your weapon as well as any weapons found on the suspect.

2. Always search suspects from the rear, never from the suspects' front.

3. Search the suspect with one hand while the other hand is in contact with the suspect.
4. During the search, keep your gun out of the suspect's reach or control.
5. Search systematically by grasping with your finger tips.
6. If a weapon is found during the search, inform your partner immediately of what is found and of its location.
7. Once the weapon is secured, the searching officer continues search for additional weapons. Never assume that a suspect is carrying only one weapon—this mistake can be deadly!

Suspects may conceal weapons or contraband anywhere on their bodies. Common hiding places or concealment for weapons and contraband include, but are not limited to, the waistband; pockets; groin area; small of back; ankles; pocketbooks, purses, and wallets; underarm areas; and jewelry designed to be used as weapons (such as necklaces and belt buckles). During the search, the covering officer's primary responsibility is to stand guard over the searching officer and protect the searching officer from outside interference. The guarding officer provides physical assistance for the searching officer if it becomes necessary. The cover officer continuously observes the suspect(s) and can secure weapons found by the searching officer.

Become familiar with your agency's policy regarding searches of members of the opposite sex. Generally, a person of the same sex as the arrested person completes the search unless an emergency circumstance necessitates an immediate search and seizure. Under normal circumstances, the arrested person can be controlled and handcuffed until the search can be conducted.

Depending on the circumstances, officers should select an approved technique in conducting a search. The "cursory search," or frisk, may be used in situations justifying reasonable suspicion searches, but not arrests. In this circumstance, search the suspect's outer garments, without putting your hands inside pockets, to discover weapons that might be used against you (*Terry v. Ohio* 392 U.S. 1, 1968). For arrest situations, the "standing modified" or "kneeling" position affords more advantage, while the "prone" (lying down) search position affords maximum control and protection for searching officers.

In deciding which position to use under any circumstances, consider, but do not limit yourself to, the following factors:

1. Number of suspects
2. Size of suspects
3. Location of contact or arrest
4. Time of arrest (day or night)
5. Suspect's past criminal record, if known
6. Type of offense involved
7. Individual officer's degree of apprehension capability
8. Availability of backup officers
9. Circumstances of the contact

Do not be lulled into a false sense of security by an apparently cooperative suspect. The suspect's apparent attitude is no guarantee that he or she will not attempt to escape when, or if, the opportunity presents itself. Always approach a suspect from a position of advantage that affords you optimum benefit of protection during the search.

Handcuff Devices and Application Techniques

The handcuff is a safety device both for the officer and the prisoner. It is used for *temporary* restraint to prevent attack, escape, destruction or concealment of evidence or contraband, and self-inflicted injury. Since handcuffs do not immobilize a suspect, you must maintain control over a handcuffed suspect to minimize his or her opportunity for action that can produce injuries or that allows escape.

The traditional metal handcuff (see Figure 14-1) can be chain-linked or hinged. Both types of cuffs have advantages, and the choice of which type is used may be designated by department policy or left up to individual discretion. Other types of devices used for restraint include plastic restraining straps, which are ideal for large wrists or for multiple suspects. Once properly applied, handcuffs should not be removed until the prisoner is within the confines of a proper detention facility.

The cuffing technique begins by placing the suspect's right arm in the rear wrist-lock position. The suspect's elbow should be just below your rib cage and trapped to body. Holding onto the suspect's thumb (palm facing outward), bend his or her wrist to a locked position, and maintain necessary pressure for control. The suspect can be ordered to place the free left hand on the back of his or her head until you are ready to cuff it.

Place the handcuff on the top of the suspect's wrist. When you

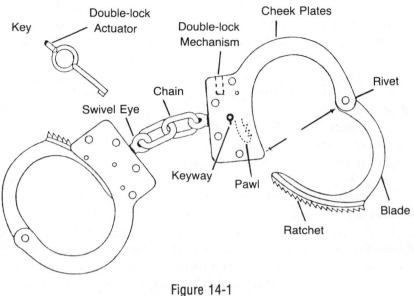

Figure 14-1
The parts of the handcuff

press the handcuff down sharply on the wrist (not "hitting" the wrist with the cuffs), the single bar will encircle the suspect's wrist and will lock. Take care not to place the cuff over clothing, wristwatches, or other jewelry. With the right hand secured, bring it to a position behind the arrested person's back while you grip the base of the empty cuff with your cuffing hand. (*Note*: Do *not* let go of the handcuff; at this point in the procedure, the suspect can use it as a dangerous weapon should he or she escape control.) Order the suspect to bring his or her free left hand down behind the back. Again, by placing the single bar of the handcuff on the suspect's other wrist (palm facing outward) and by pushing sharply forward, complete the handcuffing technique. The cuffs can be double-locked by using the point of the handcuff key to engage the double-lock mechanism, located on the double-cheek side of the cuff near the center. (See Figure 14-1.)

Although the handcuff is used for most prisoners taken into custody, there are variations to handcuffing procedure. For example, a mentally ill person should be handcuffed only when the person is not restrained by means of a straitjacket or by leather restraining straps. With a mentally ill person whose age or physical condition is such that the personal safety of both you and the individual clearly will not be jeopardized, the use of handcuffs is within your discretion. If mentally ill people are handcuffed, you may use only department-approved handcuffs and must ensure that the cuffs are double-locked. Temporary plastic restraining straps should not be used to restrain a mentally ill person. The straps can seriously restrict the flow of blood and are capable of inflicting injury (serious cutting) to the prisoner.

In dealing with multiple prisoners, a female should not be handcuffed to a male suspect except in an emergency situation. Likewise, juveniles should not be handcuffed to adults. If, in your opinion, a prisoner presents a potential danger to you or other prisoners, such an individual should be handcuffed and transported separately to the detention area.

To remove handcuffs properly, again set up an advantageous position maintaining balance and control of the suspect. Once one of the handcuffs is removed, establish immediate control of the loose cuff. Should the prisoner escape control at this point, the cuff is a dangerous weapon. Avoid improper and negligent security practices such as handcuffing prisoners to stationary objects, leaving them unattended in a patrol vehicle, or losing visual contact with a prisoner. Understand that the prisoner is the personal responsibility of the arresting officer at all times until custody is transferred to other authorized people.

Transporting a Prisoner

The time between the arrest and incarceration is critical. The prisoner, facing loss of freedom, can be extremely desperate and dangerous. All prisoners (both misdemeanants and felons) may capitalize on any relaxation of police vigilance in order to attack and escape. Undertake the transportation responsibility aware that each subject is prepared to flee custody at the first opportunity.

Officers transporting prisoners must be prepared to cope with any eventuality: "Expect the unexpected." Never attempt to transport more people than can be safely controlled. Request assistance or additional transporting units whenever multiple suspects are to be transported.

Even though an arresting officer has already searched a suspect, the transporting officer must conduct a search again before placing the prisoner in a vehicle. You cannot depend on another officer's search; after all, it is your life that is in danger while you are transporting prisoners. Confiscate any article that can be used as a weapon. Remember, a large purse, a hat pin, and high-heeled shoes of a female prisoner should also be taken away, because these accessories can be used to inflict injury.

Any person arrested for a serious offense, whether male, female, adult, or juvenile, should be handcuffed. This precaution is also taken with any person who has resisted arrest or who indicates signs of belligerence. In other circumstances, use cuffs whenever you are in doubt.

Positioning prisoners in the patrol unit for transportation generally depends on department policy. Some departments have installed a protective screen of plastic shield between the front and rear seats in patrol units; prisoners can be safely secured in back safety belts while handcuffed for transportation. In vehicles without a screen or shield, a prisoner may either ride in the rear seat with a guarding officer, or secured on the passenger side of the front seat with an officer in the back seat directly behind the prisoner. A violent prisoner can be controlled in the front seat by having him or her place his or her arms and handcuffed wrists behind the front seat and securing the prisoner with the safety belt.

Before departing for the detention facility, the transporting officer, if male, should advise communications of the time and vehicle mileage when transporting female and juvenile prisoners. On arriving at the final destination, the officer again reports the time and mileage, indicating that the transportation detail has been completed. This practice protects the male officer from allegations of improper stops and conduct during the ride from the place of arrest to the detention facility. Similar tactics are required for female officers transporting males or juvenile suspects.

During the actual transportation of prisoners, obey all traffic regulations. Excessive speeds are unnecessary and needlessly endanger the occupants of the patrol vehicle and the motoring public. Keep in mind that you are responsible for the care of the prisoners. If a prisoner is injured or unconscious, he or she must be examined by a physician and given first aid before being jailed. This precaution is taken even though there may be a strong odor of alcohol on the subject's breath. High fever, shock, brain injury, and diabetic coma are but a few of the many causes of unconsciousness that can be fatal if medical assistance is not obtained.

A patrol vehicle is not the best place to question a suspect. The driver is preoccupied with operating the unit and does not have time to take notes properly. Furthermore, a hostile, intoxicated, or emotionally upset suspect can be difficult to handle if attempts are made to question him or her *en route* to the police station. Avoid moralizing, name calling, and accusations, which serve only to arouse a suspect and make him or her more resistant. As a rule of thumb, however, officers generally inform the suspects of their constitutional rights against self-incrimination (the *Miranda* warnings) so that anything the suspect says may be used in court.

During the trip to the detention facility, officers can use the time to calm an emotional prisoner. You can often accomplish this purpose by being a good listener. Engage in general conversation to distract the suspects and prevent them from developing an alibi. Such conversation also serves to break down any defenses and make the subject more cooperative at the police station.

It is important to reemphasize that all transported prisoners should use safety belts at all times while in the patrol unit. The belt not only protects the individual while the vehicle is in motion, but also helps restrain suspects and prevents escape maneuvers or attempts. Furthermore, when all people are properly restrained, the officer is protected from potential liability in the event of an accident.

CUSTODY

Once someone is in custody, the constitutional requirements of "due process of law" are put into motion. Before people are questioned regarding their specific involvement in the alleged activity, they must be informed of their constitutional rights in accordance with the *Miranda* ruling and of their right to an attorney before questioning. Peace officers have a duty to take the person arrested to a magistrate without *unnecessary delay*.

The peace officer has several distinct responsibilities under the law. First, you must bring the person arrested before a magistrate *without unnecessary delay*. Whether or not the accused is brought before a magistrate depends, however, on the facts and circumstances of the case (such as the availability of a magistrate), your other unavoidable duties, the hour and day on which the arrest occurs, and/or the intoxication or mental condition of the subject. Generally, the test relative to unnecessary delay is based on whether or not any delay is reasonable. For example, it would be unreasonable to ask a magistrate to get out of bed at 3 A.M. in order to review the complaint alleging that a person has committed the offense of public intoxication under disorderly conduct statutes. Generally speaking, people arrested when a magistrate is unavailable can be detained until the magistrate's normal working hours.

A second requirement of statutes is that the officer submit a complaint to the magistrate stating the charges against the arrested person. To justify legal custody, you must present the facts and circumstances (probable cause) to the magistrate, who reviews your probable cause, informs the suspect of his or her rights, and sets bail or bond. The initial appearance before the magistrate and the judicial review of the arrest ensures that the ends of justice are being served in accordance with federal and state laws.

In addition to the preceding requirements, custodial officers are responsible for ensuring that commitment orders are legal and valid before placing a person in a detention facility. The custodial officer should become thoroughly familiar with proper court documents, parole and probation documents, and prisoner transfer commitment orders for prisoners(s) *en route*. Vigilance in such matters will ensure that the custodial officer is not charged with false imprisonment.

Detention and Security

The purpose of a jail is to keep a lawfully arrested person separate from society. Whenever an arrested person is awaiting an initial appearance before a magistrate or a trial, incarceration in jail ensures his or her presence at the tribunal. People are normally detained before trial if they cannot afford the price of a bail bond. During such detention, the prisoner's safety and security are prime concerns of the custodial officers. Most frequently, security during such detention is designed to prevent the prisoner's escape. However, it is also imperative that the suspect be protected against the harmful effects of contraband, such as drugs and weapons. To meet this requirement, custodial officers are required to check various forms of communication to detect any unauthorized items that might adversely affect security or the prisoner's health.

Until recently, there has been very little case law on the rights and status of pretrial detainees. Generally speaking, they are viewed as being subject to the same restrictions and privations as are sentenced offenders. In one case (*Brenneman v. Madigan*, 343 F. Supp. 128,

N.D.Cal. 1972), the courts stated that the general rule is that "incursions on a right of a pretrial detainee other than those arising from the need for custody to ensure his presence at trial are unconstitutional." Although pretrial detainees have not been convicted and have not as yet lost their "rights as citizens," security measures can and must be sufficient to protect them from harm or injury while awaiting trial.

Custody Procedures

Due process of law requires that the criminal justice system establish procedures to protect detained persons in custodial situations. Procedural law defines the extent of custodial safeguards that are reasonable for the protection of the accused, other detainees, and the custodial officer. The words "reasonable for protection" generally define the perimeters of custody procedures.

Once a person has been placed under arrest, the law enforcement officer conducts a search of him or her and the area where the person can reach to grasp a weapon or to destroy evidence (*Chimel v. California* 395 U.S. 752, 89 S.Ct. 2034, 23 L.Ed. 2d 685,1969). The custody procedures at a detention facility where the person will be held awaiting judicial proceedings likewise have reasonable safety objectives for both the detainee and the custodial personnel. Minimal control procedures should accommodate the types of prisoners to be segregated, requirements for taking personal property from a prisoner, and a peace officer "solicitation" in behalf of a bondsperson or an attorney.

Prisoners to Be Segregated. Prisoner segregation is necessary to ensure the best possible kind of integration, coordination, and continuity of care and security. Segregation in this context is not based on race, religion, or ethnic background, but rather on age, sex and type of offenders. Male and female prisoners must be segregated in confinement facilities to ensure privacy and eliminate the opportunity for sexual harassment. Juvenile offenders must be segregated from adult offenders. It may be difficult in some instances to be certain whether a young person is legally classified as an adult or a juvenile; the situation may be complicated by prisoners giving false information regarding their age. Any child initially placed in confinement with adult prisoners based on misinformation should be immediately removed when his or her real age is determined.

The alcoholic, the drug abuser, and the emotionally ill also present custodial officers with special requirements for segregation. Because prisoners in each of these classes are subject to injury from themselves as well as from other inmates, special custodial classification demands that special care be taken to protect them.

Special security measures are implemented for different classes of offenders. Security procedures will be based on both the seriousness of the offense (the felon versus the misdemeanor offender) and the risk to society should the offender escape. Classifications of offenders based on security considerations are specified as

1. *Maximum custody*. Requiring close supervision because the prisoner's escape would constitute a serious threat to society.

2. *Medium custody*. Prison security is responsible within limits because the prisoner's escape would constitute a hazardous (but not serious) threat to the community.

3. *Minimum custody*. Where a prisoner is permitted some freedom in the custodial institution under general supervision of the custodial officers because his or her escape does not constitute a threat to the general public.

A detention facility at the city, county, or state level may include each of these classifications.

Taking Property from Prisoners. Before prisoners are placed in a lockup, their personal property must be strictly accounted for by the intake officer. Custodial searches are conducted at the time of booking to prohibit offenders from taking contraband into the detention facility and to ensure that all personal property is accounted for. In some instances, booking procedures require the custodial officer to conduct a strip and body cavity search to discover contraband and/or weapons before a prisoner is placed in a cell. State penal codes specify both the application and limitations on the use of strip searches. Check your local jurisdiction for correct procedures in your area.

Once the custodial search is completed (whether the extent of the search was a general field search or an authorized strip search), any and all personal property belonging to the offender is recorded on a property statement and stored separately from all other prisoners' personal property. A copy of the personal property receipt is provided to the prisoner. If money or other valuables are taken from the prisoner, the items should be counted in front of him or her and listed by specific denominations of currency on the property document. Any property on the prisoner's person that is considered evidentiary is not listed on the prisoner's personal property record. Instead, the officer takes control of the evidentiary property and establishes a "chain of custody" by turning it over to the agency property custodian for security. In either case, once the department has taken control of the property, proper security steps must be initiated for its safekeeping until its final disposition.

Solicitation in Behalf of a Bondsperson or Attorney. Laws in most states prohibit peace officers from acting as solicitors for a bondsperson or attorney. Once a person is taken into custody, you must not suggest a specific bondsperson or attorney. The detainee may use public reference material, such as the phone book, to get information regarding people who offer such services to prisoners.

Illegal Force Against Prisoners

Illegal force against a prisoner is never justified. Willful inhumanity or oppression is obviously not condoned by the penal code, and the penalties for violation are severe. Not only can a heavy financial fine be imposed, but a custodial officer may also lose his or her job as a result of such abuse. A person is placed in confinement as punishment or while awaiting judicial review of the alleged violation; a peace officer therefore does not have the right to inflict corporal punishment that is not authorized by the courts.

A peace officer may not assault another person *under color of authority*. The words "under color of authority" mean that the officer is using his or her position as a cover to commit criminal acts against another. Whenever officers perform such acts, they are as criminal as the individual in custody. In fact, the legislative intent of the law is to punish the officer for this specific type of criminal behavior on conviction. Custodial officers are expected to be *peace* officers. Peace officers are expected to respect the law they are sworn to uphold. Therefore, you must also respect the prisoner's rights and prevent unauthorized brutal attack—not become the criminal attacker in the case. Professional peace officers are in control not only of the criminal, but also of their own emotions and actions.

Adult Booking

Booking may be the single most important data-gathering step in the criminal justice process. It is an administrative process to create a record that will be used as a central control mechanism over the whereabouts of the arrested person and his or her property. During this important process, the custodial agency will gather and store identifying information about the accused to be used at a later time. For example, the booking phase is generally used to fingerprint and photograph the arrested person. Information regarding the subject's physical characteristics or condition (sober, intoxicated, under the influence of drugs, injured, sick, etc.), place of employment, vehicle data, and legal reason for the arrest and for authority to continue detention are recorded. This information becomes the department's official documentation and provides management information regarding what happens next in the case and to the person. All the data collected help a department account for its activities, locate a prisoner or his or her property, and make administrative decisions about personnel, training, finances, and resource allocation.

During the booking process, officers must conform to the law and to minimum jail standards. Such procedures include securing their weapons prior to entering any custody facility, receiving the custody facility's medical prescreening procedures for prisoner intake, and observing the legal limitations on strip searches.

During the administrative booking procedure, officers frequently come in close proximity to the arrested person—to account for the prisoner's personal property, to acquire the subject's fingerprints, or to perform one of the other necessary functions of the custodial procedure. Thus, officers must not have firearms on their persons. The weapon must be secured before entering the custody facility. Failure to do so might result in allowing a prisoner an opportunity to grab the officer's weapon and use it on the officer, other prisoners, or even on the prisoner him- or herself. In addition to the safety precautions, jail procedures require that a prisoner's rights be protected and that the prisoner should not be subjected to unlawful force.

Secured facilities offer little or no opportunity for a prisoner to escape custody. In addition, security procedures in a jail or prison do not permit a prisoner great opportunity to threaten or use deadly force. Therefore, firearms are not permitted inside the custodial facility. Because most prison disorders can be controlled without the use of firearms, jail personnel agree that having firearms accessible to prisoners serves only to incite them to attempt escape.

Custodial facilities establish medical prescreening procedures during prisoner intake. These are especially important because the prison population is a closed community in which prisoners and custodial personnel live 24 hours a day. The potential for creating, or allowing, an epidemic in the prison population is enormous. Therefore, it is imperative that new prisoners be screened for diseases, infections, or other potentially dangerous conditions that might threaten the people inside the secured facility. To accomplish this, custodial facilities are serviced by medical personnel on a frequent basis. Custodial personnel should note any condition that may indicate that a prisoner is ill and report it to the appropriate medical personnel. In addition, custodial personnel must constantly be aware that symptoms of illness may show up in prisoners after they are placed in a secured cell. Therefore, prisoners should be checked frequently, for both security and health reasons.

Recognizing Types of Prisoners. Custodial officers will meet many different types of prisoners during their tour of duty, and each must be classified both for security and to recognize special conditions that may present custodial problems. It is imperative that intake officers be able to recognize the following types of prisoners:

- Juveniles
- Alcoholics
- Narcotics and drugs users
- Mentally ill people
- Mentally retarded people
- Sex offenders
- Homosexuals
- Prisoners who present escape risks
- People who need protective custody
- Noncomformists
- Civil and special problem prisoners

The juvenile prisoner may not be easily identifiable as a child; for their own reasons, young people may lie about their age to the arresting officer. In many cases, a child's physical appearance will be deceiving, so care should be taken to ascertain a prisoner's age as soon as possible. In some cases, a telephone call may solve the mystery. In other cases, however, the child may succeed in fooling the officer and be mistakenly placed in an adult custodial facility. As noted earlier, once it is determined that the prisoner is a child, the youngster must be immediately removed from the adult lockup and transferred to a juvenile detention facility.

Abusers of alcohol, narcotics, and other drugs require medical care. Although the legal processes define these people as having committed a criminal offense, custodial officers also recognize that these offenders are ill and need special treatment. Extreme cases of alcoholism and narcotics or drug cases can cause the abuser to experience extreme pain during physical withdrawal from the substance. In some instances, the withdrawal process can be life threatening. Such prisoners should be placed in special care units and observed carefully. If custodial officers are uncertain about a prisoner's condition, they should inform the custodial supervisor.

Mentally ill people require special handling. They may react violently to the police uniform or may submit tranquilly. In either case, mentally ill people generally do not have the capacity to understand the consequences of their acts and may not know how to notify family, friends, or custodians that they have been taken into custody by a peace officer. The statutes require you to notify a responsible person whenever you take a mentally ill person into custody. If the responsible person is not present at the moment you assume custody, you must leave a note or message in a conspicuous place to alert others as to the whereabouts of the person taken into custody.

Mentally ill people may or may not be easily identified. There are many definitions of what constitutes mental illness. However, whenever a person is placed in custody for investigation of sanity, or there is reason to believe that a prisoner is suffering from mental illness, special care must be taken to protect the individual. People in this state of mind may be dangerous to themselves or others. They may become the objects of other prisoners' assaults. Custodial officers have a specific responsibility to segregate and constantly observe these prisoners until they can be transported to hospital facilities.

Mentally retarded people likewise present a special problem in custodial facilities. Although they are not generally considered dangerous, they may easily become victims of assaults if confined with other prisoners. Whenever possible, such prisoners should be confined separately from other prisoners, and a guardian or custodian should be notified immediately.

Sex offenders may also present special problems for custodial officers. Depending on the crime for which the person is arrested, custodial officers should be aware of problems that might develop in the facility. For example, a person accused of raping a child may be viewed with hostility by other prisoners and may be assaulted. A homosexual prisoner may likewise be assaulted or may become the aggressor against vulnerable inmates. In either situation, as well as in many other similar problem situations, it is the custodial officer's responsibility to protect each incarcerated person.

Some prisoners present greater security risks than others and may therefore represent greater escape risks. The person accused of a capital offense, the habitual criminal, or the person who has successfully escaped on a prior occasion are examples of those who require special security precautions while confined in the facility.

Custodial officers must also be aware of special precautions in dealing with nonconformists and people needing protective custody, including people in civil custody. In each special situation, the protection of the person confined in the facility is of paramount importance. It is the custodial officer's responsibility to ensure that a person housed in the facility is protected from harm by following procedures to segregate special-category prisoners from other prisoners, constantly observing the prison population, and making proper notifications promptly in accordance with custodial facility guidelines. The proper notifications may include supervisors, medical personnel, juvenile custodial officers, and cooperating law enforcement agencies, to mention but a few. The custodial officer's timely actions are imperative to prevent injury, death, or escape of all the people entrusted to the officer's custody.

Booking Procedures. The first order in handling people is to respect their rights to humane treatment, including fairness, honesty, impartiality, and procedures that respect their dignity. Booking generally includes securing prisoners' personal property, confiscating any illegal property, preparing the arrest cards, and fingerprinting and photographing them.

In securing the prisoner's personal property, custodial officers must keep in mind the requirement for and limitations on strip searches. Because it is the legislature's intent to protect prisoners' state and federal constitutional rights to privacy and freedom from unreasonable search and seizures, use of strip or body cavity searches is strictly limited to cases involving weapons, controlled substances, or violence. The statutes also permit such a search when peace officers have determined that there is reasonable suspicion, based on specific and articulable facts, that a prisoner is concealing a weapon or contraband. Remember that physical body cavity searches must be conducted under sanitary conditions and only by an authorized person. Any other strip-type search must be conducted in privacy by a person of the same sex.

Once prisoners' personal property has been removed from their control, the items must be recorded on an inventory report. Money should be recorded by denominations of currency and coins. Valuables such as jewelry or watches should be accurately identified and recorded by serial numbers if applicable. Once all the property is listed on the property control document, it must be securely protected until it is returned to prisoners on their release from custody. If illegal property, or contraband, is discovered during the search, evidentiary control must be accorded it. Initiate the chain of custody over the property and subsequently turn it over to the property custodian for control and security. Should the illegal property require forensic or laboratory analysis, handle the evidence like that in any criminal investigation.

The arrest card should contain suspect identification, the offense for which the offender is arrested (including time, date, and location), a narrative of facts, where applicable, and the identity of the arresting officer(s). It should also indicate the cell or location where the suspect is incarcerated and any information regarding the prisoner's condition or state of mind. When appropriate, the arrest card should also note when notification as required by the custodial agency was made (such as alerting military officials when a soldier is arrested). The custodial officer finalizes the intake process by fingerprinting and photographing the arrested person in accordance with departmental procedures.

The statutes permit the accused person specific rights at the time of booking. Prisoners are entitled to be provided with medical care at their own expense even though a "jail" physician may be available. In addition, prisoners can be visited by an attorney when they or any of their relatives have requested the attorney's presence. Arrested people are entitled to make phone calls. The number of phone calls permitted varies with jurisdiction.

The custodial officer's primary objective must be to respect the accused's constitutional rights. Just because accused people have been arrested and are being placed in a detention facility does not abrogate their rights to constitutional safeguards, fairness, honesty, and impartiality on the part of custodial officers. On the contrary, custodial officers have a duty to respect such rights and ensure that arrested people are protected under the law. Failure to provide such protections subjects peace officers to sanctions provided by law.

Juvenile Custody Procedures

Juvenile offenders require special handling in the juvenile justice system. The U.S. Supreme Court case *In Re Gault* was a landmark in juvenile justice cases. The Court's decision stated that a child's right to "due process of law" cannot be abridged. Even though handling of children is a quasi-civil matter, rather than a criminal incident (although the child's conduct is defined by the penal code statutes), the process and procedure in handling the child's case must follow procedural correctness. In other words, the child must be afforded all the same constitutional safeguards guaranteed to adult offenders. However, the legislative dicta provide additional protections for the juvenile suspect.

Statutes generally mandate that peace officers who take children into custody (which is technically a "civil restraint") must inform them of their constitutional rights (*Miranda* warnings) *at the time of the arrest*. This is a significant difference from the adult arrest, in which officers are *required* to inform suspects of constitutional safeguards only when they intend to specifically ask them about their involvement in the criminal offense. However, when dealing with a child laws frequently require the *Miranda* warnings at the time officers take a child into custody, regardless of their intent to seek information from the child. Therefore, from the start, peace officers must be aware of the child's right to due process of law, which goes beyond the general protections provided adult offenders.

While transporting juveniles to the appropriate location of detention, many departments require officers to report the location of departure, intended destination, and beginning odometer reading of the transporting vehicle. On arriving at the place of detention, notify communications that the trip has been completed and report the ending odometer reading. In each instance, the communications officer notes the times of the radio transmissions, which are officially recorded. This procedure protects officers from allegations of improper delay in handling the child while transporting him or her to the appropriate station. (The same reporting system is used when officers transport suspects of the opposite sex, whether children or adults.)

Once at the station, or appropriate place to process children, officers have several other specific responsibilities under the law. First, contact the child's parent, guardian, or custodian and inform them that the child was taken into custody, his or her present location, and any other relevant facts surrounding the custody. If the child was taken to a medical facility or other treatment center, inform the parent, guardian, or custodian of the extent of injuries, how they were incurred, and what, if any, treatment was being provided. In the event that the parent, guardian, or custodian cannot be immediately notified, continue reasonable attempts to notify the appropriate person(s) until such contact is made.

Because the juvenile's conduct comes under the provisions of the juvenile or family court, the booking procedure is different from that for adults. Juvenile records must be kept separate from those of adult offenders. The decision to photograph or fingerprint the juvenile depends on the type of offense alleged and local policy. Generally speaking, with a felony type of offense a child may be photographed and fingerprinted. However, in handling misdemeanor offenses, authorities may decide not to photograph or fingerprint. Check department or agency requirements and policy regarding fingerprinting and photographing children.

In general, peace officers should comply with the following minimal custody procedures:

1. Give the *Miranda* warnings at the time a child is taken into custody.
2. Ensure that proper notifications are made to the parent, guardian, or custodian.
3. Respect the child's right not to be subjected to unreasonable strip searches unless authorized under the penal code.
4. Ensure that a child under 17 years of age is not confined with

an adult offender who is accused or convicted of a crime.
5. Use alternatives to custody whenever possible when handling juveniles.
6. Notify the official designated by the juvenile court that the child is in custody, and provide all necessary information.

At all times, peace officers must be aware that people in custody have rights and guarantees of affirmative protection of government. Prisoners' civil rights and civil liberties are protected not only by the Constitution but also by legislative action. Peace officers have the legal responsibility to ensure that all people's rights are protected in accordance with due process of law.

PRISONER RIGHTS AND RESPONSIBILITIES

Prisoners are afforded all civil rights and privileges that do not interfere with reasonable security and protection of the public welfare. This fact is well documented in many court cases, including, but not limited to, *Bell v. Wolfish* (441 U.S. 520), *DeCancie v. Superior Court* (31 Cal. 3d 865), and *Wolff v. McDonnell* (418 U.S. 539). However, it is also understood that prisoners have specific responsibilities by virtue of their status, for which they are accountable. Become familiar with some of the more common situations relative to these areas.

Damage to Place of Confinement

Every person who willfully and intentionally breaks down, pulls down, or otherwise destroys or injures any place of confinement, may be punishable by fine and/or additional confinement. Damage to jail(s) by prisoners tends to be a major problem and can be very expensive to the operation of the custodial facilities. The intent of the penal code is to hold each prisoner responsible for the willful destruction of property. Make prompt and accurate reports when such incidents occur, and alert appropriate supervisory personnel for filing of charges when warranted.

Right to Safekeeping

Custodial officers are charged with the specific responsibility for the safekeeping of all prisoners under custodial supervision. Any officer who is guilty of "callous disregard" for prisoner safety can be held answerable for such neglect in a state and/or federal court (*Smith v. Wade*, 103 S. Ct. 1625).

Medical Care

Each lockup facility provides medical care for prisoners. However, prisoners may decline treatment by the "jail" physician and request medical care of their choosing; the prisoner must understand that he or she will be responsible for the medical expense under this condition. If the prisoner declines the treatment available in the jail, the officer obtains and documents the prisoner's waiver of treatment.

A prisoner often wants to use his or her own physician to get prescriptions for drugs. This expense is also borne by the prisoner. The prisoner's personal physician should be searched before he or she is allowed inside the jail to examine or treat the patient. If the physician prescribes drugs for the prisoner, the medication is controlled for safekeeping by the custodial staff. Whenever a patrol officer transports a prisoner to the jail facility, the officer gives all of the prisoner's medication to the jail or medical staff for evaluation, if applicable. Each facility develops policy for the intake of medication and its control. Be aware of the policy in your jurisdiction.

Daily sick call is conducted for all prisoners by medically trained registered nurses, licensed vocational nurses, or medical doctors. Prescribed medication should be administered by the medical staff under the observation of the custodial officer. Medicine provided from outside the jail should be checked thoroughly before dispensing it. When given the medicine (either by the private or "jail" doctor), a prisoner frequently holds the medicine in the mouth rather than swallow it. When the officer is not looking, the prisoner removes the drug for future use (stores it, sells it, gives it away, etc.). The alert officer will check to see that the medicine was taken as prescribed and not be fooled by the crafty prisoner.

Right to Attorney

Prisoners have an affirmative right to be visited by an attorney whenever the prisoner or any of his or her relatives request the attorney's presence. In the event that a doctor is employed by the prisoner or his or her attorney to help prepare the defense, the doctor is likewise allowed to visit the prisoner at any time. Check local policy concerning procedures in your area.

Use of Telephone

A prisoner is entitled to free completed telephone calls made in the local dialing area, generally within three hours of arrest. If the prisoner is calling his or her attorney, the person has the right to speak to the advocate without fear of eavesdropping, being monitored, or being recorded. It is the officer's responsibility to inform the prisoner of these rights. The number and frequency of calls varies according to local laws and policy. Check the rules in your area.

Constituional Rights

Although a prisoner gives up the right of freedom of movement, he or she still retains many other rights such as freedom of speech, right to a quick and speedy trial, and the right to reasonable bail. These rights may be removed only for cause, following due process procedures (*Wilson v. Superior Court*, 21 Cal. 3d 816). The First amendment of the U.S. Constitution protects the prisoner's religious freedom. The right to counsel is well documented. A custodial officer should check with the arresting officer before any questioning relative to the arrest. If the arrested person has been given the *Miranda* warnings and has requested an attorney before answering any questions, no questions relative to the incident should be asked before the attorney has been secured. General questions for booking purposes, however, are permitted.

PRISONER RELEASE

Custodial officers must follow proper procedures when releasing prisoners from custody. Procedures for release before trial are somewhat more complicated than release after trial, when warranted. Bail is the order of a competent court or magistrate that the defendant be discharged from actual custody on meeting the requirements for release. The court may require a specific cash bail or allow a bondsperson or attorney to assume custody of the prisoner. Under the latter circumstances, the bondsperson or attorney guarantees the defendant's appearance at the trial. If the defendant does not show up at the trial, the bondsperson or attorney is responsible for the amount of the actual cash bail. If the prisoner requests the assistance of a bondsperson, the prisoner pays a fee (usually about 10 or 15 percent of the cash bail) to the bondsperson, which is nonrefundable. If a cash bail is provided by the defendant, he or she receives a refund of the bail at the time of the trial or when appearance is required. The court may increase or decrease the bail as it sees fit.

Release on a person's own recognizance can be initiated from several sources. If the release is stipulated by a judge or magistrate on the phone, use a callback system to ensure that the person calling is actually the judge (prisoners may use a friend to call the jail and impersonate a judge). Certain citations permit an officer to release an offender on his or her own recognizance when the person signs a "promise to appear" at a specific date. In some instances, an officer is authorized to release a person from custody when insufficient grounds are established for the arrest, when the person arrested was taken into custody for intoxication only (and no further proceedings are desirable), or when the person was arrested only for being under the influence of a controlled substance or drug and such person is delivered to a hospital or medical facility for treatment (and no further proceedings are desirable). In such cases involving insufficient cause for arrest and people released to a medical facility for controlled substance abuse, (1) an officer makes a record of the action, (2) his or her agency describes the action as a "detention only," and (3) any record of such arrest is required to include a record of release. Other appropriate releases involve a citation in lieu of physical arrest and dismissal of the case by the district attorney.

Certain situations require the release of the defendant after he or she has been to trial. On a court order of competent jurisdiction, a custodial officer would release the prisoner under the following situations: after preliminary hearing, a "not guilty" verdict at trial, order of probation following trial, transfer to another installation of detention, or on completion of sentence.

KEY TERMS

Booking
Bondsman
Complete (strip) search
Criminal homicide
Custody
Deadly force
Defense of others
Fleeing felon
Frisk search
Handcuff
Imminent commission
Immobilize
Innocent third person
In Re Gault
Justifiable homicide
Last resort
Maximum custody
Medium custody
Minimum custody
Reasonable force
Segregated prisoners
Self-defense
Under color of authority

STUDY QUESTIONS

1. What is the basic rule regarding the use of force to make an arrest?

2. Research your state penal code laws, and outline the rules regarding law enforcement use of force and deadly force.

3. Define the concept of *reasonable force*.

4. What is "deadly force"? When is such force justified?

5. Is the use of force ever justified in response to "verbal provocation" alone? Justify your response.

6. Define the concept of self-defense.

7. Describe the officer's duty to defend other people. Under what circumstances may an officer use deadly force in defense of another person?

8. When may an officer shoot at a nonviolent fleeing felon?

9. Under what conditions may an officer fire warning shots?

10. Relate the five steps to properly restrain and arrest a subject. What is the rationale behind the order of these actions?

11. Should arrested women and children ever be handcuffed? Why or why not?

12. When you search a suspect, should you stop searching because you find a concealed weapon? Why or why not?

13. What is a *frisk*, and under what circumstances would this type of search be more appropriate than a field search?

14. Describe the proper way to handcuff a suspect. Once you apply one handcuff, what precautions should you take?

15. Describe the proper way to transport suspects to a detention facility.

16. Under what circumstances should you report your vehicle mileage to communications at the start and end of transporting a prisoner? Why should you follow these procedures?

17. What are your responsibilities in transporting a prisoner? What special precautions should you take at such times?

18. Should you conduct a suspect interrogation while transporting the person to a detention facility? Explain what appropriate procedures you should take.

19. Why should an officer take an arrested person before a magistrate without *unnecessary delay*?

20. What is the purpose of jail?

21. What types of prisoners should be segregated? What is the rationale behind such separation?

22. What determines the classification of offenders? Define each security classification.

23. When is a complete (or "strip") search justified?

24. Describe the proper way to conduct a "strip" search.

25. What is the general policy concerning solicitation of a bondsperson or attorney on behalf of an arrested person? Why should this policy be a concern for law enforcement officers?

26. What does "under color of authority" mean?

27. What is booking, and why is it an important step in the criminal justice process?

28. Describe the proper way to "book" an adult.

29. What special problems do juveniles, alcoholics, and narcotic users create for custody situations?

30. Why should custodial officers take special precautions in handling mentally ill or mentally retarded people?

31. What special precautions should be considered in dealing with sex offenders and homosexuals?

32. What types of prisoners may require special security or protective custody?

33. What was the result of the Supreme Court case *In Re Gault*?

34. What special rights and responsibilities apply to prisoners?

35. What actions should a custodial officer take to ensure proper release before releasing a prisoner from custody?

ACTIVITIES

1. Under supervision, practice handcuffing techniques.

2. Demonstrate the proper method to immobilize and control a suspect.

3. Conduct a prisoner search, and demonstrate the correct ways to seize weapons and evidence.

4. Visit a custodial facility, and observe custodial procedures at first hand.

5. List your state's laws justifying use of deadly force.

6. If your state defines guidelines for conducting "strip searches," outline these guidelines and make an oral report to your class.

Glossary

Abnormal person. A person who does not act according to rule, or who is considered different from the average person according to society standards. Such a person requires special handling to ensure that he or she will not be injured or injure others. Many human conditions may fall under this category.

Accident report. An investigative record of the cause and circumstances of an accident that includes information from the driver(s) and accident scene. It contains complete statistical information as required by local agency forms, and documents who, what, when, where, why, and how the accident occurred.

Acquisitive mob. A group of people whose main purpose is to acquire some desired object. Examples of this behavior include a run on a bank or hunger riots.

Addiction (drug). A state of periodic or chronic intoxication produced by the repeated use of a drug.

Admission. A confession, statement, or acknowledgement made by a party that could be offered against the party in court.

Aggressive mob. A group of people with aggressive tendencies that result in violent actions.

Alcohol. A depressant drug that dulls the reactions of the brain and nervous system.

Alcoholic beverage. Any liquid or solid material, intended to be ingested, that contains ethanol (also known as ethyl alcohol, drinking alcohol, or alcohol), including but not limited to intoxicating liquor, malt beverage, beer, wine, spirits, liqueur, whiskey, rum, vodka, cordials, gin, brandy, and any mixture containing one or more alcoholic ingredients whether ingested separately or as a mixture.

Alcoholic person. A person addicted to alcohol.

Alert. Keenly watchful; vigilant; ready for sudden action.

American Sign Language (ASL, or Ameslan). The "native" language of the prelingual and early-onset deaf; it has its own grammar and vocabulary. It is a completely visual language.

Amphetamine. A stimulant taken orally as a tablet or capsule or intravenously to reduce appetite or to relieve mental depression.

Anonymity in mob behavior. Members of a mob use the large group as a cover and believe that their identity will not become known to others; thus, the individual may perform acts under the cover of the group that he or she would not openly accept responsibility for.

Apprehension patrol. Patrol methods using covert or low-visibility tactics and techniques designed specifically to locate, identify, and apprehend law violators and criminals.

Arrest. Taking custody of a person in order to bring him or her before a magistrate.

Arrest report. A police report that outlines the probable cause and circumstances of an arrest. Depending on departmental policy, this report may be included in the investigative report or filed as a separate document.

Arrest warrant. An order from a magistrate directed to a peace officer, or other person specially named, commanding that a particular known person (or if not known, then a specifically described person) be taken into immediate custody and brought before the magistrate, and then to be dealt with in accordance to law.

Automobile patrol. A motorized patrol vehicle designed to provide increased protection for officers as well as quick response capabilities.

Autopsy. A coroner's examination of a dead body to determine the cause of death.

Awareness. Observation that permits specific perception of situations and hazards.

Bail. A security deposited with a competent court or magistrate to assure that the accused will appear for trial when summoned. Failure to appear when summoned results in forfeiture of bail.

Bail bondsman. A person who provides bail service to arrested persons for a fee. The bondsman signs a "bond" that promises to make the arrested person available for trial. If the arrested person "jumps bail," the bail bondsman forfeits the required bail established by the court.

Balance. Includes mental balance as well as physical balance. Requires thorough training and practice to control one's emotional and physical selves and thus be prepared to control violators and situations.

Ballistics. The science of projectiles. The use of guns, shells, powder marks, and bullets in tests as a means of criminal identification.

Barbiturate. A depressant drug usually taken orally as a small tablet or capsule to reduce or relieve tension.

Baton or "riot" stick. A defensive weapon used to strike another, with the intention of stunning or temporarily disabling, rather than injuring.

Batterer. A person who commits domestic violence; such conduct generally results in assaults on spouses and other family members.

Blood/alcohol concentration. The percentage of alcohol in the bloodstream, measured by using a sample of blood, breath, or urine.

Booking. Administrative step, taken after the arrested person is brought to the police station, that involves entry on the police "blotter" of the person's name, the crime for which the arrest was made, and other relevant facts that may also include a photograph, fingerprint, and the like.

Breath test. An analysis of a person's breath to determine the percentage of alcoholic concentration. In order to be admissible in court, the test must be performed by a certified person who has training in the use of specific instruments.

"Breather" fire. Usually identified by an absence of flames accompanied by dense smoke pulsating from cracks in the structure. It is the most dangerous kind of fire because it is oxygen starved and can literally explode when a door or window is opened.

Burglary. When a person enters or remains in a structure or a conveyance and intends to commit an offense therein, unless the premises are at the time open to the public or the defendant is licensed or invited to enter or remain.

Capias (Latin, meaning "that you take"). A generic name for writs that order the arrest of the person named. Similar to an arrest warrant in many respects, this writ may only command a peace officer (*note*: arrest warrants may be addressed to a person other than a peace officer) to take custody of the person named in the order and bring him or her before the magistrate in order to be dealt with in accordance with the law. Frequently used following indictments by a grand jury, this writ may be signed by the district clerk or a magistrate.

Carotid restraint. A technique used to restrain a violent person or an individual under the influence of drugs or controlled substances. The tactic is used by applying pressure to the sides of the subject's neck—the carotid artery (not the trachea)—which results in a decreased supply of blood to the brain, thereby causing temporary loss of consciousness.

Casual crowd. A group of people without unity or organization who happen to be present at a specific place; for example, shoppers going from store to store.

Chain of command. The lines of supervision that exist within any agency. Each person within an organization is directly responsible to one supervisor who in turn answers to other supervisors up the chain of command. The police chief or sheriff is at the top of the command and has total responsibility for overall departmental function and its policy. The lines connecting persons in the chain represent both lines of supervision as well as communication.

Chain of custody or possession. A log or record of people who collect, make, package, and store all evidence. The log includes all those who have access to evidence and positively proves the whereabouts of evidence from the time it was collected until it is introduced into a court as legal evidence.

Chemical agents. Nonoffensive chemicals used in proper concentration to produce various effects on people; frequently used in riot control or hostage situations. Most common law enforcement chemical agent is CN, which produces an abundance of uncontrollable tears and temporarily incapacitates with no harmful aftereffects on people exposed to the agent.

CHEMTREC—Chemical Transportation Emergency Center. The chemical manufacturer maintains a 24-hour telephone service to aid people involved in a hazardous materials incident to effectively and efficiently control spills or mishaps that could endanger life and/or the environment. The telephone number for this agency is (800) 424-9300.

Child abuse. Intentional physical or mental injury to a child usually inflicted by a person related or close to the child. The injury can be neglect (a failure to provide care), sexual abuse, willful cruelty, unjustifiable punishment inflicted as corporal punishment, or emotional abuse and deprivation.

"Chop-shop" (stripping vehicle) operation. Operation by motor vehicle thieves to remove and resell parts from stolen vehicles.

Chronological notes/reports. Incidents and events organized in sequence that permit the reader to understand what occurred first, second, third, and so on. A fundamental aspect of criminal investigations is to determine *when* events take place, as well as who the actors were, what was done, or where, how, and why the events took place; by arranging notes and reports chronologically, officers can offer both oral and written evidence of the chain of events.

Circular patrol pattern. Patrolling either from the approximate center of the patrol beat in ever-increasing circles or from the outside of the beat in ever-decreasing circles.

Circumstantial evidence. Conditions and surroundings that lead an investigator to infer the existence of the principal fact(s) logically and reasonably.

Civil liability. One's responsibility for conduct in a civil court of law. A plaintiff may recover monetary damages through a civil suit if the adverse or harmful conduct can be proven by a preponderance of the evidence.

Classification of fires (A, B, C). Various types of fires are classified to determine the type (source) of the fire and the appropriate way to control it. Class A fires involve dry combustibles such as wood, paper, and cloth. Class B fires involve petroleum products such as gasoline, oil, solvents, and so on. Class C fires are electrical fires created by generators, electrical panels, appliances, or wiring. Know which type of extinguisher is used for the appropriate type of fire.

Code of ethics. A set of standards that outlines professional behavior for members of the group or association.

Code 3. Operation of authorized emergency vehicle with red or blue lights and siren; used for emergency situations only.

Commitment. A court order that officially directs taking a person to a jail, prison, or other institution.

Communicate. To cause another or others to partake of or share in, impart, or transmit or exchange thought or knowledge.

Communications. (1) The act of imparting or transmitting; the transmission of ideas, information, and the like by speech or writing. (2) A message or means of passing or transmitting messages between places or persons. (3) As used frequently in this text, the radio control center responsible for knowing the whereabouts and status of law enforcement patrols; provides patrol support and coordinates patrol activities.

Community participation. Taking active roles in the community by participating in community service organizations or programs designed to build a better society.

Community relations. Establishing and maintaining two-way communications between persons (peace officers and citizens) to ensure an open atmosphere in which ideas and information can be exchanged, and to create an arena for problem solving.

Complainant. The person who makes a charge against another person. If the complaint is substantiated through investigation, a formal charge is filed in the appropriate court having jurisdiction over the alleged offense.

Complete (strip) search. A search of the body and clothing of a suspect conducted in a private place by more than one person of the same sex as the subject. A physical search is made of all clothing, and a visual search is conducted of the entire body, including body cavities, for contraband and/or weapons.

Concealment. Any condition (such as darkness) or object (like a bush) that hides a person from view but does not necessarily provide protection from an assailant's firepower. Concealment may or may not be cover.

Confession. A voluntary out-of-court admission of guilt, oral or written, following due-process-of-law guidelines outlined by the procedural rules that include informing a suspect of his or her constitutional rights (*Miranda* warnings) prior to making the admission.

Consent. Voluntary agreement to do something proposed by another; the consenting party must be in possession of and able to exercise sufficient mentality to make intelligent judgments and choices. "Expressed consent" is that which is directly given orally or in writing, giving positive, direct, unequivocal consent and requiring no inference or implication to supply its meaning.

Consolidated emergency communication operations. Consolidated communications centers for police, fire, and other emergency response teams. Frequently, cities with "Emergency 911" network systems use consolidated communication facilities for improved efficiency and reduced operating costs.

Constructive seizure. An arrest secured by a verbal order and nonviolent submission to custody or control.

Contraband. Merchandise that the law forbids to be sold, purchased, imported, exported, or possessed.

Corpus delicti. The "body of a crime." The body (material substance) upon which a crime has been committed; for example, the corpse of a murdered man or the charred remains of a house burned down.

Corpus delicti rule. A rule of law which requires that confessions must be supported or corroborated by independent evidence. Without the independent evidence the confession is not admissible in a court of law against an accused.

Corroborating information. Independent physical or testimonial evidence that supports or reinforces known facts or other evidence.

Corrosive poisoning. Includes strong acids or alkalis that destroy local tissue externally or internally by burning the skin or the stomach lining.

County sheriff. (See *Sheriff.*) This person is responsible for operations of the county jail and many civil processes assigned by the county court.

Court protective order. A writ of a court of competent jurisdiction issued as a "stay-away" order to a person or persons involved in domestic violence complaints. The order is designed to protect victims of domestic violence from a batterer.

Cover. A protected area that provides security from an assailant's firepower. Examples are large trees, fireplugs, mailboxes, and the like; the officer's primary consideration concerning cover is whether or not it can stop bullets or other destructive devices from harming him or her. Cover is also normally considered to be concealment.

Covert patrol. (See also *apprehension patrol.*) Nonconspicuous patrol techniques using cover and/or concealment to mask the patrol presence; tactics vary depending on circumstances. The low-visibility techniques are used to apprehend persons who are committing, or are about to commit, a crime or violation.

Crime. A public offense against the state punishable upon conviction. It may be committed by an act or omission in violation of a law forbidding or commanding a duty to act.

Crime-in-progress. The current commission of a crime. This term is frequently used with "burglary-in-progress" or "robbery-in-progress" to indicate conduct that is occurring in the present as opposed to a past or completed crime.

Crime prevention. The anticipation, recognition, and appraisal of a crime risk and the initiation of action to remove or reduce it. Crime prevention is *pro*active, which means that officers take positive steps to prevent crime rather than just react to it.

Crime repression. Law enforcement efforts instituted for identifying offenders through effective investigative techniques.

Crime scene. The place where a crime occurred. It includes the location of the crime and any overt act associated with it. The most productive source of evidence.

Crime scene sketch. Rough or finished drawings of a crime scene indicating relationships of objects and people at the scene. It includes necessary measurements and notes designed to depict the area as accurately as possible.

Criminal homicide. Unlawfully causing the death of an individual.

Cursory search. A rapid and superficial warrantless search of areas in plain view, or "arms reach" search conducted of suspects and specific areas where victims or suspects may reasonably be located.

Custody arrest. A legal arrest; the state of being held in keeping or under guard.

Cycle of violence. Defines the three phases of conduct in domestic violence. The first stage is the tension-building phase. The second stage involves acute battering behavior. The third part of the cycle is the remorseful or "asking-for-forgiveness" phase. The cycle repeats, resulting in repetitive conduct of ongoing assaults.

CYMMBALS. An acronym used for standard descriptions of motor vehicles in radio communications. Each letter represents the first letter of a descriptive element: *C*olor, *Y*ear, *M*ake, *M*odel, *B*ody, and *L*icense number, followed by the *S*erial number (if known).

Damage rating. A standardized system to rate damage to vehicle(s) involved in collisions, based on the severity of the accident and the location of the point of impact.

Deadly force. Force that is intended or known by a person to cause, or in the manner of its use or intended use is capable of causing, death or serious bodily injury.

Deadly force policy. The agency's guidelines and directives outlining the circumstances in which peace officers are authorized to use deadly force in the performance of their duties. Each assigned officer must know and obey this policy.

Dead spots. Places where hand-held radios (sometimes called "walkie-talkie" radios) will not function because radio signals are limited or restricted. Mobile relay repeaters and more efficient radios can compensate for this problem in communication.

Decode. As used in two-way communications, the understanding of communications by the receiver.

Defense of others (peace officer's duty). A legal responsibility that all peace officers carry to safeguard the lives and property of innocent persons in violent situations.

Defense wounds. In assaults and homicides, wounds found on the victim's hands and arms produced when the victim tried to ward off the assailant's blows.

Defensive tactics. Efforts used to ward off attack and eliminate or reduce the severity of potential or actual injury.

Delirium tremens. Also called "DTs." Symptoms of physical withdrawal associated with withholding ethyl alcohol from a person addicted to alcohol.

Departmental policy. Administrative policy guidelines that regulate the actions and conduct of people in the organization. These rules limit and guide personnel in discretionary decisions as well as outline the chief administrator's policy on such issues as use of force, emergency driving, and professional conduct, to mention but a few.

Detention. A temporary police restraint of a suspect without a formal arrest; most common form of temporary detention is a "stop and frisk."

Directed enforcement. Patrol coverage designed to anticipate where trouble is occurring or most likely to occur.

Discretion. The ability to diagnose or analyze a problem and make mature judgments in accordance with the spirit of law, department policy, and extenuating circumstances.

Disorderly conduct. Acts that could corrupt public morals, outrage the public's sense of decency, or affect the peace and quiet of people who may witness them. Or engaging in brawling or fighting or in such conduct that constitutes a breach of the peace.

Domestic violence. Abuse committed against a spouse or family member. The abuse can result in bodily injury or placing another person in reasonable apprehension of imminent serious bodily injury.

Double-back patrol pattern. Implemented by varying the starting point and occasionally either looping a block or making a double-back run on the street just covered.

Driving under the influence (DUI) or while intoxicated (DWI). The conduct of a driver when he or she does not have the normal use of mental or physical faculties because of the introduction of alcohol, a controlled substance, a drug, or a combination of two or more of those substances into the body.

Drug. Means any substance or combination of substances that could so affect the nervous system, brain, or muscles of a person as to appreciably impair his or her ability to drive a vehicle in an ordinarily prudent and cautious manner.

Drug addiction. A state of periodic or chronic intoxication produced by the repeated use of drugs; can result in either physical or psychological dependence.

Drug tolerance. When the body physically adjusts to taking a certain amount of a drug; in order to obtain the desired result of the drug, a person must take increasingly larger doses.

DUI or DWI presumptions. Legally defined presumptions of intoxication as applied to blood-alcohol content analysis. A content of 0.10 or more by weight of alcohol in a person's blood legally establishes that the person is under the influence of alcohol. However, states can set lower limits by law.

Duress. Restraint or force on a person to do something against his or her will.

Duty weapon. An officer's authorized handgun or sidearm that he or she is certified to carry on and off duty.

Dying declaration. An exception to the hearsay rule; a statement made by a person who believes that he or she is going to die without hope for recovery. The statement concerns the physical cause or instrumentalities of what the person believed to be his or her impending death, or the circumstances surrounding the impending death.

Emergency audio and visual equipment. The siren and red/blue lights activated on emergency vehicles to alert other motorists that the driver of the authorized emergency vehicle requests right-of-way when responding to an incident or accident.

Emergency call. Any act or event that reasonably requires emergency response under a given set of circumstances and department policy. Emergency action may or may not require Code 3 driving response—this decision may be made by communications or supervisors if not otherwise dictated by departmental policy.

Emergency medical services (EMS). Ambulance and other first responders skilled in first aid tactics and techniques.

Encode. As used in two-way communications, the process of expressing a thought by using verbal, nonverbal, or written forms of communication in order to be able to transmit information to another.

Escape mob. The behavior tendency involving escape in panic situations, usually driven by overwhelming fear. Persons may react emotionally and irrationally to avoid the source of danger and often ruthlessly disregard the welfare of others in the crowd.

Esprit de corps. A spirit of enthusiastic devotedness to and support of the common goals of the group.

Evidence. All the means by which an alleged fact is established or disproved. Evidence consists of testimony of witnesses, documents, and other physical matter that can be seen. Evidence may be direct (verbal), real (physical), or circumstantial (a conclusion based on direct and/or real evidence).

Exclusionary rule. A United States Supreme Court ruling that any evidence seized in violation of the Fourth Amendment will not be admissible in any federal or state trial.

Exigent circumstances. Urgent situations that require immediate attention; a pressing need or necessity.

Ex parte restraining (court) order. A temporary court order restricting a person from doing some act or returning to specific named locations until a formal hearing can be held to determine if a "protective order" is warranted. Both orders are frequently used in domestic violence situations.

Explosive ordnance disposal (EOD) units. Personnel specially trained and equipped to handle bombs and other explosive devices.

Exposure (Johari Window). A method of sharing information with others or expressing sympathy, concern, or thoughtfulness. In police work, exposure must be controlled to prevent disclosure of vital investigative details unless necessary in the instance. However, proper attitude and compassion results in expanding the "Arena" or area of mutual information.

Expressive crowd. A group in which the people are held together by some common purpose—usually with an attitude for or against something. They ordinarily are under the direction of well-defined leadership.

Eyewitness identification. A witness who personally observed an event or person is an "eyewitness." When this person identifies a suspect in a lineup, from photographs, or at the crime scene, such identification is valuable evidence to the criminal investigation. However, investigating officers also know that eyewitness identification can be faulty and requires corroborating evidence.

False imprisonment. Any unlawful violation of the personal liberty or freedom of another.

False pretense. A deceitful and fraudulent act unlawfully used to gain money or other property owned by another.

Feedback. In communications, the ability or opportunity to clarify information by asking questions and reexamining data. As used in the "Johari Window," the opportunity to ascertain what another knows that you do not know; thus, expanding the "Arena" or body of shared information.

Felony. A major crime that is punishable by death or imprisonment in a state or federal prison.

Felony traffic stop. A high-risk traffic stop that requires extreme caution. When peace officers have probable cause to believe that one or more of a vehicle's occupants is a wanted felon.

Field identification. When an eyewitness identifies an offender soon after the commission of an offense. Done without benefit of a lineup or photographic identification.

Field inquiry contact. Documented information about persons with whom the patrol officer has had contact but otherwise does not require a formal report. Gathered data create a record of the incident for future use and information.

Field notes. The work product of an investigating officer at a crime or accident scene that serves as the basis for reports.

Fingerspelling (signed English). Communication method of the deaf, often used in conjunction with American Sign Language.

Fire bomb. Any item that contains flammable liquid or combustible liquid with a flashpoint of 200° F or less, and has a wick or similar device capable of being ignited or by other means capable of causing ignition. But, no device commercially manufactured for the purpose of illumination, heating, or cooking is considered a fire bomb.

Fleeing felon. A suspect in immediate flight after commission of a felony-type offense.

Foot patrol. A patrol method used by officers on foot for close observation of small areas. It can be combined with motorized patrol to maximize patrol coverage.

Forcible entry. An announced or unannounced entry into a dwelling or building by force for the purpose of executing a search or arrest warrant in order to avoid the needless destruction of property, to prevent violence and deadly force against the officer, or to prevent the escape of a suspect.

Fragmented police systems. Various law enforcement systems (federal, state, county, and local) having concurrent or overlapping jurisdiction of people and offenses. No one body of government oversees the totality of organizing and controlling law enforcement efforts.

Frisk search. A patting down or minimal search accomplished by crushing a person's outer garments to determine the presence of a dangerous weapon.

Gas mask. A protective mask with an air filter worn to prevent poisoning or irritation by noxious gases.

Hallucinogen. A drug whose physical characteristics allow it to be disguised as a tablet, capsule, liquid, or powder. Hallucinogens produce distortions, intensify sensory perceptions, and lessen the ability to discriminate between fact and fantasy.

Handcuff. Temporary physical restraining device used by law enforcement officers to control arrested persons.

Hazardous material. Any substance, material, or device posing an unreasonable risk to health, safety, or property during transportation; includes explosives and hazardous waste or substances.

Hazardous materials incident. An accident or incident in which the general public is exposed to hazardous materials under circumstances that may endanger life or the environment. Requires special reporting and handling to eliminate or reduce the possibility of injury.

Hazardous materials placard. A diagonal sign 10 3/4" square that is placed on the exterior of vehicles transporting hazardous materials. The placard must indicate the symbol, the name (or ID number), and the color assigned for the material being transported.

"Hit" on wanted person or vehicle. Acknowledgement that there is an outstanding want or warrant for a person, vehicle, or property as listed in the law enforcement or court record.

Horizontal communications (coordination). Lateral exchange of information between peers and other people to assist in achieving common goals and objectives.

Hue and cry. In old English Law, a loud outcry to alert the community to pursue felons (such as robbers, burglars, and murderers). All who heard the cry were bound to take up and join in the pursuit until the malefactor was taken.

Human relations. Interaction and communication among people.

Illusion. A false or misleading impression that can occur during observation.

Imminent commission. About to happen; threatening conduct.

Immobilize. Positioning or tactics to limit the mobility of a suspect prior to implementing control (handcuffing) techniques. Frequently involves using an interrogation position in the field contact situation.

Implied consent. A presumption of law that favors the state. Whenever a person drives a motor vehicle, the driver is presumed to have already given his or her consent to have his or her blood, breath, or urine tested to determine its alcoholic content. Manifested by signs, actions, or facts that raise a presumption that the consent has been given. In the event of driving under the influence (DUI/DWI) of alcoholic beverages, drugs, or controlled substances, a driver who operates a motor vehicle on the public highways is deemed to have already given his or her "consent" to provide a specimen of breath or blood for analysis to determine the degree of intoxication.

Incident report. A law enforcement officer's account of the facts and circumstances surrounding any reported event.

Informants. Persons who provide information to peace officers regarding past, current, or future crimes.

"Inner" and "outer" perimeter—hazardous materials incident. The appropriate locations where ingress and egress traffic should be controlled. The inner perimeter—where the command post may be located upwind, should not be closer than 2,000 feet from the hazardous spill; the outer perimeter should be located at the most convenient point to keep unnecessary people from entering the affected area.

Innocent third person. A person or bystander who becomes involved—either purposefully or inadvertently—in an incident.

In re Gault. A landmark Supreme Court case that held that a child is entitled to the same due process of law guarantees as an arrested adult offender.

Inspections. On-site services provided by law enforcement officers to determine the security and safety of property.

Instanter (traffic ticket). When a person is immediately ("instantly") brought before a magistrate without unnecessary delay to answer for a violation of law. Frequently occurs when a person refuses to sign a traffic citation, is involved in DUI/DWI, or requests immediate appearance before a magistrate.

Interpersonal communications (body language). Nonverbal communication that results from actions or nonactions of a person. Conduct is frequently controlled by a person's subconscious reaction to stimuli and may indicate what a person is feeling or thinking, but not verbally communicating.

Interrogation. Questioning or subtle compulsion by law enforcement officers of a criminal suspect that is likely to bring about incriminating responses.

Interview. An informal discussion with victims, witnesses, and, in some cases, suspects to obtain general information concerning identification and information relative to an investigation. The interview seeks to collect all available facts about an incident, to substantiate information already obtained, or to provide additional information.

Inventory search. Conducted whenever officers are authorized to store or impound a vehicle. Peace officers are procedurally required to prepare a detailed inventory report of the contents in a vehicle, in order to protect the owner against loss and to protect officers against civil liability.

Investigative stop. A high-risk traffic stop under circumstances that lead peace officers to believe that a crime has been or is about to be committed by one or more of a vehicle's occupants.

Jaws of Life. Equipment designed to force entry into a damaged vehicle or enclosure to rescue trapped occupants.

Job fatigue. Also referred to as "burn-out"; when a person allows the duty to become "routine." Those subject to job fatigue lose sight of their goals and objectives to be professional; such people take unnecessary risk, get out of shape, and succumb to an unhealthy lifestyle.

Johari Window. A communications design whose purpose is to explain the relationship of known or unknown information to oneself and to others. The diagram uses the concept of feedback (seeking knowledge and understanding) and exposure (sharing information or using compassion/empathy) to expand window I, the "Arena," which is information that is known to self and to others. Other windows are defined by known or unknown information: window II, "Blindspot," represents data known to others but unknown to self; window III, "Façade," is data known to self but unknown to others; and window IV, "Unknown," represents information unknown to self or others. The design has multiple applications to law enforcement patrol, supervision, and management.

Judgment. The sentence or final order of a court in a civil or criminal proceeding. The official declaration by a court as the result of a lawsuit.

Justifiable homicide. The killing of one human being by another, committed to prevent imminent death or great bodily harm or to prevent the imminent commission of a forcible felony.

Labor disputes. Disagreements between management and employees of an organization over wages or terms of employment. Disputes may take the form of labor strikes and other civil actions that may involve law enforcement action to keep the peace and prevent disturbances until the dispute is settled.

Landlord-tenant disputes. Disagreements between landlord and tenant over terms of the contractual agreement, rental payments, or other conduct relative to the tenancy. Peace officers may be called to keep the peace and prevent either or both parties from committing illegal acts.

Last resort. The final or last action available when all other avenues of lesser force or behavior have been exhausted.

Latent fingerprint. The virtually invisible image produced by the friction ridges of the inner surface of the fingertips. The moisture transfer from the fingertip to a smooth surface may be developed with dusting powders and lifting tape.

Law Enforcement Code of Ethics. The code of conduct established and used as the basis of professional behavior expected of all peace officers who are granted public trust; a peace officer's position requires a consistent demonstration of a high degree of integrity.

Law Enforcement Teletypewriter Service (L.E.T.S.). A communications network that links more than 4,500 law enforcement agencies. Data on stolen property, wanted persons, and other information critical to police operations is disseminated among agencies.

Lawful arrest. Taking a suspect into custody based on a court order or without a writ under reasonably specific probable cause circumstances outlined in procedural law.

Legal show-up. A suspect identification method in which the witness or victim of a crime is allowed to view the suspect individually, without the presence of similar looking persons.

Limited immunity. Specifically defined circumstances that outline exemptions from a duty or penalty. Personal exoneration accorded to a public official from liability to anyone injured by any of the official's actions that stem from the exercise of his or her official authority or duty.

Line-up identification. A procedure of placing crime suspects with others who are not believed implicated in the crime, in a line or other position so that witnesses can view them for the purpose of making possible identifications.

Local authorities. The legislative body of every county or municipality having authority to adopt local police regulations.

Magistrate. A person defined in the Code of Criminal Procedure who has a duty to preserve the peace within his or her jurisdiction by the use of all lawful means; to issue all processes intended to aid in preventing and suppressing crime; to cause the arrest of offenders by the use of lawful means in order that they may be brought to punishment.

Maximum custody. Security classification for prisoners who require close supervision because their escape would constitute a serious threat to society.

Medium custody. Security classification where prison security is responsible within limits because a prisoner's escape would constitute a hazardous (but not serious) threat to the community.

Mere suspicion. Facts and circumstances that cause a person to doubt or mistrust a curious situation; results in an investigation that may confirm or deny that unlawful behavior surrounds the initial inquisitive incident.

Mile-per-minute distance rule. Used to calculate how far a suspect may travel when fleeing from the scene of a crime. Generally, a person travels approximately one mile in one minute; therefore, a patrol officer could guess that a suspect would be approximately five miles away from the scene five minutes after departing the scene. By watching key intersections on the beat, an alert patrol officer may observe the fleeing suspect.

Minimum custody. Security classification that permits prisoners some freedom in the corrections institution under general supervision because their escape does not constitute a threat to the general public.

Miranda warnings. Procedural step in an arrest that requires peace officers to warn a suspect of his or her constitutional rights against self-incrimination and affirmative rights to counsel before custodial interrogation begins.

Miscellaneous police services. Includes numerous activities of a police department that are not otherwise included in the police mission. It may include, but is not limited to, operating detention facilities, offering emergency assistance to citizens, assisting or informing out-of-town visitors, answering calls about animals, and so on.

Missing Children Information Center (MCIC). A national center that maintains data on missing children and assists in locating or identifying children who are unaccounted for or lost.

Modus operandi (M.O.). A criminal's method of operation. The specific way or method used by a criminal because he or she has success with the technique. Specific M.O.'s can be used to help identify suspects.

Modus operandi (M.O.) file. A file of known offenders and their methods of operation. The file is used to identify and locate suspect(s) in a crime where a specific unique technique was used to commit the offense.

NCIC. (National Crime Information Center—located in Washington, D.C.) Maintains nationwide automated files on missing or wanted persons, stolen serialized property, stolen securities, and embezzled property.

Negligence. The failure to use the care a reasonably prudent and careful person would use under similar circumstances. Doing something which a person of ordinary prudence would not have done under similar circumstances, or failure to do what a person of ordinary prudence would have done under similar circumstances.

NMN. No middle name.

"Noise" (in communication). Any distraction or interference that disrupts or prevents communication.

Nondirective interview. An interviewing technique that turns a suspect's statements into questions that call for more information. The method repeats the suspect's last phrase, adding a rising inflection on the last word to change it into a question.

Nonresident Violator Compact. A reciprocal agreement among various states to treat the citizens of the respective states in the same manner that a citizen of the specific state is treated in relation to violations of the vehicle code. The agreement prohibits peace officers from taking a person's driver license; the person is allowed to sign a promise to attend to the citation and continue on his or her way without appearing before a local magistrate. Member states agree to enforce settlement of the citation through use of suspensions or revocations for failure to complete responsibility in the matter.

Observation. Using all the senses to become aware of surrounding elements; it involves both receiving and being aware of information; complete observation consists of sensing and awareness occurring at the same time.

Officer safety/survival readiness. The physical and mental preparation to know, understand, and apply tactics and techniques designed to ensure security.

Open-ended questions. Interview or interrogation questions designed to avoid "yes" or "no" answers. Questions are phrased to solicit and seek informative answers.

Operational "links." The interlinking transaction and communications forms that connect various units to facilitate police operations and to ensure officer safety and survival.

Operation Identification. A police-community service that encourages citizens to mark their personal property with a driver's license number for quick identification if the property is lost or stolen.

Paraphernalia related to drug use. The tools, spoons, spikes, roach clips, and other devices used to administer drugs into the body.

Patrol beat. The specifically defined area that law enforcement officers are assigned to cover during a duty shift.

Patrol hazards. Any conditions that could lead to an incident calling for law enforcement intervention or action; the four basic kinds of hazards are persons, places, property, and situations.

Patrol operations. The largest and most indispensable element of the law enforcement agency, charged with directly carrying out the police mission. In addition to crime prevention, repression, apprehension of offenders, and recovery of stolen property, patrol operations provide service to the community and handle the numerous noncriminal matters related to public safety and support.

Patrol patterns. Tactics used to cover a beat area that are designed to make the patrol unpredictable. A "random" patrol pattern uses circular and double-back patrol tactics to eliminate the potential for patrolling in a predictable pattern.

PCP. Phencyclidine, commonly called "angel dust." Found in liquid, powder, and crystal forms, it is a highly potent synthetic drug that affects the central nervous system and can cause the user to respond and behave unpredictably, and to exhibit abnormal strength and insensitivity to pain.

Penal. Pertaining to punishment for a crime; for example, penal institution or penal code.

Peptic ulcer. A physical disabler that results from an ulcerated sore in the stomach wall, this is a common ill of peace officers who eat hurried meals at varying times. Requires attention to prevent increased illness.

Perception. The ability to understand the meaning of various stimuli that affect the human senses and command one's attention; interpreting sensations.

Personal injury. A wound or injury to any part of the human body.

Personal senses. Essential for communication; senses of sight, hearing, touch, taste, and smell are used to acquire information about places and people.

Personal weapons. Various parts of the human body that can be used offensively or defensively in weaponless defense.

Perspective sketch. Objects are drawn to show them as they appear to the eye with reference to relative distance or depth.

Phonetic alphabet. Standardized words or names used to identify letters of the alphabet; used to avoid errors and misunderstandings when spelling names or identifying license plates.

Photographic line-up or identification. Using books of photographs instead of physical line-ups to permit witnesses an opportunity to identify possible suspects in a crime.

Physical evidence. Real evidence; evidence that by its nature "speaks for itself"; nontestimonial evidence.

Physical marks or characteristics. Used to identify people. Specific marks (such as scars and tattoos) or characteristics (such as limp, speech, and habits) may be used to isolate and focus on a particular subject to the exclusion of others who do not possess or exhibit these traits.

Physical restraint. All efforts to physically control a person by use of control restraints, handcuffs, or detention.

Plain-view doctrine. Evidence that is not concealed and that an officer inadvertently observes while engaged in lawful activity can be seized. What is observed in plain view is not included as a search within the meaning of the Fourth Amendment to the U.S. Constitution; therefore, the *exclusionary rule* does not apply to plain-view evidence.

Plastic (or molded) fingerprints. Fingerprints that cause an impression in soft material such as soft clay or other matter capable of maintaining a mold of the print.

Platoon system. Personnel are generally assigned to one shift or watch. These officers may serve the entire city or district. Divisions that have personnel on duty for more than one shift divide them into platoons on the basis of the hours of the day they are on duty, without regard to the number on duty or the rank of the supervising officer; this procedure facilitates making assignments.

POI (point of impact). The place where a vehicle collides with other objects or vehicles. In some cases, officers can locate only an API (approximate point of impact).

Police mission. The specifically defined purposes a law enforcement agency is organized to accomplish. Major components of a mission generally include crime prevention, crime repression, apprehension of offenders, recovery of property, regulation of noncriminal conduct, and performance of miscellaneous services.

Police-police relations (PPR). The interaction between members of the law enforcement agency. Used in connection with the "pass-it-on" theory, it is presumed that good PPR enhances good police-community relations (PCR). Conversely, when officers and their peers/supervisors do not have positive relations, individual officers may take their anxieties out on citizens, which results in poor PCR.

Police report. A permanent written record detailing the business of a law enforcement agency. Reports can be either administrative or operational. Administrative reports are used for the internal purposes of the agency and include elements of policy guidelines, budget and control data, and so on. Operational reports record facts and details of criminal investigations, accidents, and other incidents relative to line operations.

Police systems. The various groups or alignment of personnel developed to efficiently deploy or distribute the police force in the most logical manner to effectively handle crime and violations.

Portrait parle. From the French, meaning "speaking picture." In police work, artist drawings, specifically matched facial parts of a photo-identification kit, and/or computers complete a visual picture of a suspect based on information from witnesses.

Posse comitatus. Power of the state to call upon all able-bodied men to assist in apprehending law violators. The old west "posse" was organized on this concept. Modern-day peace officers still can summon members of the community (other than members of the United States military in most cases) to assist in apprehending people who violate the law.

Precedent. The concept of "stare decisis," or "let the decision stand." A court decision that serves as a standard for future decisions unless, or until, the precedent is changed because of change in law, society, or the way in which the courts interpret law. English Common Law formed the basis of precedents and the criminal law now used in the United States.

Preliminary investigation. An observation or inquiry into allegations, circumstances, or relationships in order to obtain factual information.

Preserving evidence. Efforts taken to protect evidence from contamination, change, or destruction.

Prevention of disablers. Specific tactics and techniques used to preclude various disablers that can inhibit performance.

Preventive patrol (conspicuous). Using effective patrol techniques to protect persons and property. Reducing opportunity for criminal activity or discouraging would-be criminals by being frequently visible in the community and by varying patrol patterns to reduce predictability.

Prima facie. At first view; the evidence that, unless contradicted, is sufficient to establish a fact.

Proactive law enforcement. Taking positive preventive and enforcement actions to anticipate where and when crimes or violations may occur. Subsequent action is then taken to plan and distribute the various police systems to effectively confront and handle the anticipated problem.

Probable cause. Facts and circumstances within the peace officer's knowledge that would lead a reasonable and prudent person (another peace officer, but generally a magistrate or jury) to believe that a crime has been or is about to be committed.

Procedural law. Defines and describes the methods and processes for enforcing and protecting individual rights.

Process. A judicial writ or order issued by a court such as a summons, citation, or subpoena.

Professionalism. An attitude of pride in a specialty or skill based on education, training, and strict adherence to a code of ethics that specifies definite guidelines of behavior for members of the group.

Property. Includes both real property (lands, tenements, and hereditaments) and personal property (money, goods, chattels, things in action, and evidences of debt).

Protection and preservation of the crime scene. Steps taken to eliminate the chance of destruction or contamination of evidence. It involves all activities necessary to maintain the site in the same physical condition—or as near as possible—as it was left by the perpetrator.

Prowler calls. Request for law enforcement service and protection when a building occupant or homeowner believes that trespassers are near.

Psychopathic personality. Mental disorder when a person is totally detached from reality. A person exhibiting this disorder is dangerous and may exhibit traits of paranoia and manic-depression.

Public relations. The degree or success of open communications to discuss topics of mutual concern.

Public service. In relation to law enforcement work, the ability to effectively carry out the police mission within the community.

Radio discipline. Proper use of the law enforcement radio by following departmental policy; the ability to remain calm and professionally communicate information using appropriate codes and phonetic alphabet when required.

Random patrol pattern. A combination of circular and double-back patrol patterns that consciously averts establishing any type of "routine" for the patrol beat.

Reasonable force. Sensible use of force by prudent persons under special circumstances outlined and authorized by statutes.

Reasonable person. A person who would act as most other people would in the same or similar manner under the same or similar circumstances.

Recidivist. A habitual criminal who has been convicted more than once of a crime, misdemeanor, or delinquency; most aptly describes a confirmed criminal such as a repeater.

Regulation of noncriminal behavior. Service efforts designed to ensure a safe and secure environment for citizens. Examples of the service include traffic direction and control, crowd control, and assisting motorists.

Relevant. In the law of evidence, relevant means relating to the case at hand; pertinent, meaningful, and having to do with the matter before the court.

Res gestae. Things done; refers to the entire transaction or event. Includes words and acts done immediately after the incident that are usually spontaneous and considered to be part of the act or event. This can be an exception to the hearsay rule when proper foundation is presented to a court of law.

Response time. The amount of time required for a patrol unit to arrive at the location of a crime. Apprehension of offenders is directly related to the amount of time it takes for officers to arrive on the scene.

Response zone. The specifically assigned area to which a patrol unit responds to calls for assistance or to investigate criminal activity.

Riot. Any use of force or violence, disturbing the public peace, or any threat to use such force or violence if accompanied by immediate power of execution, by two or more persons acting together and without authority of law.

Robbery. The felonious taking of personal property in the possession of another, from his or her person or immediate presence, and against his or her will, accomplished by means of force or fear.

Rough sketch. A preliminary drawing of an accident or crime scene depicting the area and evidence. The drawing also includes measurements and other vital data regarding the incident.

Routine patrol. The normal activities of a law enforcement patrol officer, which should be *anything but* routine. The patrol responsibility to be "predictably unpredictable" and apply flexible concepts designed to confuse would-be criminals.

"Routine" traffic stop. Vehicle pullovers for traffic violations or other reasons (not otherwise considered high-risk), where officers use great care for their own safety.

Safety belts. Seat and shoulder restraints that, if properly used, can reduce the harm caused by the forces of an accident and safely retain the vehicle's occupants inside the vehicle's occupant compartment.

Safety/survival tactics. Assembled from years of experience in law enforcement operations, safe and logical techniques and procedures include mental and physical preparation, shooting skills, and tactical approaches to hazardous situations. Successful officers learn these tactics and techniques so that they instinctively apply learned responses under stress; the officer who relies on training, skill, and good common sense will have a better chance to survive threatening situations.

Schematic sketch. Employed to describe a small area that is not illustrated due to the scale chosen for the rough or finished drawing; drawings might include bullet holes, toolmarks, blood spots, and other details.

Search incident to a lawful arrest. The U.S. Supreme Court held in *Chimel v. California* (1969) that in order to find weapons and/or contraband, peace officers may lawfully search the person of the individual arrested and his or her "wing-span" area (the area in which the person can reach).

Search strategies. Techniques and patterns used to conduct methodical searches of the crime scene or area. Methods include point-to-point search, the sector or zone search, the concentric circle or spiral search, and the grid search. The object of each method is to locate and identify evidence and people.

Search warrant. A written order by a justice or magistrate authorizing an officer of the law to search a specific area for certain unlawful goods concealed in a house, store, or other premises. The recovered personal property, if any, is brought before the court for legal disposition.

Security barriers. "Target hardening" or use of fences, landscaping, lighting, alarms, and locks to reduce a criminal's ability to enter a building or habitation.

Security bond. One that is posted by pledging securities or other property of value as collateral.

Security survey. A police service designed to determine the crime risk to a building or location. Surveys generally include determination of security operating and closing procedures, degree of target hardening or security barriers present, and alarm or other safety devices present.

Segregated prisoner(s). Persons who by reason of youth, sex, or status are separated from other prisoners for their safety or as required by law. For example, women and children are required to be housed separately, away from adult male prisoners.

Seizure. To take possession and control of a person or property by authority or right.

Self-defense. Using force against another when and to the degree one reasonably believes is immediately necessary to protect oneself against another's use or attempted use of unlawful force.

Sensory memory. That part of the brain that conveys or produces sense impulses that affect the part of the psyche that is part of one's immediate awareness. A person can observe large areas at any one time; while the person may not be consciously aware of an observation, hypnosis and other methods can be used to enable the person to "recall" the observation at a later time.

Sheriff. The principal head of county law enforcement. The term was derived from Anglo-Saxon England where a reeve (the King's peace officer) was in charge of a "shire" (an area equivalent to a county); the term "shire reeve" eventually evolved into the word "sheriff" used today.

Sketch (crime/accident). A drawing of a crime or accident scene depicting relevant data in relationship to the scene. The sketch may be a preliminary (rough) sketch or a formal scale drawing of the area.

SLAP method for assessing suicide risk. An acronym used to help determine how to best intervene in an attempted suicide situation: S—specific details of the suicide plan; L—lethality of the proposed suicide method; A—availability of the proposed method; and P—proximity of helping resources.

Specialized unit. Specially trained personnel assigned to a specific duty within an organization.

Specimen. A sample of physical evidence taken for analysis and diagnosis.

Spiral search pattern. A search pattern whereby searchers follow each other in a spiral pattern, beginning on the outside and spiraling toward the center.

Stealth approach (crime-in-progress). Secret or covert movement to avoid detection; moving or acting secretly or slyly in order to gain advantageous position and cover over subject(s) involved in illegal behavior.

Stockholm Syndrome. A condition that may exist between hostages and their captors resulting from interaction and empathy established between them. Hostages affected by this condition generally have positive feelings for their captors and negative feeling for police, whom they may fear because of the danger involved in a potential raid to free hostages.

Stop and frisk. A cursory, protective search for weapons of the outer clothing of a lawfully detained suspect by a law enforcement officer, based on the officer's reasonable suspicion that the person has committed, is committing, or is about to commit a law violation.

Stress. The nonspecific response of the body to any demand made on it. Stress can be either positive or negative, depending on how an individual perceives the situation. Negative stress can cause illness. Positive stress can push a person to achieve goals and make accomplishments.

Strip search pattern. A search pattern whereby searchers divide an area into rectangular strips and search in coordination with one another.

Suicide intervention. Positive steps taken to safely prevent a suicide attempt. Success is measured by the personal safety of both the person intervening in the situation and the individual attempting suicide, and is attained by removing the means of lethality without injury. Good communication skills are required for successful intervention.

Supplemental reports. Follow-up investigative reports that provide additional or corroborating data relative to an investigation.

S.W.A.T. Team. Special weapons and tactics team; a specialized unit trained and equipped to handle high-risk situations in an attempt to restore order with no or minimum injury to all involved parties.

Tactical units. Specialized patrol units generally used in covert operations for apprehension patrol.

Team area. The specific zone or district assigned to a patrol platoon or squad. The team works together and is responsible for the police mission in the specifically assigned location.

Tear gas. Includes all liquid, gaseous, or solid substances intended to produce temporary physical discomfort or permanent injury through being vaporized or otherwise dispersed in the air. Tear gas does not include substances registered as an economic poison in the Agricultural Code, provided that such substance is not intended to be used to produce discomfort or injury to human beings.

Telecommunications. All the methods and means used to transmit communications—radio, computers, television, teletypewriter, and so on.

Ten-code signals. Specifically assigned meanings to codes and phrases that begin by using the number "10" plus another number. The purpose of the codes in police communications is to shorten radio transmissions and ensure clarity of messages.

Terrorize. To create a climate of fear and intimidation by means of threats or violent action, causing sustained fear for personal safety in order to achieve social or political goals.

Three-way communications. As related to the police radio system, the ability of a mobile unit to talk both with headquarters and other mobile units at the same or different times.

Tolerance. When the body becomes accustomed to ingesting a certain amount of alcohol or other drugs; more and more of the substance is required to cause the same reaction to the item.

Tombstone courage. High-risk actions that fail to use safety and survival tactics and generally result in an officer's death. Some individuals mistakenly believe that they cannot, or will not, be hurt simply because they are "right" and the badge and uniform will protect them from all danger. Such individuals usually end up with a tombstone for their effort.

Trachea (bar arm) choke. A control technique that should be used only if deadly force is justified. The front of the suspect's throat (trachea) is collapsed using the force of the officer's forearm (bar arm) on the suspect's throat while standing behind the suspect. This choke hold is not recommended when other means using less force (such as the carotid restraint hold) are available.

Traffic citation. A traffic ticket or official notice of a traffic violation directing the person to appear in court to answer the complaint. The citation includes pertinent data to identify the driver, the vehicle, the alleged violation, the officer citing the violation, as well as the time, date, and location of the incident.

Traffic control. Methods and techniques to create a harmonious flow of vehicular and pedestrian circulation. When traffic signals or devices are not operational, patrol officers temporarily use tactics of hand and whistle communications to allow for efficient circulation until defective signals or devices can be reestablished.

Traffic stop hazards. A combination of persons and things that present potential danger. By understanding safe tactics used during the stop and being alert to specific hazards that may present risks, officers can execute measures to limit harmful effects during the encounter.

Traffic wand. A colored cone that attaches to a flashlight to aid while directing traffic.

Trauma. An internal or external injury or wound brought about by an outside force. This term also applies to psychological discomfort or symptoms resulting from an emotional shock or a painful experience.

Triangulation measuring. A dimensioning method used to specifically fix an object at any one place; it consists of making two measurements from a fixed point of the object to another fixed location such as a permanent light pole or fire hydrant.

Two-way communications. A system of exchange of ideas involving feedback during the processes of encoding, transmitting, and decoding stimuli.

Under color of authority. Conduct accomplished under the actual or assumed power that seeks to control another person.

Under restraint. A condition resulting from being taken into custody and control.

Unethical conduct. Behavior not accepted or condoned for professional law enforcement officers. Conduct such as dishonesty, brutality, racial discrimination, accepting gratuities, perjury, civil rights violation, and misusing public property or violating privileged communications—to mention but a few—may result in an officer's dismissal from office.

Vehicle search/inspection tactics. Specific guidelines designed to ensure that a complete inspection is made both of the interior and exterior portions of a vehicle.

V.I.N. (vehicle identification number). Number assigned to each motor vehicle by the manufacturer. It relates information regarding the vehicle and the manufacturer. This number is important in identifying the vehicle and its registration information.

Violator contact. The interaction between the driver of a motor vehicle and a peace officer who observed a violation or has other probable cause to identify the driver. This is one of the most dangerous moments of the driver-officer interview.

Walkie-talkie radios. Portable radios carried on the person during foot patrol or search operations.

Wants and warrants files. Information systems used to determine if persons or property are sought pursuant to a criminal investigation.

Warning ticket. A discretionary courtesy notice given to the driver or operator of a vehicle regarding an observed minor violation; this notice does not require the person to appear before a court to answer for the violation.

Weaponless defense. Tactics involving physical and mental balance to control a suspect without the use of weapons. Specific tactics may involve "come-along" or "takedown" holds designed to put a suspect in position to be handcuffed subsequent to arrest.

Weapons retention. To prevent unauthorized seizure or loss of a weapon. Specific weapons retention techniques are designed to ensure that a suspect will not obtain the officer's duty weapon. In addition, correct attention to the holster and other equipment ensures securing the duty weapon until needed in the line of duty.

Weapons takeaway. Used only as a last resort tactic, these are methods designed to remove a weapon from a subject who intends to take your life if you do not immediately act.

Wheeling a driver. At an accident investigation, being able to prove that a specific person was driving a vehicle.

Without unnecessary delay. The legal requirement of a peace officer to bring an arrested offender before a magistrate and show probable cause for the arrest. The facts and circumstances of the arrest, along with the immediate availability of a magistrate, will determine whether a magistrate should be called or if it is permissible to wait until a later reasonable time when the magistrate is in court.

Writing for the reader. A writing technique used to ensure that reports are understood. Police reports are written in chronological order to "tell a story" of what occurred and the sequence of events. When completed, the report should be comprehensible to any person who reads it.

Zone search. A pattern that divides a room or open space outside a building into smaller sections appropriate for thorough searching.

Index